REALITY:
FUNDAMENTAL TOPICS IN METAPHYSICS

Reality

Fundamental Topics in Metaphysics

PETER LOPTSON

UNIVERSITY OF TORONTO PRESS

Toronto Buffalo London

© University of Toronto Press Incorporated 2001
Toronto Buffalo London
Printed in Canada

ISBN 0-8020-4816-1

Printed on acid-free paper

Toronto Studies in Philosophy
Editors: James R. Brown and Calvin Normore

Canadian Cataloguing in Publication Data

Loptson, Peter
Reality : fundamental topics in metaphysics

(Toronto studies in philosophy)
Includes bibliographical references and index.
ISBN 0-8020-4816-1

1. Metaphysics.   I. Title.   II. Series.

BD111.L66 2000   110   C00-932582-4

This book has been published with the help of a grant from the Humanities and Social
Sciences Federation of Canada, using funds provided by the Social Sciences and
Humanities Research Council of Canada.

University of Toronto Press acknowledges the financial assistance to its publishing
program of the Canada Council for the Arts and the Ontario Arts Council.

University of Toronto Press acknowledges the financial support for its publishing
activities of the Government of Canada through the Book Publishing Industry
Development Program (BPIDP).

This book has been published with the help of a grant from the
University of Guelph.

To Kay and the memory
of her five McCulloch siblings

Contents

Preface

I want initially to situate this book and its themes in the widest possible way. Since metaphysics means such different things to different people, and evokes such differing attitudes, this is peculiarly difficult to do, and in the end I will settle for incomplete success. Before coming to that end, let me make an attempt.

Metaphysics is the study of the nature of reality: the investigation of the most fundamental kinds of things that there are and what are the – or some – basic sorts of relationships among those kinds. It means to explore what things are like in fundamentals independently of us: that is, whether or not we humans had ever existed, except where the target of investigation is ourselves or some basic feature of ours.

This is the conception of metaphysics that guides this book and which it aspires to justify and exemplify. There have been other conceptions of metaphysics, and significantly differing views as to its possibility. Among those who accept that metaphysics is a serious and viable project, there are widely differing views as to the results the projects achieve. My view is that metaphysical results which are close to basic common-sense views of the world, and even closer to fundamental results of the natural sciences, are the most plausible views to reach and defend. I take these results to include the reality of physical objects and processes; also the reality of consciousness, some meaningful degree of freedom of action, and the secure and unproblematic place of human beings among the species, kinds, and phenomena of a theoretically unitary natural world. I take them also to include the unlikelihood that there is anything outside, beyond, or behind that natural world or that there are reasons for the world's existence. I hold as well that there is good reason to accept a taxonomically rich and diverse account of the sorts of things there are.

One of the very deepest and most important divisions in post-Kantian philosophy is, I believe, the gulf between those who regard as viable, at least in principle, an essentially unitary project of theorizing about the world and its diverse constituents (including middle-sized physical objects, such things as quarks and fields, abstract entities, and free rational conscious agency), and those who think otherwise. We may style these large stances unitarianism and anti-unitarianism. For most anti-unitarians the principal line of fissure lies between free, conscious, rational agency and its products and institutions, and all of the rest of reality. Some anti-unitarians think that the former has its own 'logic' and rational structure, unbridgeable to those of the physical world; and some anti-unitarians think there is no systematic structure for conscious agency at all. At any rate these are dense issues. Positions philosophers take on them may usefully be aligned with commitments with respect to Sellars' (1912–89) well-known contrast between the manifest and the scientific image. Sellars, an anti-unitarian like Davidson and Putnam, held that unitarianism was a child's philosophy.[1] Like a child, then, I espouse and avow the unitarian hope.

All of these matters and issues they generate are explored, elaborated, and defended in the discussions that follow. However, before taking on these tasks, I want to approach the concept of metaphysics from further back, with a greater awareness than the foregoing declarations may express how tenuous, variable, and contested an undertaking this project will be.

The very history of metaphysics and its ahistorical location in the world are both conceived in extraordinarily contrasting ways. For some metaphysics represents human arrogance, desires to control and command the world; for others it signifies otherworldliness, dissatisfactions with the embodied reality of our lives and circumstances engendering a yearning for something alternative; for others again it is not perhaps quite so normatively charged but represents naïveté, the immaturity of the childhood of the mind, thinking its forms and contents the model and mirror of all else; and yet a distinct constituency thinks metaphysics represents something cognitively pathological, suggested in metaphors of flies in fly bottles and language on holiday (the literal clinical description of the disease harder to provide). For more or less all such views the impulse to metaphysics, and the products that impulse yields, are old-fashioned, pre-modern, something some people used to do or think they did; not something contemporary fully-in-the-swim people would allow it to be thought they were engaged in. Unless, perhaps, they were engaged in what is called 'new age metaphysics'; in which case, in the right circles at least, they may be on the cutting edge of modernity, even of futurity.

Within philosophy – that is, academic, Western philosophy, especially as practised in the vicinity of universities, especially in English and other Germanic languages – metaphysics has had a fate of smaller though still divided compass. Either you think metaphysics was something done in a philosophical past, until shown to be impossible or incoherent in some manner or other, by Hume (1711–76), Kant (1724–1804), or Wittgenstein (1889–1951) (or all three); or you do not. If you don't think this, you are in considerable company, at least within academic philosophy. This is the company within which the substantive topics this book will explore finds its home. Yet some (not all) of the views I come to on those topics are not currently fashionable ones; and I feel out of synch with much of the current academic philosophical culture, and do like the old ideal (never of course other than an ideal) of universal or general intellectual culture, of the informed reflective citizen. I really want to undertake the folly of trying to persuade new historicists, the several sorts of post- ... ists (postmodernists, poststructuralists, etc.), the disciples of Rorty, MacIntyre, Foucault (1926–84), and Derrida, as well as those of Wittgenstein, that what is attempted here is worthwhile, even unavoidable.

For those whose historical prisms are not filtered by Kant, positivism, Wittgenstein, or the several postmodernist hermeneutical contenders, there is a continuous metaphysical tradition – with distinct streams, and varying quantity and quality of fish swimming in them as the centuries have gone by – from Thales (ca. 624–ca. 545 B.C.) to the present. For this historical view Aristotle (384–322 B.C.) is a far more apt conceptual archetype than Plato (ca. 428–348 B.C.) (or any Presocratic), and central, paradigmatic figures in the march of the philosophical ages are Locke (1632–1704), Leibniz (1646–1716), Hume, Reid (1710–96), Mill (1806–73), Russell (1872–1970), Moore (1873–1958); and less well known ones, like Arnauld (1612–94), Conway (1631–79), Broad (1887–1971), Chisholm (1916–99), Richard Cartwright, Armstrong, Stalnaker.

Metaphysics in this model is most-general-science; and it means to yield knowledge – truth, the truth about things in themselves, how the world is, in itself and apart from us – but also with regard to us, since we too are a part of the world. I'll not enlarge on this theme here, since this is the subject of one of the chapters to come. Yet it may be valuable to set an antecedent historical and conceptual stage.

This book has been several years in the writing. As already intimated it aspires to be an historically sensitive treatment of a wide range of fundamental topics in metaphysics as that subject was conceived uninterruptedly, certainly well into the twentieth century, which would respect and react to many contemporary currents and perspectives on those topics. Its goal is to be an independent, original, and correct or true, treatise in metaphysics, and only secondarily a survey of metaphysical positions of the present or past. In what is I hope a wide, indeed generous sense, its stance is naturalist and analytic. My nearest doctrinal affinities and debts are to Russell, Hume, and Aristotle (among the historical giants, and perhaps in that order); contemporary philosophers whose work I admire, and who have influenced my thinking, include Quine, Prior (1914–69), Putnam, Armstrong, Stalnaker, Cartwright, Broad, and Michael Devitt. I identify myself as a metaphysical realist, affirming both of the constituents of the position that Devitt differentiates, viz., common-sense realism and scientific realism. Since I affirm as well the reality of more than one kind of abstract entity, and hold that their reality is independent of consciousness or language, I am also a Platonic realist. The reader will see in what ensues in the body of the book what sorts of justifications I offer for these and other positions.

A few remarks on the selection of metaphysical topics for this volume may be appropriate. My treatment of what have been major concerns involving a wide diversity of often subtle attention in the history of metaphysical inquiry will be seen to be uneven. I wanted each of the chief historical metaphysical topics to receive a chapter. What determined that a topic was of this status was, to a significant degree, whether Kant had so identified it. Kant was my Virgil as I attempted the Dantean project of investigation of a different sort of underworld. Virgil, it will be recalled, is the 'virtuous pagan' in Dante's account of the afterlife. Since he 'did not believe,' he is denied participation in Paradise, although he otherwise has the relevant qualifications, indeed is outstandingly sensitive and acute in navigating the moral and conceptual contours of the higher (and the lower) thought-world. So it is with Kant. Whatever Kant said was a fundamental question metaphysics dearly (and of course according to Kant, vainly) sought the answer to, the present book has a chapter attempting to answer; and all fundamental concepts Kant identifies as transcendental (giving them this title in his new Copernican sense) occupies a chapter. The perspective of the book will be seen to be generally quite anti-Kantian. However, Kant recognized the deep yearning for fundamental and comprehensive understanding of the world that is the central motivation to metaphysical inquiry, and had a detailed and specific awareness of what that yearning seeks to know. It seems appropriate that he play the role he is here assigned.

There are other metaphysical topics explored here which Kant had little to say about. And there are metaphysical topics, which some view as fundamental, which are not accorded the independent investigation which some believe they deserve. One of these is theory of truth, which for some is the defining issue of metaphysics and its possibility. My view is that the correct view of truth is somewhere in the correspondence/deflationary range, and that there are not metaphysically important differences between plausible versions of these two formally incompatible treatments of truth. Paul Horwich's deflationary theory,[2] for example, concedes most that a correspondence theorist would reasonably insist on, and affirms little that he or she should mind; and the plausible theses of correspondence theory are so anodyne that a delationist will rightly see them as without significant explanatory content.

Note

To facilitate historical identification, deceased philosophers or thinkers with philosophical significance are provided at their first reference in the text with the dates of their birth and death (where known). No dates are given for persons who are still living. Given names are provided only where there is more than one prominent figure with that surname, or (sometimes) in cases of living philosophers.

Acknowledgments

First drafts of most of the chapters of the book were written during a sabbatical year spent at the University of Bristol, in Bristol, England, in 1990–91. Those chapters, and the remainder that followed them, have undergone extensive rethinking and rewriting over the years since then. I would like to express my gratitude to the Bristol Philosophy department for their cordial hospitality, and useful and stimulating discussions of first versions of some of the ideas developed in these pages. I have also received helpful and suggestive reactions to the work from my former colleagues at the University of Saskatchewan, in particular David Crossley, who read through the entire manuscript and had all manner of valuable responses, stylistic as well as philosophical. Valuable comments and reactions have also been provided by my colleagues at the University of Guelph, Michael Ruse and John Leslie. Barry Allen gave me helpful reactions to the chapter on Existence, as have graduate students and other philosophical audiences who heard versions of different chapters, at Guelph, McMaster University, the University of Western Ontario, and the University of Waterloo.

REALITY:
FUNDAMENTAL TOPICS IN METAPHYSICS

Chapter One

What Is Metaphysics?

'Metaphysics,' F.H. Bradley (1846–1924) remarked in a famous passage, 'is the finding of bad reasons for what we believe upon instinct.'[1] This isn't quite my view. I doubt if there is much of anything we believe on instinct; and the fact that metaphysicians disagree so deeply would be at least a little surprising if their views were truly instinctive, innate, or anything similar.

Still, I think there is something fundamentally right in Bradley's aphorism. I believe that we – metaphysicians and others – arrive at general pictures or conceptions of the world (and sometimes pictures of our pictures) in a highly complex interplay of teachings that we receive on authority, or because of temperamental leaning, location in history, culture, class, gender (perhaps even where in an ordering of siblings we were!), together with argument and evidence of differing kind and quality, to which we attach differing significance. Often views are adopted simply because they are currently prevailing ones. The whole picture, which will vary in its systematicity and our consciousness of it, then undergoes processes of articulation and development, under stresses and constraints only some of which are rational or evidentiary. It may seem surprising for a philosopher, still more for an analytic one, but my view is that there is an exaggerated, artificial, and largely historically and biographically untrue conception among philosophers of the role and importance of *argument* in reaching, retaining, and discarding metaphysical positions.

Having affirmed this, one might expect that I would go on to advance an historicist, relativist, or at least sceptic's and agnostic's stance on metaphysical topics and the competing plausibility of metaphysical systems – as many do. In fact, I am far more sanguine and optimistic about human intelligence and cognitive skill than that. I think that the knowing hominid is – or is able to become – rather good at negotiating his and her way through the thicket of subrational, pre-rational, and sometimes irrational epistemic predispositions, and charting through to at least a relative autonomy from those forces, and to at least a relative receptivity to argument and evidence. Of course, this is a matter of degree and will vary by case – the republic of letters is not, for good or ill, a democracy – and an impressive consensus is never achieved in metaphysics. However, the topics are difficult and it takes a while for *free*, creative intelligence to become engaged, and people become wedded to their views, not always in rational – or very laudable – ways. Hence, I think that much metaphysical posturing and dissent is inauthentic and often the expression of vanity – we want to hold on to what we think others believe we discovered or published first. This too will speak more for a Sartrean than a Whorfian conception of our philosophical estate.[2]

Metaphysics is often characterized in two distinct ways. On the one hand, it is called – as I have already called it – the study of the nature of reality. On the other hand, it is said to be a study of our most basic concepts of reality. There may or may not be important differences between these characterizations. The second seems to indicate that if *we* weren't around, there would be no such subject and that, in a special way, metaphysics is a study of *us*; the first characterization doesn't seem to have this limitation.

In general, the first of these descriptions appears preferable. This seems to accord better with what we say about other kinds of inquiry. Botany, for example, is the study of plants, not of our concepts of plants. Entomology is the study of insects, not of our concepts of them, and so on. Of course, when human beings study or investigate something, it would appear that they necessarily utilize their concepts of whatever it is they study, and of related things; and it will matter a lot what those concepts are, how they work and are interrelated. Perhaps describing metaphysics as a study of our concepts of reality is or ought to be taken as just another way of referring to the study of reality. At any rate, if there were a difference between investigating reality itself and a bunch of our ideas or concepts (of anything), and we could choose which inquiry to explore, I think the first would be the more interesting and philosophical.

Let us try to be more explicit and more specific. One way to distinguish between inquiries, investigations, and disciplines is as follows. In the cases of some inquiries, from a reasonably accurate description of what the inquiry explores or studies, it follows that there are conscious beings, and from others it does not. For example, botany seems accurately describable as the study of plant life. From the assertion that there is such a thing as plant life, it does not follow that there are conscious beings. History seems accurately describable as the study of major* human actions in the past. (*Major is problematic, and left unexplained here. One of the problems of defining or characterizing the historical enterprise is in determining with which past human actions historians should concern themselves.) From the assertion that there have been such things as human actions, it follows that there are conscious beings, for action-performing human beings are necessarily conscious beings. We could call inquiries of the second type necessarily-consciousness-involving inquiries; and those of the first type not-necessarily-consciousness-involving inquiries. The question, then, is which type is metaphysics?

The answer, I think, is quite definitely that it is the first type. This does not, of course, imply that there are not conscious beings nor that metaphysics doesn't study them. Metaphysics studies whatever is real. If conscious beings or their artifacts (including their concepts) are real, then metaphysics will, *inter alia*, study them. Now, it will be observed that if there were no conscious beings, then there would be no metaphysics. Of course, this is also true of botany, geology, and every other discipline, inquiry, and theory.

This book is intended as a contribution to metaphysics. I have already had a number of things to say about what is meant here by metaphysics, and will have still more to say as the book develops. One further indication is that I mean approximately what Aristotle did and what he identified under this head in his predecessors, and what central philosophers in the Western tradition have meant, or been taken to mean, from Aristotle to Leibniz; then, more selectively, from Leibniz to the present day.

I will write as though the reader has at least a rough sense of the Western intellectual tradition in religion, literature, and science, as well as philosophy. No significant details will be assumed, and relevant critical features of the tradition will be explained as we proceed. However, I want the fact of this enterprise's historical context in a literature that extends from at least the fourth century B.C. to the present to be clear and to invite the reader's participation in it.

There are thinkers and writers with diverse points of view – what is called postmodernism is one of them – among whom I hope this book will find readers, who may be surprised at the claim of continued value and the possibility of genuine results in the project that engaged Spinoza (1632–77) and McTaggart (1866–1925). I hope, by example, to persuade them to think otherwise but I appreciate that this may be an uphill struggle.

Apart from trying to change the views of those who think that metaphysics in the Western philosophical tradition is misguided, pre-modern, and even immoral, I have to differentiate the central tradition's metaphysics from its misinterpretations. In addition, within the house of philosophy, there will be those without quarrel with metaphysics who won't share the results I reach but whom I shall try to persuade.

I cannot do justice to all, or equal justice to many positions. I assume a certain interest in, and acquaintance with, philosophy and a broad rationality, openness to argument and persuasion, and similar virtues – and that they are virtues (at any rate not the opposite of virtues). Convincing those hostile to metaphysics will be undertaken indirectly, by what I hope will be the example of successful metaphysical theory-construction and argumentation; though one chapter will be devoted to direct consideration of the case against metaphysics, and the plausibility of a rebuttal of that case.

Like so much else in philosophy, metaphysics has been different things to different thinkers, both friends and foes of the subject. There does seem accord that the subject is supposed to investigate, and offer conclusions as to 'what things are really like' or 'what the world is really like,' perhaps with a qualification for a sufficient degree of generality, or the 'really like' being required to be at – whatever this may mean – a 'fundamental (or ultimate) level.'[3]

So, it seems, metaphysics is agreed to be concerned with – possibly alongside other matters and in a particular way – what exists and its nature. One of the metaphysical positions, monism (in one sense of this term), holds that there is, in a strict and literal sense, precisely one thing that is real. (The earliest thinker who explicitly took this view was the Pre-Socratic philosopher Parmenides (fl. 501–492 B.C.)) Accordingly, we will be insufficiently inclusive if we characterize the metaphysical inquiry, as Kant did (and others, often polemically, continue to), as the investigation of 'things-in-themselves.' However, if we understand the latter phrase as implying not a plurality of objects, or entities of any sort, the Kantian conception – of how things are apart from appearance, and how they may be conceived by us (although appearance, or our conceptions, and reality, *may* coincide) – seems apt, and often useful.

Beyond this, we seem to find conceptions of metaphysics that are incompatible or divergent. Thus, there is a conception of metaphysics as (by definition, if one likes) a wholly a priori, or non-contingent, subject, that would, if it were actual, produce results that were necessarily true, in the strongest possible sense. Or, while this conception is in fact logically distinct, though it usually accompanies the latter characterization, metaphysics is conceived as a subject that would yield results that would 'transcend experience,' identify what is real as well as its nature, in a manner 'beyond' or 'above' (whatever precisely these may mean in this context) the reality and nature of things we are held to be aware of in familiar or even scientific experience of the world.

An alternative conception, which I favour and advocate, sees metaphysics as what might be called most general science.[4] This notion of metaphysics is essentially that of Democritus (ca. 460–ca. 370 B.C.), Aristotle, Descartes (1596–1650), Locke, Leibniz, and many nineteenth- and twentieth-century philosophers. Aristotle uses the term *first philosophy* for what appears to be similar to this conception. The general idea may be explained as follows. The notions of a species and of a genus have both a *logical* (or categoreal) and a *biological* use, for grouping classes of things and larger classes in which they fall. The biological use is just a special instance of the logical use. Let us use the species-genus pair in its logical sense, not forgetting, of course, that it is also able to be applied to classes of living things. There is noted an ascent in species-genus characterizations of things we think we are acquainted with, or, in some cases, reasonably hypothesize the reality. For example, it is reasonable to identify both beagles and collies as dogs, then both dogs and cats as mammals, mammals and birds as vertebrates, etc. This involves, and illustrates, species-genus ascent. It will be reasonable, indeed, important, to ask whether there is anything mandatory, or specially appropriate, in starting off with items like beagles. Would numbers, finger snaps, or death, have served? Or served as well? These are difficult questions, as well as being important ones. I ask the reader's indulgence in deferring them to a later stage. I return to species-genus ascent launched from breeds of dog. At quite high locations in such ascent, we achieve pure natural science – physics and chemistry. The relevant genera are of physical objects (actually or potentially) in motion – bodies, in the older natural philosophical vocabulary, elements, the things identified in the periodic chart of the elements, and perhaps compounds of them – and states and processes involving such things. Metaphysics, from this point of view, involves the idea of getting still more general, and comprehensive, than even physics ever gets (that is, in its theoretical categories, for kinds of things). So we reach, in the ascent model, kinds like existent thing, and possibly stuff, property, relation, space, time, mental thing, physical thing, and other sorts of reality. The examples given are meant to be illustrative of possible metaphysical genera; some of them, at least, might well be empty, or non-basic categories.[5]

This latter conception of metaphysics, which seems to be the one first self-consciously articulated by Aristotle (whereas the former, the a prioristic and transcendent one, looks to be the legacy of Plato), doesn't, at least at first blush, say anything about 'transcending' experience, or affirm that its results will characteristically be non-contingent. After all, when we go from investigating dogs and cats to investigating mammals, it is hard to see why we should be regarded as 'transcending experience,' whatever exactly it would be to do that; nor is it obvious why we should be thought to have gone from contingent results to ones that will be like truths of logic.

One further component of metaphysics, as historically practiced and as meant in these pages, may contribute to understanding how at least a part of the subject is a matter of non-contingency. As well as exploring what in most fundamental terms the world contains – this is the special proper part of metaphysics usually called ontology (the study of being) – and what, in most fundamental terms, is true about the world, metaphysics also studies (in particular cases and in general terms) the limits of possibility. Thus, metaphysics studies not only what there is and what is the case, it studies also what *could* be and what *must* be, in the widest conceivable senses of these terms. Possibility, necessity, and contingency are the fundamental varieties of modality. So this part or dimension of metaphysics is sometimes called modal metaphysics.

One is engaged in metaphysics in our sense then, whenever one thinks about what there is, or what there may be, and what the natures of things that are (or might be) themselves are (or might be). Metaphysicians tend to be preoccupied with being (existence, reality), and what things are like – i.e., how things are. In Aristotle's sense, this sort of concern was a part of what he would have called, and also what we would call, science; only – possibly – more general, comprehensive, and foundational than actual natural science. Whether metaphysics might include subject-matter, themes, content, and results, that were substantively additional to anything to be found in (natural) science, is itself a substantive matter of metaphysics. On the whole, my own view is that metaphysics does not go very substantively beyond science, but this is not supposed to be true 'by definition.' The idea of metaphysics includes and permits the idea of scientific (or naturalistic) metaphysics but does not do so necessarily or automatically. This will be a matter of investigation and argument. To disclose my own view a little further at this stage without argument: I think that it is quite possible (even if I believe that it is unlikely) that a naturalistic metaphysics is indefensible, and possible in fact that first philosophy (first science) will necessarily need to include kinds of entities (irreducible mental phenomena, perhaps abstracta, gods, even God) that could not be included within the framework of modern natural science introduced into our world (mostly) by Galileo. I think that there are good arguments for naturalistic metaphysics but they are not proofs; indeed, they fall sufficiently short of being proofs that metaphysics as an enterprise remains for the foreseeable future significantly different from natural science.

Until relatively recently in the life of the mind, there was little conscious, explicit, systematic thinking about theoretical projects themselves, meta-level, self-conscious probes of what the inquiry involved. As in other supposedly more practical spheres, the aim was to get to the matter at hand, and produce its desired outcome, rather than ponder (still less to ponder in a systematic way) the nature and point of that aim was in the first place. Aristotle may be a singular exception to this generalization, for his inquiries did extend to inquiry itself. However, between Aristotle and the eighteenth century, there was little self-conscious reflection of a systematic kind, on the character of inquiry in general or its varieties. Ideas of science, and the pursuit of knowledge and truth, certainly appear but largely within a broadly Aristotelian conception. In general, no marked contrast between what we would now identify as science and metaphysics can be found before the eighteenth century.

The idea of such a contrast does certainly appear in the writings of Kant, and perhaps implicitly in earlier thinkers of the Enlightenment. The explicit Kantian notion is that metaphysics seeks to produce results that are absolutely necessary, non-contingent, and transcendental, or independent of and in some manner inaccessible to experience. Though the idea that metaphysical claims will have these two properties subsequently becomes almost commonplace, it is nonetheless not easily located before the generations following Leibniz. It was perhaps encouraged by features of seventeenth-century rationalist metaphysics. The Cartesian ideal of an absolutely certain foundation for general inquiry about the world (*science*, for Descartes, for he certainly didn't distinguish metaphysics from science) helped lead to this notion. Even so, as beginning students in philosophy working their way through Descartes's classic work, the *Meditations,* are taught to see, certainty is not at all the same thing as necessity. The Archimedean Cartesian results – the existence of self and thought – are supposed to be incorrigibly certain, but nonetheless contingent: worlds can be conceived lacking me, selves of any sort, and thought.

On the other side of the matter, fundamental principles of metaphysics will be, many of them at least, of non-contingent character. What is to be resisted here is the idea that necessity is essential to metaphysics, that a claim cannot be metaphysical unless it at least purports to be non-contingent. This notion is absent from Descartes, and pre-Cartesian philosophy. Some form of it appears in Spinoza, but with some uncertainty (whether just for his readers, or in his own confusions is arguable) whether the necessity Spinoza conceives metaphysical results to have is strongly modal, or what would now be called natural (or causal) necessity. Spinoza does conceive the notion of setting out a metaphysical system after the model of Euclidean geometry, and certainly conceives the latter as a priori and strongly necessary. Even with Spinoza, no commentary on the procedures assures us that a system of his type, even that of the *Ethics*[6] itself, couldn't introduce axioms that would be, in fact, logically or metaphysically contingent, as indeed some of Spinoza's axioms are, whether he recognized this or not.

Descartes brought an old idea, the idea of certainty, to a kind of logical extreme, and in the process managed to ruin it, but the notion that scientific (or widely ranging theoretical) results should be certain is a respectable, and defensible, part of the central tradition. Certainty, in this sense, does not imply non-contingency, or something all-powerful deceivers couldn't lead cognizers to disbelieve or believe falsely. Rather, a result is certain if no case for rejecting it is something like what William James (1842–1910) was to call a live option: doubting it is frivolous, or non-serious, and it is known that this is the case. I do not mean to suggest that these ideas are themselves secure or clear. How what is known to be certain, serious, or frivolous, to be so known, is genuinely problematic; as is the eliminability of the normative from these themes. Some notion of public, intersubjective, or communitarian warrant for results judged certain seems to be involved, whether or not this requires a fully coherentist grounding of the idea. Examples of certainty in this central, respectable, pre-Cartesian, and, I suggest, enduring sense (Descartes notwithstanding) seem easy to provide. Death is certain, for human and other living beings; it is certain likewise that human beings have fought wars, and paid taxes, and that they need oxygen to live.

As for transcendence, the idea of being outside or beyond anything experienced: this appears above all as something that comes late to conceptions of metaphysics. A contrast between appearance and reality is there from the start. Since Thales, this is an absolutely central and fundamental notion for the project of metaphysics. However, the appearance/reality contrast as such doesn't require that things cannot, ever, be as they seem, or that reality cannot be experienced (as Thales' metaphysical system will itself nicely illustrate[7]). Again, the tradition may be thought to help encourage the idea of reality as beyond or behind a veil of appearance, the latter necessarily differing in character from the former, and acquaintance, in experience, only possible with appearance. Platonic varieties of metaphysics may seem especially to nudge conceptions of metaphysics in this direction. But even here the notion is that reality – or that which is most real, in Plato's conception – can be experienced; even if it may require some non-standard kinds of experience (perhaps only available to mathematicians, or mystics) for this to occur.

The idea of metaphysics as essentially transcendent comes about more, I think, from eighteenth-century convictions of metaphysical failure – failure to yield science, results that can be publicly known as certain – than from any central or defining notion of the enterprise as aboriginally or historically constituted. No agreed results? Perhaps that is because what had been sought, and which alone would have been acceptable as results, were beyond the possibility of experience. This is Kant's view, and that of other eighteenth-century, and later, thinkers. I will argue, indirectly (i.e., by example), that it is a mistaken view, but that what prompted it is understandable.

I conclude this introductory chapter by noting that there is also widely held the idea, in this case perhaps more widely without academic philosophy than within, that metaphysics necessarily involves beliefs in the reality of abstract entities, or of souls (the latter regarded as non-physical substances that human beings, among other creatures, either have or are). However, these views of metaphysics are quickly and easily disposed of. Many philosophers are nominalists, i.e., they don't believe that (any) abstract entities are real; and there are systems of nominalistic metaphysics. Further, many philosophers are materialists, who believe that all states of human beings and other thinking organisms are physical or material and who certainly don't believe there are souls; and there are systems of materialistic metaphysics.

In subsequent chapters, we will go on to try to decide whether, among other questions, nominalism or materialism are plausible views.

Chapter Two

Metaphysics and Its Critics: Realism, Antirealism, and the Possibility of Metaphysics

The aim of this book is to discuss and advocate views – those that seem most plausible – in metaphysics. With anticipation in antiquity, some philosophical thinkers, since the eighteenth century, have claimed to regard metaphysics as impossible, meaningless, primitive, pre-scientific, or anti-scientific, naive and pre-critical, or anthropocentric (sometimes, in recent years, androcentric). These are not of course all the same charges but they are all charges, affirming that metaphysics is bad, and not doable (or seriously doable).

I do not propose treating the case against metaphysics, in detail. It would be wrong, however, to ignore anti-metaphysics altogether. Many philosophers and nonphilosophers, including many scientists, have explicitly ranged themselves against metaphysics, and a considerable number have been educated to regard metaphysics as out-of-date and intellectually irrelevant for a serious modern mind. In recent years, new arguments and positions have been developed by foes of the metaphysical enterprise which have generated a considerable literature which it would be inappropriate to pass by without some discussion.

I

One simplified account of the development of anti-metaphysics goes like this: until the seventeenth century, philosophy, which might be better labelled speculation and theory, enjoyed a unitary and somewhat privileged position in Western culture. For plain and practical folk, it was alien and artificial, but sanctioned by its intimate relation to theology, an ideological support for that culture. Philosophical topics were curiosities, brain puzzlers, and sometimes matters of deadly earnest, as they involved individuals' and states' concerns about possibilities of power and intelligence beyond human life. Candour acknowledged that there was, for humans, at least, only one genuine systematic body of theoretical knowledge, and that was geometry. For some, (Aristotelian) logic was a second science. Piety and institutional power insisted, that there was much more of a theoretical kind that was actually known; but behaviorally people betrayed, as Hume was shrewdly to point out,[1] that philosophical convictions did not go deep. Hardly anyone really believed that they knew much at all about the extra-quotidian world, or even underlying structures of the quotidian world. If they did they would have behaved differently than they did. Along with much else, the seventeenth-century scientific revolution changed all this. Galileo (1564–1642) and his confrères, and finally, supremely, the 1687 *Principia* of Newton (1642–1727), showed that humans were capable of more actual science than just geometry and logic. There were other branches of mathematics that could be established to constitute actual bona fide systematic knowledge – i.e., knowledge in the praxis sense, things that, once you understood them, you could see to be correct, teachable to others, and not seriously doubtable. And, most remarkably, actual systematic knowledge, rather than mere speculation, about the world was achievable, namely, Newtonian physics.

In the intellectual environment these developments engendered a distinction came to be drawn between the philosophy (speculation) that was turning into, or seemed to hold promise of being turned into, (systematic) knowledge, or science, and the philosophy that looked to be dead-end, really condemned forever to remain speculation. Thus was born the distinction, as many have acquired and transmitted it ever since, between science and metaphysics. For this distinction, so conceived, and its advocates, metaphysics has chiefly survived since 1687 as an historical curiosity, or at best as a source-pool for possible proto-sciences of the future (e.g., a genuinely scientific psychology). If such a proto-science were able to be drawn from that well, it would show that it hadn't properly belonged with metaphysics in the first place; if the effort proved abortive, then it was correctly lodged, i.e., sunk, in the swamp of speculation (metaphysics).

II

The next major phase in the development of anti-metaphysics is due to Kant. The so-called critical philosophy that he developed involves a detailed and specific case against the possibility of metaphysical knowledge, and in favour of Kant's distinctive and complex account of rational psychology. The Kantian argument is complicated and also, I think, unpersuasive. Kant argues, by reductio, that if there were knowledge of the world (i.e., of reality, as it is in itself), it would follow that various contradictions would be true. For example, we would be able to prove both that the world had a beginning (in fact, must have had a beginning), and that it did not (indeed, could not have). Since neither these nor any other contradictions can be true, it will follow in turn, by modus tollens, that we do not have any knowledge of the world. As indicated, these Kantian arguments are entirely unsuccessful. They involve question-begging or quite implausible premises. Not even devoted Kantians nowadays suppose otherwise. Rather, a Kantian case for the inscrutability of the world is typically held more seriously to rest on other grounds – less formal, but no less decisive – than these so-called antinomies. Two such basic grounds seem identifiable. One is that we cannot think outside of our own structures of thought, hence whatever we did suppose was an objective (part of) reality would actually be a projection from those structures. This is the Kantian 'Copernican' general idea, that we ought to come to the view that we can have no satisfactory basis for believing that we can escape, or think beyond, the cognitive filters and screens with and through which we apprehend the world. Earlier versions of the Kantian anti-metaphysical position appear with Gassendi (1592–1655) and Malebranche (1638–1715), and among British empiricists, who give focused attention to the idea that if one wants to know about something, one should accord some critical study to the instruments, and their user, with which the desired object of knowledge is to be pursued. In this regard Hume plays something like Galileo to Kant's Newton.

There is a strong and a prioristic Kantian argument, and also a weaker position. The former enlarges upon the Berkeleyan case for Idealism,[2] which argues that trying to conceive of an object that would not be screened and conditioned by our experience-filters, our categories, is like trying to conceive of an unexperienced experience. Many undergraduate students of philosophy have been persuaded by such lines of thought, as have some mature philosophers of the past and many students of the social sciences. In fact this case for Berkeleyan idealism seems quite confused. Just because I learn of the planet Neptune through books does not make Neptune a bookish object; and in general there seems no difficulty with conceiving an object really to have a property even if object and property are screened or filtered by my mind.

The weaker Kantian position may fare much better. As Russell put it, with special reference to sense perception, 'from the fact that the perceived qualities of physical objects are causally dependent upon the state of the percipient, it does not follow that the object does not really have them. This, of course, is true. What does follow is that there is no reason to think that it has them. From the fact that when I wear blue spectacles, things look blue, it does not follow that they are not blue, but it does follow that I have no reason to suppose they are blue.'[3] Can we honestly, and seriously, suppose that we can come to knowledge about the existence and nature of constituents of reality, that would be accurate independent of our existence and nature? Won't such supposition necessarily involve a variety of cognitive *speciesism*, an anthropomorphism, that we can have no adequate reason to assume?

The second basic argument for anti-metaphysics grounded in the Kantian critical philosophy is independent. It asserts that different conceptions we come to about what the world is objectively like are irreconcilably in conflict, and we can have no hope of a rational basis, a decision procedure, for preferring one, or some, of the contenders over others. This second argument is, it may be said, a much modified, and weaker, version of the argument from supposed antinomies. It purports to prove not that metaphysics is contradictory but that it is undecidable – radically and comprehensively so. In irreverent capsule form, we may call this the Gershwin case against metaphysics: 'You say tomato, and I say tomato ... So, let's call the whole thing off.'

III

I do not want to respond yet to anti-metaphysics, rather to identify its chief modes. But the general character of most post-Kantian, post-positivist advocacy of metaphysics – currently usually taking the concrete form of advocacy of what is called metaphysical realism – may be indicated. It involves attacking Kantianism itself as a dead end, an a prioristic body of theory there is no defensible reason to confine to experiencing subjects. It goes on to argue that anti-metaphysics may rest in scepticism: the denial that any serious knowledge is obtainable about anything. However if it does not – if scepticism is refutable or is simply bi-passed – then anti-metaphysics seems to become committed to some variety of philosophical idealism or psycho-physical dualism. For if our knowledge can go beyond ourselves, the character of what is then knowable is either as-with-us or not. If the former is the case, then idealism is the result: reality is as we, as our minds are. If the latter is true, then the real divides into two broad classes; that which is as we are, as minds, and the other: nature, independent of mind. It is, contrary to the views of some contemporary materialists, almost certainly a mistake to regard psycho-physical dualism as incoherent or a priori wrong. However it certainly is mistaken to assume without argument that it is true. There has to be a reasonable chance that we are a part of nature, that categories we employ for thinking about and characterizing that which is without mind may serve finally to usefully and accurately have application to things with mind, possibly to mind itself. This general perspective is what is usually meant by naturalism. Probably a majority of philosophers now, even those professing to be anti-realists, see themselves as naturalists. The case against anti-metaphysics is going to be, ultimately, the argument that one cannot reject scepticism, idealism, dualism, and embrace naturalism, without countenancing, and tacitly advocating, metaphysics as general project.

It should be noted, to avoid misunderstanding, that metaphysics is not identical to metaphysical realism. Michael Devitt, a leading contemporary metaphysical realist, identifies this position as the conjunction of two other views: common sense realism, and scientific realism.[4] The first is the view (as he puts it) that tokens of most common-sense property types – his favourite examples are stones, cats, and trees – are real. More colloquially, then, a common sense realist is someone who thinks that there are such things as stones, cats, and trees. The second is the view that tokens of most unobservable physical theory types – e.g., quarks, electrons – are real. So, scientific realists think such things as quarks and electrons are real. 'Real' for Devitt, and for me, is synonymous with 'actual,' 'existent,' 'possessing or having being,' and 'being among the things that there are.'

One way that someone could endorse metaphysics as a cognitive project, but reject both common sense and scientific realism as literally correct metaphysical positions, is the following. The history of philosophy is in fact replete with views to the effect that, in one sphere or other, appearance diverges from reality; and such views show up, perhaps most frequently, and strikingly of all, in metaphysics. Many a metaphysician has wanted to affirm that things are not as they seem, that what the vulgar suppose to be real is not, or that it is quite otherwise than they think. There are some also who have wanted to affirm that things are not as theorists, including scientific theorists, think they are. Such metaphysicians typically want to proceed to indicate what they think the correct character of reality to be. In the twentieth century such metaphysicians have pre-eminently been scientific realists who rejected common sense realism, or else what might be called scientific 'meta-realists' – thinkers who take the nearest thing to literal description of reality available outside philosophy to be locatable in the writings of physicists, but who think physicists' reality in need of re-description in more fundamental or perspicuous form. Russell, in most phases, is an outstanding exemplar of this latter type. Berkeley, in the eighteenth century, was a metaphysician who explicitly repudiated the adequacy of physical theory for world-description.

There are common sense realists who reject scientific realism, scientific realists who reject common sense realism, and metaphysicians who think that the common sense and scientific accounts are both defective, though (perhaps) corresponding to or approximating, the literal truth about the world.

IV

Returning to our central theme, four post-Kantian phases or variants of anti-metaphysics may briefly be noted. First is nineteenth-century positivism, as expressed above all in the work of Comte (1798–1857) and Mach (1838–1916). This current largely renders more explicit what appeared earlier in the wake of Newton, especially in the writings of Hume: a conviction that metaphysics is naive, unsophisticated, representative of the childhood of human thought, really only a terminologically more ornate form of animism. The very idea that one could hope to know what would transcend human experience! All genuine, non-chimerical knowledge is founded in interpersonal observation: it is paradigmatically scientific knowledge.

The second module of late nineteenth-century anti-metaphysics is pragmatism, the most distinctively American contribution to philosophy, though it has European affinities ancient and modern. Pragmatism is a close cousin to nineteenth-century positivism, although it is perhaps more the opposing dual of common sense realism than, as positivism is, of scientific realism. For positivism the ground, the standpoint from which the intellectual terrain is to be assessed, lies in natural science, whereas for pragmatism it is in common sense. In both cases, that ground does not involve or rest on a metaphysical conception according to its advocates. So to suppose, for both positivism and pragmatism, would be to put cart before horse, or worse. And though markedly different from each other, both positivism and pragmatism share a degree of esteem for the other's grounding, and both repudiate metaphysics as antediluvian, as involving a childlike fixation on a 'magical' view of the world.[5] All of this is of course rather vague, more picturesque than precise. Moreover, that is the basis for the most forceful of the responses to positivist and pragmatist anti-metaphysics: that the latter falls apart when the attempt is made to say (more or less) literally, or with precision, just what the problem is supposed to be with metaphysics, why it is a problem, and how positivism or pragmatism manage to avoid metaphysics in their own enterprises.

The third movement of anti-metaphysics is the logical positivism of the 1920s and 1930s. It differed from earlier positivism, for our purposes, chiefly in bringing a semantic dimension to the repudiation of metaphysics, something largely missing in Hume, Comte, and Mach. Though verificationism,[6] the distinctively semantic dimension continues to reappear in muted form, especially in British analytic philosophy, a consensus – a justified consensus, in my view – is that it is a wholly mistaken and thoroughly refuted semantic doctrine.

The fourth and most recent phase of anti-metaphysics has appeared in the

work of several chiefly American philosophers, most notably, Nelson Goodman, Hilary Putnam, and Richard Rorty. The positions developed tend to be
eclectic and considerably divergent. Some of them, Rorty for example, identify themselves explicitly as reaffirmations of selective parts of classic American pragmatism. The most philosophically substantial position has perhaps
been the one defended by Hilary Putnam, and usually called, internal realism.
Although Putnam repudiated internal realism in 1994 for what he calls natural
realism, both positions involve opposition to metaphysical realism. Putnam's
views are eloquently stated and yet somewhat elusive; it may, in fact, be reasonably doubted whether Putnam's position has ever been anti-metaphysical
(or anti-realist) at least in the sense of metaphysics that will be articulated
and defended in these pages. However, it is explicitly declared to be anti-
metaphysical by its author, and possibly with justice.[7]

Putnam thinks reality is 'underdetermined' by any theory that we can produce, i.e., that several theories could be equally adequate to any consideration
that could rationally motivate the quest to know about the world. This being
so, there could be no sound reason to prefer one metaphysical theory to indefinitely many others logically incompatible with it. Moreover the project of
wanting to know the nature of things-in-themselves, what things are really
like, is, Putnam argues, intrinsically flawed, and possibly genuinely incoherent. So whatever it is we can do in cognitive inquiry, it certainly isn't
metaphysics.

V

Let me proceed to a brief response to some parts at least of the arguments
against metaphysics, general and specific. Recall that we have conceived
metaphysics as first or most general science. If there was anything the matter with metaphysics under this, Aristotelian, conception, it might perhaps be
that there was something wrong with getting that general. Rather as though it
was perfectly okay to talk about beagles and collies, and maybe even dogs
and cats, but that things get tricky, and dangerous, if you start to talk about
mammals and birds. Something along these lines is indeed what some anti-
metaphysicians, at least, have had in mind. They think that things go wrong
if you get too general – i.e., apparently, more general than physicists get. J.S.
Mill said, pithily, that this was a special trait of English minds: 'The English
invariably mistrust the most evident truths if he who propounds them is sus-
pected of having general ideas.'[8] Whether this is so or not there definitely
appear to be minds that find extremely general kinds troubling. One reason,
apparently, is because the complements of very general categories lack

exemplification, at any rate in their category. Thus, there is nothing in the category that includes only substances that is a non-substance; similarly, for properties. *Existent entity*, it would seem, has no exemplification for its complement at all.

It is not easy to see however why this is a serious objection to metaphysics as most general ('first') science.

It is also held that the content of alleged first science would be in fact merely 'semantic,' analytic, at any rate non-contingent, in contrast to real science. This, if correct, would make Aristotelian first science converge with the first, Platonic, conception of metaphysics discussed above, save for the latter's supposed 'transcendent' character.

Again it is unclear why, even if the charge were sound, this would be a good reason to object to metaphysics. It would no doubt justify demarcating metaphysics from science. That part of the Aristotelian characterization would be indefensible – metaphysics as empirical science but simply more general and comprehensive than physics. But non-contingent theoretical content seems unproblematic, as logic and mathematics of course demonstrate.

In any case, the charge here seems plainly wrong. That or whether there are material objects, or states, or mental ones, and the natures of both, are contingent matters; it is likewise for the reality and character of time, space, causality, and other very fundamental entities that metaphysics has investigated. Doubtless some of the things to be said – even among things substantive and contestable, at any rate, contested – about such things as these will be non-contingent. However that is true of some of what there is to say about clocks, and the Franco-Prussian war, and arsenic.

VI

As I have intimated, what I would like to call 'empirical Kantianism' seems in fact to offer the strongest case against the possibility of metaphysics. I do not think I will ever offer a fully successful refutation of this position. Its rejection must I think be tentative, or perhaps hypothetical.

I shall assume that no one is going to adopt a position of radical scepticism; or of solipsism, ontological or epistemological. One kind of anti-metaphysician roots his or her stance in semantics. This individual means to set off neutrally, as neutrally as he or she can, at least, and see what metaphysicians, qua metaphysicians, *say*. He or she finds or claims to find that metaphysical *talk* is in one way or other defective. This was the position of logical positivists, late-Wittgenstein, late-Wittgensteinians, ordinary language philosophers, Michael Dummett (apparently), and, it seems (providing some novel arguments), Putnam. I do not mean to suggest that these different individuals or schools had similar things to say about metaphysical discourse.

Without entering into the details of particular arguments and positions to be found in what I am calling semantic anti-metaphysics, two bases for those arguments and positions seem identifiable (apart from verificationism which I take it we have dismissed as refuted and non-serious). One may be called linguistic concept empiricism, and the other may be called linguistic/conceptual contextualism.[9] Both yield theories of meaning, as well as a certain kind of anti-metaphysical stance.

Concept empiricism is the thesis that anything that can possibly be a content in or for our mind has to have come from our experience. The early (British) empiricists, outstandingly Locke, were particularly focused on whether some mental contents might be innate or such as we began with experiences already furnished. Locke, and others, argued against innatism and for a sort of tabula rasa view of the mind, as there to be imprinted upon by experience. At the same time Lockean cognitive psychology imputes so much potentiality for a plethora of contentful states as already built into the mind that critics have widely, and plausibly, seen his views as crypto-innatist. While relevant to central themes, the anti-innatist issue is to some degree on a secondary plane of inquiry. The core idea here is that we've got to work with what we've got, and what we've got is to be found in us – in the furniture of the mind – whether it was already in the house when it opened for operation (habitation) and forays outward, or whether it was stocked in the course of these forays (including rummaging that didn't go beyond the doors). From that core idea stems the notion that all of the contents of the mind, the furniture, are ineradically stamped with the place, manner, and generation of their acquisition. Their reality, and identity, consists in the matrix of their creation. Since this is true of all of the mind's content, it will be true also of concepts (or ideas) of object, property, existence, identity, reality, world, and all the other concepts that purport to be concepts of metaphysics. Were metaphysics a bona fide enterprise (so the argument will go), these concepts would have a status, and a security of anchorage, that would permit the mind to consider their applicability independently of the matrix of their creation. But no concepts, on this view, have the privileged status of anchorage.

So far, this will furnish a partial basis for something like the Kantian and proto-Kantian, empiricist, anti-metaphysical positions already identified. What will make this an especially semantic stance is the fusion of claims to it about relations between thought and language – concepts and words. Plato said that thought is the soul's dialogue with itself, and like other Platonic ruminations, this struck – and continues to strike – a resonating note in much subsequent philosophy. Some argue that thought without language is naturally impossible for creatures we could recognize as thinkers like ourselves, while others argue the stronger thesis that thought without language is metaphysically or conceptually impossible (occurs in no possible world) for anything that could be a thinker, of any type. Those with the latter view usually believe also that language without a community – necessarily, for them, with more than one member – is conceptually impossible. *Loquor ergo alii sunt* ('I speak therefore others are'), they hold, is a priori and certainly true.[10] In any case, if concept empiricism is united with the view that thought is essentially linguistic in character (a thesis that may be understood in more than one way), the result will be a variety of what I call, linguistic concept empiricism. I take it to be clear how anti-metaphysics will result from this merger; and that it will be concept empiricism, and not the necessarily linguistic character of thought thesis that will yield this result. So it is concept empiricism that requires a response, in the defence of metaphysics, even though the people persuaded of this variety of anti-metaphysics see their position as a matter of meaning and language.

Concept empiricism (particularly if it permits innate mental contents) can be made wide and bland enough that it will be incontestably true – and not a priori or trivially true. Who can suppose that the contents of our minds have been placed there miraculously or otherwise than as a cross-product of the workings of the world – the experienced world – on us and our own operations; with us and world making widely differing contributions quantitatively, depending on the case? However world input is standardly critical. Indeed the so-called revolt against Frege (1848–1925) (i.e., against the Fregean semantics of *Sinn*, or sense, and *Bedeutung*, or reference), in favour of referential semantics,[11] which has figured so prominently in philosophy of language of the past few decades, is in part the expression of a conviction of a hitherto misplaced and under-identified world component in the understanding of what it is to think and mean. This does not imply that classical empiricists supposed otherwise. Having affirmed this, why should the fact that our contents are significantly by-products of the world's operations on us prevent us from reaching a stance permitting the factoring out of what we have contributed, so that we might hope to know what the world, in advance of or independently of doing whatever it did to us, is like in itself? Now, this may be impossible. If it is, then it will be impossible for Kantian or proto-Kantian, Copernican kinds of reasons and not because of something about what it is to mean, to speak, or to think.

Linguistic/conceptual contextualism is a more radical stance than linguistic concept empiricism, according to which the whole idea of theory-as-to-what-is-true, as something that thought or language can achieve and articulate, in some manner significantly contrastive with other things that thought or language can do, is an illusion. Linguistic contextualism is rarely articulated in such a way that this can explicitly be seen to be one of its consequences but that certainly is the idea. According to it, language is misconceived when conceived as containing sentences among its elements, with those sentences having truth conditions, or states of the world conferring or corresponding to their truth. There being facts of the matter, conditions of the world independent of us, would be entirely sufficient to launch metaphysics in our sense; at least provided that some of these facts of the matter or conditions of the world were ascertainable. Rather language should be conceived in terms of contexts of use, rule-governed clusters of behaviour, with sounds and inscriptions produced in them for which the idea of literal, objective, or factual meaning is a chimaera.

There would be a good deal more to say about linguistic contextualism and, in particular, distinctions to draw that are not elaborated here. Apart from taking us too far away from our central themes, further elaboration of either base to anti-metaphysics is unnecessary, since there are devastating objections to both, or to the claim that what is true in either implies any significant anti-metaphysical result.

There is simply no reason to believe that ideas – mental contents – got from one sort of context – experienced or innate – cannot, in principle, serve to permit the mind whose ideas they are to extend them in thought to contexts beyond their origin. This will not of course imply that extending ideas to origin-independent contexts will be justified; only that the idea of extending them in this way is shown to be coherent by our experience. Thus our own introspective phenomenology makes it abundantly plain that we can do what an anti-metaphysics derived from linguistic concept empiricism says we cannot do; and we can know that we can. How we can do so is of course another matter; the mechanisms of our psychological abilities are mysterious. That we can apply ideas, imaginatively to unexperienced and after-birth cases, where we conceive the application as remaining unexperienced, is past serious doubt.

Contextualism, as understood here, seems still more directly refutable. Like every species of relativism, it faces a genuine *tu quoque* problem. It is plain that the advocate of the theory thinks that it is true. He or she may refrain from using the word but there can be no serious doubt that contextualists think that something is gotten right, captured accurately, or something of the kind, by their contextualism. No special brief for truth-condition semantics is made in claiming this. Whatever theory of truth someone sincerely advocates, or none at all, I submit that contextualists, and relativists generally, in fact, really do believe (when they are sincere in their view) that their view is true. However if their view is true, then it will be false, since their view implies that no theory, or set of propositions is true.

The sort of self-referential problem posed here – and held to refute contextualism – is often forwarded with a kind of smug 'village rationalist' finality. There may be formal ways around this type of objection and meta-level distinctions that could be drawn to encapsulate and preserve the spirit of the contextualism. However – and it seems to me important to make this matter deliberately ad hominem, to speak to the eyes, as it were, of the advocates on the other side – there is something in the content of the objection that the contextualist *hasn't seen*, viz., the applicability of the theory to itself, and the phenomenological fact that there occurred actual occasions of (alleged) *insight*, where something, contextualism, was judged to be correct, i.e., true, objectively, and if it is, then something is true objectively, hence it cannot be.

Let us move on from semantics and return to generic anti-metaphysics briefly.

VII

The interesting (or more interesting) anti-metaphysician is not a sceptic or a solipsist. He or she is some kind of empiricist. He/she grants – insists, in fact – that it will be wrong, foolish, not to regard key fundamental concepts we employ, the very ones central for metaphysical categorial analysis, as pointing to, standing for something. Kant held that there is such a thing as mind-independent objective reality; only (as he supposed) we can't have the foggiest idea of what it is actually like. The empiricist anti-metaphysician, at any rate the one I am thinking of, enlarges the Kantian stance in certain directions. Our fundamental concepts of features and constituents of the world all doubtless correspond to realities. There is something like time, space, material objects, persons, thoughts, causality. Only we have no hope or chance of recovering what this something is like apart from us. Our concepts are not mirrors of those realities, or that reality; indeed, they aren't even coded representations that we could hope to decode. Something is out there all right, and it is some way or other (or we can not unreasonably conceive its being so); but we haven't any serious chance at all of finding out what and how it is. We can reasonably talk of cats, trees, stones, and people, for it is with the notions we have of such things that we organize and group our interactions with the world. And it will be correct to think that, like physical object, cat, trees, etc. do correspond, approximately, to something that is genuinely real. But so does sunset. The fact will be, as with sunset, that the fit between our notion and the outer realia is rough and ready, approximate; and, more importantly and inter-estingly, we can have no reasonable hope of sorting out how accurate the fit is, for the systematic edifice of concepts. We can know we are representing a real world, know we operate with some kind of code (or set of codes) by which we do so, but we're doomed forever to lack the keys to decode the system. This general position, in all its several varieties, Humean, Kantian, Putnamian, and others, may be called inscrutabilism.[12]

At the same time, it does not seem to register among anti-metaphysicians quite how much, and what, they are asking themselves and their opponents to give up. Let me remark parenthetically that some anti-metaphysicians, anti-realists, at any rate, particularly of pragmatist bent, insist emphatically that they do not dispute that there are stones, trees, cats, planets, people, time before there were minds, and in general the matter and stuff of ordinary con-viction and that we have at least basic information about them. Sometimes they insist, that no one has ever seriously denied such matters; that it is a red herring, to raise such themes, which just obfuscate or deflect what is really at issue, between themselves and metaphysical or metaphysical realist oppo-nents.[13] On this position I will content myself with saying that at some point philosophers must be left to explain that their words do not mean what they seem, and particularly when many of their own philosophical allies affirm that they really do mean what they seem to.[14]

It asks a lot of a serious mind to give up the idea that there would be time, space, material objects, and a world system, to which physical science has some genuine access and information, even if there were no people, concepts, or theorists, and independent of all three of the latter. It is reasonable to ask for compelling arguments for giving up such convictions.

It may seem that contemporary anti-metaphysics has often identified its target with what historically has only been a proper part of the subject: the quest for knowledge of what things are like in themselves. The metaphysical quest embraces additional concerns, as Kant was aware. It is instructive to note what he took to be the central core topics of metaphysics. He itemizes six: 1) whether the universe had a beginning, 2) whether space is infinite, 3) whether there are ultimate simple particles, metaphysical atoms, of which all composite things are composed, 4) whether there is free will, 5) whether there is a God, 6) whether there is an (indefinitely continuing) afterlife for per-sons. (Kant collapses the first two of these into a single topic.) Kant was quite clear about his own view: he was prepared to bite the bullet to which the criti-cal philosophy committed him. He thought that either an affirmative or a neg-ative response to any of these six questions, if held to apply objectively to the world, led to contradiction; that it was impossible to suppose one had located here a topic having application to reality (rather than features of our concepts).

For him reason is powerless to reach a result, even a tentative or (merely) probable result, on any of these metaphysical matters.

Will many – any? – contemporary anti-metaphysicians really side with Kant in this? Kant in fact takes a position like Pascal's (1623–62), committing himself to the view that the evidence is always 50/50 on every metaphysical topic, or at best that the probability of any affirmative metaphysical thesis is less than 50. Like Pascal, Kant was particularly concerned that philosophy leave some kind of intellectual space for the central tenets of Christian theology. Both thought that a modern – i.e., a post-Galilean – perspective precluded a serious belief that rational inquiry can prove, even render probable, these tenets. Both sought a way (very different ways in each case) to permit a serious modern mind to have religious convictions. 'I have ... found it necessary to deny *knowledge*, in order to make room for *faith*,' Kant says.[15]

Few contemporary anti-metaphysicians are similarly inclined. Most contemporary anti-metaphysicians are secularists and anti-teleologists. For them traditional theism is in no sense a serious option, not even for the sheltered perspective of 'faith.'[16] Let us focus on Kant's specific metaphysical issues. Putnam aside, I would submit that Rorty, Goodman, and their chief anti-metaphysical allies do not really believe that it is unknowable, or beyond the possibility of inquiry, whether there is a disembodied afterlife. Rorty, I would be willing to bet, does not believe that there is one, and certainly does not believe that it is probable that there is one. This is a metaphysical belief or opinion. He believes that it is highly probable that consciousness ceases with biological death. I suspect a similar negativity with respect to the existence of God. Further, I suspect that Putnam and at least most (other) anti-metaphysicians believe that human beings have something adequately recognizable as a power of free choice, or free action; most contemporary anti-metaphysicians will be compatibilists – believers that free actions can also be causally determined – , or if they are not, will hold nonetheless that it is probable that humans have (something like) freedom, in something like the sense, or a sense, that traditional advocates of metaphysical freedom have intended.

There does seem then to be something to the idea that contemporary anti-metaphysicians consciously or otherwise limit their opposition to what has historically and traditionally been only a part of metaphysics. On other parts of metaphysics they will have, and sometimes defend, very metaphysical positions (viz., against God and immortality, for freedom; with Kant's other questions being left as difficult but in principle answerable scientific questions).

I will conclude this discussion of anti-metaphysics and responses to it with some specific remarks about Putnam's views. In all phases of recent decades in his work, including his latest 'natural realism' stage, Putnam has claimed that metaphysical systems and projects have typically supposed, or implied, that there is an exact cardinality of objects, somehow identifiable (even if never identified) in the system or project, and that there is a single correct, true, or adequately perspicuous description of reality. There is so far as I can tell no support at all for the former of these ideas. Some metaphysicians have certainly claimed that there are infinitely many objects, and at least ancient atomists supposed that every macro-object is built up, without remainder, from the micro-objects that are the atoms. And Aristotle unquestionably 'privileged' middle-sized individual objects, especially living ones, like individual human beings, cats, and tulips. However just one true description of the world? (Would even the most theoretical botanist claim to offer, even in principle, the one true description of plants?) Most historical metaphysics has been silent or agnostic about such a thing. It is only after philosophy took the so-called linguistic turn, after, roughly, 1900, that even tying metaphysical systems or projects to such things as descriptions would have begun to occur to anyone.

Even when it did, the idea on which Putnam has so long been fixated, of a must – the notion that earlier twentieth-century analytic metaphysics insisted that there must be a unique true description of reality – is quite alien to the spirit, and the declared or implied views of most of the targeted philosophers. The one closest to such a position is, I think, Wittgenstein in the *Tractatus*, where we do find some rigid a priorism of a sort at least approaching Putnam's imprecations. Russell might also seem to be a candidate for such claims. Russell certainly had the metaphysical realist idea that, if the world is a certain determinate way – and (according to him) it is – then there may be identified a mode of conceptualization, at least of a Platonistic sort, that will represent that way; and with it in train the aspiration to a mode of symbolism, an actual linguistic system that could ideally, in its structure, give concrete shape to that conceptualization. However Russell was anti-Procrustean in this idealized project: he welcomed problems, and was the first to acknowledge complexities of fact that the tentatively and heuristically proffered theory looked to have a hard time fitting. The completed logical atomist project, if it could have occurred, would have involved sensitivity to whatever varieties of structures of fact philosophical analysis seemed to show needed to be countenanced. Russell was at stages of his work more sanguine about a simple or simpler reductive project than subsequent developments showed was defensible. For him philosophical analysis – philosophical logic – was an unending complex of attention to details. The whole edifice was supposed to give a special location, to be sure, for certain metaphysically conceived adumbrations of the first order predicate calculus. However this is still quite some distance from the Putnam bogeyman of 'one true description of reality.' With this I turn from considering the views of opponents of the enterprise to the enterprise itself.

Chapter Three

Metaphysical Systems

Of the many individual metaphysical systems – organized structures of views about reality – that philosophers have developed over the course of the history of Western philosophy, from Thales to the present day, some deserve highlighted attention for setting out on the metaphysical odyssey the present book invites its reader to undertake. My aims are not chiefly historical; but certain of the systems were and remain sufficiently influential or original that it will be helpful to give them special focus at the beginning of the journey. Sometimes a thinker or a school came to a key idea which no one is known to have formulated earlier which had continued influence thereafter and which still resonates in metaphysical inquiries of the present. That idea may be a whole way of looking at the universe or it may be a more particular insight (or supposed insight). In either case these are conceptions that have made a difference that has not gone away, and that it is useful to have available as iconic labels or nameable models that can be reaffirmed or reacted against.

Let me emphasize that this chapter is not intended to provide an overview or digest of the history of metaphysics. Rather its aim is to be a kind of glossary of terms where the terms are positions developed in the history of metaphysics that are directly involved in or pertinent to contemporary discussions and debates in (chiefly) analytic metaphysics. Who, for example, can engage in those discussions without encountering and utilizing notions of psychophysical dualism, abstract entities, determinism, materialism, teleology, common sense, naturalism, and others? In some cases the idea itself bears an historical cloak – Platonism, Cartesian dualism, etc. These ideas have, I believe, an historical contextuality which should – at least at one stage (and this chapter *is* that stage) – be brought to the centre of focus. The ideas developed within, and are key parts of metaphysical *systems*. Another metaphysical conviction brought to these pages is that metaphysical ideas are system-embedded;

this view also guides the manner of presentation of the chapter. Several very important thinkers, and systems, are omitted in this diachronic glossary. They are omitted because they do not constitute, in my view, players, or direct antecedents of players, in a contemporary play of ideas. Obviously in some cases there will be dispute about the continued significance of a system presented, as of some that are omitted. That is, in a way, part of the point. History of philosophy is part of philosophy, and is (to paraphrase Hegel (1770–1831)) a kind of court of justice of its contents. Other chapters also represent a metaphysician author's defended perspective on a problem or topic. In the very same sense this chapter means to be, not a propaedeutic, but a contribution to metaphysics. On a more prosaic plane, it also means to help the reader or enrich his and her understanding as that reader proceeds to subsequent chapters.

I hope that beginning metaphysical inquiry in this way – with some patchy history – will seem reasonable. It risks offending scholars with its patchiness in the cases of those discussed, and with its selectivity, for many other systems than those presented may also be held to be critically important. And it may seem to be a waste of time for those who would prefer plunging right in to the issues straight and neat, without anticipatory historical filters. The proof will be in the pudding. If these systems, presented in this way, provide useful archetypal backdrop, the endeavor will have been justified.

The aim is to be brief, synoptic, encyclopedic: accurate, but with more attention to what a system has been taken to be in the course of the years of its influence than with what may have been the deepest or truest intention of its original creator. More often than not, these coincide, but doubtless not always.

The Pythagorean System

The earliest metaphysical system which may be said to have had important long term influence is that of Pythagoras (ca. 580–ca. 500 B.C.). In fact Pythagoras's metaphysical ideas have had profound impact, on literally millions of people, only some of them philosophically minded, and they continue to do so. Not all of Pythagoras's views have been very influential. In fact some of them are extremely obscure. We do not really know with confidence just what he meant in the case of some views attributed to him. No doubt this reflects the fragmentary nature of our evidence about what Pythagoras and his disciples believed.

A full view of the Pythagorean system is not intended here; rather, an indication of the distinctively Pythagorean views that endured (which of course is not intended to imply that all philosophers have thought these views deserved to endure).

Pythagoras is the first metaphysical dualist in the history of Western philosophy. He taught that there are two kinds of individual substances in the world: thinking individual substances, called persons or minds (or souls), and physical individual substances. We do not know how fully developed Pythagoras's version of psycho-physical dualism was. He believed that persons or souls are eternal or immortal – in fact he thought their eternity went in both temporal directions, i.e., souls (or persons) never had a beginning of their existence as well as never having an end. In this they differ from bodies or material individuals, which, without exception, begin, last for a while, then perish. Still Pythagoras did think of persons or souls as at least normally or usually existing in a state of union with animal bodies, of human or other type. He believed in what is called reincarnation (literally, the reappearance in a body – sc., of a person or soul) or metempsychosis (the transference of a mind or soul from one (animal) body to another). This view reappears among some later philosophers, most importantly the extremely influential and productive Plato; and has been very widespread among various population groups to the present day. The primary religions that came to power in the Mediterranean world, notably Judaism, Christianity, and Islam, all incorporated a more restricted version of Pythagorean dualist theory, according to which persons (or souls) are created, out of nothing, by an all-powerful God, and are thereafter immortal, but only 'incarnated,' at least on earth, in one (human) animal body.[1] These religions have all tended to be rather exclusive, and to have tried to suppress or eliminate alternative metaphysical systems where and to the degree that they have had the power to do so. As such power has been available to organized adherents of one or other of these religions in the Mediterranean world, and then the territories Mediterranean culture spread to, from A.D. 313,[2] a somewhat uniform variety of Pythagoreanism has had a remarkably central place in the metaphysical thinking of most of the world, for a very long time.

Some philosophical writers pretend (or, in ignorance of the history of philosophy, actually believe) that this Pythagorean-Platonic conception of two substances, one material, the other immaterial but housed or lodged temporarily in the other, only appeared in human thought in the seventeenth century. These writers see Descartes above all as an important conceptual innovator, who introduced a picture and a notion of persons, their nature, and their deepest ontological relationships, that was novel and – for these writers – as deeply implausible as it was alien to a non-dualist conception of these same things that humanity had otherwise more or less uniformly and universally held. We were all materialists, or at 'worst' what we will later identify as dual aspect theorists, before Descartes came along; so these writers say. In fact, though, belief in the self as a 'ghost in a machine,' in a manner to which Descartes

made in fact only extremely modest contribution, has been very widely mani-
fested in human thought, wherever Pythagorean philosophy or Pythagorean
religion have had impact; which is to say, by 1596 (the year Descartes was
born), over half the planet.

This may be effectively illustrated by citing a passage written by a Roman
historian in about the year 41 B.C. This non-philosopher is introducing the
theme of his work, a war the Romans fought with a Moroccan king. We find
him saying the following:

> As a man consists of body and soul, all our possessions and pursuits partake of
> the nature of one or the other. Thus personal beauty and great wealth, bodily
> strength, and all similar things, soon pass away; the noble achievements of the
> intellect are immortal like the soul itself. Physical advantages, and the material
> gifts of fortune, begin and end; all that comes into existence, perishes; all that
> grows, must one day decay. But the soul incorruptible and eternal, is the ruler of
> mankind; it guides and controls everything, subject itself to no control. Where-
> fore we can but marvel the more at the unnatural conduct of those who abandon
> themselves to bodily pleasure and pass their time in riotous living and idleness,
> neglecting their intelligence – the best and noblest element in man's nature – and
> letting it become dull through lack of effort; and that, too, when the mind is capa-
> ble of so many different accomplishments that can win the highest distinction.[3]

There could be no more vivid illustration of the Pythagorean philosophy
of person and mind; and one could find something comparable, in the non-
philosophical as well as the philosophical literature, of virtually every century
since the fourth century B.C. Descartes was in fact a plodding and unoriginal
conservative, at least in this department.

The other distinctive and important feature of the Pythagorean system has
been no less durable, though its influence has been largely confined to philosophers, and philosophically-minded mathematicians. Pythagoras was the first
philosopher to articulate and advocate the view that there are things that are
real that are neither physical nor mental, namely, abstract things ('abstract
entities,' as they are generically called). Rather anachronistically, this view is
usually called Platonism – sometimes Platonic realism, or realism – and came
to be identified as one of the rival positions to take on the so-called 'problem
of universals.' As with psycho-physical dualism, it is not clear how fully
developed a version of 'Platonic realism' was due to Pythagoras or his school;
or whether we should assign to Plato a more significant originating share in
the bringing to metaphysical awareness the phenomenon or alleged phenomenon of *the abstract*. At any rate Pythagoras seems to have thought of numbers

and geometric objects as ideal abstract things that are real and quite distinct both from physical realities that may embody or exemplify them and from the minds or souls that may think about them.[4]

Plato was to augment the category of the abstract, in fact more luxuriantly than the later fundamental position generally called Platonism generally does. For Plato believed in what he called Forms, which are evidently supposed to be perfect archetypal cases of abstract entities. 'Platonists,' and really, they should be called 'Pythagoreans,' tend to hold, and typically in the history of philosophy are found to hold, more restricted 'abstractionist' views, according to which some or all of the following are regarded as real non-mental non-physical things that, at least in most cases, have being whether or not thought or language or persons do: mathematical entities (numbers, geometrical objects, functions, etc.), properties, relations, classes, concepts (in a non-mental sense of this term), propositions, meanings, expression types, and possibly other items. Several of these kinds of things, and abstract entities generally, will be explored more fully later in this book.

Psycho-physical dualism, and the belief in abstract entities (conceived, again, as non-physical and non-mental) are logically quite distinct from one another. One could believe one and not the other, and various metaphysicians have. Yet, they have seemed often, both to advocates and to opponents, to have a certain 'natural' affinity to each other, as 'appropriately' accompanying each other. What genuine conceptual basis this may have is unclear. At any rate, philosophers who have opposed both have tended to see these positions as extravagant, frivolous, not seriously credible, incoherent, diametrically at variance with what a robust, feet-on-the-ground, common sense would suggest or dictate.

For all that, both have persisted and persisted, and are no less genuine features of the metaphysical landscape today than they were when Pythagoras first developed them. This is perhaps especially true of 'Platonism.' 'Mind' as a distinctive and irreducible category of the real has been under close and sustained assault in the Western empiricist tradition for decades now; and may genuinely have been vanquished. Platonic realism has been diminished – not all of the kinds of abstract things that have at times been supposed real seem particularly to need being so supposed – but, to this hour, it is more successfully and typically ignored than refuted. These are some rather hardy metaphysical flora from so early in the philosophical saga.

The Democritean system

Democritus was a junior contemporary of Socrates (469–399 B.C.), hence not strictly a 'pre-Socratic,' though he is standardly placed in that catch-all category for early Greek philosophers whose works and theories survive only fragmentarily. Enough of Democritus's work survives, directly or by report, to put together a reasonably full picture of his views; sufficient to establish that he was an extremely original and important thinker, indeed, sufficient to make it appropriate that he be identified as the foundational iconic figure for a basic philosophical point of view which has continued ever since his lifetime, and is, at present, one of the leading contenders for having things right metaphysically or as nearly right as we can achieve.

Democritus is the first fully recognizable advocate of a naturalist philosophy. He developed the first atomic theory, and while this is important in the history of science and the history of ideas, it is less significant than his conception of the universe as a self-contained, unitary, causal system, without guiding purpose, and including mind and its products as among (and wholly among) its parts. From its beginning with Thales, Greek – Western – philosophy has explored the world by reference to the appearance-reality distinction, and Democritus's atomism is only a more sophisticated instance of this theme. Atoms do not appear; by hypothesis they are imperceptible, but they are the base and root of everything that does appear, and of everything that is real.

The Democritean system is materialist and it is reductionist. Familiar – and not-so-familiar – 'macro' objects and processes, the sorts that we encounter with our senses, are constituted out of smaller, and eventually of smallest parts. In principle to understand those smallest constituents will be to understand the objects and processes that we know experientially, including ourselves and our states.

In the history of Greek atomism we find a sequence with curious parallel to features of modern physics. Democritus was a determinist, who explicitly identified all the events of the world as occurring as instances of exceptionless general laws of nature. Ironically, this position is frequently, and still at present, misinterpreted as the view that events occur randomly, or by 'chance.' Dante, who names Democritus as the fourth important non-Christian philosopher, has things more nearly right, when he says that Democritus 'ascribes the world to chance.'[5] For in the Democritean system, the world is eternal, without beginning or end, and it is both without purpose and without reason for its existence. It is brute fact, neither having nor needing explanation; a system of eternal reinstantiation of general causal principles.

The second great ancient atomic theorist was Epicurus (ca. 342–ca. 271 B.C.). Sharing Democritus's materialism and his anti-teleology, Epicurus baulked at his predecessor's determinism. With vehemence – indeed strong moral fervour – Epicurus held (like so many since him) that exceptionless general law covering all of the events of the world including our own thoughts and our own actions, would necessarily preclude the possibility of genuine free agency. Convinced of the reality of free choice, Epicurus denied that all events are causally determined. Rather, he held, the atoms sometimes 'swerve' in their otherwise lawlike trajectories, the swerve being wholly random and causeless. Through the concept of the swerve, Epicurus sought to explain collisions of particles as well as free choice. Neither is very convincing. As 'Democritean' critics have asked ever since the third century B.C., how can a random event, one wholly without cause or explanation, be one for which we are responsible?[6]

Returning to Democritus, his most important characteristics, as a metaphysician, are his advocacies of materialism, naturalism, determinism, reductionism, and anti-teleology. Seen within this framework, and by virtue of his atomic theory, Democritus is the direct intellectual ancestor of what is now called scientific realism – the view that the postulates and postulated entities of theories of the physical sciences purport to (and when accurate, successfully) characterize or apply to reality.

Plato

If, as Whitehead (1861–1947) said, all of Western philosophy is little more than footnotes to Plato, it is striking how little of the book the footnotes actually retain. Plato lives on, and will do so for the foreseeable future, because Plato has something to say about so much of philosophy, and because he gives arguments (of very uneven merit, to be sure) for the positions he takes. Perhaps he lives on most of all because of the quantity, variety, and literary grace of the Platonic texts, and above all the central eternal philosophic archetype of Socrates who shines, sometimes engagingly, sometimes not, but always full-bloodedly, in almost all of them.

The Platonic *system* – Plato's metaphysics – is primarily an enlargement upon Pythagoras. The most arresting distinctive feature, which would appear to be at least implicit in the Pythagorean system, is – for virtually all non-Platonists – the odd and counter-intuitive doctrine of degrees of being or reality. Plato holds that the aggregate of the real is a hierarchy, in which the things at the top are not only more important, more explanatorily efficacious, but in a literal sense *more real* than those lower down. That being or existence should be regarded as admitting of degrees, like tallness, being rich, or being old, is, as indicated, a hard saying. If we have two things, and both, by agreement and hypothesis, *are*, how can one *be* more than the other?

The best that can be done with this idea, and it does seem to be somewhat

what Plato had in mind, and what helped prompt it, is to think of things like a physical object and the shadow it casts on a sunny day. The shadow is real, yet, we can perhaps allow, or almost allow, less real than the object it is shadow of. So too with echoes and ripples in water. Plato also seems to have been thinking of all varieties of representation in coming to the doctrine of degrees of being. A painting, an image, an idea, a word for something, and the something of or for which it is a representation, may both be granted or held to be, at least in the primary or normal case, real. However – so it may seem, and so it seemed to Plato – the something has a more concrete, and therefore (apparently) a greater, reality than that which (merely) represents it. Ironically, as Plato's system actually developed, it assigns to some cases of what other thinkers would call representations a greater reality than that which is represented. This occurs in the case of concepts of things, in a sense (which Plato developed from partial anticipations in Pythagoras) of concept which does not identify them with or make them depend (logically or causally) on thoughts. For Plato the concept of something has a fixed and permanent reality whereas the referent does not (though of course it may).

This latter idea seems to point to part of what Plato has in mind with the doctrine of degrees of being. Something has more reality in so far as it does not change. (One drastic change is of course ceasing to exist.) Some things, it seems, never change. Plato operates with an implicit contrast between what are sometimes called internal, or intrinsic, states (or properties), and external, or extrinsic ones (called also relational states). Many find this contrast intuitive, even obvious; and perhaps it is. At any rate if we pay attention only to intrinsic properties, we may agree with Plato that there are things that never change. These will have for him the highest degree of reality, all others some lesser degree, a function of their changeableness.

There is one other central Platonic conception which, so far as our evidence goes, seems more or less original with Plato, and which went on to have a very great influence and importance in Western philosophy. Plato's great successor (and opponent) Aristotle is even more famously associated with this theme than Plato is, but it appears in fact more or less fully formed in Plato's writings, and one of the (relatively few) doctrines Aristotle took over from Plato without much altering it. This is the idea that objects (animate, inanimate, natural, contrived), and possibly also activities, have purposes (*telea*, in Greek) or functions, that is their point, what they are here, in the world, *for*; where there is no idea that such purpose or function is relative to concerns or purposes some conscious being may have with regard to the object or activity. The telos of the object or activity is not supposed to be relative to conscious beings' purposes, but natural, in the nature of things. Those unsympathetic to this idea –

and they appeared first in the ancient world, among the atomists (with some anticipations in Anaxagoras (ca. 500–428 B.C.) and Heraclitus (fl. 500 B.C.)), and now are near-universal in at least secular philosophy – have tended to regard this idea as confused, and also as inappropriately normative. Confused because it involves imputing to things other than artifacts what may make sense for them – having a purpose or function – but seems not to for things that were not made by somebody; and inappropriately normative because it involves saying of something that it *ought* to be doing something (being rational, aiming at producing offspring, heading for the surface of the earth) that it may well not be doing, even where there may be no one at hand with an interest or concern that it do that something.

It is important to add that apparent purposiveness in parts of nature where there are not in any obvious way minds whose purposes are involved remains a significant complex of empirical and conceptual issues. The functions – as we continue to call them – of organs and processes especially in the biological world pose still living challenge for understanding, and for integration with a wider comprehension of nature as a whole. The biological component of teleology is more distinctively Aristotle's than Plato's contribution to the topic. Purposes and teleology will be discussed at greater length later in the chapter on 'purpose.'

The Aristotelian System

Aristotle was one of the most original and influential thinkers who ever lived. He more or less single-handedly founded the disciplines we continue to identify as political science, logic, and biology, and had something distinctive and systematic to say about another half-dozen fundamental areas of inquiry. He is, in the broadest recognizable sense, a scientist: a dispassionate, impersonal curious inquirer into the nature of things. This in no way implies that he is without prejudices or unexamined assumptions. He has both. He draws on experience, reason, and the theories of other serious inquirers, and he himself produces systematic theories about everything he investigates.

In assessing Aristotle it is important to include in the picture the immense shadow of his influence; indeed there is something irresponsible in merely trying to convey the most important features of his views – difficult and important as that is. Nor is the influence of Aristotle only something of the past. There continues to be extremely great interest in his work, from more than one perspective, and this interest shows no signs of lessening. His greatest doctrinal impact has been on Roman Catholic theology and philosophy, if we measure impact demographically. While only Catholics would reasonably be viewed today as in some sense Aristotelians,[7] Aristotle's ideas are taken seriously by a wide range of philosophers of non-Catholic persuasion. For a great many contemporary philosophers he remains, on many topics, a genuinely living mind.

Metaphysics is of central importance in Aristotle's work, and in the currents of thought it engendered. In fact the word itself comes from a title given by Alexandrian editors long after Aristotle had died to one of the great philosopher's most important works. This lengthy treatise seemed appropriately to be placed, in its subject matter, after Aristotle's work *The Physics* – that is to say, in Greek, *meta ta phusika*. It became called in Greek therefore *ta Metaphusika*, which becomes, in Latin, *Metaphysica*, or the *Metaphysics*. Metaphysics itself, many would say, is about just the things discussed in the latter work.

Aristotle's system is one of compromise and common sense, and is an early variety of a 'scientific philosophy,' identifiable – perhaps even conceived by its creator – as a sort of middle ground between Plato and Democritus. It also involves many important innovations in metaphysical theory. It is possible to exaggerate both the common sense and the science in Aristotle. Many of its features do not really seem very common sensical at all, and other ancient schools, notably those of the atomists and the Stoics, have in many ways much better claim to being what we would call scientific or empiricist philosophies. The Stoics, for example, like Democritus before them, advocated determinism in a fully developed way, recognizably similar to the determinism of the modern scientific age; whereas Aristotle never brings together his views on the causation of events (including human actions) in a systematic way. And the ancient atomist school – the first empiricists – were explicitly and systematically anti-teleological, unlike Aristotle. In any case, there can be little doubt of Aristotle's novelty.

Aristotle sees the universe as consisting of individual substances – particulars, in a later vocabulary. There are two dimensions to the substances: their form and their matter. In Aristotelian philosophy great complexities or subtleties are posed by what the philosopher apparently takes to be special cases of form and matter. The idea in its most straightforward form is readily grasped and plausible (both quite possibly because of Aristotle's great influence and long historical shadow). Individual physical objects, living or non-living, will be made or composed of some elements, or stuff, in one quantity or other; and that stuff will have been constituted in a particular way. The former is the matter that the object contains and the latter is the form of the object.

As with some other Aristotelian concepts, the notions of form and matter seem clear and straightforward for 'paradigm' cases, but less so with other varieties of things to which the notion is supposed to apply. I will not engage the subtleties form and matter pose, because the central idea seems plausible, and that was responsible for its influence.

Part of Aristotle's creative and constructive insight stemmed from his reflections on his philosophical predecessors. The first at so much else, he was also the first substantive historian of philosophy. The earliest metaphysicians – the Ionian cosmologists, beginning with Thales – had produced theories as to the stuff, or the elements of the world, what things are made of, really and in themselves, in spite of what may be appearances to the contrary. Only gradually did the theoretical articulation of the idea of an individual, a this particular item, appear in ontological inquiry. The idea considerably antedates Aristotle, but no one before him had the notion that metaphysical theory needs to unite an account of the elements, and the constitutedness of an individual as the particular thing it is. Plato dealt with a related but distinct problem, the so-called problem of the one and the many, e.g., how does redness, or horsehood, manage to be one thing, yet also in a sense many things, as we find it exemplified in the several red things and horses. Aristotle's theory of form and matter is a simple and persuasive union of these two components of the world as we seem to find it.

The Stoic System

By the Stoic system I mean to refer chiefly to metaphysical views developed by the three early leaders of the ancient Stoic school (Zeno (334–262 B.C.), Cleanthes (ca. 331–232 B.C.), Chrysippus (ca. 280–ca. 206 B.C.) – and especially the latter) in the third century B.C. These views are less well known than those of Plato, Aristotle, and many later philosophers, since the Stoics' writings mostly perished. We know about them primarily from fragments and later summaries and references. And for present purposes, which are only partly historical in any strict sense, I need to bring attention to only a subset of Stoic metaphysical positions. Scholars may think the selection so partial, and the use I make of it sufficiently anachronistic, that they might see doubtful accuracy or utility in identifying it with the Stoics.

However, there are particular metaphysical views which have proved remarkably persistent in philosophy, in spite of what has sometimes been opponents' incredulity, and which first appear in something recognizably close to the persisting pattern in the Stoics.

A central aspect of the strict Stoic position appears in fact to anticipate the early twentieth-century Austrian philosopher Meinong (1853–1920). He is famous (infamous, for many) for holding that the matter of being a something – an it, or object, that can be thought about – is more fundamental than, and independent of, the matter of being real. Objects, for Meinong, are so whether or not they are real (have being). Some objects have being, others (like Pegasus, the winged horse of mythology) do not. Some of the objects without existence, for Meinong, are abstract or ideal things. For Meinong the latter items have *being*; he distinguishes existence and subsistence (the sort of being that abstract things have) as the two species of being.

The Stoics anticipated much of the Meinongian view, with this difference – for them being has a single species, and abstract things aren't members of it (that is, they are, for the Stoics, strictly unreal). Nonetheless, having drawn the distinction between the really existing items, which for them are material objects and their (material) states, and the *somethings* we can individuate, think and talk about – sometimes using them in theories (of logic and language, for example) – but that aren't actual and material, the Stoics proceed rather as though the strictly unreal (ideal non-material) things were real but very different kind of things.

I have put it this way but others would see inconsistencies or differences between Stoic thinkers. Without more original texts it is hard to decide with any confidence.[8] At any rate it is important to acknowledge the Stoics' formal Meinongianism (to so dub, anachronistically, a theory *they* invented), and with it – part of its justification, apparently – their materialism. As I have indicated, though formally or strictly 'Meinongian,' the Stoics proceed to write, consistently or not, as though abstracta were an immaterial but real (indeed, irreducibly real)   kind of thing. So understanding them, we find the school (and Chrysippus above all) going on to give expression to a broad range of ontological views prominently represented by a large constituency of nineteenth- and twentieth-century analytic philosophers. Among its members (and these philosophers definitely affirm the reality of abstracta) are Frege, Alonzo Church (1903–95), Roderick Chisholm, and Alvin Plantinga. There are many others, and their ideas – these ideas – are only sometimes identified in their commonality. They deserve to be, and the reader will thereby know more about a major position on the contemporary intellectual map if they are.

I call this position Stoic, but it is more usual to style it Platonism. Pythagoras, however, preceded Plato in affirming the reality of abstract things. Moreover, Plato's particular theory of the abstract is not the one that survives and appears in medieval philosophy. Plato believed in ideal or perfect exemplars of all real abstracta. Medieval and contemporary 'Platonists' do not believe this. The theory that they advocate is the one, or a variant of the one, developed in the third century B.C. by Stoic philosophical logicians, and it is for this reason that I identify the system to be described presently as Stoic. There is no harm in calling it Platonist as long as it is clearly realized that only a very approximate resemblance to ideas of Plato is meant.

Whether we should or should not take the set of entities as coinciding with reality, all that there is, the Stoics divided entities into corporeals and incorporeals. Interestingly they included souls or minds among corporeals and thought of mental states as physical. The incorporeals were of four kinds: meaning, place, void, time. Meanings are (and were explicitly identified and discussed in a more or less contemporary way under these discriminations) mind-independent language-independent concepts, propositions, mathematical items, properties, relations.

For good or ill, and with arguments offered in their behalf by Stoics as by modern philosophers, the position holding such items to be real, and of such a nature, endures centrally in metaphysical inquiry and theory. Still another view held by the Stoics which also finds modern expression is the conviction that free will and determinism are compatible with each other. Another is the view that all existent entities are causes or effects. This idea – the notion that to be is to be part of the causal structure of the world – will be explored in a subsequent chapter, as will compatibilism.

The Cartesian System

The Cartesian system was developed by René Descartes. During his lifetime and for a few decades afterwards, it was extremely influential in Western Europe. There were then, and there probably have been ever since, a considerable number of people, in addition to Descartes, who believed that this system is true.

The Cartesian system holds that reality consists of a large number of individual substances, each with essential and accidental properties. These individual substances divide into two fundamental categories or groups: the substances that are essentially thinking things, and the substances that are essentially extended or physical things. The system holds that nothing is or could belong to both types. A property is essential to something only if it would be absolutely or metaphysically impossible for the thing to exist but not have the property. Absolute or metaphysical impossibility cannot be explained non-circularly in the system, although Descartes offers an alternative explication for it. Something is absolutely or metaphysically impossible if and only if an all-powerful being would lack the ability to make it occur or obtain or be true. It appears that it would be impossible to explain the concept of being all-powerful or omnipotent without reference to the very notion of impossibility it is here used to analyse.

The system holds further that the thinking substances (i.e., the substances that are essentially thinking things), or persons (sometimes misleadingly called minds or souls by Descartes), divide into two classes. The first of these has but one member, God. God is essentially a perfect being. From this it is evidently held by Descartes that it follows that God is a thinking being, all-powerful, all-knowing, entirely good, internally changeless; and that he necessarily exists. The other class of thinking beings or persons has a large number of members. Among them are the referents of many familiar proper names for persons, e.g., René Descartes, Aristotle, Stalin, Margaret Thatcher. Each of these, and evidently each person or thinking substance is a self, an 'I.'

The material or physical or extended substances are necessarily (or essentially) unthinking, just as the thinking substances are necessarily (or essentially) noncorporeal and unextended. The latter are simple and indivisible, without parts; although this seems either rather trivially obvious if physical parts are meant, since a nonphysical and unextended thing could hardly have physical parts, or unclear and obscure if some other variety of part, e.g., logical parts, were meant. Extended substances are indefinitely (physically) divisible, and indefinitely malleable or alterable, into any possible physical shape or structure.

Descartes also affirms that in a special sense of essence, each of these substances has a single or unique essence, viz., thought or extension. The special sense is evidently that of general kinds of extremely wide type; but the idea is not adequately developed or analyzed in the system.[9] At any rate, it appears to follow from this view, together with earlier theses, that for Descartes any physical object or substance could in principle become an object of any other physical kind. Thus, a croquet mallet could become an ashtray, a styrofoam cup an asteroid, or a lion become an aluminum can. They would cease to be croquet mallets, styrofoam cups, or lions, respectively, but they would continue to be the individual objects that they were. The sole essence of physical substances is their extension.

Persons or thinking substances are, in the Cartesian system, free, capable of free actions and choices. Hence, Descartes supposes, they are undetermined, not subject to deterministic general law.

The Humean System

The historical David Hume was, in my opinion, primarily and essentially what is later called a positivist, although not what still later came to be called a logical positivist, nor a particularly extreme example of the original or classical type. But he is, I believe, a positivist nonetheless; apparently the first of the breed. Positivists, in Hume's sense, are sceptical about the possibility of meta-physical knowledge. They do not reject its possibility a priori. Their position is one of agnosticism and avoidance. Let him or her who may wish to make out a case for metaphysical knowledge seek to do so; but such claims, like all cognitive claims, must confront the tribunal of experience, where, Hume believes (though acknowledging in principle the possibility that he is in error), they will be found wanting and condemned. Meantime the cognitive enter-prise, rational and empirical inquiry, can actually make good progress if it is cautious, and confined to questions of experience. Its great success in this regard, for positivists, is to be found supremely and paradigmatically (for some positivists uniquely) in the natural sciences.

Though a positivist, Hume does make interesting, important, and innovative metaphysical assumptions. He seems less than aware, however, that he is doing so. Nonetheless they point to a conception of the nature of reality that no earlier philosopher seems to have delineated, and it is this, with apologies for its partially anachronistic or inappropriate imputation to Hume, that I am calling the Humean system. Its importance lies not just in its novelty. Some-thing like the Humean system may be discerned, explicitly or implicitly, in a number of twentieth-century empiricist philosophers (perhaps most explicitly, as metaphysics, in Russell).

For the Humean system the fundamental ontic category is the event or state. No distinction of logical significance is drawn between them. A lump of sugar dissolving in water is an example of an event/state; so too is the sky's being blue on a particular occasion; and sensing something triangular and luminous. In addition to apparently straightforward cases, others are problematic. Though events/states are necessarily complex in structure, it requires logical or empirical investigation to determine what structure they have in individual cases. In particular, it cannot be assumed that they have object-having-property or objects-being-in-relation structure. It appears that states need not have subjects, or things of which they are states, for example. Thus, that it is raining at time t and place p does not seem to imply that something is raining then and there; 'it' may be a 'dummy' pronoun, a place-holder required by the rules of English syntax but not corresponding to anything in the nature of things. So it may also be with other states, including many for which we stan-dardly assume an ontological subject – a substance. Thus, that there is some thinking going on at *t* and *p* should not be taken necessarily to imply that something is doing that thinking; that there are thinkers, in other words. That there are events – states or episodes – is taken as given and certain but their analysis, structure, and whether they require substances (objects) as constitu-ents will be for investigation and considerations of theory to determine.

Further, the events or states of reality are taken, in the Humean system, to be, in general, at least, enumerable and discriminable. It is possible to determine objectively that this event is not that one, that some episode has begun, is taking place, has transpired and what the boundaries of episodes are. Reality, in this system, is a sequence, system, or structure of such states, each of them intrinsically indexed to place and time; though the Humean system is open to reductive analysis of both place and time. A more elaborate – and more appropriately positivist – version of this conception would see such structures of event/state sequences as relative to a perspective, with doubtful intrinsic (or 'absolute') reality apart from any perspective.

For the Humean system all distinct and discrete states are only contingently connected to each other. If states in a sequence S_1, S_2, ... , S_n are found to be states of the world, a sequence with any or all of them missing would equally have been possible, as would any alternative ordering of the sequence; and so it is for all such sequences, including the maximal sequence comprising the whole set of all actual events and states. Thus, the very first event of the universe could have been an eighteenth-century-garbed fop sipping tea from a porcelain cup, and its successor event – at the same (or some other) place and an instant later – a collision of purple and white billiard balls. And so on. Moreover, a possible, complete sequence of events consists of idealist, even solipsist idealist,[10] sensings and thinkings, in every possible order and without subjects. For example, events accurately describable as 'blue being sensed here and now' then 'pain being felt here and now-plus-one-time-unit,' then 'wondering whether 97 is prime here and now-plus-two-time units,' could constitute a part, indeed the whole, of some 'world.'

It is always and only through experience that we find that *this* is the world we have discovered ourselves to be in, and that it is of *this kind*. Contrary to some interpreters, I do not think that Hume, or his system, are in any very strong sense foundationalist or incorrigibilist.[11] This is an epistemic, or epistemological, matter, and something we can avoid here. However, it can and should be affirmed that the picture of reality Hume offers is fundamentally one of contingently related states, with no assumptions made about whether such states are immediate deliverances of consciousness, or exemplifications of human theories of varying degrees of sophistication, or neither.

Hume is important then, for metaphysics, for his posing the possibility of metaphysics without substance, for the notion of an event (or state) ontology, and for the notion of a radical inherent contingency in the nature of things. As indicated, a number of twentieth-century empiricist philosophers have taken up, and extended, these metaphysical views.

Reid

I mean to identify under the name of the Scottish philosopher, Thomas Reid, what I want to call the common-sense view of reality. What is common sense? Haven't radically differing conceptions passed, in different times and places, for what common sense says about fundamentals of the world as well as anything else? This may be so; that is what the critique of the system now presented may insist. It is clear nonetheless that there have been metaphysical theories that have claimed that the real nature of the universe is significantly different from its experienced appearances. Equally, there will be philosophies that hold that appearance and reality fundamentally or significantly coincide; moreover, that we can justifiably assemble a systematic account of the world that begins and ends with what is encountered in everyday human life.

A case can be made for Socrates as the first common-sense philosopher, just as a better case, in my view, can be made that Socrates was the first analytic philosopher. The historical Socrates seems to have held firmly to the basic and ineliminable reality of standard physical objects and processes as well as of individual human beings and their states, including their mental states. Still, such common-sense theory as we find here is undeveloped. Socrates' contemporaries, the Sophists, were common-sense *philosophers* – they are the intellectual ancestors of modern pragmatism – but not common-sense *metaphysicians*, since they denied the possibility of a coherent or achievable project of understanding the world objectively. More plausibly than either Socrates or the Sophists, Aristotle has some claim to being an early common-sense metaphysician. For Aristotle, however, the authoritative ground of the results he comes to as to the nature of things, while it gives what 'the many' know (or think they know) in their commonality a consultative status, it gives this status also to the (supposed) experts who have gone before, and, finally, definitive authority only to Aristotle's own deployment of reason, as he understands it. The many, and their views, have a place in this account (which was not the case in earlier Greek philosophy, apart, perhaps, from Socrates); but independent rationality, which can and sometimes does depart from the views of the many, is sovereign.

Thomas Reid seems, in fact, to be the first self-conscious champion of the idea that we have, over the course of our existence as a species experiencing and thinking about the world in relatively uniform ways, achieved accurate, shared apprehensions of basic features of our world. Reid's primary aims were epistemological: to contest and refute the scepticism implicit (as he saw it) in rationalist and explicit in empiricist philosophies of his day, and thereby justify knowledge claims about the world. If scepticism is refuted, however, it follows that knowledge is possible, or actual, but not what constitutes the content of that knowledge. It is a contentful addition to the refutation of scepticism to argue, not that some esoteric theory only delineable with specialized categories and in a technical vocabulary, is the truth of things but rather that we always possessed, out of quotidian experience and with familiar, elemental, and universal modes of thought and speech, all that was needed to set out that truth.

The common-sense system holds that there are physical objects, some animate, some not; living plants and animals, and dead or never-living particular objects; all with qualities that we directly sense (this last, at least, was part of Reid's version of common-sense realism). This allows that there may be imperceptible qualities that objects have, as well as imperceptible objects. For common sense too, thought is real and so is our freedom of choice and of action. Real as well are time and space, with an objective structure that corresponds to our experience of them: beyond every space and time, whatever the magnitude of either, is another of comparable magnitude.

Still, there are issues on which common sense does not speak with a single voice, and on some issues it may be altogether silent. The existence of a God is at least not ruled out by common sense, and along with that hypothesis (and perhaps others) would be allowed possibilities of a beginning of time. Common sense would insist on the reality of general causal regularities, in at least much or most of nature; but be silent or contrary whether causality's writ also extends to everything that conscious beings think or do. Whether a material object could think, whether there could be immaterial (or disembodied) personal existence for a once living human being, whether so-called secondary qualities (colours, sounds, temperatures) could fail to be objective qualities of physical objects, are just some of the philosophical issues on which the views of common sense are unclear or divided. Even direct perceptual realism is not universal among common-sense philosophers. Reid was a perceptual realist but the greatest representative of common-sense philosophy in the twentieth century, G.E. Moore, was not.

Nonetheless, a common-sense, metaphysical perspective, in many cases still remarkably close in detail to the philosophical ideas and commitments of Reid, continues to be a living and active part of contemporary metaphysical investigation and debate.

Chapter Four

Categories and First Principles

I

An orderly way to proceed with the project of investigating reality in the most basic and general terms (and with candid acknowledgment of a selective leaning toward topics of special interest to humans) is to try to set out at the start fundamental concepts and principles, and matters of method. This is somewhat how Aristotle proceeded. At any rate, alongside his major metaphysical treatises, the *Metaphysics* itself, the *Physics*, and *De Anima*, we find a set of writings called collectively the *Organon*, concerned with procedural and foundational things. This is where most of what we know as Aristotle's logic is to be found. The *Organon* also houses a work particularly important for metaphysics, called the *Categories*, which seeks to set out various fundamental ways in which substances can be classified and investigated.

Aristotle had a metaphysical bias or predilection for substances. It seemed clear to him that they, and above all individual living substances, like Socrates and Fido, have a centrality and in some manner a logical priority in investigating the world that other existing things do not. We may possibly come to some version of Aristotle's view, but, at least at the outset, we are trying to be more neutral; at any rate, to devise a set of organizing concepts of categories of things that will be as comprehensive as possible, and not just confined to things like individual human beings or dogs (or, for that matter, electrons).

We want, then, to borrow the idea of a systematic outlay of categories from Aristotle, but to use the idea quite independently of his practice or purposes. This indeed has seemed methodologically appropriate and desirable to many other metaphysical inquirers. Alfred North Whitehead, for example, in his ambitious (and often obscure) metaphysical treatise *Process and Reality*,[1] devotes his first post-introductory chapter to developing a highly involved 'categoreal scheme,' in whose terms the system of his book is to be understood.

II

Something else called category theory has developed a life of its own, as a specialized philosophical discipline concerned with fundamental kinds and classifications of things, and what it may or may not be meaningful to ascribe to something of one category in the language (or concepts) of another distinct category. (One especially prominent category theorist, of this sort, has been in recent years Fred Sommers.[2]) I shall have things to say in this chapter about both kinds of category theory – that is to say, about category theory as an autonomous field in ontology and the philosophy of language, and about category theory as a preliminary to metaphysical inquiry. Both can be expressed in distinct idioms: either as a matter of language or as a matter of concepts and things. The view held throughout the present book is that quite often philosophical views can be expressed in a 'linguistic mode,' as a matter of words and how they work (practically or for purposes of theory) or, alternatively, as a matter of actual or possible things and their actual or possible properties and relations, and what might or must hold in respect of the latter. These alternatives, as I see them, are not actually equivalent, but they by and large 'amount to the same thing.' Characterizing things as a matter of words is not (contrary to the views of many twentieth-century philosophers) an advance upon putting things as a matter of things. Indeed, where 'language mode' and 'reality-mode' diverge – certainly where or if they conflict – the latter is always to be preferred. In general, I would argue that philosophy of language (which for the most part would reverse that preference ordering) has gotten 'too big for its boots.'[3] However, it will often be convenient, and especially in the present context, to phrase our inquiry and its results as a matter of what we do or should prefer to say about the world and its divisions, rather than as a matter of the world and its divisions themselves. This, then, is a first statement of method for the present inquiry.

Returning to category theory in its particular twentieth-century form, it should be noted that its advocates have characteristically adopted a view which virtually defines their subject for them but about which I want to be largely non-committal. This is the idea that some things said about things not only do not but cannot apply, and only produce incoherence if applied to some other things. The idea, for them, is that concepts come in families, such that certain attributions (true or false) make sense for items in those families, which don't make any sense if someone tries to apply them to items in categoreally distinct families. Although category theorists are sometimes incautiously extreme in their claims of this kind, the most reasonable view to assign them appears to be that *some* things can be intelligibly said of anything at all – for example, *being found interesting (or boring) by someone, being discussed in such and such a book,* and, perhaps, *being real,* or *being such that p* (where *p* is any true proposition); but that some things cannot intelligibly be said of items from distinct categoreal families: for example, *having just been photographed* might be said intelligibly of Bill Clinton (whether truly or falsely), but (a category theorist might affirm) is unintelligible, or meaningless, if said of, say, the number 7 or the property of self identity or 5:35 p.m. yesterday, all of which, in turn, would have things meaningfully sayable of them, that would be incoherent if said of Clinton.

Linguists sometimes approach these matters in a more heuristic or empirical manner, noting varying degrees of dissent or discordance a speaker of a natural language may feel on being presented with sentences that are syntactically well-formed – subjects, predicates, etc., in appropriate places – but which seem or are informationally bizarre. From (say) *That tree wanted to talk to me about his law practice* to (a particularly famous example: Chomsky's) *colourless green ideas are sleeping furiously* there seem to be formulable sentences along a continuum of ever-increasing oddity, but that remain syntactically well-formed. What is to be said of them? There are quite a few possible positions to adopt, along different parameters. Most acknowledge that a proposition can be not merely false but necessarily false; so some would prefer to say that every syntactically well-formed sentence is meaningful, but some of them express necessary falsehoods. So in this view, it couldn't be that colourless green ideas sleep furiously, because it is logically (or metaphysically) impossible to sleep furiously, to be colourless and green, and to be green and an idea. Others, category theorists among them, would prefer saying that, e.g., being a round square is different from being a sleeping idea, and while the former is necessarily something not obtaining the latter doesn't (even) manage to be that. ('We can't understand,' is a standard formula, what could possibly be meant by combining these two ideas.) Yet no one, it seems, wants to say that the Chomsky sentence is literally unintelligible noise, just gibberish.

As indicated above, I don't want to take a stand on this matter (though it may have emerged that I lean toward the necessary falsehood position). There certainly seem to be degrees of strangeness that can attach to or be felt at the perception of what, formally speaking, can count as well-formed natural language sentences.

In any case, it does not seem to matter very much metaphysically what view we prefer on the Chomsky sentence, or what I have called the defining feature of category theory. Even if *7 is asleep* involves a category mistake, we have to have a way, and plainly can avail ourselves of some way, of saying that being asleep does not apply to the number 7. So, even if, as Sommers would hold, *7 is asleep* and *7 is not asleep* both commit category errors, we need something which we may as well call *7 is non-asleep*, to express the desired idea. Some reserve non-*F* for complementarity within a category. If that usage is adopted, we simply need to, and can, construct another formula to indicate that a certain predicate doesn't apply to a certain subject, either because it happens contingently not to, or necessarily fails to, or because it would be unintelligible to assert that predicate of that subject.

III

I may have diverged at unnecessary length into twentieth-century category theory. However, some of its advocates have argued that its defining feature is of metaphysical moment, so it seems appropriate to show that it is not. Also, I do want to make use of other features of category theory, namely, those it shares with Aristotle's original launching of the subject.

So conceived, categories will be fundamental groupings of things that are or might be real. The 'might' just indicated is important. Initially, at least, it would seem to need to be an epistemic 'might,' since we might delineate a metaphysical category – see a point in having one – at an early stage of inquiry, which in fact (we later concluded) was a category of metaphysically impossible things, that necessarily fail to be real. Suppose *F* was such a category. We might initially place *Fs*, or *Fness*, on the conceptual map, because there was a long tradition of doing that, or because some particular philosopher we held in high regard utilized such a category, or because it looked somehow promising to think, provisionally, of there being such things. But this would not preclude coming, after argument and investigation, to the view that not only are there no *Fs*, there couldn't be; even, possibly, that the concept of Fness is incoherent, the illusion of a clear notion of a kind of thing there could be.

It seems that (metaphysical) category theory should have two basic stages. One is the absolutely preliminary one just now discussed partly where all theoretical options are under consideration. The other, later stage is where some commitment has been made to a conceptual structure held to provide a blueprint for thinking accurately about what is real. Even at this later stage, there need be no formal commitment to the reality of entities falling under the categories adopted. That will be a third stage of categorial (and methodological) development, for which we can utilize Quine's well-known phrase, and concept, ontological commitment. Roughly, ontological commitment is the idea that the kinds of things implied to be real by a set of statements that are accepted and affirmed constitute the ontology for that set, to whose actual reality the set's advocate is rationally committed. So, if someone S holds that a is F, and that a is F implies that some G thing is real (because a is necessarily a G thing), then S is ontologically committed to the reality of G things; or (alternatively) S's theory containing the claim that a is F implies the objective existence of Gs, as one of the kinds of things the universe contains.

Let me illustrate all three of the stages identified above.

At the first stage we might consider the plausibility of assuming items of a variety of kinds (or alleged kinds). Candidate cases, with sample exemplars of each, might be: spatio-temporal particulars (e.g., Bill Clinton, the wooden table my hat is on, the sun); abstract entities (e.g., the number 7, the property of being an electron, the class of fish); temporal entities (such as the fourteenth century, last week, the first three minutes following the big bang); Meinongian possibilia (like Aphrodite, Batman, the golden mountain); and stuffs (e.g., snow, styrofoam, hydrogen). As it happens, I have great difficulty believing that the category of Meinongian possibilia can survive initial scrutiny. It isn't, it seems to me, a case where one group of ontologists thinks there are items of kind K, and a rival group denies that there are. There is, I believe, insuperable difficulty in seeing that this particular putative group is genuinely on offer, at the ontologists' market place. Of (nonactual) Meinongian possibilia we are supposed to be able to say, intelligibly: there are things that there aren't. I don't know what the first occurrence of the copula in this formula is supposed to mean, and nothing in the Meinongian literature seems to help. It is apparently not supposed to mean something *ontic*; and sometimes it is described as a formulaic phrase answering only requirements of grammar. But, ... I can't see it. I can't see how it can help but be something ontic; and if it is ontic at all, Meinongianism is bound to be a logically contradictory position, since Meinongianism will be unable to prevent (indeed, must endorse the possibility of) the second copula in the formula being understood as the first was.

Now, this will alert the reader that I am not sympathetic to Meinongianism; which is indeed the case. In the present context, though, it is of more important to see that one can consider, and either accept or reject, the conceptual viability of a category of entities, well in advance of any commitment to the actual reality of any such entities.

IV

Another dimension to categoreal choice should also be mentioned, and then deferred to later discussion. Sometimes an ontologist will regard entities of a certain type as reducible to entities of another type. (This may obtain whether or not the ontologist regards the entities as actually real.) The concept of reduction is, I believe, more complex than often supposed. Some account of reducibility will be given below. At this phase of inquiry, it seems reasonable to say that we are seeking a set of categories for the real, some of which might possibly turn out to be subsumable under, or reducible to others. That possibility will be, initially, at least, of less moment than achieving an adequate, and clear, conceptual stockpile.

Without claiming that alternative approaches may not also be fruitful, I offer a categoreal schema which is intended to be exhaustive, but perhaps skeletal only. We will have for each category the matter of what it is to fall under the category, and separately the question of whether or not anything does. That is, to reinforce what has already been affirmed, we offer categories of ontological type, without presupposing in the cases of any of them that there actually are entities of the type in question. I want even to allow – to insist in fact – that all (or some) of the entities of a given type might actually turn out in the end to be 'logical constructions,' 'logical fictions,' or (in that curious phrase of Russell's which, in his usage, violates or ignores the use/mention contrast) 'incomplete symbols.' An entity is a logical fiction or construction if it is the case that truths in our language seem to imply that there exists such an entity (or type of entity), whereas in fact these truths are analysable into statements with no such (even apparent) implication. 'The average consumer' is an example of an entity sometimes held to be a logical fiction; according to some views so also are numbers, as (for some) are persons.

The character of much of the discussion that precedes, laying the groundwork for setting up a categoreal scheme for ontology, may make it appear that the enterprise is to a very considerable degree heuristic or ad hoc, and this, in turn, might be thought to suggest that the categories to which things are to be assigned are contingent items, or that it is contingent whether something falls under the category in which it is placed. Reflection should suggest, however, that the categoreal results, if plausible, hence, true, will not be contingent, but necessary. Much foundational work in formal enterprises is tentative, and exploratory. There will seem at the outset considerable room for trying out whether a conceptual option can prove fruitful. This will provide, in fact, no reason whatever to suppose that a preferred conceptual option is merely contingent or empirical. The best way to see this will be to try, after the conceptual scheme has been laid out, to see whether an item in one category can be transferred to another. And with this last preliminary set of remarks, let us proceed with the outlines of our ontological schema.

V

Our most general and comprehensive notion will be that of an *entity*. Anything that exists or has being is an entity. Everything, in short, is an entity.[4]

The entities divide up into five alternative bipolarities of which we shall take notice. It doesn't matter which of these we start or finish with. Each is a bifurcation of all the entities that is exclusive and exhaustive.

First, every entity is either abstract or concrete. There may not be any abstract entities – so some wish to maintain – or there may not be as many, or of as many types, as has sometimes been supposed. However, there appears to be general agreement about what are intended as the abstract things. If there are such things as these, properties, relations, classes, concepts, propositions, numbers, geometrical and other mathematical objects, are abstract entities or *abstracta*.[5]

Formally defining what it is to be an abstract entity is a difficult challenge. Three paths may briefly be mentioned. First, it might seem plausible to identify abstracta as the entities that *cannot be experienced*. A lot of initial objections, or questions, come immediately to mind. We need first to make clear that we talk not just of sense experience, but of experience or awareness of any sort, so long as it is what we may call *direct*. We need also to make clear though that there can be (direct) experience in the sense intended that involves processes of *inference*. (Thus, for example, if I see someone wearing a white coat and holding a stethoscope, in a (normal) hospital setting, it may seem reasonable to say that I have (directly) seen, or at least experienced, a doctor; even though I clearly have made inferences from what I have directly observed if I am to know this. For some philosophical views comparable inference is involved in concluding that a physical object has been observed, or an animal.) These poles will constitute the Scylla and Charybdis of attempting to define abstracta along this line, and I frankly do not know whether both can be avoided simultaneously. If inference can be an element in (direct) awareness, why then can abstracta not be directly experienced? And if the experience really must be direct, how can such a thing as the fact that this piece of sugar is soluble in water not turn out abstract? I think on the whole that it ought to be possible, with a great deal of work, to set out programmatically notions of experience and (possible) objects of experience, such that just the entities we have in mind antecedently as the abstract ones will be incapable of being experienced (by any possible 'mind' or thinking subject), according to these notions, and all the other entities will be capable of being experienced. Carrying out this program would constitute in fact the defence and justification of (one version of) *empiricism*.[6] Conceived in still larger terms it would comprise the defence of reductionism (Quine's second 'dogma of empiricism')[7].

A second line of approach to defining abstracta departs from the idea that the abstract entities are the things that are neither directly nor derivatively physical, mental, or temporal in nature, and that they are the only things of which this is true. Here again a good deal of work is required to specify what one will want to mean by *physical*, *mental*, and *temporal* in this context. I won't attempt to say anything at all about time in this context, except to say that by 'is a temporal thing' we won't want to mean (even in part) 'is a thing that occurs or exists at some time.' Some philosophers certainly have had the thought that some things, and if some things then surely abstract things among them, do not exist at a time, are 'outside time,' 'atemporal,' or something of the sort. Other philosophers, though, while agreeing that of some things it may always be false to assert that there are specific instants of time at which they begin to exist, endure, and cease to exist, nonetheless profess to find extremely obscure the idea that a thing exists 'outside time.' My own convictions certainly are with this second contingent. I think that if the number 7 or the property of redness exist, then they existed at 4:00 o'clock yesterday afternoon; likewise for things like God. Similarly, it seems to me that 7 was greater than 5 yesterday, and has continued to be so today. (The issue of whether anything can exist outside time will be taken up more fully in later discussions.) However, a useful concept of *being a temporal thing* shouldn't have to take sides on an issue like this. By a temporal thing we will more usefully want to have in mind temporal items as such: instants of time, seconds, minutes, hours, days, centuries, etc., and possibly time itself.

In general, with matter, mind, and time, adequate explicative success ought to be possible. One will want to specify a notion of 'is a physical thing' such that events, facts, and states, as well as 'substances,' will fall under the extension of the term; and likewise for 'is a mental thing.' Defining and classifying the realms of the physical and the mental respectively in this way (and without, of course, prejudging whether these realms exclude each other) should in fact be perfectly possible, even relatively easy. Less straightforward surely will be the conviction one could have that only abstract entities could be non-mental, non-physical, and non-temporal. Perhaps we will want to say that the abstracta are the entities that are essentially non-physical, essentially non-mental, and also essentially non-temporal. How sure can or should one be though that the universe doesn't or couldn't contain other sorts of things that are essentially non-physical, non-mental, and non-temporal, than abstract entities? (Though clearly abstracta *are* essentially non-physical, non-mental, and non-temporal.)

A third path to this distinction between abstracta and concreta seeks to define abstracta simply by ostension. Thus, we aim at providing an exhaustive disjunction of the kinds of abstracta. This approach may also be promising (though also in need of labour). Perhaps properties, relations, propositions, information (what information theory is supposed to be about), concepts, sets, numbers, pure geometrical objects, actual geometrical objects (the points of physical space, and such items as the North Pole and the equator),[8] linguistic expression types, series, functions, and any other mathematical 'objects' really are all the abstract entities there are. Something will be abstract then if and only if it is one of these.

In a notable discussion of the contrast between abstract and concrete entities, David Lewis raises doubts whether this contrast can be plausibly and clearly drawn.[9] Lewis considers four ways in which the contrast might be argued, and finds difficulty with each of them. None of Lewis's four precisely coincide with the three putative grounds of distinction explored here, though two of them are close (Lewis's 'negative way' and his 'way of example' are similar to my second and third putative grounds). My own discussion, as will be noted, affirms the difficulty of drawing the contrast. However, unlike Lewis, I take the distinction, even if its precise grounds are elusive, to be intuitive. Lewis is particularly concerned to determine whether a (possible) world will turn out to be an abstract or concrete entity. It seems evident that a world is concrete, even if it has parts or constituents that are abstract. In this respect a world is like a fact, or a state of affairs, both of which are complexes (see below) which may consist of a concrete individual particular's having a property (which is abstract).

I see no good reason to doubt then that the distinction between the abstract and the concrete is conceptually well-grounded, and intuitive (however difficult to state). The concreta, of course, will be defined as the entities that are not abstract. We may state again that we do not maintain or imply that there *are* abstract entities. It may be that there are none in one of two ways. It might be that abstracta, or some – perhaps most – abstracta, simply do not exist; or it may be that they are 'logical constructions': things that seem to exist, that our discourse seems to imply to be a kind of thing the universe contains, but that can be shown to be such that discourse apparently about them is always analysable as discourse that is not about them but something non-abstract. On either view it will be held – though some philosophers seem unaware of this in the case of the second view – that there are no abstract entities. The second view though will show (if it works) both why (though there are none) there seem to be abstracta, and that lots of propositions apparently about abstracta are perfectly true. But our concern here is with none of these matters; rather only with what it would be actually to be an abstract entity, i.e., and exist. Again, then, we take it we know what this does mean.

VI

A second distinction we draw that is often confused with the first is between universals and particulars.

There appear to be entities that are universals which are not abstract, and almost certainly there are abstracta that are not universal. And at least with the notion of *particular* intended here – the term is used sometimes in other ways – everything in reality is quite certainly either a universal or a particular, so we may find a use in our ontological schema for this traditional contrast as well as the division between the abstracta and the concreta.

What is a universal? Intuitively, although crudely, a universal is an entity that has or can have instances or cases. The clearest cases of this notion are afforded by properties and relations. Thus, we may say that the individual red things are instances or cases (exemplars) of the property of redness.[10] The ordered pairs of things such that the first loves the second are the instances of the (binary) relation of loving. (And in general, the instances of an *n*-ary relation will be the ordered *n*-tuples of things of which the relation is true). We note that it appears that there is a difference of type between the instances of properties and relations: the exemplars of the former are standardly individuals, of the latter ordered n-tuples, i.e., classes or sets of a certain special sort.[11]

As well as properties and relations, other kinds of abstracta seem reasonably construed as having cases. Thus, it appears appropriate to regard the sentences (sentence *types*, that is) that express propositions as instances or instantiations of those propositions. Similarly sentence tokens may be taken as instances of sentence types.

However, not all abstract entities are universals. A class for example surely is a particular thing. True, it has members. We could perhaps not unreasonably stretch the notion of exemplification to have application to class membership. Yet intuitively a class is just the specific collection of things that it is, not something that is (as it were) wholly repeatable in each of several different cases. The individual points of space may plausibly be taken as other abstracta that are not universal.

It may seem too that some universal entities are not abstract. Thus it may be reasonable to take some facts as instances or cases of other facts. Perhaps the fact that *this* piece of copper expands when heated is an instance or case of the fact that *all* pieces of copper expand when heated.

Some universals cannot in fact have instances. Contradictory properties, for example, cannot.[12] So we must modify the initial approximate characterization of a universal we gave above. We may say that a universal is an entity that can have instances or cases, or that is analysable as a conjunction of entities that can have instances or cases. ('Conjunction' remains without, but clearly in need of explanation here, since we obviously don't mean by it a binary sentential connective – i.e., an expression which may be applied to two sentences to produce one compound sentence. All the connectives are in fact extendable to apply to relations between properties; in this particular case what one has in mind should be fairly obvious.) In one usage particulars are (Aristotelian) primary substances; or else – a more catholic usage – possible values of individual variables in first order logic;[13] in yet another, the one suggested here, any entity that isn't a universal is a particular.

VII

As indicated, we are offering here just the outline of an ontological schema, with details where they seem readily forthcoming, and beyond that some pointers to possibly promising approaches to such details. We have then the concept of an entity, and the pairs abstract/concrete, and universal/particular. A particular is any entity that cannot have instances or cases (and cannot be analysed as a conjunction of entities that do), and we saw that some labour, and some semantical decisions, were needed before we could be content with the concepts of having or being an instance (or case).

Our third bipolarity divides entities into the simple and the complex. Although the general idea seems easy to state and illustrate, and appears a wholly intuitive notion, this is perhaps the most difficult and opaque of our ontological category sets. Yet it is one that has seemed sound and intuitive to philosophers since Aristotle. That doesn't make it right, or coherent, and it certainly doesn't make it easy to define or explain. Yet something like this contrast seems hard to resist when trying to grasp the most fundamental categories of things.

We want to say that there are the *objects* as such, the individual things – whether abstract or concrete – and there are complexes that contain objects as their constituents. Thus, for example, if apple *a* is red, there appears to be something highly plausible about saying that the apple is one (kind of) thing, and its being red – apple *a*'s being red – is another, with both of them real entities. The apple, in the example, will be the simple, and the apple's being red will be the complex. One way to define this contrast might be – and a certain begging of the reader's indulgence is required here – to take the concept of *being a constituent of* as primitive. We can then define a simple thing as an entity that can be but cannot have a constituent. A simple is an entity that can be, rather than one that is, a constituent, because it may have failed to enter into a complex, may have remained, so to speak, a free atomic object, but will be no less a simple for that. In fact, though, if facts and states of affairs are complexes, and they are of course paradigm cases of them, then something can be a constituent if and only if it is a constituent, for it is a necessary truth that if something exists then there are facts about it or states of affairs in which it figures (e.g., the fact that the item has some property that it does). Still, it may be held, the *idea* of a simple is the idea not of actually being an element of a complex, but of being capable of being such an element. Correlatively, if something could have a constituent, but just happened not to, it would seem persuasive that it wasn't a simple. Being unable to have a constituent won't mean that a simple thing will be incapable of being divided into parts (for example into physical parts). Provisionally, at least, I want to count ordinary physical objects (such things as an individual horse, or a rock, or a tree) as simple concreta,[14] and they, of course, will have parts. But they don't have constituents. Facts have constituents, events and processes have them, states and states of affairs do, propositions have them, so do sentences. (Sentences also have parts.)

Some might find the idea of taking the concept of a complex, in our sense, as primitive (but clear). It will still be necessary also to have a notion of constituency, or no analysis or explanation of what complexes are like will be possible. Only with the concept of constituency can we define a complex as an entity that has constituents.

What can we say about the relations between being a constituent and being a part? I take the former to be a broader notion. Facts, for example, have constituents. It seems at best unclear whether they have parts, or whether and in what sense anything non-physical can have parts. Or perhaps they are just different (if, in some respects, similar) notions. Possibly it is attractive to say than an hour has parts, its first half and its second half, for example. However, these are surely not constituents of the hour. Are the members of a set constituents of that set? Maybe so. We can continue in metaphor. We might say that whereas divisibility into parts 'implies' the possibility of some act of division which has not yet taken place, a complex is already 'divided' into its constituents. Moreover, we may assert that there is only one possible specification of the constituents of a complex. However, there may be and standardly, there are, many possible specifications of parts of a thing divisible into parts.

This may not make it an easy thing (nor have I claimed or implied otherwise) to itemize the constituents of a complex. Doing so is, indeed, the very project of what has historically been meant by philosophical analysis. Like so much else in philosophy, philosophical analysis appears first among the ancient Greeks, in the attempts that Socrates and Plato considered (and sometimes offered themselves) to formulate accurate and theoretically informative definitions or explications of fundamental concepts. Although Socrates has a good claim to be the first 'analytic philosopher,' the usual historical picture accords the foundational roles to Frege, Moore, and Russell, in the late-nineteenth and early-twentieth centuries. All three deeply original philosophical thinkers, with the youthful Wittgenstein's *Tractatus Logico-Philosophicus* providing a fourth important exemplar from this early modern period of philosophical analysis, worked with a model of logical or conceptual 'space' within which clear, careful intuition was to seek and with good fortune find structures of facts of common sense, science, logic, mathematics, or theoretical metaphysics. Russell's special version of this enterprise produced what he called the philosophy of logical atomism (and of which Wittgenstein's early work is a variant). Classically, philosophical analysis is then the attempt to delineate and explain the structures of complexes, like belief, propositions, facts, and to itemize and distinguish the elements or constituents of those complexes. I avow here a classically logical atomist conception of this enterprise, and undoubtedly betray also an equally logical atomist credence in the chances of success for it. I do not conceal the conviction underlying everything written here that few philosophers have come nearer the truth of things, in their methods or in their results, than Russell (and to a lesser extent Moore and the author of the *Tractatus Logico-Philosophicus*).

VIII

Our fourth bipolarity divides entities into necessary things and contingent things. A necessary being is an entity that exists in all possible worlds, a thing that couldn't not exist. A contingent being is any non-necessary being, i.e., a thing that exists but doesn't in at least one possible world. We will have a great deal more to say subsequently about necessity, essence, possible worlds, and related notions.

As our final pair of ontological categories, we include the bifurcation of entities into individuals and sets (or classes). This classification may not be thought necessary to our purposes or symmetrical with those we have distinguished above. For the sets are a subclass of the abstracta. Yet this contrast has traditionally been found a very important and intuitive one to draw, and we too will I think find use for it.

The concept of a set or class is standardly held to be so basic that it is not noncircularly or nontrivially definable. At any rate, the intent here is to mean by a set (or class) just what the investigators of set theory mean by one. An individual is any entity that is not a set.

Our basic ontological categories itemized, we can proceed next to consider combinatory classifications of entities. I note first that sets are entities that are abstract, particular, and complex. (We saw that we had simply to decide whether we wanted to count 'is a member of' as a case of 'is a constituent of'; that it would have been reasonable enough not to count class-membership as constituency, but that there was sufficient analogical intuitive conviction to doing so that we would.) I note also that some sets are necessary and some are contingent.

Sets disposed of, we can proceed to combinatory classifications of individuals.

There will be sixteen of these, as some simple arithmetic will show. Some of these, however, will certainly not have any instances. The sixteen follow, together with examples where there are some.

Individuals	Examples
(1) Abstract particular simple necessary	natural numbers[15]
(2) Abstract particular simple contingent	points of space
(3) Abstract particular complex necessary	facts about sets
(4) Abstract particular complex contingent	mathematical facts about specific points of space
(5) Abstract universal simple necessary	non-haecceitous properties[16]
(6) Abstract universal simple contingent	haecceitous properties
(7) Abstract universal complex necessary	non-haecceitous propositions
(8) Abstract universal complex contingent	haecceitous propositions
(9) Concrete particular simple necessary	none (instants of time?)
(10) Concrete particular simple contingent	physical objects; persons (instants of time?)
(11) Concrete particular complex necessary	none
(12) Concrete particular complex contingent	physical facts, processes, events
(13) Concrete universal simplex necessary	none
(14) Concrete universal simple contingent	none (?)
(15) Concrete universal complex necessary	none
(16) Concrete universal complex contingent	universal physical facts (?)

Let us further illustrate our categories with a specific case, and use them to 'explain' what goes on and what elements are present when a (certain) sentence is true.

Suppose some individual a is red. This, we will say, is a fact. An individual and concrete fact.[17] Facts are complexes. That is, they have constituents. This one has for its constituents the simple individual concretum a and the property of being red. (The latter is an abstractum, which might be thought to compromise the concreteness of the fact. I shall say not, however, until compelled to say otherwise; and I do not think such compulsion will be forthcoming. Why can't a concrete fact have a nonconcrete constituent?) Apparently, these two – simple concretum and property – are the only constituents of this fact. The fact is not, however, the set or aggregate of concretum and property. It is the concretum and property concatenated together in the entity-having-property way; and that is primitive and unanalysable.

At the other end of the ontological telescope is an individual (English) sentence token, 'a is red.' This too is a complex. Its constituents are word tokens, in a certain order. The sentence type 'a is red' is an abstract entity, consisting of what is common to all 'a is red' sentence tokens. It is a complex, whose constituents are word types, in a certain order.

All sentence types synonymous with 'a is red' express the same proposition. This too is a complex, its constituents are concepts, one for each constituent of the fact that a is red. These concepts are the concepts of those constituents. (The concept of a and the concept of redness, in this case.)

As well as being abstracta ('ideal objects,' in one older idiom), word types, sentence types, concepts, propositions, and properties, are also all universals. That is, each has instances or cases or exemplifications: respectively, word tokens, sentence tokens, word or expression types (in the case of concepts), sentence types, and facts (or states of affairs). The exemplification relation is not perhaps quite the same in each instance. If so there is at least in each case an exemplification relation, similar to the other cases.

IX

After a great deal of classification, and combinations of such classification, we may note that we can, with the machinery we have developed, do something that may be thought rather exciting from a metaphysical point of view. We can define the concept of a substance.

We will utilize in doing so the concept of being temporal (mentioned in what was said above about abstracta), as well as our ontological categories. For it seems appropriate to assert that instants of time and the like are not what we will want to mean by a substance.

We will define a substance then as an individual that is concrete, particular, simple, and non-temporal.[18]

Most philosophers who have been interested in essentialism have been primarily interested in the essential and non-essential traits of substances, just as there has been a preponderant attention throughout the history of metaphysics to substances. This presumably reflects metaphysical orientations that are at least as old as Aristotle. Very, very few philosophers have denied that there are substances, except perhaps in the way that Descartes does in the *Meditations* (i.e., with attempts at the exercise of radical doubt or scepticism). On the other hand, virtually every other kind of entity has had its non-believers.

It seems very difficult to believe that there are substances, but not also to believe that there are facts, states, events, or processes, of which these substances are constituents, participants, or elements. It may even in fact be easier to believe in such complexes as these than to believe in substances. At any rate one of the few philosophers who did doubt the 'ultimate' existence of substances, Russell, did not find it possible to jettison this final most basic of categories (i.e., the category of the concrete, particular, complex, non-temporal individuals).

X

Other categoreal contrasts, and basic categories, than those delineated above can be set out. We have referred to the categories of the abstract, the physical, the mental, and the temporal; and indicated the challenging character of formally defining all of them. Other fundamental categories that suggest themselves are the categories of the causal – entities that can have causal efficacy in the world – and the representational – entities that can depict, represent, symbolize. For some philosophers only causal entities, entities that can act or be acted upon causally, are real (or 'fundamentally' real for theorists for whom there are degrees or levels of being).[19] This seems a prejudice difficult to make intelligible, much less justify, but many philosophers have held it, including many on the contemporary scene. In any case it seems important to identify, even highlight, things that are capable of producing results in the world.

XI

In addition to category theory in our two senses – the Russell-Sommers enterprise of (alleged) incommensurable meaning clusters, and an actual ontological taxonomical scheme – at the same stage and on the same plane of metaphysical inquiry, it is appropriate to engage First Principles. Classically, metaphysical theorizing involved the explicit or implicit setting out and utilizing of fundamental conceptual insights and constraints that were supposed to be self-evident, non-trivial, and that could guide the formation of the body of a metaphysical system or the determination and resolution of particular topics of metaphysical investigation. In its purest form, perhaps supremely exemplified, at least in intention, by Spinoza's *Ethics*, these insights and constraints were conceived as 'axioms,' from which the subsequent truths of the system, and truths about the world, would follow deductively. More often something much less comprehensively result-producing was envisaged, or at any rate articulated.

Some of the First Principles of earlier instances of the metaphysical enterprise, the causal principle, for example, have come to seem problematic, or false, in the light of developments in modern physics. Some of anti-metaphysical disposition have drawn the invalid inference that all first principles will prove problematic or false; or vacuously analytic. I will make a case that some are true and possess substantive content. There does seem to be value in at least partly recasting the undertaking of formulating the elemental principles of first science.

Some fundamental conceptions should be regarded not as axioms, or elemental truths we think we see by a natural light of reason necessarily to be so, but rather as postulates, or methodological directives necessary to inquiry, metaphysical or otherwise. Every axiom of a formal system can be reconstituted as a rule or imperative. This truism seems applicable to some metaphysical 'axioms.' The difference is not trivial. While axioms readily turn into rules, the converse is not universally and unproblematically the case, at least if the resulting modal status is supposed to be one of alethic necessity (i.e., the strong 'in principle' absolute necessity of logic and mathematics).

Take what many classically saw as the fundamental and central first principle, the so-called principle of sufficient reason. (Not the principle of the analyticity of all non-existential subject-predicate propositions, which moderns standardly assign to Leibniz under this label; rather the principle Leibniz, like other classical metaphysicians, accepted, and which he took to imply the latter.) The principle of sufficient reason was the principle that there is a *sufficient reason* for everything: an explanation, causal or logical (conceptual), as to why any true proposition is true, any existent exists, or any fact or state of affairs obtains. This is a principle of ultimate universal intelligibility, according to which everything makes sense, at least in principle.

Now, there are complexities in the idea the principle is supposed to express. What does 'in principle' mean, for example? Must everything be intelligible for us? Couldn't there be explanations intelligible for some extra-terrestrials that we couldn't grasp? Mightn't there be some requiring an infinite mind? And what, precisely, is an explanation, given that minds substantially different from human ones might entertain one?

Complexities aside, it remains problematic whether we have adequate reason to believe with confidence that a principle of sufficient reason is actually true. We seem able to conceive of utter unintelligibilities, things that could happen, or be true, where there was no reason at all for their being so. (It seems possible to conceive, for example, of a world that would be entirely deterministic save for one occurrence in it, that was random and causeless.)

A principle of sufficient reason may fare better as a postulate or directive, an assumption guiding inquiry, which it will be supposed there will never be reason to challenge or surrender. *In investigating any matter, proceed as though there is a reason (explanation) that would render that matter intelligible.*

Other principles of explanation that in the older vocabularies would have been (and sometimes were) phrased propositionally, also seem more plausibly construed as directives to be assumed, and where we cannot readily conceive what it might be like to give up (or what could be a good reason for giving up) the rule. Principles of simplicity in explanation, for example. Occam's razor – prefer, ceteris paribus, the explanation with the fewest kinds of entities – and cognate principles as to what makes one explanation better than another, seem unjustifiable as axioms of reason, for we seem able to conceive falsifying cases, but not improvable as guiding directives in constructing explanatory theories.

A number of postulates do seem, however, beyond the possibility of conceiving of a counter-instance. (By which I do not mean to imply that no one has thought they had counter-instances to them.) One in particular seems to be a distinctively central conception of a set of major twentieth-century metaphysical perspectives. This conception, formulated long before the twentieth century, has its opponents, ancient and modern. Nonetheless it is, I believe, defensible, meaningful, and important.

This principle is the postulate expressed in Quine's theory of ontological commitment. Like much in Quine, this doctrine is a loan, extended a little bit, from Russell. Russell had argued against Meinong's central supposed insight, the so-called principle of the independence of *Sosein* (the having of characteristics) from *Sein* (being). From something's being thus and so, Meinong held, it doesn't follow that – it will depend on the case whether – it is real. Russell denied that this is so, and the result is encapsulated in the logic of *Principia Mathematica*. From $\ulcorner Fa \urcorner$ one validly infers $\ulcorner (\exists x)\ Fx \urcorner$. Only real things have properties, stand in relations, etc.

Ontological commitment extends this insight to sets of propositions (or sentences, as Quine would prefer). Excluding contexts where reference is what Quine calls opaque (i.e., where a truth is capable of being turned into a falsehood, or conversely, by replacing one apparently referential expression with another for the same item), existential generalization on sentences held true will yield an ontology, by kind or type, depending on the kinds or types of the entities generalized ('quantified over'). This idea alone makes Russell and Quine among the most important twentieth-century metaphysicians.

XII

Before leaving our consideration of metaphysical theories, in the previous chapter, and views about the kinds of things that are or may be real, in the present one, I want to identify and give a name to a position which I think a substantial constituency of philosophers have held, though seldom consciously. I call this view Andersonian Platonism, or perhaps Andersonian inflationism, after Alan Ross Anderson (1925–73), who I think held the view to be described, though I know of nowhere in his published writings where it is set out fully or explicitly. (I recall it rather as a view he expressed in his classes in which I was a student.) As indicated, I am sure that several other philosophers have also held the position to be described; it seems innocuous to assign it specially to Anderson.

Andersonian Platonism is a metaphysical realist position which takes seriously and literally the theory of ontological commitment. The latter implies, as already noted, that we ought to take our ontological, or existential, affirmations, which we would not, on reflection, regard as metaphorical, as affirmations about what exists and is real. Ontological commitment also involves the affirmations that being, or existence, is a single kind of thing, whatever it is that has it; and that (excepting such cases as may be successfully explained away) *apparently* existential or ontological claims or remarks are always in fact *really* existential or ontological. To ontological commitment is conjoined what might be called a passive or pessimistic Occamism. Occamism is the theory that kinds of entities that can be eliminated from metaphysics ought to be. Everyone, I take it, will pay at least lip service to Occamism. Everyone, that is, will agree that if there really is no particular need of a category of things, that everything we suppose true and everything we want to say is perfectly well secured without that variety of thing, and we can see how to do without such items, then by all means we should dispense with them. For some, however, Occamism is a sort of 'motherhood' position, like the view that the good ought to be augmented. Passive or pessimistic Occamism (these positions may differ) is dubious about the prospects of large-scale or interesting ontological elimination, or else just largely indifferent to devoting much energy or attention to Occamist projects.

Furthermore, Andersonian Platonism (or inflationism) holds that plausible assertions of natural language, and natural thought, which we have excellent reason to accept, imply that there are such things as numbers, relations, government policies, bank accounts, ways of life, smiles, sidelong glances, and all manner of things of an 'ordinary' and not obviously physical type.[20] Andersonian inflationism is happy to accept all of them, with cheerful insouciance, in fact.

Andersonian inflationism, as I intend it, holds finally the *methodological* position that one should not accept as philosophically intelligible or perspicuous what may be called scare-quoted discourse. Scare-quoted discourse is typically used in two ways. In one the intent is pejorative: the idea which is 'scare-quoted' is viewed as dubious – incoherent, problematic, or risible. In the other use of scare-quoted discourse, the writer is suggestive, allusive, brief, or (in some instances) tentative and uncertain. While the first use is typically adversarial, the latter may well be sympathetic; the writer thinks it may be difficult to spell out fully or literally what the scare-quoted language is supposed to convey. 'The relation of *betweenness* is no doubt in "Plato's heaven"' is a piece of scare-quoted discourse, presumably of the first type.[21] Andersonianism refuses to regard such discourse as philosophically perspicuous unless some alternative mode of expression is found to say what it purports to say. This applies to views one opposes, even to those that one regards as ludicrous or incoherent, as well as to views one advocates. Andersonianism persists in a dogged literalism and will not acknowledge that anything seriously pertinent to its doctrines, or to any philosophical topic, has been said as long as the statement remains in scare-quoted mode. (Of course some philosophers who write in scare-quoted mode do so because they hold that the positions they obliquely characterize in this way are intrinsically unintelligible or incoherent. The Andersonian may be sceptical or agnostic about such views as the latter. At any rate, he takes seriously and literally the Wittgensteinian behest, 'Whereof one cannot speak, thereof one must be silent'[22] – i.e., really silent; without snigger or scare characterizations too.) The question naturally arises whether, if scare-quoted discourse is philosophically unacceptable for the Andersonian, metaphorical language will be also. As outlined here (and no fully developed position is intended in this account) the Andersonian is the literalist, ontological one-worlder, who does not mind ontological profusion and diversity. Metaphor is itself a complex theme. The Andersonian might need to reserve judgment on it.

I have no doubt betrayed some sympathy for Andersonian inflationism in the above characterization. However, I think that if reasons were offered for being actively Occamist, the Andersonian view ought to give way to such enterprise. Failing Occamist success, perhaps it is a reasonable view to hold.

The Andersonian is a Platonist, but views the affirmation of the existence of abstracta – indeed all existential affirmation – as a pedestrian matter. Yes, he or she will say, numbers exist, and properties, classes, relations; and perhaps propositions and other non-physical non-mental items as well. But so what? They are causally inert (are neither causes nor effects). Moreover, there is no place they exist. (And he will recognize nothing coherent in queries as to a 'place' or 'status' they might have.) But they are real.

If there is a 'Fido'-Fido fallacy – and presumably there is[23] – there should also be identified a fallacy that involves supposing that because something is, there must be some place that it is, somewhere it is. This fallacy is committed, for example, by anyone who supposes (or who supposes that anyone else must suppose), that if there are properties, concepts, numbers, or other abstract things, there must be some place where they are (apart from places, if any, where their exemplars are); hence that there must be thought to be, if standard physical space won't do, some other kind of place, typically referred to, with derisory scare-quotes, as 'Plato's heaven.' But – so it can be believed if this is indeed a fallacy – there is redness, but no where (apart from where red things are) it is; numbers, but no where they are, and so on; and not even quasi-places, or metaphorical ones, at which they must be conceived as locatable.

Let me remark finally that battles between Platonists and anti-Platonists have filled the history of philosophy, and are by no means settled yet. A strong Platonism – and Plato himself – holds, that different varieties of abstracta not only are *real*, but play a fundamental explanatory role in making sense of the universe; perhaps even a sort of causal, and certainly a rationally, grounding role, for understanding the nature of things. Strong anti-Platonists have tended to view abstracta as items of an essentially childlike fancy: silly, and both ontologically unnecessary and explanatorily vacuous. There is more than one (possible) position between these extremes, and what I have sketched as the Andersonian view means to be a particularly anodyne, but ontologically affirmative case. To be does not require being at (or even vaguely near) a place. Nor does it require having a causal role. Nor does it require being particularly useful in some theory or some explanation. Being can be and be utterly useless. Of course, some abstracta may turn out to be good for something (as well as to be). We shall see.

Chapter Five

Existence

I

In this chapter I want primarily to explore three themes focused on existence. It is the peg they will all be hung on, but in fact they are largely independent topics. The first of the topics is the question (or apparent question), Why is there something rather than nothing, i.e., why does anything exist?[1] Some have regarded this as one of the deepest and profoundest – some, in fact, as the very most important – problem of metaphysics;[2] and some have viewed it as a pseudo-problem, not a coherent topic at all. The second theme concerned with existence is less easy to formulate with precision. I am tempted to phrase it in terms of the question, What is the big deal about existence? But that is too frivolous and not very revealing of what is meant. Instead, I will call this second existential topic, Is ontology in principle different, as a kind of inquiry, from, e.g., botany, chemistry, or psychology (and if so, why)? The third topic is, How should we conceive, and analyse, judgments of existence and non-existence? Or – in one sense anyway – what *is* existence?

I should indicate from the outset that the first and third of these topics will be explored, not, I fear, conclusively, but at any rate as sober and independent queries about which much ink has been spilled and dissenting views honestly defended. In the case of the second of my topics I have, it is candidly acknowledged, a partly polemical intent as well. The aim is in this case to drive a wedge between some of the views of prominent anti-metaphysicians and anti-realists (Putnam and others), and to argue that they in fact are guiltiest of what they accuse their opponents. The polemic is intended more or less for its own sake, as blows against a particular kind of philosophical position, method, and style, all of which seem to me wrong, and counter-productive. The substantive burden of this part of the chapter aims to buttress and reinforce the Aristotelian conception of metaphysics – viz., realist, most-general science – that this book broadly advocates.

II

Let me mention also some 'existence topics' that I will not explore in detail but to which other philosophical writers have given a lot of attention. I will say a few words about why I think those topics have not deserved as much energy as they have generated and why they will be largely marginal to my concerns. One of these is the old and vexed question whether existence is a property, or as it is too often, rather unhappily put, whether existence is a predicate. The latter formulation seems unfortunate, since 'predicate' is standardly used to denote a linguistic item. There is no doubt at all that 'existence' is a predicate. It occurs in the predicate part of grammatical sentences, e.g., 'Clinton exists.' Some predicates express properties – 'is prime,' 'is wise' are examples. Some predicates do not: e.g., 'is so-called because of his size,' 'is universally feared under that name,' and, so I hold, all predicates containing indexical expressions (that is, expressions – 'I' and the other personal pronouns, 'here,' 'now,' etc. – whose sense is more or less invariant, but whose referent shifts from speaker to speaker). The question is whether 'existence' is a predicate that expresses a property, or one that does not. A subordinate question sometimes asked in this quarter is whether, even if existence is a property, it is a property that particulars have: some philosophers form the idea that existence is a 'second order' property, that classes, or propositional functions, have.

Much of the literature on existence as a property or a non-property seems vitiated by a failure to indicate what a property is, so that one could hope to be in a position to have an intelligent opinion on the matter. If any care is taken to indicate what it takes to qualify for propertyhood, it seems to fall out more or less automatically that existence will be a property, or not, depending on the conception of propertyhood preferred. I prefer regarding a property as something that may be affirmed of or ascribed to something.[3] It seems plain that existence can be affirmed of things, so it develops directly that existence, according to me, is a property. Of course, there are properties and properties. Some are arguably simple, while some are certainly complex. Some can be analysed as something other than what on the surface they seem to be. If so that isn't necessarily a good reason to say that one wasn't concerned with a property; rather the contrary. If metaphysical assumptions are made with regard to a perspicuous or fundamental level of facts in the world (I will have more to say about such assumptions below), then there may be argued to be properties that appear at the surface level but not at the perspicuous or funda-

mental level. Perhaps *being reminiscent of a Tuscan summer* is such a property. *Existence*, I believe, is not. At the deep level, as well as at the surface, it
is true to say of some things, really, literally true, that they exist. This theme
will be further explored under the heading of my third topic on existence.

Another existential topic that won't be discussed, however, is whether the
ontological argument for God is significantly affected by the investigation of
existence. My view is that, Kant notwithstanding, no version of an ontological
argument for the existence of God needs to depend on whether existence is a
property. This is due to the fact that any premise in an ontological argument
that says or implies that existence is a property can be straightforwardly
replaced with an approximately equivalent premise (perhaps then with adjust-
ments elsewhere in the argument wherever that premise occurs, as a part of
another premise), that won't have this implication; the justification for the
replacement premise being more or less the same as it was for the original.
Thus, for example, in the Cartesian version of the ontological argument,
'Existence is a perfection' can be replaced with 'Anything that had every perfection would, necessarily, exist.'

III

I turn, first, to the grandest and deepest problem of metaphysics: the mystery
of being itself. Why *is* anything real? Why is there something, rather than
nothing?[4]

There have been two kinds of attempts to show that this query really isn't
the fundamental question it purports to be. One involves the claim that the
question is incoherent and meaningless. What does it mean to ask why anything at all exists? We can handle specific queries about particular cases and
kinds of cases. We can ask why there are flowers, why lions exist, or comets,
or wars, or love. However, why anything exists, it is held, does not have, and
cannot be supplied, *context*, to make it a meaningful query. Put differently,
there is no sense in which what could be sought under this heading would be
an explanation of anything. Explanation presupposes that something be able to
qualify as satisfaction for the inquiry, and nothing here could do so.

This seems wrong and dogmatic, however. To be sure, it appears to rest on a
version of a principle of sufficient reason: viz., that there is an explanation, in
principle, for anything. Such a principle may be a reasonable assumption in
undertaking inquiry in any domain. However, it does seem thinkable that there
be nothing, and the fact that there is indeed something to deserve explanation
if possible. To be sure, something can *seem* (coherently) thinkable, and not
really be so. In such a case, the greater burden is to show incoherence, and the

premises for doing so in the instance at hand seem either question-begging or less plausible than the result they mean to unsettle.

What might an explanation of why there is something rather than nothing look like? It is indeed not easy to say. In fact I want to defend a position similar to the one that Hume defends, in *Dialogues Concerning Natural Religion*, on what is fundamentally the same topic. Hume envisages one deeply popular and philosophical route to theistic belief as prompted by a desire for an ultimate explanation, an explanation of the world that would be final, definitive, self-justifying, something one could see to be the achieved destination of all explanatory pathways. He points out that this desire for ultimate explanation is in fact something that can never be satisfied. For, of any postulate offered as providing explanation for something one wants explained, one can always meaningfully ask, why *it*? Why is that thing real? It is not only that if an explanation is regarded as self-justifying (*causa sui*) then the explained can be so regarded also. More importantly it is that we can always probe beyond any point our inquisitions have reached. We can say the words – self-justifying; *causa sui* – on our lips, but we cannot mean them in our hearts. We can think the query, and know what we mean, when we ask, Why it?, of anything at all.

Thus, I am arguing that the question, why is there something rather than nothing? is meaningful, sensible, and, I suppose, deep and profound in its way, but it is not a question we can hope to answer. If there always have been things in existence in the past, then the answer is something like, Well, that is how the world has happened to be, which isn't really a definitive or complete answer at all. If there have not always been existents, if existents appeared out of nothing, then, no explanation of the fact would seem to be possible. In any event, even if we had an explanation, we could ask of it, why it held.

The second attempt to derail 'the problem of being' occurs on a more prosaic plane. It involves the claim that some things – no extraordinary persons among them – have necessary existence. They couldn't not be. Candidates for this status have been some abstract entities and time. For this point of view, the problem of being is a genuine query, and it has an immediate and straightforward answer. Why is there something rather than nothing? Total nonexistence is not a thinkable or possible option for all of being.

Even if there are necessary beings – properties (some of them, at least) or times – and it seems reasonable to believe that there are, this would not appear to resolve the mystery of being. Why are there necessary beings, if there are? There just are? Well, but why? It seems possible and thinkable to ask these questions. There seems to be something in the idea of ultimate surprise and ultimate mystery. Some things happen to be thus and so and we shall be forever unable to explain why they are thus and so; and if that apparent mystery is solved, another waits in the wings to take its place, and always will.

IV

So what is the big deal about existence? If I affirm that at least three Germans won the Nobel Prize in the 1920s, that seems factual, straightforward, and true. If I affirm that those or other Germans exist, that Clinton, the number 7, or hydrogen exists, have I asserted anything either more metaphysical, or problematic, or altogether different in kind? I want to say, No.

Basically the view I wish to promote is that results we accept as more or less literally and more or less objectively true should be conceived as on a par, with respect to metaphysical as well as epistemic status and kind. I take this to be compatible with something like the classic conception of philosophical analysis (the conception, above all, of Russell and Moore, with significant input also from Frege and Wittgenstein), according to which a proposition (or sentence) might be regarded as approximating something true but requires rendering into a form that will be viewed as perspicuous: the elusive idea of a form and structure that exhibits, on its surface, the form or structure of a fact of the world that makes the proposition or sentence true or false. This classic conception of philosophical analysis in its metaphysically declared form is logical atomism: the thesis that there are determinate (and knowable) facts of the world, that are things in themselves (in something like Kant's sense), independent of a cognizer's perspective. And for the historically developed logical atomism of Russell and Wittgenstein this involved the specific view that these determinate, knowable facts constitute themselves into a structured hierarchy, with a most elemental or fundamental level consisting of particulars-having-properties and particulars-in-relation. The project of philosophical analysis need not presuppose logical atomism (though both Russell and Moore were logical atomists); for someone could undertake formulations that were conceived from the less to the more perspicuous, with no assumption that any ideal state of perspicuity was possible. At any rate, I take logical atomism to be a plausible metaphysical option, and nothing affirmed in this context or anywhere else in this book should imply otherwise. So I might affirm that being more or less literally and more or less objectively true implies being perspicuous or able to be rendered so.

The general result I advocate might be called the holism or the characterological unity of the true. This is a somewhat vague thesis. It is meant to contrast with what I elsewhere call cognitive pluralism and its special case, cognitive dualism. It is also intended to draw the serious, reflectively endorsed results of all inquiry (all the things we think we know) into metaphysical legitimacy; that is, to affirm them as metaphysical, as truths about reality. Botanists, algebraicists, investigators of seventeenth-century Polish history, theoretical engineers, all make in their professional capacities, metaphysical remarks and contribute to the metaphysical enterprise.

Still a further purpose this conception is intended to serve is the subsumption of (true) existence claims in the general forest of truths about the world. Whether or not existence is a property affirming that something exists or is real is just another kind of thing to say about the world and its occupants. Existential affirmations do not have to meet a higher stricter standard than other affirmations; theirs is the tribunal of all truth-seeking discourse and inquiry. Further, existential affirmations do not importantly contrast by kind from non-existential ones. A practical, almost ad hominem, implication of this is that philosophers shouldn't worry so much about what they or their colleagues might let through the (ontological) door; apart from a general methodological concern to get things right, to proceed from evidence to results that are well-grounded.

The obvious targets of these remarks are projects of severe ontological economy and reduction, and conceptions that contrast what is real with the *really* real (or primarily or most fundamentally or basically so). Such conceptions seem to be problematic: either something technical will turn out to be involved, sufficiently so that it will be unclear whether it genuinely gives expression to basic intuition; or there may be no coherent conception involved. This is not to quarrel with Occamism (i.e., in this context, advocacy of Occam's razor), even energetic Occamism, per se. It can be interesting, challenging, mind-bending, to try to see what might be able to be done without, or how lean, or hierarchical, an ontological or categorial edifice can be proposed for the world. The quarrel here is with those who think such enterprise common sensical or deeply intuitive. I believe that its guiding note should be heuristic, constructional, and pragmatic. One should dispassionately look to see whether a particular reductionist proposal appears to be successful – and three cheers if it is – with a minimum of prior partisan engagement on the outcome. Russell here, as elsewhere, seems to me to embody the right perspective; and of him it may truly be said no one ever in the history of philosophy was more energetically or imaginatively imbued with the Occamist impulse.

Alongside philosophers who feel certain that there are no such things as *Fs* (for some kind or sort, *F*); and sure that there exists nothing other than the things that their theories say there are, where they are sure they are on the side of Science or Robust Common Sense (or some other variety of angel), I mean to target Hilary Putnam, and like-minded neo-Kantians. Their error, I think, is to tacitly assume one of the very things their theories are supposed to assault and dislodge; namely, a notion of ontology as a project with a kind of Archimedean anchor that (contrary to the supposition that they unthinkingly share with the view they oppose) there is no reason to conceive or to want it to have.

A model for existence quests, hence, by implication, for how ideally to think of existence when those quests succeed, is supplied by cases of figures of legend about whom historical inquiry legitimately may differ. Was there a real Robin Hood? Did Agamemnon exist? King Arthur? Guinevere? Helen of Troy? In spite of the convictions of some scholars who investigate such questions, the answer appears to be, in the present state of evidence: quite possibly, or even probably, but the confirming evidence is not at hand, nor, perhaps, likely to be.

Suppose there really was a Robin Hood. What is known about the world if it is known that Robin Hood existed? Presumably that there was a flesh-and-blood man living in medieval England around whom stories developed that viewed him as an outlaw, an impressive archer, etc., with those stories eventually appearing in documentary record. But that he *existed* as such under the supposition made? Well, that he was as we take our current human selves to be, and each animal, physical object, and other items of the universe, with respect to being something that is.

It is only if certain assumptions are made, characteristic of particular varieties of early twentieth-century, empiricist philosophy – assumptions that are an anathema to the current repudiations of that philosophy (like those of Putnam, and Rorty) – that anything problematic will be forthcoming with regard to the fact of something existing. Assumptions of a programmatic project of construction and correspondence, between theory and world, from atoms of the one to atoms of the other, must be operative, otherwise the assertion that a certain item exists will not be very troublesome or interesting. Another way to put this point is to say that ontology need not be foundationalist; but it seems that the current neo-Kantians (the neo-neo-Kantians, we could call them) haven't grasped that fact. I have spoken in favour of what may be called heuristic foundationalism: logical atomism conceived as a project not intended to be based in alleged immediate deliverances of sense perception; instead, like a scientific theory, though of 'first science.' Putnam and Rorty, I think, need to suppose that someone seeking to identify classes of existents must think of those existents as fitting into a hierarchy erected upon a base level, which is transparently world-mirroring (and knowably so); but not even logical atomism, of Russell's type, need suppose (or, I think, historically did suppose) this. That some item is affirmed to exist does not, by itself, involve a commitment to any such hierarchy; and if a theoretical project seeks to devise a construal of all existents into such a hierarchy, some class of items taken as elemental or foundational, the entire edifice can be provisional, tentative, or contingent. It by no means need be tied to subjective phenomenologies but can instead admit the possibility of alternative schematic models with relevant adjudications to be made on their merits like theoretical adjudications in science.

This second existence theme may deserve further restatement for, if I am right, the implications of the view I am defending will be far-reaching. No eyebrows are raised nor suspicions of otherworldly disconnection from what are otherwise sober and plain topics and people, if someone (e.g., a paleontologist) says that reptiles antedate mammals, or water contains hydrogen; not even if the person adds emphasis and says that these things are really so. The same prosaic character should attach to assertions (and denials) of existence; and should do so even if the propositions of being (the relevant German term of art, *Seinsobjektiven*, may be helpful) are said to be true of reality, or things in themselves. Was the claim that water contains hydrogen relativized to our conceptual scheme, or a merely phenomenal order, or otherwise bracketed, qualified, or subjectivized, when put on the table? If not, the claim that clouds, plants, numbers, sense data, or gods exist should not be treated in those ways either. Of course particular existence-claims may be untrue, not known to be true, or simply unclear; they may also be found in everyday life, and in contexts of varying theoretical character and generality (from basket-weaving to pure metaphysics). The preceding is true also of propositions that are not *Seinsobjektiven*.

If this is correct – if, that is, propositions about being, and the rest of the propositions, are on all fours with respect to each other – then fundamental ontology does not need special justification. Nor, at least in principle, should its practitioners be relegated to the ranks of the pursuers of forlorn or outmoded hope. Lest any reader suppose that this is not something that anyone would deny, I would claim that the foregoing is definitely contrary to the views of postmodernists, Kantians, neo-Kantians, Putnam, Rorty, and numerous other individuals and schools, inside and outside university philosophy departments. To be sure, the argument here rests on the premise that conceptual territories do not become conceptually problematic as they become maximally general, that is to say, as they are conceived as parts of the study of reality.

This, in sum, and admittedly in a vague state (partly justifiable by the vagueness in the positions it means to unsettle), is the central idea in the assertion that existence isn't such a big deal. I proceed to the third existence topic.

V

What is existence? It seems, on reflection and consideration of what have been proposed as alternative views, that existence is just exactly itself, and not something else – that it is in short a basic or primitive thing (or our concept of it is basic or primitive). I take it that existing, being, being real, being among what there is, being part of the universe, are synonymous, and strictly equivalent[5]; and that the core idea they express cannot be rendered in substantially different language.

Still, even if some concept is primitive, there will be things to be said about its kind, and its logic: its semantics, the kinds of relations that its instances will have to instances of other concepts. Being primitive never implies characterological silence. How is it then for existence?

Classical logic, the logic of *Principia Mathematica*, involves a view of existence similar to the redundancy and, more recently, disquotational views of what truth is (associated with the names of Frege, Ramsey, Strawson, and several recent philosophers). According to this conception, while we may use an existence concept that is strictly uneliminable from our discourse, nothing quite or precisely matches this conceptual item in the world itself. In Russell's logical atomism, at the ground level of fact there are no facts of the (putative) type ⌜*a* exists⌝ or ⌜*Fs* exist⌝. At the ground level there are just facts of type ⌜*Fa*⌝, ⌜*Gab*⌝, ⌜*Habc*⌝ (and their negations). Then there are, among other constructions upon, such facts, quantifying generalizations on (some of) them. Of special interest, in the historical development of classical logic, and for us, is the so-called existential generalization on an atomic fact. Suppose *a* really is *F*. Then – it will follow – something is *F*. That is, we say (for classical logic), there exists at least one thing such that it is *F*. *It is F* is a so-called propositional function (or open sentence), something that turns into a proposition (or sentence) by something being done to its unspecified (open, variable, ambiguous) pronoun ('it'). Among the things that can be done to the pronoun (apart from its replacement by a proper noun) is that it can be tied down by the introduction of a quantifying phrase, like the existential quantifying phrase, that will make the pronoun refer to that which this quantifying phrase talks of. For Russell, as philosophical logician, the existential quantifier is less perspicuous than the universal ('everything is such that ...') because the latter does not contain even the appearance of expressing an existence-idea. For him, 'there exists at least one thing such that it is *F*' is more perspicuously rendered with 'it is not true that everything is such that it is not *F*.' The topic of the universal quantifier is the whole universe. Something like the foregoing is the central core of Russell's idea about existence. When we say that such-and-suches exist, according to him, we aren't really talking about the such-and-suches, we are talking about the universe (or reality), saying that it contains such-and-suches. Existence gives way to *instancing* or *exemplifying* a propositional function (or property/relation – for the propositional functions of *Principia Mathematica* are ambiguous between, or else do double duty for, open sentences and universals).

In classical logic, a non-synonymous strict equivalent for individual existential assertions is also available. With the addition of the identity relation to elementary first order logic, that (object) *a* exists can be rendered as ⌐there exists at least one thing such that it is identical with *a*⌐. Russell rightly insists that the latter is not genuinely synonymous with ⌐*a* exists⌐. (Thus his insistence that the latter is 'strictly meaningless.') However, it will be strictly, i.e., necessarily equivalent to it, from within the framework of pre-formal discourse where we locate and deploy the common-sense existence concept.

The resulting picture is spare and economical. It is also elegant and beautiful. As with other concepts of the common-sense framework, of quotidian or 'natural' philosophical consciousness, the Russellian program displaces where it does not utilize: existence is displaced with existential quantification (and identity), any degree of absence of fit being simply ignored and abandoned. That is, this is enjoined by the enterprise itself and is part of its claim to render philosophy scientific.

While Russellian displacement analysis seems plausible and attractive in mathematics and, at least as a project, seems viable with respect to the categories of substance and universal, it seems to me that the cost is too high with the case of the category of existence.

Another way to put this is: can we suppose that it is even possible that existence is mere appearance and not also reality? For that is after all what Russellian displacement analysis invites us to suppose. We start out supposing that there are numbers. Russellian displacement analysis entails that we abandon this view by adopting the conviction that what we took to be numbers are in fact classes of classes (of equinumerate objects). Similarly, if only, in this case, it worked, we are invited to conceive substances as series of events or clusters of universals (Russell favoured both reductionist proposals at different times); and in another mode of Occamist enterprise, Russell considered thinking of universals as definable by reference to designated standard particulars. If such projects were successful, we would still 'have' substances (or universals) or at least enough of what prior core intuitions had wanted for them. Is existence comparable, however?

It seems to me that the answer is No. If saying that *a* exists isn't the same as saying that there is something *a* is the same as – and it isn't – there is still something it says that is clear, simple, and (if *a* does exist) true. Moreover, it is a fact about *a* that will be affirmed if it is asserted that '*a*' exists. These remarks are not intended to suggest revisions to classical logic.[6] The formula type ⌜*a* exists iff (∃*x*) *x* = *a*⌝ seems entirely adequate to any need there could be for the formalization, within the resources of first-order logic, of proper-name, singular, existential, assertions. Of course the logic of identity, plus the classical semantics for individual constants, will have the result that no negative singular existential can be true. This was part of the case Russell gave for the meaninglessness of all proper-name, singular, existential assertions, affirmative or negative. It is not news that first-order logic cannot handle, i.e., capture the distinctive semantic features of all sorts of kinds of expressions. No problem seems to be caused by the invariable falsehood of instances of formula type ⌜~(∃*x*)*x* = *a*⌝; any more than by the invariable truth of ⌜(∃*x*) *x* = *a*⌝. This is because we conceive of the constants as necessarily designating real individuals.

What of singular, negative existentials that at least appear to be true: e.g., that Pegasus does not exist? Russell famously held that all ordinary, and emphatically these story-derived, proper names are actually disguised abbreviations for definite descriptions. This seems wrong for ordinary proper names, and at least not adequately subtle in the case of names like 'Pegasus.' Russell's conception for the latter does however seem to be in the right direction. There are plainly proper names which only find themselves in employment by virtue of stories (of one kind or other) in which they were introduced but in which the name did not refer to a real individual, in the intentions, successfully realized, of the story-teller. Causal theories of names identify their semantic role by reference to histories of usage developed from successful 'dubbing' of (or reference to) real individuals by those names. It is a modest extension of such theories to conceive of causal histories whose beginnings were (fictional) stories, in which fictional apparent-proper names were introduced (without a genuine dubbing or referential role), and to affirm that some apparent-proper names are not genuine proper names but rather symbols with such histories. The semantics of these apparent-proper names will be comparable to what some claim of *exists* and *true*: they can only be provided by means of what Quine (following Russell and Tarski) calls semantic ascent, in which symbols (in either a linguistic or a Platonistic sense, as the semanticist may prefer) are the logical subject of the sentences providing the truth conditions for the sentences containing the (merely) apparent-proper names.

To sum up this stage of the investigation: existence is a property that everything has (indeed, has essentially). It is primitive and fundamental. The Russellian reductionist treatment of existence is elegant and neat, and in general provides satisfactory semantic resources for saying most things sayable and true involving existence, save for the central metaphysical reality of facts of being, and the general fact of being itself, differences which make quite a lot of difference.

VI

I go on to consider more fully ideas of levels or kinds of being, and also to present and contest what is I think a widely advocated contemporary thesis about existence which seeks to link it to causality. The former theme will emerge in the course of discussion of the latter. What I will call *extra-causalism* is a thesis of metaphysics (or ontology) holding that some entities exist or are real that are not in causal relation with other entities. These entities are neither causes nor effects of other entities; or that they are real is not a causal consequence of the reality of other entities. The contrasting position, which extra-causalism of course denies, is causalism.[7] I should perhaps remark parenthetically that by 'causality' and its variants I mean always (and only) the causality of naturalist and empiricist views of the world since Galileo, whether or not this causality is held to be Humean constant conjuction or to involve some sort of inherent necessity.

Some illustrations of causalist commitment may be useful to provide. David Lewis is a causalist, at least to a degree or of a sort (maybe more). 'The *definitive* characteristic of any (sort of) experience as such is its causal role, its syndrome of most typical causes and effects.'[8] Lewis goes on to identify the 'definitive characteristic' of a combination lock's being unlocked as 'the causal role of that state.' The suggestion of the remainder of the essay cited is that all physical events have as their definitive characteristic their causal role, and the essay's materialist avowal is that all events are physical events. I take it that this will imply that for events, and similar entities (Lewis says – ibid, p. 99, fn. – that he will 'not distinguish between processes, events, phenomena, and states in a strict sense'), to be is to have a causal role, indeed, to have the precise causal role that the item has. This will go, of course, only part of the way to full causalism.

A fully explicit advocacy of causalism will be found in the work of several recent philosophers. Prominent among them (and already cited) is David Armstrong. Others are Brian Ellis[9] and Hartry Field[10]. Still another is Bruce Aune, whose causalism is affirmed in his book *Metaphysics: The Elements*.[11] 'We can simply say: *a* exists = *df a* belongs to the space-time-causal system that is our world. Our world is, again, that system of (roughly) causally related objects with which we are, and anyone who is alert enough to understand it is, in direct experiential contact.'

Like Field's principle, cited above, Aune's explicit formula will make it appropriate to differentiate causalism from what might be called spatiotemporalism: the thesis that to be is to be part of a, or the, spatiotemporal order or the spatiotemporal network of relations, whether or not those relations include causal ones.[12] Not only are spatiotemporalism and causalism clearly distinct conceptually, actual philosophers – certain varieties of libertarian, for example – advocate the former but not the latter. I want nonetheless to assimilate at least a physicalist or naturalist spatiotemporalism – the sort of position which, like Field's, views current physics or biophysics as without a serious explanatory rival in the entire empirical sphere – to causalism. This assimilation also seems justified, and a correspondingly widened causalism illustrated in the account of existence given by Richard Sylvan (1935–96).

> As policy in arriving at an account of existence ...: begin with those items which obviously exist, not-controversially, such as medium-size material objects, and close under enlargements produced by unavoidable extensions thereof, such as compounding or summation and dissection or analysis ... The route to an appropriately minimalist definition of existence is now evident. An item exists if it stands in suitable physical relations to the paradigm existents.[13]

Although this does not appear to be stated explicitly by advocates of causalism, the thesis it expresses is evidently held to be a necessary truth by most or all of those advocates. In this respect it presumably parallels Quine's well-known ontic formula, 'To be is to be the value of a variable.'[14] The Quinean would not suppose that the latter is true in some but not other possible worlds; and the causalist will hold that every genuinely coherent or possible world is one all of whose existents are participants in causal relations.

Still, the causalism/extra-causalism contrast as intended here is a shifting continuum of opposing positions, not a single thesis and its denial. Some causalists, for example, accord universals what may be regarded as a secondary causal role. The sky's being blue or an apple's being sweet may have effects, and by virtue of those facts the constituent universals are parts of a causal story, the causal network of the world. Such a causalism as this insists only that putative entities making no contribution to this network are in fact pseudo-entities. So realism with regard to universals or other abstracta need not imply extra-causalism. Only a Platonic realism – i.e., a position affirming the reality of unexemplified universals – will do this. Causalists then need not be nominalists, and extra-causalism is not established merely by refuting nominalism. Further to these complexities: it may be, as some think, that some properties are contingent consequences of the existence of concrete particular things (for example, the properties of being a VCR, or the property of being taller than Napoleon, may be properties that only are real as consequences of the existence of VCRs and Napoleon, respectively), and while some would argue that the relevant consequence is *logical*, there may be a reasonable case for viewing it as *casual*. At any rate *some* properties, at least, will exist non-contingently if Platonism is true, and these properties will not be causes or effects of anything.

Extra-causalism does not require Platonism however. Otherwise put, there are other ontological theses which will imply or motivate it. Among them is belief in the independent reality of points, or larger units of time or space – independent, that is to say, of particular objects, states of affairs, events, or facts, to occupy them. Neither places nor times have causes or effects; not at least, if those places and times are real regardless of whether particular items occupy or are located at or in them.

VII

I have urged earlier two theses about *being* or *reality* that, while independent of extra-causalism, will make it a more substantive or consequential view than it might otherwise be thought to be. The first of these is that being or reality is a single kind or type. The second is that being or reality does not admit of degree. To affirm the first is to side, as noted earlier, with Russell, Quine, and many others against Meinong, McTaggart, and others; and to hold that being, existence, subsistence, being real, being an entity are all equivalent, and necessarily so. It is to maintain that 'being' is univocal, and is the same thing, to whatever it is applied. To affirm the second is of course to deny that well-known view of Plato's, famously met with in the 'divided line' analogy of the *Republic*. However, it is also, as it is meant here, to deny that there are things with 'basic' or 'fundamental' or 'ground-level' being, and others that *are*, but not basically. Such theses as the latter have appeared particularly prominently in both Aristotelian and empiricist philosophy – in the second case especially in the twentieth century. Daniel Dennett, for example, contrasts the items of hard science, which have fundamental reality with entities that, if real at all (Dennett seems not to care whether they are or not), have non-basic or ersatz being. Dennett's list of things with the latter include, interestingly, pains, and 'haircuts and collars and opportunities and persons and centers of gravity.'[15] The view I advocate is that there are no second class beings, either in the sense of being or in the sense of having a being that is derivative or less genuinely a matter of being at all, than the being of other things. It is not denied of course that many things only have being because of the being of other things, that in many cases things are parasitic upon or constructed out of others. The possibility and with it the problematic character of projects of ontological reduction of things of one kind to those of another is acknowledged. What is affirmed is that in all cases of parasitism, construction, or reduction the *being* that these things have is not anything other than the being that the most fundamental things have. In respect of *being*, at least, all things with participation in it do so altogether, equally, and on all fours with each other. There are no such things then, in my view, as what Sellars called 'Pickwickian' senses of being. I will call the thesis about being that I advocate, with its two distinct components, the unity of being thesis.

The unity of being thesis will, if true, make extra-causalism more substantive because it will eliminate what would otherwise have been the option of treating items without causes or effects as things with attenuated being. The latter contrast would permit a modified extra-causalism which would allow that some real things lack causes or effects but only the second-class ones; all the entities with basic being would be causes or effects.

It will be appreciated that in the nature of the theses being advocated – they are very basic theses – somewhat special kinds of argument could alone be marshalled, on one side of the theses or the other.

The best argument for the unity of being thesis is, I think, that in respect of its first component thesis, denying it violates Occam's razor and confuses subclassifications of reference with subclassifications of sense. That beagles and collies are dogs does not make 'dog' equivocal as applied to each. Similarly with 'is,' 'is real,' and putative synonyms, as applied to comets, neutrons, Bill Clinton, numbers, and symphonies. Senses should no more be multiplied beyond necessity than any other sort of thing.[16] The second component thesis is best defended by the argument that its complement or denial is only problematically coherent; or only has such coherence as will make it succumb to the first argument. That x's are reducible to y's doesn't – so long as x's are still granted to exist – taint x's existence. Similarly if x's are parasitic upon y's.

One very direct reason for believing that extra-causalism is true is that entities which do not appear to have any role in the causal structure of the world nonetheless seem to be real. For example, there really seems to be such a thing as what it would be to be an intelligent Martian or a world war fought in the third century. This is of course to be saying, in general terms, that extra-causalism is refuted by the fact that Platonic realism with respect to properties is true; and it will not move nominalistic philosophers who have heard the (best) case for Platonism and remained unpersuaded by it. Another kind of case may fare better. The point of intersection of the Greenwich meridian and the equator at a given nanosecond seems to be an actual location in space. A helicopter could hover directly above it. Yet it seems causally inert.

It was suggested earlier that versions of causalism might successfully encompass some abstract or immaterial things under the umbrella conception of being constituents of facts or states of affairs that have a causal role in the world. Possibly ingenuity, and a sufficient degree of counterfactuality (a willingness to assign something a causal role if it were in principle possible that it be a part of a complex that would have a causal role, or if it itself was wholly comprised of constituents with causal roles), might permit construing anything someone wanted to assimilate to the causal in this attenuated way. However, it will be clear, ontic conviction precedes the applicaton of ingenuity and survives any reverses with which ingenuity may meet.

This suggests a kindred argument for the extra-causality position, which may be conceived as a version of Moore's open question argument.[17]

(C) *x* exists iff *x* is a cause or effect

is, if true, informatively so. It is certainly not analytic. The *sense*, or *Sinn*, of 'existence' is extra-causal. Moreover, we can think the thought of something existing but being outside the causal network of the world. Thus, we can think the thought of unicornhood existing, or the centre of gravity of the solar system at the first instant of the twenty-second century. (C) might, of course, if not analytic, be a synthetic a priori truth. In fact, though, it seems clear that, affirming (C) involves and expresses, resolve and decision. Some metaphysicians say that they mean to take as real only what is in the, or a, causal chain. However, the very resolve belies the necessity of so proceeding. And if (C) is contingent, as this will suggest that it is, then there are worlds where it fails to be true, i.e., where some things exist extra-causally. However such worlds will be indistinguishable from the actual world, save, allegedly, for (C) and its consequences. That is, if in the actual world x exists and is a cause or effect but in other worlds is not, among the latter will be worlds whose event structure mimes the actual world save for its causal relations. So, at least, it would appear. However, if this is so, there would seem to be no reason not to hold (C) false of the actual world too. We would have reason then to conclude that (C) is false.

We would have reason in turn then to conclude that extra-causalism and the unity of being thesis are both true. Why, it will reasonably be asked, affirm them? What views, or whose, are denied if they are held true? And what will it matter anyway, one way or the other?

The numbers of contemporary causalists are large.[18] Most varieties of physicalism (or materialism) are also instances of causalism, insofar as the physicalist position is affirmed comprehensively as offering an exhaustive inventory of the real. Many empiricist and naturalist philosophers have supposed or have argued that their views of the world require or are enhanced by a particularly lean or sparse ontology and specifically one that will countenance spatio-temporal particulars and some minimal set of additions to them. Such convictions appear with the first empiricist and naturalist philosophy, in Democritus and Epicurus, and in a modified form in Aristotle. Ever since lean ontology grounded in the perceptible has been a hallmark of empiricism and naturalism. In recent decades this focus has been displaced merely laterally and in the same spirit, by metaphysical commitments to the world's causal structure.

I want to defend the idea that while Occam's razor is a sound principle, and both clarity and linkage to the observable are understandable and plausible, exclusive commitments to spatio-temporal particulars or to causes and effects are more expressions of what is an essentially romantic and aesthetic sentiment than of a scientific, naturalist, or empiricist ontology.

Extra-causalism, as I wish to use it, is not part of an agenda that would weaken an essentially scientific, physicalist, or naturalist view of the world and our place within it. The agenda to which it contributes, for me, is part of a claim that science does not in fact have an attention so clearly focused on *existence* as does philosophy. Philosophers want deeply and centrally to know what exists, what is real and what its character is. Scientists do also – or so advocates of realist views of science (I am myself one) hold – but not in the same paramount way. They want to understand and explain the world and its experienced constituents. This need not lead directly to fundamental theories about the whole of existence. Few scientists, for example, feel any challenge in the question of the ontological status that ought to be accorded numbers or other mathematical entities. It does not seem right to say that that is just because they haven't yet got around to the physics of mathematical objects. Rather the inference to draw is that fundamental physics only partly coincides with fundamental metaphysics or ontology; more specifically, that fundamental physics does not seek to produce, and does not even operate with identifiable assumptions about, an elemental set of existence postulates.

My aim here then is not simply to refute or puncture causalism. The latter is prompted not merely by what we might call ontological minimalism: heroic commitment to the smallest stock possible of kinds of things. More important, causalism is meant to express the scientific point of view. It is supposed to affirm (part of) how metaphysics should look if we suppose that (metaphysically realist) scientific naturalism is the soundest guide that there is to the objective character of the universe. If putative entities are problematic proportionate to their distance from the core items of theoretical physics, it is understandable that the causal structure of the world, and the items necessarily involved in it, should be 'privileged' for ontology.

Though this outcome is understandable, I want to suggest that a genuinely scientific, naturalist, or empiricist point of view, or set of commitments, does not require or even significantly lean to causalism. This aim has only been intimated and sketched in this chapter with, I hope, the beginnings of plausible argument in the direction of its realization. It is in any case largely independent of the investigation of the character of being or existence, as such, to which my concluding remarks return.

VIII

A consequence of the unity of being will be that, if affirmations of being are ever ontological, or existential, they always are. Since some affirmations of being are certainly ontological, then they all are. If anything is ever said to be, or if anything implies that something is, the being involved is a matter of being an actually existing, genuine part of reality. To some these remarks will be banal truisms. However, to others they definitely are not. In addition to those who have differentiated categories of ontic status, such that (for them) the being that physical objects have is a different sort of thing, even if somehow related, than the being that abstract entities (for example) have, there are also philosophers whose positions imply that being-affirmations aren't significantly ontological at all. Usually philosophers with this view hold that no genuinely clear and perspicuous discourse is ontological, metaphysical, or indeed philosophical. One constituency with this view are positivists. The greatest of twentieth-century positivists is Carnap and he, in a celebrated paper,[19] argued that questions of being that are internal to some adopted framework, or language, have typically automatic and trivial answers, whereas those external to it don't make any sense.

The positivist stance is reasonably well-known and it will be clear that it conflicts with the unity-of-being view. Less well-known, or explicitly articulated, is the other view of the broad type under consideration, which may be connected to philosophies grounded in (certain ideas of) common sense or shared common life. There may be, I think, phenomenological versions of such positions but I am primarily meaning to identify adherents of 'ordinary language' philosophy and, even more importantly, of pragmatism. The 'ordinary language' school was prominent, especially in Great Britain, in the 1940s, 1950s, and early 1960s, but has few unadulterated advocates now. It is otherwise with pragmatism. The distinctively American philosophy developed with Peirce in the 1880s and 1890s, and has had revivals at different times ever since, and is quite prominently advocated in the present. Philosophers sometimes are pragmatist *to a degree*, it should be remarked. I hope to identify a reasonably pure type. Rorty may plausibly be held to fit the mold tolerably well. At any rate, for pragmatist views, we are clearer about the meaning and deployment of basic (and many nonbasic) assertions of common life than we are about philosophical theories or indeed aspirations to philosophical theorizing at all. We say all sorts of things, they work well for us, and it is by no means self-evident that theses that (non-pragmatist) philosophers tie to them really have those links or, indeed, that they really make good sense at all; and these observations attach themselves to at least some instances of what I am calling being-affirmations. We know and say that there are swans in Australia, that there are numbers higher than 96, that there are smiles which have sunk kingdoms, that there are market trends that bode ill for the next economic quarter; and, according to these pragmatists, it is not obvious, and probably untrue that anything very interestingly metaphysical is to be made of any of them, as to what reality in itself is like for example. One should be suspicious of people making claims about what is 'real,' and certainly should scrutinize those claims, demand to know what they mean by 'real,' and not necessarily expect that there will be a univocal or persuasive answer. Our bedrock grounding in what we say and what we know is independent of and will survive the passing array of philosophical theory as decades, and centuries, march by.

All of the latter is deeply at odds with what is argued here. Others have argued for the theory-ladenness of most or all discourse, even when it is not visible on its face that it has this character, and others again for the normativity of much or most discourse, even when it appears otherwise. I argue for the metaphysicality of the things that we say and believe: this is precisely what is intended and implied in Quine's thesis of ontological commitment, and the views of Russell's from which it stems. What we say and think carries with it inherent implications as to what there is, and the relevant 'what there is' is strongly ontic, existential, or metaphysical, in a single univocal, primitive and not otherwise explicable sense.

Chapter Six

Essence and Possible Worlds

I

The concept of essence has figured in metaphysics since Aristotle. However it is unclear whether any ancient Greek thinker attached to the notion of *ousia* (the Aristotelian term translated as 'essence') or whether any Roman philosopher attached to the subsequent term *essentia*, an idea that is more than a distant relative of what Western philosophers have meant by essence since the twelfth century.[1]

Essence in this sense (or senses) has been a part of what we can identify as a family of strongly modal concepts: concepts of what might or must be, in a manner independent of what humans or other cognizers *know*, or might know, and independent of features, even of the most general kind, that happen to apply in or to the world we inhabit. Some philosophers have been sceptical about this whole family of concepts; and it certainly seems to be the case that it takes considerable motivation, and prompting from philosophical texts and teachers, for the laity – the extra-philosophical community, and initiates to the subject – to get the hang of what is intended by this family and its members.

Nonetheless there seems something there to be found, something that can be seen to be both clear and important for metaphysics. Indeed there has developed in recent decades in analytic philosophy a view that out of reflection on strongly modal concepts, definitely including *essence*, the heart of the most plausible positions to take on most metaphysical questions can be discovered. This rather vaguely stated thesis is sometimes called the thesis of modal metaphysics.[2] Whether or not it is true, modality is one of the provinces of thought and reality to which metaphysics gives attention, because it is there and it is basic; similarly for what has also been called the metaphysics of modality, i.e., the metaphysical implications of the most plausible views on modality.

The central anchor for the position advanced in these pages is that a 'strong' variety of possibility, what was dubbed, in the middle ages, *de re* possibility, is conceptually primitive and indefinable. Some things are able to be the case and we need to and can take ourselves to have a clear metaphysical intuition of this kind of fact. These possibilities typically include situations of something's being able to have a property (whether or not it actually does). We have a clear intuition, so the modal metaphysician claims, of the idea of what we are saying when we say such things. We might be unable to tell with confidence what really is possible in this sense.

Thus, we might be playing a guessing game where one of us is to think of something that the other is to try to identify by indirect questions. You are thinking of the number 7. I ask if what you are thinking of could be photographed. You say that it could not be photographed. I ask whether it is divisible by two. You say that it could not be divided by two. I ask whether it could be prime. You say it could be and is.

Such conceptual focus and verbal interchange seems to identify a 'could' that is 'in principle,' and non-epistemic. It is also not linguistic or even propositional; at least, not obviously so. If it is a 'logical' possibility, it is not clear what that means or what utility there is in calling it that. No formal logical system – certainly not first order predicate logic – could produce a contradiction from 'the thing you are thinking of is non-prime' or 'that thing has been photographed.'

If this is a matter of logic, then it wouldn't seem to be a matter of formal logic. (And it also isn't informal logic.) Some things simply couldn't be; it is impossible, in principle, that they be, however the world has been, whatever its history, constituents, or natural laws. In this same sense other things can be, it is not impossible, in principle, that they be; at any rate, we have the idea of what it would involve for this to be so. This possibility is what we call *de re* possibility: possibility concerning a *thing* and not some way or other that the thing may have been referred to or classified.

This conceptually primitive possibility seems to attach primarily to states of affairs (or – a little confusingly – possible states of affairs). By a state of affairs, in this sense, will be meant something that need not actually obtain or occur. This comment is intended to explain the apparent confusion in indifferently referring to states of affairs and possible states of affairs since in some lexica a state of affairs, 'by definition,' does obtain. *Aristotle being an olive merchant* is a (possible) state of affairs; so is *Aristotle being a philosopher*. Aristotle was, of course, a philosopher, but was not an olive merchant. Primary or particularly clear cases of (possible) states of affairs are complexes involving objects (substances) having properties or standing in relation to each other.

(Possible) states of affairs need not be viewed as ontologically irreducible. They can be conceived as modal properties of substances, other individuals, or the universe as a whole. This interpretation is adopted here and elaborated below.

Independent of possibility in principle, some things must be so, they are necessary, in principle, as they are; at any rate, we have the idea of what it would entail for something to be necessary in principle (whether or not anything really is or whether we know if anything really is so). The orthodox view in modal logic, and the philosophy of modality, is that 'in principle' *must* and 'in principle' *could* are interdefinable and interintelligible. Something will be necessary just in case it is impossible that it not obtain and something is possible if and only if it is not necessary that it not take place. For reasons that will emerge below, the same reasons that motivated A.N. Prior[3] to the same view, this equivalence is rejected in the position on modality advocated here.

II

Further, there is the central focus of metaphysics as such: the world, reality, the universe, the aggregate of all things real or that have being including the facts, states, or events that occur over time in the course of the world's history. The aggregate sum of everything existing, everything obtaining, occurring, or being true. I will call it reality, the universe, or the actual world. And I will affirm that reality exists.

Like everything that exists, reality has properties. It has the property of containing human beings, for example, oxygen, and chemical processes; also the property of containing Bill Clinton. Some of reality's properties are complex, like containing animals, if there are horses. Others are modal: for example, being able to contain people (it actually contains people, so it must also be able to), and being able to have had a hundred billion planets with intelligent life.[4]

For reality, as with everything else with properties, there is the total aggregate of all its properties. Some properties are the complements of others. Being red and being nonred are examples of such a complement pair. The total aggregate of a thing's properties may be represented schematically in the form being F and G and H and ... – where some of the letters will represent property complements. For reality (as for everything else with properties) there are aggregates of compossible properties – properties able to be jointly satisfied or had by the same thing (representable schematically as being able to be F and G and H, for example). An aggregate of properties is maximal if and only if every property or its complement is included in the aggregate. If we regard a_1, a_2, a_3, ... as logically proper names[5] for all actual individuals – i.e., all individuals which do, did, or will exist – then we may consider complex properties of the form: being able to contain as the only individuals that there are, a_1, a_2, ... and to be ϕ, where ϕ is a maximal property (aggregate) and where the entire property aggregate is satisfiable, i.e., able to apply to something.[6] Such a property will apply to reality and apparently only to it. Each such property will be said metaphorically to constitute a possible world.

This construal of possible worlds bears a significant resemblance to one that Chisholm developed in a 1986 paper[7], with some important differences. Chisholm does not explore the idea of a maximal property of reality conceived as an individual; and in consequence, he does not consider whether, as suggested earlier, a (possible) state of affairs can be regarded as or reduced to a modal property of reality. For Chisholm a possible world literally is a maximal (possible) state of affairs. Hence, for him, an indefinitely large number of possible worlds literally exist. This view will have the unattractive consequence that the actual world is not a possible world, since the actual world is not a mere (possible) state of affairs (even a maximal one), that is to say, not an abstract entity.

III

My account of possible worlds will diverge to a still greater degree from others in the literature which identify worlds either as (maximal) ways or maximal compossible sets of propositions. As with Chisholm's treatment, the problem with both of the latter is that the actual world is a possible world but the actual world is not literally a way or a set of propositions; and all possible worlds should be entities of the same ontological kind as the actual world. My view is that there is only one individual of the sort that the actual universe or reality is, namely, it itself. There are no possible nonactual universes or worlds. However, there is the complete actual way that the actual universe is – the aggregate of all of its properties – and these include constituent modal properties that are likewise complete and maximal within the scope of the possibility that governs them and that identify the individuals they include (as the only individuals that they include). These latter complex modal properties of the actual world may be isolated, separated from each other, and from the non-modal properties of the universe. What is within the scope of each of these complex modal properties may be described accurately as a way that reality could have been. As a number of philosophers rightly and importantly point out, an object is to be distinguished from its properties; hence a way is not literally to be identified with a thing of which that way is, might, or would be true (under appropriate conditions). Possible nonactual worlds would be, if they were real, such things. They aren't real nor do the ways obtain or hold in any respect or of anything (except of course for the actual way); what obtains or holds are the properties of these various ways being able to obtain; and these properties are true of reality.

This is how matters are strictly. However, we allow ourselves to speak as though there were entities that were the things of which these several ways were true and we call them, and the actual world, possible worlds. Yet everything said in this vocabulary must always be rephraseable in principle in terms of the actual universe and its properties including its modal properties. We use the possible worlds vocabulary – speaking as though there were such things literally – because it is convenient and expressively powerful to do so. Henceforth, then, I proceed (when convenient) *as though*.

IV

In the view advocated here all the possible worlds that there are are – or are 'determined by,' or paired with – a total compossible aggregate of how things could be for reality, involving all and only actual existing individuals. This is another respect in which the treatment of possible worlds adopted here diverges from more usual accounts. My view is that since there cannot be logically proper names of non-actual individuals, there cannot be facts about them, including modal facts. A possible world, in the sense explained, with non-actual individuals would be incomplete, a non-maximal way. (More along these lines will be developed below.) Exactly one of the possible worlds is of course the actual world, the way that things could have been for the whole set of things that there are, that is the actual way things are for them.

What of proper subsets of the actual individuals and reality-possibilities with respect to them? It appears natural or intuitive, at least initially, to think that there are possible worlds containing some but not all actual individuals. As will be seen below, I think there should be identified a family of world-like entities, rather than a single possible world notion (even if a possible world *simpliciter* is given a specially valorized status), and one of these world-like items could be devised for ways things might be for proper subsets of actual individuals. However, there appears to be a compelling case for denying such world-like items as the latter a full possible world status. If every (genuine) possible world is maximal, i.e., for every proposition p and property F the world contains either p or not-p and has F or non F, then the world will contain propositions and properties involving identity with or diversity from every actual individual (i.e., not merely every individual found in the putative world but every actually actual individual) for these are in fact among the propositions and properties that there are. Suppose our candidate world-like item w fails to contain a_{19} but does contain a_{47}. Then not being a_{19} would need to be (it would seem) a property of entities of w (a_{47} among them). But then a_{19} will be in w – since 'a_{19}' is a logically proper name – contrary to the hypothesis. We could of course revise relevant maximality, to fail to include properties involving individuals other than the relevant world's set. The problem is that in this case linkage appears lost or compromised with regard to the idea of a world as a total way things could be. If we do stick to this latter idea, then possible worlds contain all and only actual individuals. If we are going to put this as a matter of a possible property of the actual individual Reality – if, that is, we are going to say that Reality could have been like this and the *this* includes a total (maximal) story of things – so that, for example, the story will always provide an answer to the question whether Aristotle is or is not in the story – possible worlds will turn out as indicated.

Of course there could also have been things that there aren't. Each human being, for example, could have had a sibling additional to all those he or she does have. So we need to identify another sort of 'world,' namely, incomplete ones: worlds in which the individuals of the world are not necessarily all identified. These will be modal properties of reality of the form (where zero or more of a_1, a_2, ... appear in the instance of the form) *being able to contain a_1, a_2, a_3, ... and to be such that* ϕ, where ϕ will include at least one property and may – but need not – include every property or its complement. Such worlds as these are incomplete in that they allow it to be said that there are individuals other than actual ones (i.e., individuals actual in the real world) without naming them. So, for example, if a and b are actual siblings, and they have no others, an incomplete world might include as constituents *being able to contain individuals a, b, c_1, c_2, ... and to be such that: a and b are siblings and there is an x such that x is sibling of a and x is sibling of b.*

It seems then that it is a mistake to suppose that there is a single possible world notion. As affirmed above, I think there is only one world in the literal sense. Otherwise worlds are metaphorical heuristic devices or constructs, to be explained literally in terms of properties of the one actual world. As devices or constructs, there are different kinds of worlds, serving different theoretical purposes and answering to different semantic or metaphysical intuitions.

Some indeed make use of impossible worlds not constrained by having to be consistent or possible, like stories with details that contradict each other.

These I leave wholly out of account for the present purpose, though a full theory of worlds would need to encompass them too. All worlds explored here are possible ones – situations able to obtain. Among these some include as well so-called fuzzy worlds, with indeterminacies or vague-boundaried states of affairs or objects. If such things are possible and in spite of some impressive formal theory, it remains controversial whether they are: also whether, if they are, the actual world is such a world; but if they are possible, worlds theory of the type I sketch here would include them.

V

One fundamental distinction to discern is a contrast between a possible world as a way things might seem, feel, and be, if that world were real – a world from within, as it were – and a possible world, as glimpsed from without. These spatial metaphors are not to be taken literally, nor is the phenomenological one. The difference between a possible-world-from-within and a possible-world-from-without may be illustrated by the case of an arbitrarily chosen contingently existing particular – Aristotle, for example. We want to affirm that possibly Aristotle does not exist, in the sense of meaning that reality could have lacked Aristotle, could have failed to contain him. From without, we want to be able to identify possible worlds lacking Aristotle, ways reality might have been about which we can say that they lack Aristotle. If reality actually had lacked Aristotle, there would be – according to the view taken here and elaborated on below – no Aristotle of which any assertion could be made, including the assertion of his non-being. There could be no such proposition as the proposition that Aristotle doesn't exist, to be able to be true or false, or even to have an indeterminate truth value. Such worlds as those in which the latter situation obtains are what is meant by worlds from within.[8] Similarly, if there were an enumeration of all contingently existing actual entities a_1, a_2, a_3, ... (in fact there are arguments for thinking that there are non-denumerably many contingent actual entities but let us for argument's sake suppose contingent realia countable), *there are possible worlds lacking all of* a_1, a_2, a_3 ... will be a true proposition if incomplete worlds are meant and meant from without, but not otherwise.

The stance taken here on possible worlds then is a version of what Graeme Forbes[9] and others call reductive realism (in contrast to the absolute realist view especially associated with David Lewis).[10] More precisely the view I advocate is close to reductive realist positions that identify possible worlds with maximal states of affairs (as with Chisholm, and with Alvin Plantinga)[11] or with maximal possibilities (as with Lloyd Humberstone).[12] It is closer still (as is a great deal in the present chapter) to the concept of a possible world, and related concepts, discussed in Robert Merrihew Adams' paper 'Actualism and Thisness' (*Synthèse*, 1981). Adams' view, and mine, differ from other reductive realist views in holding that the only possible worlds that there are are ones containing actual entities. Of course, in addition to the possible worlds that there are, according to me, there could have been possible worlds that there aren't, that is, had other individuals existed than those that do, and there could have been such individuals, there would have been other possible worlds, in addition to the ones that there are. In other words, reality could have had properties which it does not have.

This particular position is incompatible with views of possible worlds I would call generically Meinongian (Adams calls them possibilist): views according to which possible non-actual individuals have a kind of ontic status, other than existence, or being, or at any rate really do have properties, whether or not they themselves are real.[13] According to some views of the latter type, such possible non-actual individuals include worlds, conceived as something other than possible properties (more accurately: properties consisting of something's being possible) of the actual universe or reality. (If one is not a Meinongian or possibilist, one is probably what Adams and others call an actualist – as I am. 'Actualism is the doctrine that there *are* no things that do not exist in the actual world.'[14])

The most theoretically 'serious,' and fruitful, family of cases of at least apparent Meinongianism occurs in formal contexts of mathematics and logic where abstract models are utilized with domains of entities whose reality or irreality is a matter of indifference for the model. 'Suppose we have a domain of individuals a, b, and c, where a is F, b is G, and c is neither F nor G.' Is a F? Do a, b, and c, exist? Of course not. (Or if they did – if it happened that there were or for some reason, theoretical or practical, it had been appropriate to choose real individuals as referents of the constants – it wouldn't matter for any formal purpose.) That is to say, this formal allowance of unreal individuals having properties is only apparent Meinongianism. It is a kind of story-telling, for purposes rather different from more familiar story-telling. At the same time, it deserves emphasis that it is a considerable challenge, one that will not be taken up here, to think what a metaphysically perspicuous and literally accurate rendering of the semantics for almost any formal theory in logic or mathematics might look like.

VI

The view taken here also firmly embraces and extends the Russellian position on logically proper names, as Russell and, later, Prior, developed it in philosophical logic. According to this view, if a is a logically proper name, a genuine individual constant, then its bearer or referent is automatically and necessarily real. Such symbols as these are only lexically available, only appear as items of vocabulary, where they denote actual entities. Unlike Russell, we allow logically proper names for actual individuals not currently existing. (Indeed, Russell views them as language-user-relative, requiring that there be an individual with whom acquaintance is present and occurrent, for a logically proper name to be deployed.) We do so by utilizing a so-called causal theory of (proper) names, whereby present genuinely-naming use is secured if suitable causal chains go back to occasions of purer Russellian acquaintance-experience type. There will be then no genuine naming of future not-yet-actual individuals, any more than never-actual individuals.

What is true of logically proper names will be true of concepts appearing in expressions involving them. Without a real (at present or in the past), 'a' has no meaning (at any rate as a genuine name), and there is no such concept as being a, being brother of a, b being taller than a, etc. In such circumstances, situations, or worlds, lacking a, there are no propositions (true or false; or even there, truth valueless) about or in any way involving, citing, or referring to a. This is the view Alvin Plantinga calls existentialism.[15] It is here cheerfully endorsed and advocated.

The logic of existentialism I, and others earlier (above all Prior), have set out elsewhere.[16] Here I want chiefly to fill in the picture of possible worlds and essence it will involve, then to go on to some particular essentialist views I advocate, and others (which some contemporary philosophers defend) which I dispute. I will remark though that in this logic the standard $\diamond\, \alpha \equiv\, \sim \square \sim \alpha$ principle[17] will not be valid, since α might contain a logically possible name for something contingent. If it did, $\diamond\, \alpha$ might be true, but $\sim \square \sim \alpha$ would not be, since in this logic any proposition with a propositional part that is formally truth-valueless is itself truth-valueless. If α were 'Aristotle is an olive merchant,' then $\diamond\, \alpha$ will be true, since there are worlds in which he is. But the proposition $\square \sim$ (Aristotle is an olive merchant) is truth-valueless since there are worlds at which the proposition *Aristotle is an olive merchant* is truth-valueless (strictly, meaningless), since he doesn't exist at those worlds. And of course the negation of a meaningless proposition will itself be meaningless. By similar argumentation it may be seen that the standard modal rule $\vdash \alpha \rightarrow\, \vdash \square\, \alpha$ will also not hold in this logic. Save for its deviation from standard $\diamond$ and $\square$ interdefinability, this logic very closely resembles the standard modal system S4.[18]

VII

I want to make use of one other possible world notion in addition to those already described. I will call this a Ramsey world after the philosopher and logician F.P. Ramsey (1903–30), who had a similar idea. In the general view adopted here, some propositions – the ones containing logically proper-name concepts – exist only contingently. (Other categories of proposition may also be argued to exist only contingently but that matter is left open in the present context.) Other propositions, however, exist necessarily (whether or not they are true necessarily). The proposition that 7 is greater than 5, for example, could not not-exist. So too the proposition that substances are not times. And many others (possibly – i.e., we do not yet presume one way or the other on this matter – all propositions save those containing logically-proper-name concepts). If we consider the class of all non-contingently existing propositions, there will be constitutable from them maximal compossible sets of propositions: sets such that every proposition or its negation is in the set, and that are compossible or able jointly to be true. Such a set of propositions determines a Ramsey world. (The latter is named after that philosopher because he developed the idea of the existential generalization of all the atomic sentences of a language that would wholly eliminate proper names from it.)[19]

The concept of a Ramsey world permits an account of ways the world might have been that is not anchored in, or that does not take its point of departure from the actual world. It permits both the question and the answer to the query, What is a possible world-story?, without reference to the particular named (or nameable) individuals and entities of our universe. This is, I believe, the concept of a possible world that Leibniz originally had in mind. It affords a God's-eye view of how the world, or a world, might go, and what it might contain. A Ramsey world is not a possible world since it does not contain or lack Aristotle, or Cuba, or any other individual; but it also fails to be asymmetrically tilted, as possible worlds are, in favour of the entities of the actual universe. We will utilize Ramsey worlds where convenient, as the modal story enlarges.

VIII

Some people have thought that there is a major metaphysical or epistemological problem with identifying an item in one world with one in another. However, I take it, with Kripke, that the so-called problem of transworld identity is a pseudo-problem, at any rate in most of the ways it has been formulated.[20] Possible worlds are not epistemic items, nor epistemically generated or motivated. They aren't new terrain for inquiry with (inter alia) a view to discover whether things they contain are already known. To have affirmed that Aristotle could have been an olive merchant is already to affirm the possibility of states of affairs in which he is one or that reality has the modal property of Aristotle's possibly being an olive merchant. Since full possible worlds-from-without – the relevant perspective from which to consider 'transworld identity' – are necessarily *complete* with respect to every proposition and property (i.e., they contain every one of the former or its negation, and every object in them has every one of the latter or its complement), if a candidate for such a world contains a person called Bartholomew, then one of the things true or false of the latter is that he is (or isn't) Aristotle. Being Aristotle is of course distinct from being called 'Aristotle.' In many possible worlds Aristotle exists but isn't called 'Aristotle.'

So objects, all of them, exist in many possible worlds and this is held to be quite unproblematic. At the same time what the properties objects may have in non-actual worlds containing them is by no means automatically determinable. The great issues, discussed since antiquity, of the conditions of identity over time for different individual substances, kinds of substance, and other individuals constitute the heart and central content of this inquiry. It is also the issue of the essential properties of a thing, the properties an entity has in all the worlds that contain it (i.e., in all the ways the world might have been such that that entity remains real and self-identical). These are simply alternative vocabularies for the same topic.

Most attention to the essential properties of entities has focused on substances or spatio-temporal particulars. Historically, these were the only entities whose essential features or essences were investigated. In recent years a certain amount of essentialist inquiry has also been accorded events, sets, and other entities.

IX

The first kind of essential property I will discuss is one about which few essentialists would differ with me although it is a category of property that seems rarely identified or explored. This is the category of what I will call *ontic type*. If something is an *event*, there is no possible world, I believe, in which it is a number, a triangle, or a property. It is essentially a non-number, a non-triangle and a non-property. Similarly, giraffes, I would affirm, essentially fail to be sets, points of space, or propositions.

One of the many currents in twentieth-century, analytic philosophy triggered by a conception of Russell's inventive genius is called category theory.

It is especially associated in recent years with the work of Fred Sommers and earlier with Gilbert Ryle; still earlier Russellian type theory (in mathematical logic) gave theoretical expression to a form of this idea. (The idea also owes something to common sense or folk semantics for natural language.) Generally category theory is the idea that concepts come in clusters or groups such that certain things may be said of one cluster that cannot meaningfully be said of others. If the attempt is made, the result is supposed to be something not false – not even necessarily false – but meaningless. Famous examples abound in the literature: for example, *Saturday is sleeping furiously* and *7 is green*.

Category theory was, of course, explored in Chapter 4. The features that group entities in the categories under which they fall are what I mean by properties of ontic type. (I will evidently have committed myself to at least modest dissent from strong versions of category theory in holding as I do that an entity of one category can meaningfully and truly be said to possess the complement of basic features of entities of other categories, e.g., I take it that *7 is non-green* is meaningful, indeed, true.)

Entities are essentially lodged in their features of ontic type, both positive or affirmative and negative features. A simple thing – if there are any – is in no possible world a complex one. Similarly being abstract and concrete absolutely and essentially exclude each other.

At the same time there are complexities and grounds for dissent in this terrain. Many philosophers of mathematics believe that numbers are sets, which might be thought a violation of category or ontic type. Many philosophers in the 1920s and 1930s (and some before and since) have believed, applying what they supposed were results or insights from modern physics, that physical objects were a series of events, which would definitely be category errors for some philosophers. The philosophers who viewed physical objects as series of events were not, it is important to recognize, regarding physical objects as abstract entities. They often, as many philosophers do, failed adequately to distinguish sets and aggregates. The real view in question is that physical objects are temporal aggregates of event-aggregates (World War II is an example of a temporal aggregate of event-aggregates) localized at a series of spatially adjoining places. Of course many philosophers in recent decades argue that the whole category of the mental is simply a specialized variety of the physical, in spite of what had been confident assurances (advanced most famously perhaps, by Gilbert Ryle, in his book *The Concept of Mind*) that such identifications were bound to be conceptually confused.

In general a variety of constructivist philosophical projects would seem to constitute challenges to what many suppose to be categorial or ontic-type boundaries between kinds of entities. Some of these challenges and projects seem quite plausible, prima facie, commonsensical intuitions or convictions notwithstanding. Nonetheless it seems quite wrong to believe that ontic borders are completely fluid.

I will not undertake to delineate the ontic boundaries that are immoveable, i.e., that indicate essential properties of ontic type, in any systematic way. They seem to definitely distinguish abstract, physical, and temporal entities. We can, I think, confidently predict that no future constructivist project will show us what it would or could be for the planet Jupiter, for example, in some possible world to be identical with the fourteenth century – or with *a* century. Similarly, no abstract thing is capable, even in principle, of becoming a physical object. Nor could *yesterday* have been an isosceles triangle. I think ontic distinctions are still finer than this. Yet how finely-grained, and along what bases of theory or system, remains work for future inquiry.

In any case, I think that there would be near-unanimity among the essentialist community, at least at the conservative end of the spectrum, about the essentiality of properties of ontic type to their bearers. I will proceed then to the areas of essentialist investigation or conviction where there is definitely not unanimity and where in fact I want to defend a view which most other contemporary essentialists would not share.

X

With the classical tradition (ca. 1100–1900) I focus chiefly on individual substances or particulars. In recent decades four specific essentialist views – convictions as to the essentiality to particulars of four kinds of properties – have been advocated. The leading proponent of these four varieties of essential propertyhood has been Saul Kripke.[21] Others share his views or argue independently for similar results. I want to argue emphatically against three of the four and raise doubts about, or complexities with, the fourth. The four kinds of properties frequently argued to be essential to the particulars that have them are:

1. Natural kind properties, like *being a horse*, *being a tree*, and *being a human being*.
2. Properties of material composition, like *being wooden* (or *being made of wood*), and *being composed out of hydrogen and nitrogen*.
3. Properties of origin, or causation, like *being son of Ralph and Mary* (had by someone who is in fact son of Ralph and Mary), and *having developed as the result of interaction between sperm and egg*.
4. What were earlier (by Carnap, for example) called individual concept prop-

erties, and are now – sometimes (though others use this term importantly otherwise) – called haecceitous properties (or haecceities), like *being Aristotle*, and *being Cuba*, together with appropriate complement properties, like *not being Socrates* (or *being diverse from Socrates*).

Sometimes arguments of sophistication and some considerable degree of formalism are offered for the essentiality of one or more of these four property groups to their bearers. I believe nonetheless that all essentialist argument comes, sooner or later, to the coherence or intelligibility of allegedly possible situations, in which a suitable particular is found to have or lack the relevant property. Accordingly what will be given here will not purport to be a thorough review of all arguments in the literature for (or against) these four essentialist positions.

Some additional comment on the four will however be desirable prior to evaluating them.

1. Some philosophers do not trouble to distinguish or attach metaphysical significance to the contrasting cases of kind terms characteristically expressed by a count-noun expression and a mass term. Others, as earlier discussion has indicated, this book among those others, do. The examples given above are all of count-noun type. I will however also address allegedly essential properties like being gold and being oxygen.

2. I see a difference between being gold and being made of gold, although others don't. Both are held essential to their bearers by some philosophers. Both will be discussed here. It is also important to note that not just any material stuff or element a thing may contain or be composed of is held essential (typically) to the thing. Some who think being wooden essential to wooden tables or containing hydrogen essential to water or to glass of water *a*, or to the English Channel, would baulk at similarly viewing containing styrofoam or including cognac to things with those properties. If it is essential to something to have the chemical elements it does, is it likewise essential that they be in the proportions they are? This would seem improbable. So there will be a range of essentialist positions, weak and strong, falling under this rubric, and aligning themselves with what we might call philosophical chemistry.

3. On the face of it, Kripkean essentialism as to origins seems pronouncedly – even anachronistically – Aristotelian. Causes here seem to be or at least to require particular prior substances that engender the substance whose essence is being determined and inspected. Whether there is room to manoeuvre here, as far as the advocates of such essentiality are concerned – whether, for example, my existence could have been brought about by a causal chain of events that might fail to include all actual substances in that chain – may need to be

addressed. If it is, we address unavoidably the question of the essential qualities of events as well as substances (particulars).

4. It should be noted that an individual concept or haecceitous properties are not to be confused with semantic properties or with self-identity. Being Aristotle is distinct from being called 'Aristotle' – and whether or not Aristotle could lack the former he could certainly lack the latter. Moreover, being Aristotle is different from being self-identical. Everything has the latter trait but only Aristotle has the former. At the same time it needs to be said that it is not obvious that everything has an individual concept property. Doubtless everything with a proper name does but what of those which happen to lack one? Do things with more than one proper name have more than one individual concept property? It seems clear that the essentialist intention, whether or not it is able to succeed, is that everything (named or otherwise) has exactly one individual concept property. Some philosophers (Adams among them) have talked also of the 'thisness' of a particular, others of what makes something be just this particular thing that it is. And it is typically assumed that both of these are the same as an individual concept property. More of these matters will be posed and addressed below.

An additional comment on substance and essence in more general terms ought to be made. It seems right to say, as Aristotle and traditions stemming from him evidently do, that a particular (or individual) substance could undergo things it did or that were done to it that destroyed the substance but preserved the elements of which it consisted. As with identity over time and essence, quite different vocabularies have in different contexts and times probed what seems to be a single theme. One of these vocabularies talks of substantial change: the idea that something might happen to a particular such that it, that particular, could no longer exist, even though all its parts, or all of the matter that had composed it, continue. Aristotle's standard example is the bronze statue of the god, which is melted down and recast, perhaps now as a cauldron. The idea is not that the statue has been transformed, but it, the object or substance, continues to be real. Change here has been too great (unlike the statue being painted over or losing an arm). It is not just that there is no longer a statue; there is no longer *it*, *that thing*, as a statue or anything else. Instead, a new substance has come into being, though composed of the selfsame matter as the old. Similarly, if there were a wooden table somewhere, and it were pulverised, smashed to dust, the heap of dust that resulted would not be the table, now transformed, but a new individual, or heap of individuals, composed of the elements that had composed the table. By contrast even some dramatic changes are held to preserve the identity of the particular. For example, we might see Carl the caterpillar on a sidewalk one day; and a few weeks later

Bob the butterfly, which has developed from Carl. We can, or should, suppose that Carl is identical to Bob; Carl has passed from caterpillar-phase to butterfly-phase.

I don't want to comment on these or other cases. It is the idea that is critical, of a distinction between a case where a continuing particular has been changed, even quite radically changed, and one where the particular has ceased, and a new individual (or individuals) – which we can call a *successor* individual (or individuals) – have come into being out of its remains. So we shall need to be able to decide in particular cases whether an alleged change has permitted the continued existence of a substance, or rather necessarily has produced a successor to that substance.

Let me now provide the general contours of method, argument, and position. First, the position: I advocate a variety of what Forbes and others call haecceitism. Others use this term quite differently, it should be noted. Haecceitism is the view that a distinct individual substance has a thisness, a matter of its being just the very thing that it is, that is logically[22] independent of its being known or knowable (verifiable or falsifiable) that it is by the substance itself or by any community of substances. Moreover, for haecceitism, the concept of a substance's thisness is not constituted by (or of) such natural kind, material, compositional, and causal traits as the substance may have. So understood, haecceitism does not as such deny that some natural kind, compositional, or causal properties may be essential to the substance. Haecceitism as such is neutral about whether a certain horse may not be essentially a horse, or a gold ring be essentially made of gold, or the Queen have had George VI as her father. Haecceitism, rather, denies that the identity of a substance at a time or its continuing identity over time is constituted by, logically a function of, or dependent on such properties. Metaphysically, there is the matter of that particular substance *a*, say – being *a*, and continuing so, and that is a logically independent matter from what else may be true of *a* regarding *a*'s nature, composition, or origins, and logically independent also of any matter of evidence anyone might have as to whether or not *a* existed, or had continued to exist, or had ceased and been replaced by some other object *b*. A particularly clear advocate of heacceitism, in this sense, in recent years is R.M. Adams.[23] A much earlier thinker who championed the doctrine, and in a form particularly close to the version (and its extensions) in these pages, is the seventeenth-century philosopher Anne Conway (1631–79).

Let it be noted also that haecceitism, as I have explained it, should not be identified with the claim that the haecceity of a substance is essential to the substance. Even if some will certainly argue that if a haecceity is what we have said it is, it must then also be true that a haecceity is essential to its bearer. Indeed, haecceitism as I mean it, is as such neither an essentialist nor an anti-essentialist position. That substance *a* is and continues to be *a*, in fact, in the actual world – if it is a fact of the actual world – does not tell you what the options are for other possible worlds.

Haecceitism as such does not imply that there are haecceitous properties that every individual uniquely possesses. Maybe there are such properties and maybe there are not. I will provide reasons, which I do not myself regard as necessarily compelling, for believing that some individuals at least do not possess haecceitous properties. Among the issues at the centre of deciding the matter is what exactly it is (or should be held to be) to be a property. If a property is or necessarily involves a conceptualizable content, a definite and specifiable something which can be asserted of or ascribed to the property's bearer, then perhaps there are things other than properties – thisnesses, possibly, among them – which are had by entities or true of them.

As for essence: in addition to haecceitism, and partly because of it, I think the natural kinds, material composition, and origins essentialist views are all mistaken. Then I work the other side of the street. I argue that there is no clear haecceitous property that every substance has and that should be viewed as essential to its bearer. Moreover, a substance's continued identity, when it occurs, is, from an essence or possible worlds point of view, entirely fortuitous, a matter of what I will call (adapting a phase of Thomas Nagel's, from another context) *metaphysical luck.*

My general stance on substance, then, is in a fundamental sense anti-essentialist, although it accepts and advocates the conceptual framework and tools of essentialism, and holds that substances, and all entities, have at least properties like self-identity, existence, and properties of ontic type essentially. Approximately my general line is that essentialism is true but only trivially so.

Method: in general, as I remarked above, matters of essence are decided by possible cases, exercises of the conceptual imagination; and I believe that many such exercises are quite compelling. Many of the possible cases devised and assessed by philosophers of essence are of course remote from the normal conditions of human life or those that science describes. That fact is in my view not a serious reason for discounting their value for metaphysics or thinking that they may not yield decisive results.

A more concrete matter of method is that I assume that phenomenological or introspectionist evidence and hypotheses are legitimate, empirical, and often (evidentially) weighty. With Nagel, I believe that there are matters of fact, that consist of how something feels to, or for, an experiencing subject. I do not assume that facts of this kind are not also facts of brain chemistry; in fact, I suspect that they probably are. Nor do I assume or believe that facts of this kind are incorrigible or unable to be mistaken. However, there is such a thing as what it feels like to enjoy strawberries, to find someone hauntingly evocative of an old flame, or to imagine yourself in *that* situation, and many many other facts of similar type: facts of a what-it-feels-like type.

Now the arguments: Though the four cases are substantially different, they exhibit commonalities, especially the first two, which will reduce some of the labour of refutation.

XI

First, then, natural kinds. I do not take for granted that the concept of a natural kind is wholly clear or unproblematic. (Nor, I think, need an advocate of the essentiality of natural kinds to things they apply to take this for granted.) Straightforward cases of what is intended are supposed to be properties like being a bat, being a human being, and being a pine tree, though how things are supposed to go for non-living things, and whether a natural kind can be something other than a biological species (or something resembling one) is unclear. At any rate, being an F, where F stands for any Linnaean species, would seem to be the form of a large number of natural kind terms, whether or not other kind terms will qualify.

Recalling that it is the essential properties of individual substances we are exploring – Tom, Dick, Harry, and every other particular individual object (including of course non-human ones) – the idea then is that each such individual, if a member of a biological species, is essentially a member of that species. Every horse is essentially a horse, every mushroom essentially a mushroom, every human essentially a human, etc.

Is this in fact the case? I think not for reasons stemming in part from Darwin (1809–82) and the *Origin of Species*. That great classic begins with a discussion of the arbitrariness and difficulties of sure classification of many individuals by species and develops and defends the now central tenet of modern biology that species are not fixed biblically static entities, but fluid and changing things bearing closer or more distant relation to each other. Granted that whole species change and become differentiated over time, what is going to be conceptually or imaginatively daunting about the idea of a single individual changing species over the course of its lifetime? Obviously this doesn't in fact happen but – of course – that is not the point for modality 'in principle.' If dogs can evolve into things that are no longer dogs but some new and distinct species, why couldn't Fido do that in a sped-up evolutionary transformation process, over his lifetime? However, if Fido could do this, then Fido isn't essentially a dog. And if Fido isn't essentially a dog, no other species-member, including individual humans, will be essentially a member of their species either.

This argument could obviously be enlarged upon and reinforced. More detail as to possible biological mechanics might be desired (the course of fetal development should suggest some possibilities). However, the central constituent idea should be clear and persuasive. The argument depends on members of actual natural kinds turning into members of not yet existent species. If this occurs in any possible world, then the argument will succeed. This will not prove that Fido could turn from a dog into a cat. Indeed there will be a weaker natural kind essence position which will remain untroubled by the argument, that every member of a species is essentially not a member of any alternate (actual) species – i.e., every dog is essentially a non-cat, a non-butterfly, a non-human, etc.

This weaker position will be a good deal harder to refute, since doing so requires – as the previous argument did not – addressing the very prominent, widely held view of the semantics of natural kind terms developed by Putnam and Kripke, according to which natural kind terms are almost purely referential terms, like logically proper names, all successful use of which requires causal linkage to original occasions of baptismal application of the term to real live members of the relevant species. So, if this view were correct, no matter how feline Fido became, even if he acquired biochemical traits making it impossible to distinguish him from a cat, he still wouldn't be a cat, since no kind term applied to him (even if it phonetically exactly resembled 'cat') could have the ancestry of its usage traced back to ostensive references to actual real live cats.[24]

My response to this objection will be, at least initially, indirect and general. The method in metaphysics advocated throughout this book has been to downplay the importance of language and meaning; and certainly to keep them always well differentiated from the rest of reality. There is undoubtedly the fact of what it is to be a cat, in nature, apart from how possessors of human or other minds conceive of or refer to cats. If Fido could acquire all of what nature has to offer regarding what a cat is biochemically (even if not historically or causally), we can give Putnam and Kripke the term 'cat.' Essentialism is about *res*, things, not *dicta*, or intensions.

If Fido turned into a cat, or something biochemically indistinguishable from a cat, why shouldn't we think of this as Fido ceasing to be, and a new successor individual appearing on the scene? The answer, I think, is that there would simply be no sufficient reason to believe that a substantial change, in the metaphysical sense, had occurred; any more than there is when a caterpillar becomes a butterfly. We are supposing uninterrupted biochemical and physical (and for that matter psychological) continuity, and this would seem sufficient, in the absence of any other candidate for identity with Fido or with an earlier stage of what we are now supposing is the cat Fido has become.

If dogs become cats, in some possible worlds, it is difficult to see why there would be a barrier, essentially, to any living individual substance evolving, without loss of identity, into a higher thinking being, a being with experiences, memory, consciousness, and a conceptual life. This is a bold and sweeping claim. It also reflects what children's stories, and mythology, widely suppose is conceivable and imaginable. Why should we believe those conceptions incoherent?

If they are not, then we become well-armed for the rejection of the second essentialist position under consideration, the claim that every individual substance has essentially the material composition that it has.

XII

We have seen already that more than one claim may be intended with the latter idea, some more plausible than others. Clearly a material substance does not need to continue having exactly the same matter as formerly. For one thing, no material substance does so. Uninterruptedly acquiring and losing matter, some of the new matter a material substance acquires may well be of a new material element. Ralph Robinson does not cease to be he because his body assimilates formerly alien quantities of lead. Plastic or metal organs or organ parts do not diminish personal or animal identity, when they replace dysfunctional or destroyed protoplasm. Inanimate objects too seem plainly able to acquire at least parts of previously alien material without ceasing to be.

What might seem to be difficult is the idea of a central or controlling material part of an object coming to be of different stuff. Even if all other parts of a human body were replaced with plastic, silicon, and copper wiring, we might seem unproblematically able to have the same person so long as the original brain remained intact and made of the same stuff. Similarly, perhaps, for other animals. And while inanimate objects do not seem typically to have such a central or controlling part, possibly – it might seem – one molecule more than 50% of the object must remain of the original stuff contained in the object.

I will defer much of the discussion of the case of persons to the chapter concerned with persons, chiefly indicating here that continuity of consciousness in a material body where fission – division of the substance into two or more successor substances of the same type as the original – has not occurred, seems entirely sufficient for personal identity. There are many complexities in the concept of a person and many ingenious diabolical hypotheses that the philosophical imagination has produced for reflection on that concept make for difficulty and befuddlement. Here our concern is with situations that are reasonably smooth and easy. All is normal save that the person now has no living parts, none of the original biochemistry it began with. Can that individual still be our Fred?

I think the answer is Yes. It seems particularly easy to think so if the situation has been one of gradual replacement of bodily parts, and there has been continuity of consciousness, an ongoing series of experiential states that permit a subject's evidentary claim. That is, I can imagine that it is to me that it all happens; I can project and identify a sequence of experiences occurring uninterruptedly for me.

What will be true for human beings in this regard would seem unproblematically to hold also for any other substance capable of having experiences, which we now see – at any rate, believe – encompasses at least all animals.

What about inanimate and nonliving material substances? Could that table, in fact made of wood, have been made of glass, or iron, instead? An enlarged and more detailed account of all of our cases would doubtless be desirable. However, why doesn't gradual replacement of material parts permit preserved identity, even after the 50% point has been passed, and then up to and including total replacement? This seems to be the moral of the most sensible view to take of the Ship of Theseus, where we imagine a wooden ship transformed into a steel and aluminum one (and no rival candidate ship created). I conclude then that material composition – being made of the same kind of stuff – is not essential to any material substance.

XIII

What then of the alleged necessity (essentiality) of origin? I shall defer most of the defence of this view to my chapter on persons but I want to argue that persons are not essentially material (as well as not being essentially of the sort of material of which the ones we are familiar with are made). There is in any case a principle which seems highly plausible and which, if true would settle decisively the issue of the supposed necessity of origin.

In setting up this principle, let us confine our attention to properties the possession of which does not imply relations to or, indeed, the reality of, other individuals or times than the possession by that individual of that property. Let us call such properties intrinsic properties. So being red, being equiangular, being a horse, being a human, being wise, would all seem to be intrinsic properties since an individual's possession of any one of them would not seem to imply, by itself, that any other individuals are real or that there are times before or after the time of that individual having that property. (I don't mean to imply by this that one individual really could have such a property wholly without other individuals or times obtaining; just that it wouldn't follow semantically, from the content of what such ascription says, that there are other individuals or times.) This seems a natural and clear notion to use. By contrast being seventh person to climb Mt. Everest, being taller than George, being eleven years old, will all be non-intrinsic – extrinsic – properties.

The following, then, seems highly plausible to believe.

If a property F is intrinsic and if it is possible (*de re*) for something x to have F and finally if it is also possible (*de re*) for something y to have F at all times at which y exists, then it is possible (*de re*) for x to have F at all times at which x exists. (That is to say, if something could have an intrinsic property which something could always have, then it could always have it also.)

Applying this principle to the kinds of cases we have been discussing: if there are worlds where a human being (for example) becomes wholly composed of plastic and copper wiring, then – since there are worlds where some things are, throughout their existence, composed of plastic and copper wiring – there will be worlds where that human being is never not composed of plastic and copper wiring. However, in such worlds as those that human being will not have – at any rate need not have – its terrestrial biological parents as progenitors. From which, as may readily be seen, the argument will be generable that no material substance need have had the origin or causes it did have.

Even on physicalist assumptions it is difficult to see why the belief that a substance must necessarily have had the causes it had should be compelling. Presumably every material substance is at the beginning of its existence a unique aggregate of a finite number of molecules. Surely there will be worlds, with different laws of nature than ours,[25] where the existence and conjunction of that aggregate, producing the developed substance that actually exists, comes about through different causes than in our world. Kripke, in brief, is wrong.

XIV

I turn now to the fourth essentialist claim, that every particular has exactly one individual concept or haecceitous property that is essential to it.

I do accept and agree that some particulars, at least, have exactly one individual concept property. Aristotle had, for example, the property of being Aristotle, and, so far as I know, he had no other haecceitous property than this. Of course Aristotle's name, in Greek, was not 'Aristotle' but Aristoteles; but this seems to me not to modify the truth of the ascription of the property of being Aristotle. The property of being Aristotle is distinct both from being called 'Aristotle' and from being self-identical – everything having the latter, where only Aristotle has *being Aristotle*, and Aristotle could easily have lacked being called 'Aristotle' whereas if he could have lacked being Aristotle it is certainly not a trivial matter. Further, from the fact that Aristotle had the property of being Aristotle it does not follow, but from the fact that Aristotle had the property of being called 'Aristotle' it does follow that words and language exist.

So far then I share the view (as some others do not) that there are genuine bona fide properties that some things, at least, have, that consist in the thing being that thing; moreover, that such properties, when they occur are not matters of language, or more precisely, are not linguistic or semantic properties. It seems quite reasonable to identify such a property as being Aristotle with the (putative) property of being identical to Aristotle; even though the latter might seem to be a relational property and the former not. At any rate, one has said something about Aristotle when it is affirmed that he is Aristotle just as when it is affirmed that he is a philosopher (though one is not of course affirming the same thing).

What about all the other individuals named 'Aristotle' (Onassis, for example)? I take it that when it is said of Onassis that he is Aristotle or that he has the property of being Aristotle, and it is said of the great philosopher that he has the property of being Aristotle, the same thing has not been said of these two individuals (as it would have been if it had been said of each that he is Greek, for example). That is, the wide replication of proper names constitutes a sort of ambiguity. It is not altogether unlike other varieties of semantical ambiguity ('bank,' 'bore,' etc.), where context, or possibly some systematic enumeration, is necessary, easily adequate, and successful for determining what the term is supposed to mean, signify, or represent on a given occasion, or in a given context.

Beyond this point I should say that I do not so much refute the fourth essentialist view as harbour doubts, hesitation, and perplexity, leading to what I think are problems with it.

First of all, if an individual has two quite distinct proper names – 'Cicero' and 'Tully,' for example – it seems to me not at all obvious that this individual doesn't have two individual concept properties. Something different seems to have been said about the man when it is said that he is Cicero than when it is said that he is Tully. This seems right even if these names are denied to have any descriptive content. Of course they must in some manner amount to the same thing. For, of course, Cicero = Tully. However, it isn't simply something that stems from the fact that someone can know that Cicero is an orator but not know that Tully is but being Cicero seems to be a different property from being Tully. At any rate, that Cicero = Tully doesn't seem sufficient reason to think otherwise.

If this is correct, then individuals will have as many individual concept properties as they have distinct proper names. This in turn may suggest that those more than a trillion individuals with no proper name have no individual concept property at all. A nameless individual could, perhaps, acquire an individual concept property but unless and until it is properly named, it is hard to see why it would now have one.

The view of individual concept properties we are coming to slightly reluctantly does see them as more closely linked to proper names than strong advocates of the idea would desire. However, we seem still more forcibly nudged in such a direction by another phenomenon of nomenclature: changes of name. Take Jacqueline Onassis, for example. She was born Jacqueline Bouvier, became Jacqueline Kennedy, then subsequently Jacqueline Onassis. When she was eleven, did she have the property, then, of being Jacqueline Onassis? I submit that this is implausible to suppose.

I shall not pursue this line of investigation further. The idea was supposed to be that there is this feature that things have by being themselves, each thing with a different such feature. Trying to tie down this feature has turned them into functions of social or institutional conventions of proper naming, which one wants to see as a mistaken course. On the other side, however, it is clear that not every predicate expresses a property. (An example famously pointed out by Quine is the predicate 'is so-called because of its size.') My view[26] is that no predicate containing an indexical expression can express a property, an autonomous feature or characteristic of something. *Being it* or *being that thing* can't literally, as they stand, be properties. (They may be property functions, incomplete properties, or property schemata but they aren't properties.) Someone may feel a conviction that there is such a thing as being it or that thing, a unique such thing for each individual, but that will not show that such conviction or intuition points to a genuine property.

I infer that it is problematic that there are individual concept properties for everything (and only one such property for each individual). A fortiori it is doubtful that individual concept properties are essential to their bearers, since everything could, and in some world does, undergo a change of name.

XV

I conclude by remarking that things other than substances would seem to have more in the way of a non-trivial essence than substances. Exploring the essences of properties, other abstract entities, events, temporal entities, and other things, is not undertaken here although it is certainly of interest, value, and content. Events, for example, would seem essentially to contain their constituents. Further metaphysical inquiry must investigate these dimensions of essence.

I referred earlier to something I want to call metaphysical luck. By this I mean that there are possible worlds where individual substances do not manage to continue to exist, to preserve their identity as time passes, because of things that happen which are, at least in a sense, external to these substances. The most obvious such phenomenon is fission, the sort of thing that happens to amoebas. There are worlds where this happens to human beings, for example. In such worlds there may continue a genetically appropriate 'representative' or 'identity-candidate' for an earlier existing human that nonetheless cannot be that earlier human because there is a rival claimant (possibly more than one) with equally impressive credentials not merely epistemically or in point of evidence but metaphysically. Commitment to haecceitism might allow one to insist that one of the claimants is (though unknowably) identical to the earlier human; but sober and metaphysically honest reflection on the case will make it clear that this is not genuinely an option. I am therefore numerically the same as a child once living in Ottawa partly because the sort of fission envisaged didn't happen to me (even though it could have). My identity through time is not only a function of spatio-temporal continuity with continuity of consciousness; it is also a function of fission not having occurred. It is a matter of metaphysical luck. More on this in a subsequent chapter.

Chapter Seven

Substance

Accounts of pre-Socratic philosophy rarely seem to comment on a curious and metaphysically significant fact about the systems of the earliest philosophers. These early thinkers were concerned with what the world is made of but not with that of which the world is made *up*. The world is made of elements, substances of one or more sorts; it is made up of particular individual things, also substances of one or more sorts – but where the substances are of a different kind.

Twentieth and twenty-first century philosophers who have taken 'the linguistic turn' have often found it convenient or appropriate to distinguish between two kinds of nouns or noun phrases: so-called count nouns (and noun phrases) and mass nouns (and noun phrases). 'Atom,' 'horse,' 'philosopher,' 'angry elephant' are count nouns (or noun phrases); 'snow,' 'blood,' 'hydrogen,' 'wet cement' are mass nouns (or noun phrases).

Not all mass terms are terms for substances (the ancient Greek term for substances in the 'mass noun' sense, *stoicheia*, may be helpful to employ sometimes). For example, love, folly, philosophy, poetry, being, substance, justice, music, art, are all mass nouns (some of them also have count noun use). None presumably is a term for an element, stuff, or substance.

It seems desirable though to utilize a wide conception of what might turn out to be the *stoicheia*. All of the items referred to in the periodic chart of the elements should of course qualify and all of their compounds. Other things should be able to be stoicheion candidates, at least: for example, matter. Some dualists have believed in an immaterial mind-stuff, an element mind, out of which persons and/or thoughts are composed. Anaximander's (d. ca. 547 B.C.) neutral *apeiron*,[1] as with the universal element for all later neutral monists,[2] should also qualify. And the possibility of artefactual stoicheia should not be excluded a priori. If chairs and shoes are at least candidates for spatio-temporal particulars – substances in the count-noun sense – then furniture and footwear ought to be candidates for 'mass' substances in the 'stuff'-noun sense.

In general studious neutrality and liberality is the appropriate note, at least in beginning to talk about countables and stoicheia as substances; together with the unequivocal assertion that not all mass noun expressions refer to substances, in any sense, any more than all count noun expressions do.

This declared, some nonetheless believe that the distinction between count- and mass-noun expressions is trivial, and merely nominal from a metaphysical point of view.[3] Others do not. They think that there is something ontologically different about being gold and being a lion; and for that matter then, about being rock and being a rock.

And there does indeed seem to be a formal difference to draw between entities of the two types. This difference is not as straightforward as it might be supposed. For example, it might be thought that the difference between a mass entity (i.e., a stoicheion) and a particular entity is that the latter is located or locatable at a single place, while the former is not. But for it to be true that all particulars are located at a single place a place needs to be able to be a region of space (not just a point of space) and for some particulars such a region will not consist of contiguous parts. Arguably this is true of the spatial regions occupied by very standard and familiar particulars like individual lions or human beings. Physical theory appears to imply that most of the space occupied by an individual lion or human being is actually empty. Ordinary spatio-temporal particulars are actually spatially 'gappy.' That is, there is empty space between some of their parts and others.[4] It is difficult to believe that metaphysical particularhood would be a function of the detectability or otherwise of spatial 'gappiness' by beings of just our range of size and sense organs. If something whose parts are scattered over empty space in a small region of space can be a particular, why not then something – like snow or gold – whose parts are simply scattered over larger regions of space?

Another attempted differentiation, at first sight plausible, also appears to be problematic. Particulars, it might be claimed, are entities that are temporally boundaried. All of Clinton exists at the times at which any of Clinton exists, but it isn't true that all of snow exists at the times at which any of it exists. The former doesn't in fact seem true for things that live and grow. If Clinton grows a beard, that beard will be part of him. It doesn't exist until grown, so part of Clinton doesn't exist at times at which some (at least) of Clinton does. One might have a still more vivid illustration of the idea here with the case of a deer and his antlers.

However, one might think this may mean that the temporal distinctiveness of particulars simply hasn't been appropriately characterized. If a particular ceased to exist, then it could not reappear and begin to exist at a later time. Let there be a time when something doesn't exist at all, then if this something exists at times on both sides of that time (i.e., before and after), it can't be a particular but it can be a mass entity.

We need to become 'more metaphysical' in evaluating this proposed differentiation. Individual machines are, I take it, reasonably plausible cases of particulars. Ralph's '79 Mazda, for example, is a particular. Moreover, Ralph's '79 Mazda could be taken to a body shop and systematically disassembled. Every detachable part could be detached and sent to an individual in a distinct community. If it were, then after the complete dismantling of Ralph's '79 Mazda, we would reasonably maintain that it does not exist. Let all of those distinct parts be sent to all of those distinct places. And let them stay there, separately packaged, for five years. Then, after five years, let each of those parts be sent back to the original body shop and the car be reassembled. It would seem reasonable to believe that Ralph's '79 Mazda would have come back into existence. It would have existed for a time, and then gone out of existence for five years, and finally resumed existence.

The same kind of reality-profile could be experienced by any spatio-temporal particular with parts. Persons would constitute a problematic case for some metaphysical views but it seems imaginable that a human being be 'disassembled' into discrete living parts that were kept apart but living for a period of time then reassembled into the same again-existent human being. Obviously current biotechnology and probably future biotechnology would not be able to bring this about, especially if it were to involve a partition of brain segments as well. Yet in principle the idea seems possible.

In any case some bona fide particulars able to exist, then not exist, and finally exist again, are all that are needed to make the case. The case that temporal continuity is unnecessary for particular identity and hence a basis for distinguishing particulars from mass entities.

Why isn't snow, then, or gold, or hydrogen, a particular? Formally, or semantically, the reason is that, if F is a term whose range is particulars *and* mass entities, in the case of the former there can be more than one F, in the case of the latter, there cannot be. Another closely related reason is that snow, gold, and hydrogen, have instances or cases, and particulars – the horse, Clinton, the mat – do not.

I want to argue for a global categorial picture of the real, and this may be an appropriate place for its disclosure. According to the ontology I want to defend, there are three kinds of 'primary' realities: particulars, mass entities, and properties/relations. They comprise a sort of continuum, from maximal to minimal particularity, or minimal to maximal universality, respectively. Particulars and mass entities share features which properties/relations lack, and the latter share with mass entities characteristics that particulars lack. For example, particulars and mass entities are typically directly perceptible by conscious beings, while properties and relations are not.[5] Moreover, particulars don't have cases or instances but mass entities and properties/relations do.

My focus here is chiefly on substance and substances, and I don't want to elaborate or defend perspectives on properties and relations. I do want to adopt and defend a realist view of the latter. However, for the perspective of this chapter, it is unimportant whether the realism preferred is that of Aristotle or that of classical Platonism. (It should be recalled that classical Platonism is a position implied by the views of Plato on abstract entities but that doesn't in turn imply them. Plato believed in perfect archetypal exemplars of the properties that are real. Classical Platonism is agnostic or sceptical about such things. Frege, Moore, Church, and Chisholm are twentieth-century, classical Platonists.) Classical Platonism holds that properties and relations are real, mind-independent, and do not require examplars to be either. Aristotelian realism holds that properties and relations are real and mind-independent but only either if exemplified. Strictly Aristotle would dispute the allocation of *primacy* – the claim made above that there are three kinds of things with 'primary' reality – for properties and relations. For the Aristotelian perspective, primacy is reserved for particulars and perhaps mass entities.

There have been a number of thinkers in the history of philosophy who have wanted to accord some things – usually abstract entities of one sort or other – second-class ontological status. Either the reality in question is regarded as derivative or parasitic, or it is said to be an altogether different ontic status than existence, which is reserved for spatio-temporal entities. Aristotle took the former view for such abstract things to which he granted reality while the ancient Stoics (apparently) took the latter, as did a number of late nineteenth-century thinkers (among them McTaggart and Meinong).

As indicated in earlier chapters, the perspective favoured here is quite unsympathetic towards ideas of degrees of reality or being, and favours an Occamist conviction that since meanings, like other entities, shouldn't be multiplied beyond necessity, there has to be a good reason for multiplying the senses of 'being' or 'existence,' and that something is abstract or parasitic is not a good reason.

Why then talk of *primary* reality at all? I want to distinguish what one lexicon calls *individuals* including particulars, mass entities, and properties/relations all as individuals from complexes of individuals (like facts, states of affairs, events, possibly propositions, etc.). This will to some degree parallel type ascent in classical (i.e., *Principia Mathematica*) logic, though this is not its chief motivation or justification. Individuals have primary reality, concatenations of them have secondary reality, concatenations of *them*, tertiary reality, and so on. The reality in each case is equally genuine and of equal ontic degree.

Niceties about varieties or degrees of being aside then, I want to count anyone who thinks that properties or relations are real as a realist. So Aristotle and his perspective are realist. As indicated, for the purposes of this chapter it doesn't matter if Platonic or Aristotelian realism is preferred. That is a matter to be considered and decided on its merits. Likewise that there are entities of any other category will not imply, or suggest, that all entities of that category that anyone has proposed are real also. For example, maybe there are facts but not propositions.

Let me return to the pre-Socratics. The Ionian cosmologists, Thales, Anaximander, Anaximenes (ca. 585–525 B.C.), produced theories of the elements of the world, i.e., of fundamental mass entities, with no hint offered that there are things such as particulars at all. Water, the apeiron, air, are mass entities. Who first included particulars in his account of the world?

The question is complicated by the fact that the earliest metaphysicians, the Ionian cosmologists, were also the earliest proto-scientists, and the latter dimension to their concerns took a practical form: Thales predicted eclipses; Anaximander is supposed to have devised the first map of the world. Moreover, all of the cosmologists had ideas about the formation and character of the sun, the moon, the earth, and the soul. These would all appear to be individual substances, i.e., particulars. (The soul, as such, is not. But while some metaphysical theories have believed in mind-stuff, or world-souls, it does not appear that the Ionians did (unless we see something along such lines in Heraclitus's cryptic remarks about soul as fire); otherwise to believe in soul is to believe in individual particular souls.) It is unclear whether the Ionians thought of the perceived world, including its particulars, as mere appearance, the *stoicheia* as the reality that so appears; or whether they engaged in totally distinct cognitive enterprises, as pure philosophy on the one hand, and astronomy/natural history on the other, without trying to connect them. (Cf., in either case, Parmenides' Ways of Being and Seeming.) At any rate, there is missing in Ionian speculation, as in that of Pythagoras – the world's first Cartesian dualist – a self-conscious or theoretical awareness of the category of the individual particular, that one finds explicit in Aristotle.

The first philosopher who gives expression to the contrast between the two kinds of substances – the substances that we refer to by count nouns, and those we refer to by mass nouns – seems to be the pre-Socratic thinker Empedocles (ca. 495–435 B.C.). Much in his system is obscure, and it is difficult to interpret with confidence the fragments of his writings. Nonetheless there does appear a definite sense of the individual *thises* of the common sense, physical object-world, and the contrasting elements of which these individuals are formed.

Count noun substances are the metaphysical innovations which it seems justifiable to assign to Empedocles. From Thales onwards the idea of *stuff*, elements out of which the universe is composed, is central. One may well suppose that theories of fundamental elements must rest on or at any rate be accompanied by, notions of particular things those elements form. Still, the idea that you and I, and all of the other particular human beings, are real – part of the order of being, and not just appearance – together with particular and individual non-human animals and inanimate things, is not clearly articulated in philosophy before Empedocles. He is the ancestral figure for what we may call ancient empiricism: the two primary wings of which are atomism and Aristotelianism.

To return to the metaphysical project under view, I proceed under the assumption that metaphysical realism – the conjunction of common sense and scientific realism (in the manner set out by Michael Devitt) is true. At the end of the chapter, I indicate briefly how we may view matters if that assumption is not made. But with it in place, I want to defend the thesis that, in a Russellian vocabulary, the distinction of entities into (at least) three – particulars, mass entities, and properties/relations – is ultimate and irreducible. More precisely, there exist particulars, mass substances, and universals, and at least one entity of each type is not also an entity of either of the other types. I am not then committed to the view that no mass entities are universals or particulars, or that no particulars are not also mass entities, etc. At the same time the idea is that all three categories are in general irreducibly distinct. The thesis would be embarrassed and problematic were many cases of reduction demonstratable.

The thesis intended is supposed to be metaphysical. As such it is claimed that its truth is not merely a function of human language or thought, or of language or thought as such. There is supposed to be something in the nature of things that makes a deep difference, in kind and in principle, between things like Dobbin, the horse, or Jones, the biochemist, and things like snow or gold, and finally things like the property of being perceptible or the relation of being older than.

As indicated, it seems somewhat problematic how precisely intuitions about the referents of mass terms divide their subject. Our target group is stuffs, elements, substances – conceived liberally. Plainly some referents of mass terms – e.g., justice, poetry, music – are not stuffs or substances. What about sound, though? (It is of course something the mass term for which is also a count noun. There are many such cases.) Or porridge? ... smoke? ... or toxic waste?

What is needed are broad categorial guidelines with minimal infusions of ontological ideology. Let us first have some wide groupings of potential cases, then see what arguments there may be to begin eliminating putative stuffs. There seem distinguishable perhaps six categories of referents of mass terms: 1) institutional/normative (e.g., 'justice,' 'law,' 'technology'), 2) artefactual (e.g., 'furniture,' 'footwear'), 3) colours, 4) categorial (e.g., 'being,' 'substance'), 5) material stuffs (e.g., 'gold,' 'mud') and 6) forces (e.g., 'love,' 'energy'). Only the second, fifth, and sixth categories seem arguably taken to be, or to include, candidates for *stoicheia* of things, elements of which the world's items are composed.

In order that they be emphatically excluded from the category of mass substance, some attention to colour is advisable. As far as I can tell, colour terms are unique, or almost unique, in the entire vocabulary of predication.[6] They behave in fact in a way that is highly idiosyncratic. In spite of the fact that they are so unrepresentative of the class of predicates, or maybe because of it, they can easily mislead and confuse. They involve the particular danger of misleading and confusing because they designate so vivid and prominent a feature of perceptual experience.

Virtually alone among adjectives, the colour words can occupy, quite naturally and unproblematically, the subject position in a sentence. They behave very similarly to mass terms and, indeed, are sometimes (by Quine, for example[7]) taken to be mass terms. They are unlike standard mass terms however, in being able to behave quite normally as adjectives. Thus, compare:

(1) I don't care where I live so long as there is plenty of *red* there.
(2) I don't care where I live so long as there is plenty of *snow* there.

(1) supports, it may be said, a conception of red (and *mutatis mutandis* of every colour) as a genuine mass entity, a stuff. That this conception is illusion seems demonstrated by appropriate extensions of (1) that lack analogues for (2). The wish expressed in (1) could not be fulfilled unless

(3) $(\exists x)(x$ is red$)$ – at least one individual thing is red

were multiply true of the environment desired. The difficulties with grafting 'stuff' discourse on to the first order predicate calculus make (or seem to make) incoherent attempts to produce an analogue for snow. It does not seem to make sense to say that 'at least one individual thing is snow.' The extremity that the quoted language poses is masked, at least a little, by two features of English syntax that are not supposed to be carried into the wholly unambiguous syntax of predicate logic. Namely, first, that in spite of contrary resolve and intention, anything at all can be allowed (or made) to fit the English formula 'at least one individual thing'; but only countable individual objects or object-like things can be values of the individual variables of first order predicate logic. Second, the English copula can be taken as an 'is' of identity, or – if this differs, as some suppose – of unique predication; but the 'is' of predicate logic – so to speak – can admit only of a single interpretation, viz., the purely predicative interpretation, if the severe and exacting aim of first-order quantification is to be realized. 'Someone is a dentist' and 'Someone is Fred' rightly require quite different kinds of symbolization. The latter critically involves identity within the scope of its quantifier. *If* 'snow' and other mass terms were taken to be or could successfully be treated as singular terms – see below – then a comparable analysis for the quoted sentence would be possible. However, it should be made clear, this would require supposing that there is a genuine individual object of which 'snow' would be a proper name, something that cannot be regarded as prima facie plausible.

An alternative which some favour (Quine, for example) is to take 'at least one individual thing is snow' (and comparable locutions) as elliptical, always, for 'at least one individual thing is made (or composed) of snow' (and such). However, $\lceil x$ is made of $F \rceil$ implies that there is something of which x is made – which leads to the problem identified one step later.

Returning to colour terms: they seem in fact really to be mostly normal adjectival predicate terms that are allowed, for obscure reasons, to behave in certain contexts like genuine mass terms.

Mass terms, genuine mass terms which I contend colour terms are not, also behave similar to adjectival predicates. As well as purple flowers, and heavy books, there are gold rings, water fountains, snow shields, oxygen masks, helium balloons, bronze swords, etc.; there is also chicken soup. Such facts point to – and conceal, or at least abbreviate – interesting features of language. All of the mass term cases involve being composed (or made) of the stuff in question, or producing it, or being designed to prevent it. None of these is true of the purple of purple flowers, or the heaviness of heavy books.

Consciousness-involving mass terms are more like the rings than the flowers. A love potion does not contain love but is designed to produce it. A love potion is not a potion that is love. A love-crazed individual is, evidently, filled with love, if not in a manner usually thought of as admirable. A love song is a song about, or, possibly, expressing, love.

The view that I favour, although it would take more space than I have here to argue in detail, is that the emotions be conceived as elements of a kind. They are like force, energy, and mass. All of these are regarded, within a perspective of one theoretical kind or another, as part of what the world is made, or by which it runs. The elements, the stoicheia, need not be overtly material things.

On the other hand *being* is not an element of the world. Nothing is made of being, nor is it so conceived by anyone. The case seems similar for space and time, which are also items referred to by mass terms. What space and time are is deeply puzzling, and important, as Augustine (354–430) and others have felt. They too, with their proper parts, must be explored by the ontological categorial mind. They belong, it seems, with being, substance, and other structural or categorial mass items.

One of the essential features of genuine stoicheia would seem to be playing a causal or explanatory role in the workings of the world. Structural and categorial items seem to play no such role but the typical candidate cases considered of stuffs, whether physical or mental, seem invariably to do so. Significant work on the logic of mass entities, coming to unpersuasive views, as I see it, of mass entities as properties of nonstandard objects but otherwise with creative proposals for the internal structure of the logic, has been done by Peter Roeper, Jan Tore Lønning, Paul Needham, and others.[8] None of this work is free from difficulties, usually consisting of mass entity truths it is unable to express.[9]

Within the class of elements, in the wide sense in which I conceive them, certain subdivisions seem appropriate to draw. One is the distinction between elements that continue to compose anything else formed out of them and those that do not. Paul Needham, uniting claims of Quine, Peter Roeper, and Jan Tore Lønning, articulates what he calls *homogeneous reference* as the distinguishing feature of what he identifies as genuine mass predicates.[10] Homogeneous reference combines two conditions: (1) whatever is the aggregate of two quantities [or cases, or 'parcels'] with a mass predicate itself has that predicate [this is the cumulative reference condition]; (2) all constitutive parts of something with a mass predicate have that predicate [this is the distributive reference condition].

The cumulative reference condition seems to characterize all the things I encompass as mass entities. Thus, if this is water and that is water and they are aggregated, then the combination has to be water; similarly, it seems, for all stuffs or elements. However, the distributive reference condition is definitely not satisfied by all the mass items I discuss; and it is arguable that it is not satisfied by any mass items. Thus, not all the proper parts of footwear are themselves footwear (indeed, presumably none are); and if partition proceeds to atomic and subatomic levels, it seems that no chemical element or alloy of them, would satisfy (2). Further, some stuffs do not mix their component stuffs homogeneously or, in some cases, at all. Take some chicken soup, for example, with real chunks of chicken in it. It seems right that chicken is a constitutive part of chicken soup, in this case; yet wrong that each case of that constitutive part is such that *chicken soup* or *soup* applies to it.

Needham argues that the relevant partition can or should stop short of such micro-components. There will be a need of course for criteria by which to mark the relevant boundary. For characteristic physical stoicheia, the line of demarcation seems plausibly to be the point below which the stuff does not retain its salient chemical or phenomenological features. If this can be convincingly done, then we can distinguish, along these lines, homogeneous and non-homogeneous stuffs.

Quine develops the imaginative idea of construing mass entities as scattered particulars. This involves thinking of mass terms as very close, semantically, to proper names. There is Fred, and Barbara, Aristotle, France, Mt. Everest; and there is snow and cheese. The latter two are scattered, over space and time, but otherwise they are similar in type to Fred and Mt. Everest. Mass terms, on this view, have more semantic content than standard proper names. From the assertion that Albert exists there isn't a lot that can be inferred about reality, without ancillary information. From the assertion that carbon exists, or cheese, much can – perhaps – be gleaned. However, the situation with proper names is not uniform. 'The Red Sea' is, apparently, a proper name, and it provides considerable semantic content. Perhaps then mass terms are like such descriptive names.

This view is imaginative, and it offers tempting Occamist economy; and the fact is that mass terms do behave very much like proper names. However, the appeal of this view stops just about there. Mass entities can be quantified whereas the bearers of proper names cannot. 'Much wine is over-priced'; 'All snow is white'; 'Some cheese goes well with that bread'; etc. Yet quantifiers don't make sense applied to the referents of proper names: 'All of Bill ...,' 'Some of Martha ...,' etc., are not literally quantifiers attached to the referent of the name, the instantiations of these quantifiers are parts of the bearer of the name. Of course one can say the same of mass term quantification but only with special, and implausible, pleading. Furthermore, mass entities all seem capable of being constituents of more comprehensive mass entities. Just as water consists of hydrogen and oxygen, so other mass entities, soup, for example, contain water. No upper limit on the possibilities of constituency in some larger or more inclusive stuff seems to be internal to the 'logic' of mass entities. There appears to be nothing comparable in the 'logic' of proper name bearers.

So mass entities aren't singular particulars. Moreover, they aren't particulars of any other kind, since the latter don't have cases, instances, quantities, parcels, or units, whereas mass entities have some or all of these. Similarly, mass entities aren't properties. Here too there are resemblances. 'This stuff is snow' is similar to 'this stuff is green' and 'this stuff is toxic.' Moreover, it seems correct to want to identify a stuff not with any particular unit, quantity, or bunch of stuff. Gold is not *that bit* of gold, but that of which the bit *is* a bit; and this will be true for every bit of gold, however large or small the bit, in the universe. Gold itself, then, is like being square or being hungry, both – somehow – present in and absent from the occasions of its reality. Interestingly, in so far as mass entities are like properties, there seems to be no question that they would conform to Aristotelian, not Platonistic, norms of propertyhood. That is, whether or not there is or might be such a property as being a horse if there weren't, or never were, horses, it seems evident that if all cases of gold ceased, so too would gold itself. Though gold isn't the same as its instances – though arguably the same as the mereological sum, or better, the aggregate of its instances, over time (this is in effect the view Quine discusses) – still, the existence of gold is absolutely dependent on there being instances of it.

So why aren't mass entities properties? They are too particular, too concrete to be so. Gold can be seen and touched. It may be urged that it is instances of gold that are seen and touched. Both are, the instances and the gold itself, the one in tandem with the other. *Being gold* is of course a property, and not, by the way, the same property as *being made of gold*. Only gold itself has the former property, it seems clear, while many things have the latter. In any case, gold is not the same as *being gold*, any more than Aristotle is the same as *being Aristotle*.

It does need to be observed that the view that stuffs are properties is widely held. This was Richard Montague's (1930–71) view.[11] It is also defended by most of the other contributors to Jeff Pelletier's valuable anthology *Mass Terms: Some Philosophical Problems*.

Against so high a tide of learned and intelligent authority it may be difficult to resist. It may be that the very concept of a property is sufficiently elastic that there will be a sense of property such that identifying stuffs as properties in that sense will be altogether and rightly convincing. Supposing that stoicheia are properties need not consign them to an intractably abstract or universal status, or so it may seem. In any case I have already affirmed ontological commitment to properties. Will it not be desirable, if it is even partially feasible, to dispense with a third fundamental ontic category and collapse stuffs into properties?

As a good Occamist, I will happily reduce three to two if I can. What sustains resistance however is difficulty as to what it is stoicheia would be properties of if they were properties. Consider an eight cubic metre volume of Chardonnay in a resting barrel. The barrel is not the subject of a supposed mass-property. It is not made of Chardonnay. And it is the same object whether empty or full; before Chardonnay was put in it as after. Moreover, consider the seven cubic metre volume of the same stuff in the same barrel that is uniformly surrounded by Chardonnay. That is a parcel, unit, heap, or whatever, of Chardonnay. It is not easy to get the mind around the idea that there is an object, particular or individual, of which that Chardonnay is true, or indeed of which Chardonnay (or for that matter of which *being Chardonnay*) is true. Montague is unimpressed with this concern. Lots of objects are artificial, non-natural, constructed, or simply obscure. If we can conceive Chardonnay to be a property, and devise a category of thing to be the object-peg of which it can be said to be true, Occamist and other considerations formal or aesthetic should be unleashed and allowed to reign.

Still, disquiet persists. As noted above, being made of snow is not the same thing as being snow, and snow doesn't seem to be a property. It is a stuff, part of what makes up the world, a substance. Further, to affirm the point once more, snow, and other stoicheia, seem too concrete or material to be properties. They are part of the causal structure of the world.

The long and the short of it seems to be that there are three kinds of fundamental entities: particulars, stuffs, and properties (or relations).

Many questions of course remain. Could there be a world without substances? If substances are thought of as enduring over intervals of time, the answer seems pretty clearly, yes, for both individual and stuff substances. In that sense, at least, anti-substance metaphysical postures like those of Hume and Russell seem partly justified; although, of course, the possibility of a world without perduring substances does not imply its actuality, nor that ours is such a world.

Could there be a momentary substance? Need substances endure, over some protracted period of time? Is it part of the very concept of a substance that such a thing last, at least for a while?

As with so many comparable issues, the answer to these questions is, I think, It depends. It depends on what we mean, and what we may want to mean by a substance. At any rate, it isn't trivially self-evident that no substance is momentary. It is hard to see that any fundamental intuitions are violated by affirming that one is.

Could an individual substance be extremely small? Really quite small – smaller than a neutron, for example? Again, why not? No doubt advocates of substance have primarily had in mind what we characterize as medium-sized objects; but it is difficult to see why the very concept of a substance should be thought to preclude extremely tiny ones. And why might one not be as large as a galaxy, or bigger still?

If the concept of substance is as elastic as these queries suggest, it becomes a pointed and important question whether there could be a physical world without substances. What would it be like for there to be no substances? Perhaps an empty physical universe would qualify: infinite (or for that matter finite) space with nothing occupying it. Given the presence of any extended bit of matter, of any kind, don't we automatically thereby have substances?

The system of Hume, if regarded as coherent, may remind us not only of how bare the particularity of a particular may be, but also – though this may be the same thing – of how agnostic we perhaps can and should be vis à vis the non-universal constituents of facts, events, or states of affairs (i.e., the consituents that are not universals); if, that is, we surrender the view that appearance is in general a sound guide to reality.

And on these multiply inconclusive and incomplete notes – adrift between the metaphysical options of anchoring ourselves in the, or a, common-sense view of the world, which includes substances of both particular and stuff type, and the esoteric exotica of constructivist philosophy – I leave substance behind.

Chapter Eight

Universals

It has scarcely been possible to avoid indicating, certainly intimating, the view this book advocates on abstract entities, in the chapters that precede. In the present chapter I want to make that view fully explicit, provide something of a case for it, and make ancillary remarks on ontology and the abstract.

The view urged in these pages is that abstract entities are real. Some abstract things that some philosophers have favoured are almost certainly unnecessary postulates for existence. They can be analysed or reduced to other entities, abstract or non-abstract, or plausibly argued to be wholly chimerical. And, it now goes without saying, Occam's razor is always with us. Anyone who can make a case successfully that a type of entity that is apparently real can be analysed as something else has made a signal contribution to philosophical science; and projects of Occamist reduction are to be welcomed and encouraged. I do not believe that all abstracta can be analysed away. Yet if someone could show that this view is mistaken, the position taken in this book is that such enterprise would not be incompatible, in spirit or result, with the general stance favoured here.

What seem to me to be incontestably real are properties and relations. Other abstracta – propositions, meanings, geometrical and other mathematical entities, numbers, expression types, even sets – seem less basic or fundamental. Some of these entities may be unreal. Even if all are real, they are less fundamental than properties and relations. Facts consist of particulars or stuffs – stoicheia – having properties or standing in relations; or are truth functional or other combinational aggregates of them, quantifications of them, etc. This is logical atomism, prior to a Quinean paring away of its constituent Platonism.

Actually the position taken here vis à vis the abstract does not require or imply logical atomism. For the latter supposes that the world is determinately thus-and-so. Yet even if it is not, even if in the world itself, apart from representations of it, reality is fuzzy, vague, or indeterminate, still there will be fuzzy, vague, or indeterminate properties and relations that characterize the things that there are.

Strategically, I want to argue that properties and relations – I sometimes call them universals – are safe and reasonable things to accept, as well as being extraordinarily convenient and possibly necessary. Part of the case for showing this is repeating with emphasis the principle that something can *be*, without the requirement of a *place* at which it is. There is no need to speak, with or without quotation marks of any kind, of such a thing as Plato's Heaven (or 'Plato's Heaven'). Being wise, being prime, being a brother of, we can say, are things that there are, in addition to the things to which they apply, without locations for them – apart from the locations their cases have.

Further (this is a central thesis of Chapter 5) the affirmation that something exists or is real, while doubtless important, should not be exaggerated. It isn't such a big deal. So we say that, as well as Aristotle, Clinton, Ethiopia, Alpha Centauri, the third Interglacial Era, there is also such a thing as being gold, being a horse, being taller than. So what? If existential facts are not seen as more profound or different in kind (except as existential facts), than other kinds of facts, what are we affirming that is problematic?

Of course it had better be true that there are such existential facts. But isn't there such a thing as being a VCR, being three parts oxygen, being older than, etc.? Simple plausible existential generalizations seem quickly and easily to require their reality.

(A) (1) 5 is prime
    (2) 7 is prime
∴ (3) There is something (viz., being prime) common to 5 and 7.
(B) (1) This apple is red.
    (2) That pencil is red.
∴ (3) There is something (viz., being red) common to this apple and that pencil.
(C) (1) Socrates is wise.
    (2) Hermann Hesse is wise.
∴ (3) There is something (viz, being wise) common to Socrates and Hermann Hesse.
   And so on; and comparably with relations. (E.g.:
(D) (1) Joseph and Jerome are brothers.
    (2) John and Edward are brothers.
∴ (3) There is something true for Joseph and Jerome that holds also of John and Edward.)

Now it is sometimes argued that the so-called substitution interpretation of quantification will obviate any need to take the existential conclusions of (A), (B), (C), (D), etc., in any way that would require reality for what they say exists. According to this view, ⌜(∃x)Øx⌝ can and should be understood as meaning, 'there is a true substitution instance of the formula ⌜Øx⌝' – or, more fully, 'at least one sentence that will result from replacing ⌜Ø⌝ with a (grammatical) predicate expression, and ⌜x⌝ with a (grammatical) proper name, in ⌜Øx⌝, is a true sentence.' If there are substitutional interpretations of existential quantifications, then there can be such interpretations for so-called second-order quantifications, characteristically symbolized with so-called property variables (Ø, ψ, ...). The inference pattern exhibited above then may be represented as:

> *Fa*
> *Fb*
> ∴ (∃Ø) (Øa ∧ Øb)
> (where *F, G,* ... are 'property constants').

The conclusion schema then is just to be interpreted as 'there are true substitution instances of ⌜Øa ∧ Øb⌝.' Since the premises in the pattern have provided such substitution instances (whether true or not), the appropriateness of the reasoning will be manifest.

Substitutional quantification has been much discussed. One simple, and direct line of argument against it goes: logic is logically independent of language. Some things would follow logically from other things (and others not) even if there never had been thinking beings or expressions. *Fa* ∴ (∃x) *Fx* is one such pair of things. However, it couldn't be if ⌜(∃x) *Fx*⌝ meant that there are true substitution instances of ⌜Fx⌝, since there are no substitution instances if there is not language. And if some purely conceptual interpretation of a substitution interpretation were offered, one not making substitution interpretations dependent on language, we would be stuck with abstract entities – propositions or propositional functions – anyway.

There are other problems with substitutional interpretations of quantification. Another direct difficulty is that we want to be able to affirm and deny existence; i.e., to be able to make ontological remarks. If all quantification was substitutional, we could not do this. Some opt for using two kinds of quantifiers, substitutional and objectual ('objectual' is the term now used for the older more classical construal of quantification, as involving reference to the world or 'objects'). We would then always need to indicate what kind of quantifier was intended in a given context, an objectual or a substitutional one; and we could presumably use both, in a single statement. We could say that in $\ulcorner Fa \rightarrow (\exists x) Fx \urcorner$ the quantifier is objectual, but in $\ulcorner Fa \rightarrow (\exists \emptyset) \emptyset a \urcorner$ the quantifier is substitutional and read them, respectively, as 'if a is F then there exists at least one individual that is F' and 'if a is F then $\ulcorner \emptyset a \urcorner$ has least one true substitution instance.'

However, so opting is ad hoc, a case of it that can be prompted only by theoretical desire. There could be nothing about the two cases as such that could justify such divergent treatment. The second is chosen to avoid affirming the reality of properties. Otherwise they seem wholly parallel constructions – $\ulcorner$if a is F then there is something that $Fs \urcorner$ and $\ulcorner$if a is F then there is something that a is$\urcorner$. The substitutional-objectual combinational advocate would seem to still face the problem of how he or she will say that there exist properties which a given individual has. Legislating by fiat the sayability of it, by not allowing that $\ulcorner (\exists \emptyset) \emptyset a \urcorner$ could be construed objectually seems inappropriate, indeed, immature.

As indicated, the strategy here is twofold. If abstracta (of any kind) could be shown to be unnecessary ontic postulates, then well and good. They should definitely be dispensed with on Occamist grounds. Of course that is true of any type of entity. If someone could show that there is no need to hypostatize VCRs, fifteenth-century wars, sound, or anything else, let us refrain from hypostatizing them, i.e., taking there to be such things. As indicated, also demonstrating such things requires, inter alia, showing that inferences which seem to imply, typically, through existential generalization, that there are entities of the rejection-candidate sort, do not really do so, or else that, while valid, their premises can and should be rejected. No such Occamist case, in the cases of universals, seems genuinely persuasive.

The second prong of the strategy is to persuade the reader that universals are all right. They should not particularly be viewed as suspect items that heroic enterprise ought to be accorded to dispensing with. We affirm many things in common sense, scientific, and formal contexts, that imply universals and with which we seem to operate clearly and comfortably. For example, that there are binary relations that are irreflexive and transitive, that there are properties seldom exemplified before the invention of gunpowder, etc.

One reason philosophers have for regarding universals as metaphysically suspect is that they seem to be linked to thought and/or language in ways that other entities are not. More specifically, particulars – and possibly stuffs – seem wholly independent of mind with respect to their reality and discriminable identity. The planet Jupiter is there, real and distinct from the planet Mars, my copy of *War and Peace*, and gold, zinc, and tapioca. Yet, even if the reality of properties is conceded, for the sake of argument, their identity conditions look to depend, in a way, on *us*. Property F is identical to property G, it seems, only if $\ulcorner X$ is $F\urcorner$ means the same thing as $\ulcorner X$ is $G\urcorner$; and only if someone thinking that something was F would thereby be thinking that it was G.

Some argue, per contra, for the possibility (which is to say the actuality) of contingent identities between properties, just as there are, or are supposed to be, contingent identities between particulars. Thus, being blue is said to be identical to being (of) the colour of the sky, being red to being (of) the colour that most enrages bulls. And of course being (made of) water is said to be the same as being (made of) H_2O, and so on.

On the other side, a property is supposed to be something assertable of something; and, it is claimed, surely reasonably, if you say of something that it is red you really haven't said the very same thing of it if you say that it has the colour that most enrages bulls. You may have characterized the item in a way that is factually equivalent or that corresponds to it in some important way. However, you aren't saying exactly the same thing about the item in question.

Along these lines, it seems appropriate and plausible to affirm that it is really facts, and states, that are contingently identical; and that it is these facts, states, events that are concretely in the world and independent of mind. Facts, states, events, processes can happily be accorded reality: they are identifiable by their causal properties. Properties, if they are real, don't have causal properties, and couldn't have them. So, if this line of reflection is correct, being red isn't, and couldn't be, identical with having the colour that most enrages bulls. Rather some facts consisting of objects being red are identical with facts consisting of objects having the colour bulls least like.

However, if this view is defensible, it will certainly require expansion and commentary. We think of facts (events, states, processes) as having structure, and have already identified them as cases of what we called complexes. Such things consist of elements or parts. If a fact is comprised of a having property F, and we had, following the earlier now rejected line of reflection, wanted to say that F is contingently identical to G, we will now say that a having property F is the same fact as a having property G, even though $F \neq G$. Yet it might seem natural to say that if one fact is identical to another, and all of their elements or parts save one are identical, the remaining parts will be also.

Though natural, it is hard to see why we would be forced to such a view. Certainly we will want to say that F and G, in our schematic case, are equivalent in a special manner – factually equivalent. We expressly want to affirm this. There will be other cases of pairs of propositions (or sentences) naming or pointing to the same fact, that will otherwise not be isomorphic; and this will be quite unproblematic: likewise with our case.

Further, even if universals seem identifiable as a function of semantic or mental phenomena, this should not imply dependence on those phenomena. Jupiter was a planet before there were any human beings. That particular and that universal – being a planet – were hooked up with each other anterior to language or thought, at least in our region of the Milky Way. Properties are as objective as particulars and facts, and as fully real – as of the world (if not literally in the world) as they are.

Let us pursue and try to tease out, additional complexities in these quarters. We have assumed that facts are a similar categoreal or ontological type to events, states, and processes. Are they, however? The latter may all seem more concrete than the former. Suppose lump of sugar, l, is dissolving in glass of water, g, at t and p. This is clearly an (individual) event or process, by virtue of which it is a fact that l is dissolving in g (at t and p). At t and p, l has the property of dissolving in g. However, if I am appropriately located, I can see the event taking place. As concretely and materially as perception can be, I can observe the sugar dissolving; and it appears correct to say I observe not only l but the dissolution also. If I watch Smith run, I observe not only him but also his running. We regard it as evident, however, that I cannot literally perceive a property. So the dissolution in g that I observe isn't a property – a universal.

What is it then? It is an instance or case of something universal. I can compare that dissolution with others. This repeats what we have already affirmed. How about the fact that l is dissolving in g at t and p – as opposed to the event?

One view (endorsed, at one phase of his career, by Russell) is that a fact is a structured complex whose constituents are particulars (we will want to add stuffs to these) and universals. The fact would seem in this view to be itself then a partly abstract thing. A perceiver could not directly observe a fact, in this picture, but the concrete case of the fact: the event, state, or process.

Are facts, in this sense, necessary? Could we not do without them? And keep events, states, processes, plus universals? So long as universals are retained, this course does seem plausible for the material component of reality. We would view the world, through these ontological lenses, as consisting of structured complexes of particulars or stuffs at rest or in motion. We designate the internally unmoving complexes, states and those in motion events or processes, though this distinction clearly should not be viewed as fundamental. If we call all these complexes, states (in a primary or generic sense), then a state will consist of particulars or stuffs, and concrete cases of universals.

Apart from particular material states we still need facts. Generalizations from particular material states, aggregates and compounds of them, mathematical and conceptual complexes, all require the concept of fact, and the latter in turn requires the concept of a universal. As such it may seem perverse and implausible, even if ontologically parsimonious, to disallow a reality for the fact of a particular having a property (at a time and place), the fact of a stuff being in relation to another stuff, etc., in addition to the respective states.

What is at issue here seems to be mere parsimony. The matter appears otherwise with other putative abstract entities. My goal is not to be exhaustive but survey the major candidates. Notable among them are mathematical entities and intensions. The former seem unproblematically reducible to either special cases of the latter or classes. So I will confine my attention to the ontological credentials of classes and intensions (or concepts, including concept aggregates or clusters).

Virtually all philosophers – including even those otherwise nominalist, like Quine – affirm the reality of classes or sets. This is because virtually all philosophers want to be able to have and to do mathematics, for its own sake as well as natural science which seems to depend on mathematics; and mathematics requires (if one accepts ontological commitment) the affirmation of the reality of classes. Classical logic conceives numbers as classes (of classes). All other mathematical entities appear to be conceivable as concepts or classes of concepts.

Cantorian arguments[1] make it essential to distinguish between individuals and classes, and to give up the idea of a coherent and conceivable class which contains everything (i.e., all individuals, and classes, including that class itself). The assumption that there is such a class, together with wholly certain and unproblematic additional assumptions, will imply contradictions. At the same time, it is difficult to resist the intuition or conviction that the idea of absolutely everything is thinkable and then collectable (into a single class). Those Cantorian arguments are powerful and clear, and so, however difficult, such resistance should be mounted.

Intensions, in the sense intended here, are items which, if real, would not depend on thought, language, thinkers, or speakers. There is a range of views possible, however, with respect to relations between thought or language and intensions. We should initially mention a view which Locke may have held and which Russell somewhat more certainly did,[2] according to which there is a kind of mental entity – Locke (if this interpretation is correct) called them ideas, and Russell called a special case of them propositions – which constitute contents for thought. These items – ideas and idea-clusters – would not, if real, be intensions in our sense, since their nature is mental; a fortiori, they would only exist when and as thought with such contents did.

On the other hand it could be held that intensions – concepts and concept-clusters – while not mental in nature, exist only as contents for thought. From this perspective the existence of a concept or proposition (at a time t) implies that thought exists (at t). With still greater but still incomplete autonomy for intensions, it might be held that intensions require having been contents for thought to become real, but once ontologically launched, as it were, they no longer need this concomitance. Such a conception is not as fancifully fine-grained as it might first be supposed. It might be argued, for example, that prior to the twentieth century there was no such concept as the concept of a VCR; but that now there is and will henceforth be, whether or not intelligent life continues indefinitely in the vicinity of earth. There will always be hereaf-ter such a thing as what it is to be a VCR, whether or not anyone, very much later than now, thinks about VCRs or has the concept of one.

There is a conception of concepts classically associated with empiricism which deserves explicit articulation, especially since it is often assumed in positions not obviously linked to this conception. According to it there is a stock of primitive simple concepts out of which all other concepts are com-pounds (truth-functionally analysable or otherwise). One is a concept empiri-cist if one supposes both that the only concepts human beings can have are the primitive simple ones or their compounds, and that these primitive simple concepts are acquired by human beings from occasions of immediate and direct experience (not necessarily found directly in the world on such occa-sions – as Kant seems to have proposed for some of our concepts). Concept empiricism may be true. No stand is taken here as to whether or not it is true. I want instead to point out that positions with respect to the nature and auton-omy of intensions do not have to take sides on or make assumptions about concept empiricism.

Similarly, in affirming that intensions are real, one need not imply that they have necessary being or existence in all possible worlds. A full Platonist position would of course do so. It would hold that all intensions have existed eternally and in all possible worlds.

This particular Platonist view appears to be false and refutable. If there are logically proper names, then some intensions exist only contingently. If '*a*' is a logically proper name, then concepts and propositions including *a* (e.g., that *a* is wise, being *a*, being a brother of *a*) will – by definition of what it is to be a logically proper name – only be real once *a* is.

Of intensions, concepts seem to be more fundamental and therefore harder to do without, than the aggregates or clusters of them usually called proposi-tions.

Both, however, are attacked by their enemies in ways that are only partially appropriate. In particular, it is supposed by some critics that intensions must prove themselves useful if they are real. They must accordingly establish for themselves an explanatory role, for example, in accounting for how it is that we believe.

In some respects at least, this places the cart before the horse. Something's reality is not a function of utility. Things that *are* do not have to establish that they deserve to be real. Indeed many things that there are seem quite useless, and others very much to deserve non-being. If an entity does play a useful explanatory role, that is doubtless splendid. However it is conceptually confused to suppose that whether or not something *is* is in any way dependent on being able to make a case that the item has an explanatory role. That an item has a necessary explanatory role, or even a plausible explanatory role, will be a good, and even a sufficient reason to *believe* that the item is real. This does not make the item's reality consist of that role. Nor does the converse hold, i.e., that belief in the reality of something implies an explanatory role for it.

This affirmed, we can (and must) directly confront the questions: are concepts real? and are propositions real?

The Locke-Russell view referred to above, according to which intensions or concepts (including their propositional aggregations) are purely mental objects, is in many ways attractive. However, it bears the double liability that it would prevent the existence of truth as independent of thought and it would still involve abstract entities if it was to account for such phenomena as shared belief. With an eye lingering on the possibility that this theory might nonetheless permit development in ways that would meet all concerns, I opt, as many do (and perhaps still more fail to), for a realist position on concepts and propositions, with the signal difference that, for me, some concepts are real but only after they have been thought, or appeared as thought of or else brought into being as concepts logically implied by concepts that have been thought. Propositions as particular concept aggregates are real also. Nonetheless it seems doubtful whether they should be taken to be things with which we have in any sense a relation of acquaintance when we are in states of 'propositional attitude.' Another way of saying this is that propositions should not figure in any central way in psychology, even rational psychology, with respect to the aetiology or the phenomenology of cognitive, epistemic, or comparable mental states.

At the same time I would want to argue that propositions may serve a useful explanatory role and indeed appear in disguise in many theories, including currently popular ones, that are regarded as having high explanatory and empirical value. Any theory which uses ideas of information, information contents, or similar notions, is in fact using propositions. Information is an intensional notion. The information that p = the information that q only if $\ulcorner p \urcorner$ is synonymous with $\ulcorner q \urcorner$. It seems clear in fact that the information that p, at least in central or standard cases, is identical to the proposition that p.

As with other abstracta I want to argue that it is the opponents, not the proponents, of propositions who are guilty of mystification and obscurantism, exemplified by their heavy use of scare-quotation and similar matters of style (and not of substance) in arguing against propositions. There are no places at which propositions are located, and they have no role in the causal structure of the world. Their reality is as isolable components, or constituents, in complexes that do play a part in the causal structure of the world. Propositions explain belief (and similar states of propositional attitude) in the sense of identifying such elements or constituents in these states, which have efficacy as causes or effects. Similarly they explain shared belief and related phenomena. These are never causal explanations.

Propositions also have truth values. Some are true, others are false, and arguably some are neither: truth-valueless, or, if one prefers, possessed of a third truth value which we could call indeterminate.

That propositions have truth value is one good reason to regard them or some of them, as having eternal existence – existence at all times. Otherwise we must argue that there have been times when nothing was true. Some find this an acceptable result. However it seems plausible to hold that a thousand years after the Big Bang there was hydrogen in existence; moreover that this was something that was then the case. It doesn't seem plausible to hold that something was the case but wasn't true. If that was true at that time, then something was; it can hardly have been true if it didn't exist, to be able to have this feature. The item in question cannot have been a sentence (type or token) since there weren't any then. It seems reasonable to propose propositions as having been in existence, and true, at those temporally remote occasions. This line of thinking is, I think, resistable. One can insist that nothing was true until there were thinkers to think or language-users to speak. Why insist on that? If we allow propositions to exist now and view them as abstract extra-linguistic, extra-mental entities, and we find it persuasive to say that there were truths before there was thought or language, we will go along with pre-mental, pre-linguistic propositions. If we do that, it is hard to see what we would, or could, think of as constituting the beginning of the existence of these propositions. Perhaps there are items in the world of which the concepts contained in those propositions are concepts. So, until there was hydrogen, there was no concept of hydrogen (even in the pre-mental and pre-linguistic sense); hence no propositions about (or involving the concept of) hydrogen.

I shall not pursue this theme further. The aim here is chiefly to disclose options for theory. I want to defend a (modified) Fregean theory of meaning and concepts, conjoining with it a Russellian theory of logically proper names (but rejecting the currently popular extension of the latter to natural kind terms). So I do lean to eternally existent propositions – those without concepts that would be expressed in a sentence with a logically proper name. From a metaphysical point of view, this is a secondary issue. I share the Devitt-Sterelny view[3]: philosophy of language long ago (in the early twentieth century) became too big for its britches, or its or anyone's good. The theory of meaning can't have the weighty metaphysical (or anti-metaphysical) implications so many philosophers (by no means confined to Putnam and those like-minded) have supposed. Only a little reflection shows this. The little epiphenomenal bubbles, after-breaths, emanated from the mouths, pens, pieces of chalk, computers, etc., of this particular finite ensemble of cosmic ants – ourselves – and the content and theory of its clockwork, however interesting to (some) humans themselves, is of very parochial significance for the world as a whole. How much of Fregean semantical theory, and how much of referential, or any other is correct, cannot contain the key to the nature of reality. Hence it seems to me we have adequate grounds for holding that Putnam's famous 'brain in a vat' argument[4] is completely unsuccessful even without close inspection of its details, and even though it is interesting, important, and certainly challenging, to inspect those details. Nothing about meaning or representation could possibly show that something is or isn't a possible way things are.[5] This is, one might say, a naturalist transcendental anti-transcendental argument; and many will think it too quick, indeed, glib, and simplistic. I do not dispute that acute, indeed dazzling, analytical intelligence has enlivened the theory of meaning, and the formulation of arguments about the necessary presuppositions of the human power of representing, and the fact that we mean when we speak and think (and perhaps that what we say or think has meaning). I simply ask the reader to step back from the facts and the phenomena of meaning and representation and acknowledge that these are natural activities, that members of our species engage in (and that members of other species do not). I invite the reader also to ask himself or herself whether they would not, on reflection, agree that it ought to be regarded as surprising if it were to turn out that important, interesting, substantive general results about what is (still less, what must be) true of the world, were consequences of representation and meaning.

I close this chapter by setting out the theory of propositions that I want to defend. It is essentially that of Frege and Church (which is to say, essentially that of the ancient Stoics), together with the inclusion of propositions containing logically-proper-name-concepts. For this view, no proposition contains an indexical-concept (a concept standardly expressed with so-called indexical expressions – non-anaphoric pronouns, 'this,' 'that,' 'here,' 'there,' 'now,' 'then,' etc. – language-user-relative or 'egocentric,' in Russell's phrase, expressions). Declarative sentences containing indexicals will express proposition-like entities. Had the term not been pre-empted by Russell for entities which seem to be distinct (if similar), it would have been natural to call these things propositional functions. At any rate, things like 'it is wise,' in the theory I advocate, are not propositions but another kind of abstract object: fragmentary or incomplete almost-propositions that can be regarded as capable of doing duty for indefinitely many actual propositions.

In the view I favour the actual propositions might more appropriately be verbalized with present participles than with verbs. Thus, 'Socrates being wise,' '7 being greater than 5,' 'Clinton pushing a button at 3:15 p.m., January 15, 1998, in the White House,' etc., would be more perspicuous names or nominalizations of propositions than the corresponding forms with verbs.[6] The standard device for rendering propositions assertoric will then be the indexical suffix 'is now the case.' So ⌜Jones believes that the cat is on the mat⌝ is analysed as ⌜Jones believing the cat-being-on-the-mat is now the case⌝. Similarly it is true that the cat is on the mat is analysed as (something like) ⌜the-cat-being-on-the-mat is now the case (or: now holds)⌝. This enables the proposition itself wholly to lack indexical concepts (even the concept expressed by 'it is now the case that' implicit in normal, primary – arguably, all – declarative sentences). It also is in line with conceiving of a proposition as an aggregate of constituent concepts.

Propositions may or may not contain temporal or spatial indices or qualifiers (or quantifiers). Some do and some don't. *Socrates being wise* is one proposition, *Socrates being wise in Athens*, *Socrates being wise in 407 B.C.*, and *Socrates being wise in Athens in 407 B.C.* distinct ones. Some propositions are true at all times at which they exist. Others shift in truth value over time. There seems little or no utility in calling the former complete and the latter incomplete. The first group may be designated the propositions expressed in 'eternal sentences.' If we found persuasive the idea that propositions only exist from the time when the things to which their constituent concepts refer exist, this label would be regarded as hyperbole. At any rate such propositions have a stability that the shifting group lack. If there are vague or fuzzy concepts then there will be vague or fuzzy propositions, which will be still more unstable.

As argued earlier, the view advocated may be regarded as over-lush. Why not try to economize, pare away some of the kinds of entities allowed in the ontology? The response is that if we haven't mystified existence, it shouldn't be problematic to affirm in the world, the reality of all these things; and the door always remains open, and the invitation serious and sincere, to 'Occamize': for someone with the taste for it, as well as the ingenuity to find and show a way to dispense with any dispensable items.

Chapter Nine

Space

My aim in this chapter will be to come to conclusions about the metaphysics of space. One can hardly discuss space at all without in some manner engaging the physics of space. If certain kinds of results were reached, namely, results incompatible with what modern physics says about space, the character of the engagement would be critical, and, as I would see it, the metaphysical account would need to be very much on the defensive. It would be in fact almost certainly wrong. In any case, there would be for such an account a heavy burden of argument to try to show how physics has erred.

As it happens, no such burden will fall upon the view defended here. (It will be found to be otherwise when I come in the next chapter to time.) At least, I think this is the case. The way it is usually put is that objects, or states or events involving them, are to be identified with reference to four dimensions, not three, as common sense and older physics had affirmed. In addition to the three spatial dimensions (intuitively the width, height, and depth the object or event occupies), a fourth temporal dimension is involved, that may no more be separated from the three spatial dimensions than any of them may be separated from the other two. Still, even if this is granted, it may be noted that depth, for example, remains a distinct item – a reality distinct – from width even if inescapably linked to it. But many popular and semi-popular expositions of relativity physics claim that the latter has actually dispensed with space and with time, in favour of space-time. Taken strictly or literally, this is evidently to adopt a view analogous to the one taken about mind and matter by some varieties of neutral monism, according to which there is no such thing as either mind or matter as supposed by common sense and quotidian experience, but rather a unitary kind of reality (whether a stuff, an event, or a state). (A distinct variety of neutral monism apparently holds that mind and matter are both real, only neither elementally so, for each is a form or case of a single underlying reality, which is itself strictly neither exclusively the one nor the other.)

The relations of space, time, and space-time, are not as clear as might be desired (or as popular expositions of relativity may suggest). We have provided two options. One is the view that space and time are both unreal, although a distinct item with a displacement 'identity'[1] to them is in their conceptual vicinity. The second is the view that space and time are both real but are special cases or manifestations of a single thing, space-time (perhaps like the relations of ice and water vapour to water). Still a third option is a humbler position according to which space and time are interdependently linked so that – even though both are real and distinct – the one cannot be identified and characterized without reference to the other. In this third alternative it is space-time that will be the constructed or derivative entity, not space or time. Space-time would be a sort of aggregate or a codependent pairing of space and time.

All of the foregoing will be viewed, largely accurately, as a simplistic and distorted account of what the evidence from common sense and the history of physics should yield. Doubtless time-concepts and space-concepts arose long ago in the history of our species; and – more doubtfully but possibly – out of them emerged what we could call single concepts of space and time, constitutable as the common sense notions of these things. These concepts may possibly be underdetermined, like so many common-sense concepts; or they are rounded intuitions of space and time that the folk achieved and that commonsense philosophy could excavate. In any case Newton produced models, a theoretical structure, including space and time conceived as independent items. A considerable measure of fit between folk-space and -time, and Newton's theoretical versions, was unquestionably intended by Newton and accepted tacitly, at least as warranted by the readers of the *Principia*. Newton's conceptions are by no means conceived to stand or fall as a direct function of a perfect match. Indeed, with sufficient general success of Newton's system as a whole, his account of space and time could be and was received as augmenting, even correcting, the folk account.

This is the way all substantive science develops in relation to common sense or folk knowledge. There must be sufficient commonality to afford and justify confidence that the same terrain or items are being explored. However there will be a sufficient looseness of fit to permit science to supplement and sometimes revise common sense: its entitlement being a function of systemic adequacy and power.

When someone proposes a new model and theoretical structure – as Einstein (1879–1955) did, supplanting Newton on space and time – complex and controversial questions of commensurability arise. I favour resolutions of these questions that maximize commonality of framework and discourse; more Kuhnian[2] or relativist opponents incline otherwise. Wherever truth lies in these matters there will be no question that common sense, Newton, and Einstein should not be conceived as distinct articulations with each constituting hypotheses as to what the real nature of space and time, or the spatio-temporal, is. Newton and Einstein are theoretical proposals, whose systematicity and complexity make it difficult to isolate the spatio-temporal component of each for handy comparison with that of the other or with common sense; and even if there were a detailed common-sense view of the world which is reasonably determinate and consistent (both problematic assumptions), it does not proffer itself as a model or proposal by which spatio-temporal things might be profitably and systematically thought about.

I take these remarks to justify the idea that it remains reasonable to isolate space – or better, spatiality – as an aspect of the world, that common-sense intuitions and rival physical theories give accounts of; and likewise with time (or temporality). Even if the theory about spatiality that we ought to accept will link space more deeply with time than we had previously expected would prove the case, that theory will still give us the goods on a genuine aspect of the world. It will not show us that there is no such dimension as spatality. In short it remains even scientifically respectable to explore space and time apart from each other.

The view I want to advocate is this: (1) it is unclear whether there is a comprehensive and consistent, common-sense theory of space (or spatiality); (2) to the degree that there is, that theory seems contradicted by physical evidence; (3) common sense spatial intuitions err; (4) space could be – in other possible worlds is – profoundly different from either common sense or physics space; (5) there are possible worlds with more spaces than one, each infinite in extent; (6) there are possible worlds entirely lacking spatiality. So space itself exists only contingently, and it can have a different structure and 'metric,' than a Euclidean or a Riemannian[3] one.

For many philosophers none of the foregoing claims will be controversial. From a metaphysical point of view they may be said to relegate space chiefly to physics. Space is as physics says it is. From a metaphysical point of view, what is most interesting and distinctive about space has to do with its modal properties – what it is and is not capable of being like.

(1) Kant and other rationalist and some common-sense philosophical theorists notwithstanding, it is by no means obvious that there is a comprehensive folk theory, or set of intuitions, about space. It is true that Euclidean geometry is experienced as deeply intuitive, and its extension from two to three dimen-

sions appears a transition the mind 'naturally' makes, and finds correlatively intuitive. But the certitude of phenomenologically apprehended three-dimensional Euclidean space extends no further, at any rate as certitude and felt with intuitive conviction, than the limits of the perceptual fields (visual and tactile – but much more confidently in the first of these cases than the second) surrounding the apprehending subject. As far as I can see – and for even the most far-sighted that isn't very far – and only rather haltingly, so far as I can feel or touch my surrounding space feels Euclidean, with something approaching 'apodeictic certainty.' I can imaginatively extend that surrounding space, imagining myself continuing to see it as it extends and enlarges, and the imagined extended space will also 'feel' Euclidean, and I can infer that this would continue for me indefinitely. However this is not the same as affirmation that the whole of space is intuited as Euclidean. It isn't. I am unable to encompass such enormities phenomenologically, and my imaginative limits are real, and severe. Really, I simply go around with a sort of Euclidean proscenium accompanying me, beyond whose limits I am guessing, or projecting – but not seeing with anything like a natural light of reason.

Moreover, even within the limits of my perceptual field it is at least a little problematic whether phenomenological space is Euclidean, or fully or exclusively so. We have mentioned the specially tentative character of purely tactile spatial intuition. Visually too it is unclear to what degree Euclidean spatialization may be learned, rather than innate or automatically intuitive. It seems quite reasonable to imagine human minds coming to adulthood believing that space 'shrinks' as objects recede in the distance. Some spatializations seem inconsistent, or potentially inconsistent, with others. Awareness of the horizon and other phenomenological dimensions to a realization of the curvature of the earth seem at odds with intuitions that all of the earth's surfaces accessible to me will be, in transitive stages, in a straight line from any surface I currently occupy. The very fact that four-dimensional and Riemannian spaces are conceptually (and imaginatively) motivatable at all is evidence that Euclidean spatializations do not have as firm and automatic a grip on our spatial imaginations as Kant and philosophical rationalism (including its manifestations in Reid-Moore style common sense philosophies) suppose.

(2) The evidence from physical theory fairly decisively establishes that there is no good reason to regard space as the infinite and uniform container – infinite in three Euclidean dimensions – that Newton, and the central atomist/empiricist tradition (adopted also by Spinoza, and post-Spinozist rationalist philosophers) before and after him, suppose. The reflections expressed above are partly intended to suggest that that is not wholly surprising – i.e., that we were more agnostic than those traditions implied. Space is more accurately

depicted by a Riemannian geometry than by Euclidean. Within the framework of the non-Euclidean geometry adopted for physical theory, the old Euclidean truths remain sound; but of course they no longer have Euclidean meaning. From a Euclidean perspective, actual physical space is found to involve curvatures that are a function of the strength of gravitational fields, the speed of transit, and the relative position and motion of a potential measuring observer, of the object – most notably, the light ray – whose behaviour is held to disclose the structure of space in that space-time region of the universe; all of which results are surprises for common sense perspectives.

(3) Even if they are not fully, comprehensively, or consistently Euclidean, common sense or folk spatial intuitions are not Riemannian. We do take, or tend to take, our perceptual field spatiality as a model for spatiality in general, and to every degree of distance, and at whatever speeds, from ourselves. In this the physical evidence shows that we are mistaken.

(4) The famous science fiction novel *Flatland*[4] describes a world in which space has just two dimensions, not three like Euclidean space or four like space-time. It seems fully conceivable and self-consistent that space be like that; or any of an indefinitely large number of other ways, uniform and non-uniform, that would differ from Euclidean and real physical space. Non-uniform spatial topologies seem particularly effectively to destroy the idea that space must have particular sorts of contours, or be mappable upon a spatiality with them. Parts of the universe might exhibit a spatial curvature, other adjacent parts be Euclidean, and others two-dimensional or with a nearly random degree of spatial 'stretch' (like a mass of pizza dough in the hands of a Picasso-like artist).

(5) It also seems thinkable that reality contains 'spaces' that would be alternative to one another: each infinite, with its own special geometric properties, and not normally (or at all) accessible to one another. We can think of an Alice-through-the-looking-glass kind of world, where there are concurrently alternative 'total physical worlds.' It makes for more interesting science-fiction stories if we think of occasional possibilities of access between such total physical worlds, but for our metaphysical purposes it may be more appropriate – certainly simpler – if we conceive there to be so such contact. Again, the picture of such a reality, as consisting of concurrent total physical spatial structures – worlds within worlds, if one likes – seems perfectly conceivable. It would not be, on such a conception, that each (or any) actual location would have simultaneous occupancy, by distinct but inter-inaccessible physical realities (this too seems conceivable, though less metaphysically interesting); rather, the structures of location themselves would differ, and be inter-inaccessible.

Of course the actual possible world might be such a reality as this. We do not appear to have compelling evidence for supposing that it is; although a number of contemporary cosmologists have argued for hypotheses at least somewhat along these lines.

(6) A relativist or relationist view of space will have no trouble arguing the conceivability of an aspatial world. Such a stance need merely urge the possibility of a world without motion or matter. In such a world there would be for the relativist no space, since space, for him or her, is 'defined' by reference to motion, events, or physical particles. Without any of the latter there would be, according to this position, no space.

However, the view I advocate is 'absolutist,' in the sense that, while space exists contingently and with a metric and structure admitting of extremely wide variation, nonetheless space is distinct from – both diverse from and conceptually autonomous of – things existing, happening or moving in it. This variety of spatial absolutism is compatible also with the idea of space coming into being and growing larger of extent, gradually over time, as a causal consequence of a central event in the history of the world, like the big bang. Thought experiment seems to me rather readily to establish such an absolutist view, though of course many anti-absolutists aware of claims from such evidence persist in their view. At any rate, it seems tolerably easy to conceive all motion ceasing and all matter disappearing, leaving only empty, eventless space; and if that is conceivable with such prior history, it seems conceivable that such an achievable state of the world should have been the state it had always been in. That any total state of the world at a time (where by 'total state' we mean something involving no reference to earlier or later times) would be able to be the total state of a (complete) possible world, is a metaphysical postulate or principle which seems to me deeply plausible. In any case, whether affirmed unrestrictedly or not, the principle's application to our case – the attainability of eventless empty space implying the existence of possible worlds that at all times in them consist of eventless empty space – seems persuasive.

If so, spatial relationist arguments for the possibility of aspatial worlds will not be available to us. Nonetheless, the existence of entirely aspatial possible worlds seems clearly demonstrable or as demonstrable as these matters may be. The very claim that space exists contingently will of course formally require this view, as will the idea that space becomes larger as light travels away from the original world-foundational explosion. If there are wholly nonphysical worlds – and there are – there are worlds without space. Worlds without locations, places, here, there, a where from which observation or reflection could occur. Such worlds would nevertheless contain abstract entities, and time, and times.

Could there be a world with mind but lacking space? This is a difficult question. If there can be purely disembodied thought – a big 'if,' though one I propose cautious assent to – then it would seem to emerge that there are worlds with thinking in them but no space. Some thinking taking place – and presumably then someone doing some thinking – but nowhere this occurs and nowhere such thinking is focused upon or to which it can refer. We might perhaps conceive of the God of some of the philosophical theologians, his thinking entirely a matter of contemplating abstract ideas, and aggregates of them – some of these propositions – to try to motivate the idea posed; though with no need of such properties as omnipotence or omniscience (and certainly not omnipresence).[5]

This is obviously a sketchy and perhaps too informal account of space and spatiality. Its overall moral is that philosophers, including metaphysicians, should largely resign their claims to expertise on space, in favour of physicists. The modal queries remain to them – queries which, in my view, physicists often mishandle, with clumsy and mistaken views about definition and operationalizability. Once the modal boundary questions are settled, it is for them to tell the rest of us what space is – and they will have much to tell.

Chapter Ten

Time

The drift of naturalist and empiricist philosophy as well as twentieth-century physics generally, has been in the direction of confuting many common-sense intuitions and allegedly a priori rationalist philosophical convictions. While this is a tendency I generally share, in the case of fundamental views about time I find myself to a significant degree of contrary mind.

Let me start at the end by stating as broadly and directly as I can the conclusions I reach and defend about time. First, time is odd, and a puzzle: not just in the way that St. Augustine meant in his often repeated remarks.[1] Time is odd because a bedrock of intuitions about it is to be found at the lowest level of analysis and reflection about the world. Temporality cannot be thought away. Space can be, but time cannot. There is no level of consciousness or analysis from which temporality is absent. And in a sense, this is surprising. Time ought to be thinkable away, if we were ingenious or imaginative enough. Some have of course thought that it is. But they are wrong. Time was lurking there anyway, even if they declined to say aloud that it was.

Moreover not mere temporality as such is there admitting a plethora of structural contours or metrics. Rather, specifics of what time can be conceived to be will be found at the fundamental level of inquiry. I argue that the prevailing positions in the philosophy of time, which are for the most part empiricist, and hold that time can have a wide range of 'topologies' (structural shapes and their study) and 'metrics' (roughly, measures of structural sizes), are wrong. In fact I take on, with these convictions, more opponents than the standard, contemporary naturalist and empiricist ones, and what many argue are the metaphysical implications of modern physics. The preceding array of stances joins ranks with many varieties of rationalism in the history of philosophy (and theology), including Aristotelian ones, with respect to time, in holding that there are possible atemporal circumstances. More precisely, for these rationalist and

Aristotelian positions there are circumstances in which there is no motion. Kant held that the structure of the world as we apprehend it (both internally and externally) is necessarily temporal. Kant, to me, is right about something central. However, he is not right to take inexpungible temporality to be merely phenomenal or subjective. We cannot think time away nor seriously conceive that it fails to belong in the objective order of things-in-themselves independent of us.

There is some leeway in the contours time might have. The implications of special relativity for simultaneity and the fact that both relativistic and Newtonian temporal worlds are possible show this. Kant is mistaken to suppose a fixed, fully replete 'Euclidean' content for time. This is a third central claim. The goalposts can be moved a little and in ways that don't gibe with common sense temporal intuition.

In the nature of the claims being made, how could they possibly be defended? They seem purely (and merely) intuitive. However, my intention is that they should be defensible and defended. This can be done in two ways. First, by reductio: by attempting to conceive a universe atemporally or radically temporal – a universe with a temporal topology and metric quite different from the actual one – and running up against the impossibility of the task, feeling in the process the temporal structure of the world we are forced to affirm. The second kind of defense is to show that nothing in the physics of time precludes at least some synthetic a priori structures for temporality; more powerfully, that the physics cannot be articulated without the assumption of those structures. This second defence I will be able to provide only partly but some efforts in this direction will be undertaken. But the attempt here will be skeletal, and must be more than usually tentative. I will welcome assistance, and correction; and the challenge of specialists who think I err.

Deep convictions are held about temporality. No assumptions are made here nor have I intransigent convictions about the categorical and ontic geography of temporal things. Does time exist? What is it if it does? The eighteenth century? Now? To some degree the most reasonable account of these matters seems to me heuristic. It is temporality as such – the universe exhibiting temporality – which seems to me 'not thinkable away' and certainly real whatever the fine-grained story of the autonomous or reductive character of the temporal vis à vis particulars, facts, states, events, or other things that there are. That is what I want to urge as the most securely anchored and initial datum for our inquiry.

Another of the conclusions I argue for is that time is less like space than is widely supposed, both by many philosophers and the laity. Bergson (1859–1941) was a philosopher who made much of the claim that theoretical conceptions of time erroneously spatialize or over-spatialize time. While I certainly do not want to defend a Bergsonian account of time,[2] it does seem to me that it is peculiarly difficult and important to try to think and speak literally, non-analogically, in a vocabulary and concept-space peculiar to itself about time, as far as this is possible.

The language of time is heavily spatial. It seems correct to say that much or most of the terminology with which we characterize temporality derives from characterizations of space or spatiality. Time's features are framed by us in a largely borrowed and analogically extended vocabulary. This seems neither surprising nor intrinsically problematic. In some direct sense we both see and touch the spatiality of things rather vividly. The cognitive mechanics for temporality are themselves challenging and non-obvious. It seems natural that this multi-sensory, perceptual and experiential domain should serve as the imaginative and semantic base for the characterology of other spheres. There are other parallel cases where the characterizing vocabulary of a sector of experience is patently an adaptation from elsewhere: characterizations of the mental, especially the affective, and the language of music and musical experience, come to mind. Music is entitled to the term chromatic and the language of the emotions to cold; even though both could mislead. In none of these cases is there compelling reason to believe that the sphere characterized with a borrowed and extended set of terms must be conceived, within those terms, as the latter applied in their original setting; or that the borrowing necessitates a confining impossibility of forming clear notions of the sphere to which the vocabulary has been extended. In all cases, care, clarity, and reflective awareness are in order.

Tense logic provides many of the resources for achieving the relevant clarity, and reflective detachment, in the case of time; though it leaves the inquirer with too many choices, options for conceptualizations of time that aren't genuine.[3] At any rate, my view is that time is very different from space characterologically. This will not have an important bearing on the relevant physics, the replacement of time and space with space-time (the latter isn't really, as sometimes popularly thought, neutral monism for space and time but something like a requirement of conjoint spatial and temporal indexing, ubiquitously, for all particulars, events, and states). Saying that time and space are very different is of course quite vague. How different is very different? A sketch of an answer appears in what is to come, though I regret it will not be more than a sketch.

Fleshing this out a little, I think, as do many others, that the concept of time travel is actually problematic, and by no means simply the imaginative exercise in science fiction that it is widely taken to be. The project gets launched conceptually only as time is spatialized and if we try not to spatialize time – and we can, at least to a sufficient degree for this theme – we find it quite hard to see what it is that we are supposed to conceive; or that it merits the label of time travel.

Enlarging a little on time travel, it is travel backwards into the past that is, I think, problematic or, more frankly, incoherent. Travel into the future may perhaps be given a certain content. The future, being the future, is not a defined or finished thing – as is the past – that one might in some sense visit. In the case of the future, one might get there sooner than the normal course of events and this could be a kind of travel to the future (though, necessarily, on a one-way ticket). Apparently, by travelling extremely rapidly (in a rocket ship, for example) and then returning to the place of departure, one would, according to general relativity, be able to get to where the rest of the universe will arrive, more slowly than it: so that, in the sense indicated, the rest of the universe would arrive in the future ahead of us.

Supposed travel into the past, literally, is the idea that a group of individuals go from a situation in which they have found themselves to some earlier occasion (from, say, 1998 to 1643). The difficulties with this conception are multiple and serious. First is there a profound revision in our supposition of a non-relative or non-relational feature of ordered time. Instead of a linear succession of 1984, 1985, 1986, and so on, we would think of 1984-for-S, 1985-for-S,' and so on, for all individuals (not just those capable of experience or measurement). Being able to accommodate time travel seems insufficient motivation for considering such a revision. One way of understanding special relativity, apparently, is through this kind of conclusion: that time is relative to vicinities, and the objects and states in them. However, there still appears to be for relativity theory what one might conceive as a 'super-time,' within which vicinity-times go their independent ways. However, I will leave these matters out of account here.

More pointedly, if travel backwards in time were possible, there would be no reason in principle why someone couldn't go back and kill their own grandparent before their parent had been conceived. Indeed, there could be no reason in principle why they couldn't go back a mere week before they entered the 'time machine' they travelled in, and kill themselves. Such options have sometimes been discussed in the literature as puzzles. Indeed they are. If there is a possible world where time travel occurs, then there is a possible world where someone so travels, kills themselves – but doesn't commit suicide – and is alive at subsequent times, the killed self not revived.[4] There will be worlds where one person has become or rather, was, some time ago, for a while – two.

Something is amiss here. It seems to me it is similar to what is amiss in the possibilities created in Escher drawings.[5] In the latter, the details in the vicinity of any given stage of the picture are coherent and spatially possible; it is the larger coherence of a representation of a possible space that collapses. Similarly there may be temporal coherence in the vicinity of some individual and their experiences which disappears in the larger temporal picture.

This does not gainsay the innumerable possible worlds in which persons undergo experiences that are qualitatively indistinguishable from those of an earlier occasion. Moreover, it remains possible to claim metaphysically that what I want to call things going awry or amiss is the contemplation of worlds very different from the familiar one: where a familiar kind of world is suddenly interrupted by the uncaused arrival of a duplicate of one of its citizens, sufficiently similar to warrant the claim that this citizen from that moment had ceased being, with one of the duplicates subsequently killing the other, and then itself disappearing and later reappearing (all disappearances and reappearances of course ex nihilo) and still later getting into a 'time machine,' setting the dial to a date where records indicated an extraordinary replication had occurred.

However, something is still amiss here and it is Escher-like. For we wanted in the original (and possibly less sophisticated) versions a familiar world with a familiar past to become unfamiliar in an extraordinary future where the familiar past could be revisited. That is what feels possible in its immediate temporal details and that in ascending to the higher vantage point shows itself to be impossible. 'Saving the appearances,' by showing that we can perhaps have that desideratum by rendering the past as other than the familiar type, but rewriting it as nomically or metaphysically 'unfamiliar,' in suitable ways, so that the later temporal voyage would 'work out' is, it seems to me, to miss the point. It is being too clever by half. It acknowledges that some structural and linear features of time impose themselves on anything we can conceive for events occurring in time; and actually more, for I don't believe that I would cease to be if I, per impossibile, as I believe, returned to a time where, just before I did so, I existed (and where no one resembling me died); that is to say, I think this really will lead to the logically impossible.

Moreover, I don't mean by this or by the desire to de-spatialize our conception of time, any point about temporal language and its use or rules. What we are disposed to say or think represents only a crude and halting guide to what is the case. It is not worthless but it is only of modest utility in determining what we ought to believe. There may be intrinsic structures in language that predispose us to error or failure to discover features of the character of the world, that we may nevertheless be able to make out partly by bending, resisting, and revising those structures in language.

To investigate time as we explored other metaphysical themes, we will ask three kinds of questions: (1) does time exist? (2) what is the nature of time? (3) what modal status do the existence and nature of time have?

I said that our firmest datum must be that temporality is real even if a reductive analysis dispensing with time itself or individual times may be successful. Although this position stands, I am dubious about the prospects for eliminating time. Efforts to provide a genuinely tenseless discourse seem hopeless and, if this is the case, we seem ontologically committed to time. As with other themes, the matter is chiefly one of work and detail, but also not as important as many suppose. To repeat, existential facts are not dramatically other than non-existential facts. A thoroughness I shall not attempt here would require the assessment of reductionist programs that purport to eliminate time and times (even if they might preserve temporality). I shall assume they fail.

What is time? Or what are times? Time and times are *sui generis*. They are similar to other things, notably space and places, but only to a limited extent. Time, we may say, is the aggregate of all times, at any rate past and occurrent ones: I shall say more about the future later. A time is something primitive but whose nature can be partly conceived analogically by reference to places and numbers. Times comprise series, as do places and numbers. The formal relations between members of time series are similar to those between places and numbers. There is notably a relation of greater than with a converse lesser than between members of all three kinds of series, although in the case of times, unlike places and numbers, it is not obvious that earlier members of the series, as normally or naturally ordered, should be styled lesser. In any case for all three we can conceive an order with a parallel structure, in which earlier members of the relevant series are earlier chronologically or numerically or in extension smaller, than later members (for time, number, and space, respectively). Moreover series of times, like series of numbers and places, will involve equivalences in magnitude. One time can have the same magnitude as another as do pairs of numbers and places.

The distinctive structural feature of time series, all of whose members are progressively 'greater' in magnitude, is what is captured in the idea of time's undirectionality – sometimes called time's arrow or the anisotropy of time in contrast to the isotropy of the identity in structure in all directions of space. This idea is elusive. It is difficult to give it a clear articulation that isn't circular, and at the same time most people think they recognize what is meant. It is what is involved in the ontic status we accord the past. It is what makes the past gone, closed, sealed off in a manner even advocates of time travel acknowledge, with the idea that if the past is visited, it will turn out to be the case that whatever is done in or to the past via the visitation was already there in the past. Time is a structure of positions that extend backwards from a given position. Some analogy with the negative numbers is appropriate, the given or designated position – which for worlds with consciousness in them is the indexically identified now – corresponds to zero. At the given or zero position there is anticipated an approaching series of positions – the future – which has, however, reality only as the members of the series become, in turn, the present. I shall have something to say below about the ontic status of the past.

Otherwise we fill in, or at least augment, the complement of time with noting such things as that events occur, states obtain, and objects exist in, or at, times. We can add too that time – the aggregate of any complete series of tangential times – may be conceived as a kind of line. This line is divisible in principle, it seems, indefinitely.

I proceed to modal questions. Does time exist necessarily? My answer is, Yes. Likewise with every particular time – at least it is metaphysically necessary that each time should eventually obtain.

Time is linear and open. That is, every time series whose members are of the same temporal magnitude is such that each of its members has one successor of that same magnitude, and no member of such a series recurs. This is the case both for Newtonian and relativistic time. Are times essentially like this? To these questions I give a sketchy, affirmative answer. In this case I shall offer some argument for it, presently.

Since antiquity, philosophers have divided themselves into those who think time is metaphysically, conceptually, or logically independent of events and those who take the contrary view. Sometimes the first party is called absolutist, and sometimes Platonist; the opposing position is generally styled relativist, relationist, or reductionist. A kind of compromise holds that there could not be time before there were events but that once time and events are in place, there can be periods of time without events (that is, of course, anywhere in the universe). Whether the events, held by relationists to be necessary to time, need to be physical motions of particles or waves, is a more vexed point. One of the great classical relationists was Leibniz. He held that time was reducible to orderings of events. He is frequently interpreted also as a metaphysical idealist for whom material events and states are mere appearances; the corresponding realities are in this view mental or representational states of different kinds. This is the standard interpretation of Leibnizian metaphysics.[6] Phenomenalist positions of the nineteenth and twentieth century, some of which were relationist on time, can seem idealist. If it is sufficient for time that there are irreducibly mental states or events without physical movement occurring anywhere in the universe, it is hard to see that such states or events might not consist of a series of awarenesses of mathematical facts. A world with a mind apprehending that 5 was less than 7, and 5 was less than 8, and so on, might qualify as a temporally ordered world, a world with time. It seems an easy move from this possibility to the possibility of time existing with no events of any kind.

In fact this is the view I want to defend. Newton-Smith defends it effectively, I think, in *The Structure of Time*,[7] to which the reader is referred for details. Newton-Smith's view is that virtually all matters with respect to the existence and nature of time are empirical and contingent. As is evident by now, this general stance seems correct on space and most other metaphysical topics but not on time. The fundamental case for the possibility of eventless time, even time prior to any event, mental or physical, is that we can think of it. Similarly the fundamental case for the view which I also advocate that time necessarily exists, is that we cannot think its absence. These are what van Fraassen and others call phenomenological arguments for these conclusions. Ideally they would be supplemented by non-phenomenological arguments. As a kind of Russellian empiricist and a naturalist, I find it almost an embarrassment to defend so rationalist a position on time and primarily on these grounds. Nonetheless it seems to me the right one.

It should be noted that absolutism on time is by no means the same as the view that time necessarily exists, as Newton-Smith's view demonstrates. You can believe that time can exist without events – i.e., that what Newton-Smith calls temporal vacua can occur – even prior to any event taking place, and also believe that there are genuinely atemporal worlds. Moreover, you can believe that time cannot exist without events, even physical motions, and suppose, as Aristotle did, that since time necessarily exists, there has always been physical motion. The view I advocate then is that time can exist without events, and that time, unlike events, exists necessarily.

I have some hesitation calling the view I advocate Platonistic. Specific times – 1985 and the eleventh century B.C., for example – are wholly individual or particular, though not spatial or causal particulars. It would be consonant with my view in fact to deny that there is anything in the temporal compartment of the world other than temporal tokens; i.e., to hold that there are no such things as temporal types. No such position is taken here, but, with the right sort of ontological reductionism, it might in principle be successfully defended. At any rate, in some senses at least times are not abstract or Platonistic entities. They aren't universals, classes, or any other kind of mathematical entity; nor abstractions or constructions in any obvious sense.

On the other hand times are not spatial or extended things. They also have, and can have, no causal role. The fourteenth century, or 4:15 p.m. yesterday, doesn't, and couldn't cause anything to take place; nor could a state of a temporal entity having some property or being in relation to something do so. Moreover, in a certain sense times are universal. Individual times occur at, or are true of, or apply to, a multiplicity of states and events. Even if absolute simultaneity is rendered problematic in relativity theory, special and general, local simultaneity survives (where measurers and measured objects are not moving at extremely high speeds relative to each other), and this appears to be enough to confer the relevant degree of universality on times.

I turn now to the topological features of time and the question of whether divergent alternatives to time as an open real line, without beginning or end, are possible.

First, if time is 'not thinkable away' then it can have neither beginning nor end. For if it could, then a state of the world apart from temporality would be conceivable. Any such segment of the world could characterize an entire world. However, that would be an atemporal world and thus time could be thinkable away. This – the impossibility of beginning or ending time – would not preclude circular, branching, or epicyclic time structures: all of which have been argued as possible and to them we now proceed.

Nietzsche (1844–1900), certain pre-Socratic philosophers, and Kurt Vonnegut[8] notwithstanding, time cannot literally recur. It is metaphysically impossible that, once 1991 has passed, it could be 1991 again. This is formally assured by the logical properties of the B time series (the earlier, later, contemporaneous series of times) standardly given by the three principles (as stated by van Fraassen):[9]

1 Of any two events, either one is before the other or they are simultaneous.
2 If A is before B and B is before C, then A is before C.
3 No event is before itself.

The matter transcends, however, a mere axiom set. The date 29 May 1953 is either when a human first climbed Mt. Everest or it is not. If that occasion was the first time a human being reached the summit of Mt. Everest, then a later occasion, however closely it may resemble it, cannot be the first time Everest was scaled. So exact replication of earlier stages of world history with all of their properties is metaphysically impossible.

Of course the argument here may be held to beg the question. If there really were eternal recurrence, nothing could take place for the first time, which would mean that many characteristics we currently accept about the world would be mistaken and there is nothing problematic about that.

While replications of world history are, however unlikely, metaphysically possible, these will not be literally recurrences of either the selfsame events or times. There will be no reason to regard the replica of myself many billions of years in the future or the past, as literally me; and since these replications will be, by hypothesis, earlier or later, they cannot literally be the same events or times.

However, could time itself recur, so that there wouldn't simply be a replica of 1991, as alike as is metaphysically and logically possible but literally 1991 again? Apart from the fact that this would violate the intuition that no event precedes itself, the idea involves a spatialization of time. Only if one were thinking of a time as a place one arrives at and hence might return to can the idea begin to be motivated. If one focuses on the idea of this very temporal occasion one will see that a time is specific and unrepeatable; it is similar to a linguistic or an event token. To suppose one could return to 1991 is like supposing one could return to a spoken sentence token, after its subsequent silence.

It is difficult to believe that supposed metricizations for branching time are what they purport to be. Here too it seems that time is spatialized, but as elsewhere without a successful case that alternatives to temporality have been articulated coherently. In the tense-logic literature, and some of the empiricist philosophy of time, one finds formalisms with incomplete accounts of what they are supposed to mean as accounts of time.

At the heart of the matter is what we ought to say and believe about imaginary situations – worlds – in which parallel normally isolated orders, dimensions or realms obtain. A real world and a looking-glass world, or several of both, in tandem, with points of ingress and/or egress among or between them possibly; the entirety comprising the possible world in question. In one vocabulary such worlds afford, or can afford, a case for the non-necessity of a unity of space. That is, there can be a multiplicity of spaces, without a common or shared super-space housing them all; spaces may well be wholly disconnected from each other, each constituting a 'complete' space.

In some worlds of this type spaces have branched out from earlier unitary spaces. Fission, more or less amoeba-style, has occurred for a space itself so that the successor spaces to an earlier unitary space are wholly disconnected from each other. Maybe this has involved subordinate fission for elements or individuals in the generator space. Some particular has 'split' or possibly a whole system of particulars, together with their relationships, has 'split' one fork of which moves into one now discrete and self-contained space while another fork occupies another. Will there be any reason to believe that time has split or involves temporal branching? I want to claim something rather strong, namely, that we cannot successfully and coherently think of a situation of the kind described as involving temporal branching. At any rate we certainly don't have to think of time as having divided in such cases. We can think of these worlds with reference to non-standard spatiality and fission. Moreover, there will be no good reason not so to conceive them. So the case made here is partly an instance of Occam's razor. Time hasn't cracked asunder when an amoeba splits into two amoebas – and we don't doubt that we must take there to be two, with neither identical to the one formerly in place, however close the resemblance genetically to the original, and even though the successors are spatio-temporally continuous with the original. Why is it any different if we have larger, more systematic, or comprehensive scenarios concerned? It is like the differences between possible changes for one individual, and a whole future part of a possible world that includes that individual or its successors. There is no more reason to think that time has divided in such cases than there is to suppose that existing is different when cows do it than when numbers do.

Further, we will have difficulty if we try to think of time as having divided when it is really space and possibly some individuals in former spaces. For, we will be unable to avoid thinking of events on one 'branch' as partly simultaneous with, or wholly earlier or later than events on every other branch. Put otherwise events on one branch will be partly simultaneous with or wholly earlier or later than events on every other branch. Even with relative time, we can make temporal comparisons between one part of the universe and any other.

It is evident that I place a lot of argumentative weight on a particular variety of 'transcendental' reflection of a Kantian kind. Why should anyone be impressed by such argument or take it seriously? Well, partly because if someone is going to make a case for a non-standard topology for time we should be convinced that it is really time that is discussed and not something else (like space and fission). Moreover, I think that, though he errs deeply on other themes and even here qualification is needed on time Kant has got it right. We cannot put together the thought of what it might be like even for temporality to be a sort of Whorfian screen or filter and there be another way that what the (supposed) temporality filter does for us be able to be done or no way at all. There are of course those who say otherwise but they cannot in fact mean it in their hearts. There are certainly sincere and convinced advocates of relational, contingent, topologically plastic time. McTaggart sincerely believed that time is unreal. My claim is that we operate with a conceptual substrate where we can neither remove temporality nor coherently frame the thought of what it might be like to try.

I would like to proceed to some remarks on temporal becoming. I begin by saying that I find many of the themes posed here difficult and puzzling. Some are very difficult problems while others approach the threshold of scepticism or paradox. So I expect to make only a modest contribution to the clarification of these matters.

I take it that the part of temporality which is clearest is the structure of fixed temporal positions that constitute themselves as earlier or later, before and after, and (at least partially) simultaneous with each other – McTaggart's B series. McTaggart's own view notwithstanding, the B series seems more basic than, and in some manner conceptually independent of, the A series – the past, present, and future structure of temporal positions.

However, the A series is certainly fundamental also. Russell held, as McTaggart summarizes his views, that 'If there were no consciousness, there would be events which were earlier and later than others, but nothing would be in any sense past, present, or future. And if there were events earlier than any consciousness, those events would never be future or present, though they could be past.'[10] McTaggart argues against this view, correctly I think. That is, this view is false, whatever the merits of McTaggart's case against it. Past, present, and future – the present including, of course, being now – are not indexicals or egocentric particulars like others. They are not speaker-relative or consciousness-dependent. If we are discussing a possible history of the actual world and are focused on 1846, then earlier temporal positions will be in the past, relative to 1846, whether or not there is consciousness or language in that version of our world. Similarly, it seems true, for example, to say that even if there had never been consciousness or language, it would now be the case that the universe contained carbon and that it had now existed for many centuries.

Moreover the differences between past and future are not just differences in nature but differences in their reality, their ontic status. There is much to commend the idea that only the present is real though one confronts immediately the taxing question of the duration of the present, the extent of the now, if one affirms that view. Even if only the present is real, the past was real and is in some manner not merely determinate as it was, forever with the content it had but it is also ontically still available in a most unclear but definitely substantive sense. The present is the implements in use, the play occurring on the stage, and the past is the assembly of implements on the shelf, inspectable even if not accessible or retrievable through the museum glass it lies frozen behind. All of this is quite vague. I find completely unattractive any Platonic or later notion of degrees or varieties of being and do not want to affirm that the past has a species of being different from anything else that is. Yet I do nonetheless want to say that in one (admittedly unclear) sense the past still is and yet in another that it is not.

The problematic character of the past may be displayed in a particularly striking way by the example of the ancestor relation. James I died in 1625. His descendant, our Queen Elizabeth II, was born in 1926. How will we most accurately describe the relationship between James and Elizabeth? James is ancestor of Elizabeth? James no longer exists. There is no James to be ancestor of Elizabeth or to have any relations or properties. James was ancestor of Elizabeth then? Yet he could not have had this relation at any time during his lifetime, i.e., at any time when he existed, for there was then no Elizabeth for him to be ancestor of. A more accurate formulation – one that will be actually used – might appear to be: James *was to be* ancestor of Elizabeth. However when did he come to have this ancestral relation? Not, it seems clear, until there was an Elizabeth in existence, i.e., over 300 years after his death. How, then, could James have become Elizabeth's ancestor? How, that is, could ancestring Elizabeth become a relational property of James's, when there was when Elizabeth began to exist, no James to have this property?

Now it may seem that the problem posed is unreal or artificial. For we can after all explain and describe what is involved in James being the ancestor of Elizabeth. He begets someone who begets someone who begets ... etc., until we come to Elizabeth. A causal sequence is involved that is in other contexts quite familiar. 'X causes Y' does not require that X and Y wholly temporally coincide. X may no longer exist while Y continues. We find familiar the idea of a causal chain or sequence; and 'ancestring' is just a special instance of it. 'A ϕ-ing' may easily be in the remote causal ancestry of a current event – an event taking place now – consisting of b ψ-ing but there no longer be an a.

Logic – classical first-order logic – does encompass the past – past individuals – among the values of its variables. Our queries are metaphysical and in this case also transcendental ones, in Kant's sense, which register something equivocal or problematic in this part of classical logic about how it is possible for past and now unreal things to participate ontically with what is now real. This puzzle, the ontic status of the past, I leave as an unresolved problem.

The future, on the other hand, has no reality at all. It will, of course, have being but for now it isn't there in any sense whatsoever. It seems to me that a view and a model that is quite wrong is one that sees time as like a train (or a river) that travels through countryside. The countryside is already there but it is just that the train, or river, hasn't yet got to particular parts of it. Something like this is accurate enough, I think, for the past and present, but not for the future. Beyond where the train or the river is now there is not a settled or determinate terrain that we happen to be unable to see until we get there. Instead, one might say, beyond the train's present location, there is simply an abyss. I don't mean by this anything bearing on Laplacean determinism and its alternatives. The future might be fully determinate and fully determined. Quite certainly even we, limited cognizers that we are, know a very great deal about the future, much of it knowledge of what will definitely come to take place. It isn't the relative light or darkness of the future, or the extent to which, when it does transpire, its content will have issued programmatically from the present and the past. It is the reality of the future now that concerns us. In the strictest sense, the future, now, is not; there is no such thing, even as something that awaits.[11]

If this is right, then it will have implications elsewhere, notably for the B series and its temporal qualities. Fictional or metaphorical models aside, the world – any possible world – isn't in fact, in its ontic character, a set of ontic positions, with events, and particulars and other realia. It isn't, for example, ... 1996, 1997, 1998, 1999, 2000, ... with events, states, and their constituents clustered at them. It is 1998 (or whatever the occasion it actually is in the given world) and maybe what precedes it but not anything coming after even though there will be a subsequent continuation of the series.

These remarks about the future need elaboration that will take account of some of the implications of relativity theory. For any event there are, according to relativity theory, events that will in some frames of reference be simultaneous with the first event but in others later. So from some perspectives the second event will share the present with the first event, and from others it will be in the first event's future. I need then to affirm that the future that is unreal is any event, with its constituents (except for those which may already exist) which is, for no frame of reference, simultaneous or temporally overlapping with an event regarded as present. The present will then be viewed as having a horizon extending into what is for some purposes a future relative to it, with the complete abyss claimed above identifiable as the nonbeing beyond that horizon. I shall leave these reflections at this incomplete point.

Chapter Eleven

Causality

I

That causality, in some sense, exists in the world is not open to serious dispute. Having your head chopped off, for example, leads causally to your death and most likely, to your non-being, though that need not be insisted on here.

What has been in dispute is just what causality is; and what is its extent, including what may be called its modal extent. As for the former, there is the matter of a so-called common-sense conception of causality and what is involved in it; and the degree to which anything objectively in the world corresponds to that conception. This is a problem of conceptual analysis: what do we mean by holding that something causes something? It is also an appearance-reality problem: given that there is some degree of fit between our concept and what is objectively in the world, how close is that fit? Is it often complete, for example?

The second pole of contention and uncertainty that causality poses – extent – is the question whether anything escapes causality, and if so how contra-causal a world could be. Positions on the extent of causality have ranged from one extreme, reasonably attributed to Spinoza, according to whom every state of every possible world is wholly subject to causality, to another, rather more doubtfully attributed to Hume but plausibly assigned some twentieth-century empiricists, according to whom some states of the actual world escape causality and every state of some possible world does. I discount the positions of some metaphysicians and empiricists, for whom there is no such thing at all as causality. These positions I dismiss, perhaps dogmatically, as unserious, or as more or less immediately confuted by experience.

We must address first what we mean by causality because we could not otherwise have adequate confidence in exploring other topics involving causality nor that it is a single thing since one position argues that there is more than one kind of causality.

An anchored datum with which we may begin is that effects – the things that are caused, whatever precisely it is to be caused, and even if there is more than one sort of causality – are facts, states, processes, or events of the world.[1] Among such facts or states are that particular objects exist. However no object, all by itself, is or could be an effect. Effects are invariably what we have been calling complexes. They are also, it is clear, sometimes individual or 'singular' fact (state, process, event) tokens, in one vocabulary, and sometimes classes of facts (states, processes, events) – types. (E.g., Oswald [or his actions] caused Kennedy's death and carelessness causes accidents, respectively.) In general, in what follows, I shall talk indifferently of effects, whether types or tokens; indifferently also of whether the effects are states or events. Either term should be assumed to be meant abbreviatively (for state, event, process, or fact).

Most would certainly hold and try to argue that all effects are contingent, that is, they need not have existed or obtained, and in some possible ways of the world's being, they do not exist or obtain. That is definitely the view I would take. However, it does seem an independent matter whether a fact or state of the world might be metaphysically necessary, something that exists in every possible world. That is to say, even if some fact or event of the world were absolutely necessary in this sense, it would seem to remain possible that, in some or all worlds, such an event should have had a cause. If so, then it would be a mistake to suppose that, as we try to begin to specify and offer commentary on the frame $\ulcorner$... causes $Y\urcorner$, we can affirm it to be analytic that a relevant Y must be contingent. However, for our purposes it can be reasonably assumed that we are confining our attention to events that are metaphysically contingent. The analysis of causality for necessary events, if there are any, can be reserved for some other occasion.

Something that is caused must be a complex. Moreover, there must, if there is an effect, be a cause. We justifiably take the skeletal frame for causality to be $\ulcorner X$ causes $Y\urcorner$: causality is, or instantiates, a binary relation.

II

We note, in addition to the frame $\ulcorner X$ causes $Y\urcorner$, a comparable one, $\ulcorner X$ explains $Y\urcorner$. It seems that there will be instances of the former that will be instances of the latter. More precisely it looks at first that if something causes something, then that will entail that the former explains the latter. The converse does not seem true, as the fact of mathematical explanations, for example, will show.

However, the relations between causality and explanation are more complex than this. Explanation requires either minds or propositions while causality does not. Causal relationships in the world are concrete and typically, perhaps invariably, physical. However, an explanation is either an explanation for someone (actual or possible) or it is a conceptual structure, a complex of propositional relationships by virtue of physical relationships in the world often, but diverse from them. One or both of these, the intentional and the intensional, may be reducible to concrete physical facts and relationships in the world, as many philosophers suppose. If this is the case it would imply that ⌜X explains Y⌝ must have a more complex analysis, involving third (or more parties than X and Y), that ⌜X causes Y⌝ can safely avoid.

At any rate causal explanation comprises a variety of explanations. If our attention is confined to states of the world (types or tokens), is all explanation causal? At least two kinds of explanation (of states of the world – this qualifier should be assumed henceforth) have been proposed as non-causal or exhibiting explanatory features that are non-causal: functional explanations and explanations by reasons. The first of these purports to explain something by reference to the function or goal it serves; the second claims to explain an (intentional) action by reference to reasons an agent (typically the person performing the action) has had. In both cases many philosophers have argued that these are both special varieties of causal explanation and this is the view I advocate. In the case of functional explanation this would have to be a view involving considerable complexity in the details of the reduction of the functional explanation to classes of cases of efficient causation, together with covering laws. As my goal is causality as such, I shall ignore functional explanation.

Explanation by reasons, however, is another matter, since the obtaining of temporally adjacent states of the world – an agent's having a specified set of reasons – is involved in this case and this we take to be a central and defining feature of efficient causation. If an agent's act is explained by reference to his or her reasons, this is similar to an occurrence in inanimate nature being explained by reference to prior states.

This synopsis may run roughshod through an intricate and sophisticated literature but I do not see any reason not to regard reasons as causes, i.e., not to suppose that ⌜S having reasons $R_1, R_2, ... R_n$ for performing action a⌝ can serve as an immediate causal factor in the occurrence of action a. In so declaring I align myself with one prominent position in the literature and against others, without entering the complexities posed in that literature but doing so must stand as a promissory note for a detailed defence of the reasons-as-causes view.

III

Somewhat less promissory is the position I take on another causal topic involving persons: the idea of agent causality. Some have advocated a view according to which certain causes are not states, events, or processes of the world but a special variety of object, viz., a subject, person or agent. According to this view, defended by its advocates as identifying what they regard as the logically primary variety of causality, agents originate causal sequences. Some hold that objects other than agents can also initiate causal sequences or can serve as causes. What is argued here for agents, and agent causality, may be extended, with appropriate changes of wording, to them. In the history of causal attribution, it appeared more natural to assign causation to persons (or objects) than to events or states, until the seventeenth century. Only gradually from that fecund age did the idea of ascribing causation to complexes, rather than objects, take hold.

Accordingly I have no wish to deny a certain naturalness about affirming that persons and possibly other objects are causally responsible for things that happen.[2] What I and many others want to conjoin to this allowance is the claim that where $\ulcorner X \urcorner$ in $\ulcorner X$ causes $Y \urcorner$ is a person or object, there will be a state, process, or event (possibly an act) involving X – call it A – such that X's causing Y will be identical to A causing Y. Thus agent (and object) causality will be in this sense, reducible to 'complex' (event, state, process, etc.) causality.

I want henceforth to take both relata in $\ulcorner X$ causes $Y \urcorner$ to be complexes and shall proceed on that assumption with the acknowledgement that there are cases of agent and object causation which it is claimed are reducible to our paradigm.

IV

Whether there are deep-level varieties of causal structure, a central paradigm has features that have received more or less canonical articulation. These may be repeated here.

We need as anchor idea the notion of immediate causal factor in the occurrence of E, where E is the event (fact, state, process) whose causation is set out.

Being an immediate factor in an event E can be explicated independently of causal ideas. The idea is one of contiguity or overlap in time. The immediate factors of an event are all events occurring at any time at which that event takes place including the first and last instants of its occurrence (and, if desired, the instants prior and subsequent to them). I say 'if desired' to by-pass a metaphysical issue about which I have little to say: whether the causes of events should be thought of as operating immediately before the events they cause or whether they should be thought of as operating causally in the first instant of the occurrence of the caused event. I am unable to decide between these alternatives, though I lean toward the second, on the grounds that if cause and effect don't 'touch' in time, the former couldn't produce the latter. Causes must nudge their effects. I proceed henceforth on the assumption that this will be a structural feature of causal (and other possible immediacy) relationships but it seems easy to revise disjunctively, in the way indicated, if there were a persuasive reason to do so.

Events take place in space as well as time, and there would evidently be a possibility of spatial immediacy for an event as well as a temporal one. A reason is offered below, which does not seem compelling, for allowing the metaphysical possibility of causality without spatial immediacy involved in any way. If spatial immediacy were thought to be a desirable, or necessary, constituent in the immediate causal factors of an event, it would seem to be reasonably straightforward to add this notion. (Let S, S', ... stand for the specific spatial locations at which events occur – where they are happening then: If E takes place in S and E' takes place in S', then E and E' have spatial immediacy iff S and S' partly coincide (or [if desired] are such that there is a point at which E occurs such that no point is between that point and some point at which E' occurs).

It remains to add that temporal immediacy may confront complications from relativity theory, according to which the idea of absolute simultaneity is incoherent. If this is accurate, then the concept of the set of events occurring at any time at which a given event is occurring would appear to be problematic – i.e., there would not be such a uniquely determinate set. I don't know enough about relativity to be sure that there won't be more difficulty here than this modification addresses but, since even in relativity theory some events take place at shared times, we can revise the account above to say that an immediate factor of an event will be an event occurring at any time at which that event is taking place.

Causal factors are (causally) necessary conditions of an event's occurrence. Without them the event would not have occurred and they are logically and metaphysically independent of the event. Hence the factors could (logically and metaphysically) occur and the event not. I would argue that the event is also logically and metaphysically independent of its causal factors. Given the Kripkean essentialist position that there is no possible world containing a given human being that does not also contain all of that person's ancestors, showing the metaphysical independence of effects from their cause requires showing the falsehood of the Kripkean and cognate views. This I have undertaken in Chapter 6.

For cases of events whose causal factors have entirely obtained not later than the beginning of the occurrence of the event, the logical and metaphysical independence of causal factors from what they jointly result in is demonstrable from the fact that any physical or causal system can be conceived as ceasing to exist at any time. For any ongoing such system and a total state of that system at a given time, there will be a possible world where that state is the last state of that system. So the constituent aggregate of states that would have produced a certain effect could obtain but not the effect.

Some causal factors, hence some causes, are still in operation when the effect has begun. Some appear to involve simultaneity of cause and effect. Thus we can conceive of a pair of organisms that come into existence at the same time and whose lifespan is spent feeding parasitically off each other, culminating in the simultaneous demise of both. I dare say there are living systems exhibiting this feature though I know of none. The nurture of the one will be cause of the destruction of the other, nurture and destruction being simultaneous. Standard occurrences of fire and heat may also involve simultaneity of cause and effect.

Such possibilities teach us a number of lessons about the 'logic' of causality. While it appears correct that there cannot be backwards causation – no causal factor can be wholly subsequent to an event it is a factor of – and an immediate causal factor must obtain at a time that overlaps with or is temporally tangential to an event it is a factor of, no other temporal constraints seem necessary for the relations of events and their (immediate) causes.

Summing up so far and asserting with emphasis that this is to be understood as a principle *de re*:

X is an immediate causal factor of Y iff (1) without X occurring (or obtaining), Y would not have; (2) X is logically and metaphysically independent of Y; (3) X temporally overlaps with or is tangential to Y; (4) X is not wholly subsequent to Y.

The last of these clauses could of course be built into the penultimate one. If an event has duration then it has a maximum of two temporal, tangential points. It might have one or none because it was a vague or approximately boundaried event, as many are; that is, there might be no precise point at which it began or at which it concludes (or just one of these might be the case). Only an event with a sharp boundary of its beginning or end can have an event tangential to it. So we could have identified a first tangential point for an event as the instant at which the event occurs but which is such that no part of that event occurs earlier. We could then have replaced (3) and (4) with: (3)′ *X* temporally overlaps with or is first tangential to *Y.* I note as well that some would understand temporal overlap as including temporal tangency. If so we will have been redundant or prolix.

Because of the phenomenon of causal over-determination (situations loosely described as being such that two or more factors obtain which are both causally sufficient for the occurrence of an event), some causal factors must be conceived disjunctively.

The resultant model for causation, given the notion of an immediate causal factor, will be as follows: we utilize w for a world or sub-world (isolable part of a world); then: the aggregate of $X_1, X_2, ..., X_n$ is total cause of an event *Y,* in *w* iff each X_i is an immediate causal factor in the occurrence of *Y,* and, if *w* is deterministic, then the aggregate of $X_1, X_2, ... X_n$ is causally sufficient for the occurrence of *Y,* i.e., if $X_1, X_2, ... X_n$ obtain, then Y would not not occur, and if *w* is indeterministic, $X_1, X_2, ... X_n$ is causally sufficient for the occurrence of some event within a range *R* of relevantly similar events and *Y* is within *R.*

V

A number of comments on these conditions seem important to make. First, the notion utilized for immediate causal factors and total causes of (causally) necessary and sufficient conditions – explicated, in the case of necessary conditions as ⌜*X* is necessary for *Y* iff if *X* does not occur, *Y* would not occur⌝, sufficiency being, of course, the converse – itself legitimately asks for explication. What is meant by ⌜if *X* does not occur, *Y* would not occur⌝? What are its truth conditions?

The aim here is to exhibit the structural features and properties of (efficient) causation as we find them in our concepts and, as we suppose, in the world. Causation might prove explicable in terms of non-causal ideas. In undertaking such an analysis one doesn't know how primitive or deep the idea of a cause will turn out to be. The conditional utilized in the analyses offered is assumed to coincide with the causal conditional. Although the literature on conditionals often calls it this, it is not a counterfactual conditional since events that really are causal do take place. Nor does it seem accurate to call it a subjunctive conditional. As philosophers since Hume have affirmed, a conditional's being causal must 'support' the corresponding subjunctive conditional. Thus ⌜if *X* does occur, then *Y* would occur⌝ must, if it is causal, 'support' ⌜if *X* were to occur, then *Y* would occur⌝. The former doesn't entail the latter since the latter implies while the former does not that either X has not occurred or isn't known to have occurred or not. Perhaps 'support' means this: ⌜if X occurs, then Y would occur⌝ entails ⌜if (X occurs but it isn't known that it did or X doesn't occur) is or were to be the case, then (in that situation) if X were to occur, then Y would occur⌝.

As for the analysis of subjunctive conditionals I must offer another promissory note. Several analyses have appeared in the literature, most prominently those of Lewis and Stalnaker. Both are complex, involving technicalities that it will not be profitable to set out here. I will remark that I find the Stalnaker treatment more plausible than the Lewis one.[3] Both seem more holistic (Lewis's has still other counter-intuitive features as well) than seems to me plausible.

I attempt with this further adumbration of what is intended to be present in or absent from my analyses of causation: that something causes something does not seem to be essentially linked to anything else that takes place. It may be that this causes that this time, on this occasion but never otherwise before or since. A world, in short, could be causal, even wholly causal – every event having causes, even deterministic causes, every event having sufficient causes – but not be a uniform world. We find ourselves in a universe exhibiting a certain degree of uniformity; we could have found ourselves otherwise located. The uniformity of nature is additional information to anything knowable about the causal structure inherent in particular facts or any aggregate of particular facts of the world. To know that such and such caused such and such is to know something about that situation, viz., that the former made the latter occur, produced it, brought it about (the latter terms are of course synonyms for *caused it*).

Hence, I would deny, what some, I think, would affirm, that from ⌜E is total cause of E'⌝ it follows necessarily that ⌜($\forall E''$) (if E'' is relevantly similar to E, and no factors disrupt the operations of such effects as E'' might have, then ($\exists E'''$) (E''' is relevantly similar to E', and E'' is a causal factor in the occurrence of E'''))⌝ [a causal factor rather than total cause, since there might obtain, in some relevantly similar circumstances, causal overdetermination]. Each occasion is logically (and metaphysically) capable of being different from cases in which genuine causation occurred.

This will not, it is to be noted, have implications for the fact of causal laws or laws of nature. It will favour rather a 'bottom up' instead of a 'top down' conception of natural law. The laws of nature will be conceived as aggregative of such causal interactions as take place in relevantly similar circumstances. Arguably it will be a drawback, or at least an open query, for this conception, why nature is uniform, to the degree that it is. The approximately Humean approach advocated here has to say: that is how things happen to go in the world, this world among the many, and that happens to contain cognizing beings like ourselves.

I have called this approach approximately Humean because it involves seeing the uniformity of nature as contingent and additional to the particular facts of conjunctions of events and states of the world (conjunctions which will be, at least typically, logically and metaphysically contingent). In another respect, however, the view I advocate diverges significantly from Hume. The view I advocate – called *singularism* in a valuable article by Michael Tooley[4] – was articulated clearly by C.J. Ducasse,[5] and is defended by Tooley and Anscombe[6] as well as myself. Singularism dissents from the Humean analysis of causes as cases of constant conjunction. Tooley calls Hume's a supervenience view. In the full story a partial reconciliation with Hume is effected, I believe, in the following way. Hume's methodology involves systematic double analysis of our concepts. On the one hand he seeks to disclose what we mean by a concept. On the other he articulates what he thinks we are entitled to mean by – what experience permits us to assign to – the concept. Self and cause are two central cases of concepts subjected to this process of double analysis in the *Treatise*. Hume thinks our concept of cause includes a notion of non-logical necessity which binds cause to effect. He thinks as well that nature and experience entitle us to no more than a constant conjunction – supervenience – view without necessity. I am at this stage involved in what for Hume is the first of these modes. Whether he is right about the second awaits discussion.

VI

It is important to point out that neither singularism nor anything advocated in this chapter is incompatible with the claim that all actual events that in fact have causes must have had causes or the very causes they did. For all that is argued for here it will be possible that it is essential to some or all of the actual events of the world, and all possible events, that they should have precisely the causal properties, general or specific (being caused, uncaused, deterministically caused, indeterministically caused, being caused by factors of some kind K, being caused by precisely factor(s) F, etc.) that they do have. It is of course not implied by singularism, nor anything argued below, that their causal properties (any or all of them) are essential to actual or possible events. Moreover, my own view is that no causal property is essential to any event. This view, if true, does not follow from singularism and will not be defended in the present context. Singularism is a view about what it is to be caused and to be a cause.

It is the view that resemblances between cases of events and their causes is extrinsic to their having been caused and caused as they were.

It follows that singularism is compatible as well with the claim that, where *F* is an event and *G* is its causes, all *F*s are essentially *G*-caused. Singularism is a thesis about the concept of cause. It permits possible extrapolation backwards – if this *F* was *G*-caused, then all past ones were – but not anticipation, which of course sits well with Hume's lessons on induction. Extrapolation is the appropriately imprecise term to use: we need to have the relevant essentialist data about events to reach even this conclusion about the past. From ⌜this *F* was *G*-caused⌝ it cannot be inferred that any past *F* was *G*-caused, no matter what *G* is (so long as it is logically independent of *F*).

VII

A further comment is required on the clauses in the analysis of total cause respecting deterministic and indeterministic worlds or sub-worlds. I need to argue that both of the latter can be conceived non-holistically, i.e., such that both deterministic and non-deterministic systems are intelligible without reference to larger or surrounding systems of cases, actual or possible, that resemble the particular case in question. By contrast singularism implies that these factors can causally determine that this should occur; and these, in turn, can be maximally causally relevant to the occurrence of that other event; and both being understandable in these ways without even tacit reference to other actual or possible situations, and laws or principles that would apply to them.

I might be granted the point provisionally with an eye on my promissory note on the analysis of necessary and sufficient conditions, in the case of deterministic worlds and sub-worlds. For if that one event could not occur without another can be conceived and can be true, in isolation from any other system in which it holds, it would not be difficult to extend this idea to a whole set of such factors. What about an indeterministic (world or) subworld? What is even meant by this?

The idea is that, even if genuine randomness occurs in a system, such that no immediate causal factors are sufficient for the occurrence of the event, still, if there were factors sufficient for something to take place among a range of relevantly similar alternatives and one of those alternatives does take place, then those factors should be viewed as its (total) cause. Thus, for example, suppose there were genuinely random factors involved in who among very heavy long-term smokers gets lung cancer. So an element of quantum randomness can obtain, and smoker A gets cancer, or not, as that is the case. Positioned as we are, with the possibility of a probabilistic assessment of the

situation, perhaps we know that 97 per cent of the very heavy long-term smokers get cancer but 3 per cent don't and there is no factor – not simply unknown
but none in principle knowable – about .25 per cent of those not afflicted. If
citizen Smith were not one among the 3 per cent who escape, i.e., he or she
does get lung cancer, there will be unanimity that Smith's heavy long-term
smoking was cause of his or her lung cancer. Or maybe we have a case of the
exact position a subatomic particle will occupy following a set of occurrences
and it is indeterminate in principle which position it will be but determinate
that it will be one of a range of locations. Here too I think it is appropriate to
call the immediate factors impinging on the situation, impinging on the range,
the total cause of the event that occurs even if it is indeterminate that it should
be precisely that which occurs.

The idea of 'relevant similarity' appealed to in this part of the analysis
clearly requires explication. Something intuitive is meant here but it would be
desirable to be able to say precisely what is involved. Yet another promise of
future enterprise must be made here.

VIII

We need to face as well the metaphysical possibility of causation at a distance.
There will be immediate factors for an event that takes place far from where it
occurs. Could any of these be a causal factor in the occurrence of that event?
In intelligible mechanics for a world, there needs to be adjacency of space as
well as time in the possibility of a sequence being causal. If causation occurs
at a distance, in the somewhat loose sense in which this is possible, we normally assume mediated or indirect causation. Some distant event sets off a
chain of events that culminate in the occurrence of the event on which we have
focused. To have an interesting case of causation at a distance we need to
think of the causal factors as posed above, viz., as immediate or temporally
overlapping with the event. For this to occur we would have to conceive of a
chain of causal transmission over the space between factor and event that
occurred simultaneously with the operation of the factor. This seems odd but
not impossible.

Could a causal factor fail to involve causally at any time, events taking
place in spaces between where the factor obtained and where the event
occurred? This appears to violate intuitions about minimal constraints on
mechanics for a possible world, quite independent of the actual laws of nature.
Still, it seems conceivable that this could occur and therefore that there could
be causation without mechanics. Something causes something to occur, but
there is no chain through space from cause to effect even though effect and

possibly cause are in space. If it is metaphysically possible, this is something like divine causation (if there were otherwise the possibility of its occurrence).

IX

With immediate causal factors and total causes in place, we come now to the idea of a cause itself or a cause simpliciter. This is an exceedingly difficult concept. It is odd that it should be since this is the central intuitive concept of a cause at the heart of ordinary thought and usage. Suppose we have a situation where a window is broken because someone throws a rock through it. We find it appropriate to affirm that the hurling of the rock at the window caused it to break. However, the hurling of that rock, in those circumstances, is not by itself sufficient to break the window. It is, in those circumstances, just a necessary condition – something which if it had not occurred, the event would not have occurred. We are supposing we have not got a case of overdetermination. Another necessary condition is that the window was not opened five minutes earlier, another that the rock was not blown away or apart by something intervening – Superman perhaps – or that there should have been oxygen present within a mile of the window (since without oxygen there cannot be a human hurler and without the latter, the window would not have been broken). However even though there will be assent to the idea that the presence of oxygen and the absence of Superman may have been causal factors and even parts of the total cause, of the window's breaking, neither, we want emphatically to say, is the cause, or even a cause, of the window's breaking. There is a distinction we want to make between some necessary conditions of an event's occurrence and others. Some are necessary background factors but are not what actually causes the event to occur.

Moreover, some causal cases appear to exhibit a much simpler pattern than we have so far discerned. Let us take the case with which the chapter began, for example: decapitations cause deaths. The decapitation of Charles I was causally sufficient for his death. Don't we here have a very simple straightforward case of a single immediate casual factor which, without the need of the concomitance of any other, produces the effect and is the cause of that effect? From this extreme simplicity we find a neighbour next in a continuum of causal patterns in which a single immediate causal factor (or a few such factors) is sufficient in normal circumstances or 'ceteris paribus,' to produce the effect. For example, a piece of copper is heated and this causes it to expand; but conditions must be normal and other things must be equal. Perhaps slightly further along the continuum will be the case of the match that is struck on the matchbox, causing the match to ignite. Of course there must be sufficient force applied but not too much, the match must not be wet, there must be oxygen in the environment, etc.

My aim is not to elaborate a typology of causal patterns. The variety of causal patterns will be very profuse and the requisite typology complex. My limited purpose is to see whether there can be drawn with some precision the distinction between conditions like the presence of oxygen and the dryness of the match, in that example, and the match's being struck; so that one could call the latter the cause of the match's ignition, but not be stuck with so designating the former; and do so in such a way that continuing states of the world (or parts of it), that do not involve overt change, snow being white, a particular lump of sugar being soluble in water, for example, could also have causes in the same sense.

Some philosophers of science, Carnap, for example, regard this distinction as one that cannot be made for the objective world. These philosophers think that selective attention to some of an event's causally necessary conditions reflects human features but not those of the events independently. For them, we call some causal factors the cause because we are a certain size with brains and sense faculties of the kinds we have and special social, legal, and cultural/ historical concerns. In the world if all factors are truly necessary, then there is no basis for distinguishing systematically between some and others, that will mesh with the results of these habits and features.

This seems wrong to me. I think there is something significantly different about the hurling of the rock, in our example, and the presence of oxygen and absence of Superman. However, I stress the difficulty of justifying this claim.

Initially one may have in mind that, of the factors in the total cause of an event, one (or a small number) may be such that, given the other factors, it is (or they are) sufficient for the event's occurrence. There is the idea that, if the other factors were held stable, the cause simpliciter should be the one that then is sufficient for the event. The trouble is that this would qualify every causal factor as the cause. For every causal factor will be such that, given the rest of the causal factors, it is sufficient to produce the event.

We need perhaps to divide the cases of events or states into those involving stasis and those involving change: i.e., the ones where the cause of something continuing to be the case and the cause of something having occurred that was not previously the case are concerned respectively. I will attempt to identify the causes that may not be total causes for the latter case and then leave this whole, difficult, problem for further enterprise. For the match of causality with the world still awaits discussion.

If we are concerned with cases of change, it seems clear that among those factors which causally contribute to that change we can distinguish the dynamic from those that are static. A static factor is one where in the regions of space or time in which it obtains, in the factor interval – the time period during which the factor is a factor for the event under consideration – that factor stays as it was. It obtains during that interval and some time period prior to it, and during both intervals involves no change in the causation that occurs. A dynamic factor is a different matter. During its factor interval, it involves change that affects what occurs.

As well, we can distinguish reasonably between immediate factors that do and those that do not, involve particulars and kinds actually present at the occasion of the event. In an obvious sense, if Superman's being absent or there being no bauxite nearby are immediate causal factors of an event's occurrence, they fail to involve Superman or bauxite, respectively, in the vicinity of what occurs. We may say that an event is constituent-present iff every particular and such instances of kinds as it involves are present, in space and time, where and when the event is. We may now propose the following:

Where an event E is a case of *change*, the aggregate of its immediate causal factors $C_1, C_2, ... , C_n$ constitute the cause of E iff $C_1, C_2, ... , C_n$ are dynamic, constituent-present immediate causal factors of E.

Finally on the themes being explored here:

$C_1, C_2, ... , C_n$ are causes of E iff $C_1, C_2, ..., C_n$ constitute the cause of E, or there is a sequence of events $E_1, E_2, ... , E_K$, such that each E_i is the cause of a unique member of the sequence (save E_K), and $E_K = E$.

The account of (efficient) causation offered here will need to be a programmatic part of a general account of causality in all forms and at all levels. It is intended that all cases of causality, including complex cases of social and natural causation, individual and generic, should be reducible to the fundamental type of individual efficient causation. While this may not be implausible, demonstrating it in detail is a large task that has only been sketched in outline here.

X

I go on to the question of extent. How accurately does our concept of causality correspond to what would be in the world even if no intelligent beings existed? And how wide is the territory it claims? Can we conceive anything to escape causality, and if so, by how much?

As with the conceptual analysis of causality problem, so also with what I call the extent of causality problem (in both cases they are really a cluster of problems), what is to a large degree thoroughly covered ground will be here explored anew. Positions advocated will be not unfamiliar ones nor particularly controversial though some are contested.

I begin by repeating the opening claim of the chapter. There is causality in the world. When Charles I was decapitated, that caused his death. If we are content to regard Charles I as a metaphysically bedrock particular – an existing substance (even if, possibly, an aggregate substance, composed of constituents) and not a mere logical fiction – and we regard decapitation and death as real states of the world (even if they have the complexity of constituent states), then it seems right to regard the causal relationship between these two things that happened to Charles I as on the same plane of 'ultimacy,' as no less real or self-disclosing. There is no reason to regard causation as involving a deeper degree of appearance disguising the objective nature and structure of that part of the world (in either physical or logical space), than is the case for decapitation and death. At any rate, the challenge is at the door of those who think causality is primarily phenomenal to show this. The prima facie position is not just that causality is objectively in the world but that it is as objectively there as the events or states it links.

This does not preclude some measure of appearance or illusion in our concept of causality. The direct Hume-inspired question – do in any sense causes necessitate effects? – brings into sharp focus a central part of this concern.

XI

The analysis of causality offered above may be thought at first to have skirted the Humean question. That analysis did not involve a species of necessity in the causal relation. However the conditional at its core – the causal conditional – leads to the same conundrum. ⌐If C did not occur, E would not occur⌐, if true, invites the query, why? What could there be about C that would have the consequence that, failing it, E would not happen; rather, what could there be in the linkage between C and E that would have this result? Particularly if, as for the singularist account defended here, the result in question is not to be conceived as intelligible by reference to repetitive patterns of which it is an instance? What can there have been but a forcing (in John D. Trimmer's [1950][7] phrase), a producing (in Mario Bunge's [1959]),[8] a making, i.e., a sort of necessitating? Mere concomitance is plainly insufficient for causation, and, on our Ducassian view, we will not have recourse to the concomitance's being constant or even usual since a universe might be exhausted by a single causal event.

I cannot say often enough that my concerns here are metaphysical, not epistemological; nor are they those of the philosophy of science. I take for granted that verificationism in all forms, including Wittgensteinian or Dummettian ones, is false; that some things might be quite undetectably. Further, that where arguments or claims in semantics (and philosophical semantics) have anything other than trivial or hypothetical metaphysical implications, that is ipso facto, all by itself, a refutation of those arguments or claims.

With that reaffirmed, Hume's queries are very sensible. Granted that there would be a difference between decapitations merely preceding deaths, and decapitations causing deaths, once, usually, or always; and granted that we have in mind something for the latter idea that exceeds what is in the former, and that it is difficult to see what it would be if not a kind of necessity. As to what kind of necessity we conceive in causation, there are two options neither of which offer much illumination; either the idea is primitive, a *sui generis* notion perhaps found in connection with our own activities (willing or intending and resulting physical motions); or, as Hume evidently held, it is a transferred or analogical notion, borrowed from logic, mathematics, and conceptual relationships.

Nonetheless, Hume's observation stands: we do not observe or experience any such thing as the causal necessity that we impute to the relation between a cause and its effect. This is not a merely sceptical point. There just is not as an isolable component of what we experience when the causal relation holds or even as a more abstract, functional, or structural feature of the relation, the necessity part.

This suggests that there is something problematic about assuming necessity to be there, even though we do so and this seems to be built into our very concept of causality (and is not as Hume supposed merely an accompanying behavioural habit). We do so Hume or no Hume and we are surely right. There is a difference between something happening and its having to happen; it is thus in the world and we sometimes get it right when that difference obtains, or fails to obtain. Nonetheless we are glaringly short of holding up the mirror to nature in the case of our concept of causality and this needs to be acknowledged and resolved.

I have so far said nothing about Kant's solution or a Kantian solution to this problem. Of the two alternative accounts of causal necessity, this is a special case of a *sui generis* view. It takes the concept of causality, with its distinct species of necessity, to be innate, and also 'transcendental,' in Kant's sense of that term. However it is difficult to see how Kantian transcendentalism can avoid the subjectivism that empiricist opponents impute to it. Of course you're supposed to have gotten Kant wrong if you think the presuppositions of any possible experience are merely Whorf-like categorial filters for our species but I am unable to come to any alternative interpretation that is clearly coherent. Anyway Kant is definitely wrong to think that the world of things-in-themselves certainly fails to correspond to our concepts. It (at least) may do so, and we have powerful reasons for thinking that in the case of causality it does do so.

Provisionally I find myself drawn to a view that is a modified version of Kant's view. It could also be described as a (considerably) modified version of Hume's view. According to this revised Kantian view, a causal concept is innate. We are pre-wired to utilize one and do so without sensory cuing. We have been fortuitously constituted in this regard because we are generally right to expect causes of things that occur, those causes necessitating or nudging their effects (in contrast to cases of merely accidental correlation). Some of the ideas in so-called naturalist epistemology according to which we are naturally selected to have true beliefs, seem to dovetail attractively with this modified Kantian picture of an innatist predisposition to find causality in the world we experience and what that world actually (but otherwise undiscoverably) contains. Yet we can think of something occurring without a cause. Kant was wrong to suppose we cannot. Indeed nature can contain and possibly does contain causeless events or states. However mysterious and rationally repellent the idea seems, we can get used to the idea of such things, as the fortunes of modern physics shows.

The necessity which we assume to be constituent in the bond between cause and effect is only correctly located there (if anywhere). Thus the necessity attaches to the relation not to the relata. Neither causes nor effects by themselves are necessary in this sense. Moreover it is not ill-formed or incoherent to assert the necessity of events by themselves. Indeed this is often done, although always, I think, carelessly and misleadingly. It is coherent but always false to affirm that a given event had to occur. What is accurate (if any assertions of natural necessity are) is the claim that some event had to occur given its causes, which is an alternative though an easily misleading way of saying that causes necessitated the event, since everything modal in the situation resides in the link or the relation, rather than the events (or event aggregates). Comprehending this is the key to the truth of compatibilism in the free will-determinism issue, i.e., to seeing that determinism, even if it were true (as it seems it is not) would not preclude genuinely free actions.

If our world contains not only determinist subsystems but also indeterminist ones – hence is not, as a full system, determinist – and if we acknowledge, and indeed, emphatically affirm with Hume, that we can conceive causeless occurrences, then we must face finally the query: how contra-causal can a world be?

In fact I think the answer to this will be implicit in positions already argued for above. If the singularist view on causality is correct, and the uniformity of nature (to whatever degree) a fact additional in a world to any particular causal connections it contains, and there can be wholly causeless events, then a world could contain any proportion of caused to uncaused constituent events. Hence there will be worlds in which lots happens and nothing is caused to happen; worlds in which everything – or any number of events short of everything – merely happens to have happened (even given what preceded) and nothing had to happen (given the same). This will include the possibility of statistically improbable worlds, worlds, for example, in which there is a continuous run of 93,008 tossings of fair coins landing heads each time, even though each time 'it was an accident,' a 50/50 chance. As so many pathways seem to show independently, we find ourselves as we do, situated world-wise as we happen to be. In Margaret Thatcher's remark, as she departed from political power, it's a funny old world.

Formal Summaries of Concepts or Principles That Appear in This Chapter

Spatial Immediacy
If E takes place in space S, and E' takes place in space S', then E and E' have spatial immediacy iff S and S' partly coincide or [if desired] are such that there is a point at which E is occurring such that no point is between that point and some point at which E' is occurring.

Immediate Causal Factor
X is an immediate causal factor of Y iff (1) without X occurring (or obtaining), Y would not have, (2) X is logically and metaphysically independent of Y, (3) X temporally overlaps with or is tangential to Y, (4) X is not wholly subsequent to Y.

Total Cause
Where w is a world or sub-world (isolable part of a world): The aggregate of $X_1, X_2, \ldots, X_n$ is total cause of an event Y, in w iff each X_i is an immediate causal factor in the occurring of Y, and, if w is deterministic, then the aggregate of $X_1, X_2, \ldots, X_n$ is causally sufficient for the occurrence of Y, i.e., if $X_1, X_2 \ldots, X_n$ obtain, then Y would not not occur, and if w is indeterministic, $X_1, X_2, \ldots, X_n$ is causally sufficient for the occurrence of some event within a range R of relevantly similar events, and Y is within R.

Support

⌜If X occurs, then Y would occur⌝ entails ⌜ if (X occurs but it isn't known that it did or X doesn't occur) is or were to be the case, then (from or in that situation) if X were to occur, then Y would occur.⌝

A Falsehood

From ⌜E is total cause of E'⌝ it follows necessarily that ⌜($\forall\, E''$) (if E'' is relevantly similar to E, and no factors disrupt the operations of such effects as E'' might have, then ($\exists\, E'''$) (E''' is relevantly similar to E', and E'' is a causal factor in the occurrence of E''').

Constituent-Present

An event is constituent-present iff every particular and such instances of kinds as it involves are present, in space and time, where and when the event is.

The Cause, for Changes

Where an event is a case of change, the aggregate of its immediate causal factors C_1, C_2, ... , C_n constitute the cause of E iff C_1, C_2, ... , C_n are dynamic, constituent-present immediate causal factors of E.

Sequences of Causes (for Changes)

C_1, C_2, ... , C_n are causes of E iff C_1, C_2, ... C_n constitute the cause of E, or there is a sequence of events E_1, E_2, ... E_K, such that each E_i is the cause of a unique member of the sequence (save E_K), and $E_K = E$.

Chapter Twelve

Purpose

I

That people and other conscious beings have purposes when they do things is not seriously contestable. This is one of the distinctive features of mental life as we know it. We act often with an end or goal in view; we conceive of (or imagine) something we desire or strive to bring it about and succeed or not depending on the case (our abilities, the realizability of the goal, interfering circumstances).

So there are purposes in the world. They are best understood by reference to states of imaginative or conceptual consciousness trained on the future. It seems plausible to suppose that such goal-directedness is a much more elaborate and sophisticated variety of features of systems, living and non-living, where no attribution of consciousness or intelligence would be made. In some such cases the system was designed by intelligent beings, ourselves, to be goal-directed (heat-seeking missiles, for example), so this is just our purposiveness at one remove. In other cases natural systems not designed by conscious and intelligent beings exhibit traits that resemble goal-directedness or purposiveness. An earlier age of philosophy – supremely in the Christian thirteenth century – sought to make a case in this widely evident phenomenon for belief in an overall guiding and creative hand for the world. Contemporary inquiry tends to take an approach that wholly reverses that earlier one: rather than see apparent purposiveness in intelligent nature as pointing to unseen high intelligence behind phenomena, modern naturalist investigation seeks to show that our purposiveness derives from and resembles completely unintelligent and automatic mechanisms of the world – variations on the theme of the flower that opens its petals to the sunlight not because it wants to or because someone wants it to but because the warmth of the sunlight triggers the possibility of its absorbing the wherewithal for its survival.

There are two problems regarding purpose that have not been wholly solved and which deserve consideration within metaphysics. One is a technical topic, and the other is anything but technical. Both were introduced to philosophy by the ancient Greeks.

The more technical problem of purpose stems almost entirely from the thought of Aristotle. In assigning teleological themes to him, I am not primarily concerned with historical or textual accuracy, although I think the views I discuss fit both history and texts. Aristotle or 'Aristotle,' an imaginary philosopher who really held the views I shall assign to Aristotle, held that objects have ends, telea, as part of their nature: there is for every object an end or purpose for that object. Aristotle also held this to be true of activities or states of various kinds. It is natural to think that Aristotle has been guilty of a bad inductive inference, and attributed to all objects a trait which only applies – and only can apply – to some of them, namely the implements or artefacts, objects that have been made by intelligent beings precisely in order to fulfil some purpose that those intelligent beings had. For example, the purpose or end – the what-it-is-for – of a lawn mower is to cut grass because that is what people made them for. The lawn mower has that telos derivatively: it has that purpose only because we have that purpose.

Aristotle's idea, however, seems more plausible than this. Just as machines and artefacts have purposes even though they are unthinking, so we attribute purposes to bodily organs and other inanimate parts of nature. In these latter cases – unlike lawn mowers, there is no intelligent being (apart at any rate from a God if there were one) whose purpose it is that these objects have the purposes which we assign to them and which many say they objectively possess. The purpose or function of the heart is to pump blood and that of the liver is to secrete bile while the colouration of animals serves to camouflage them from predators and so on.

Aristotle seems to have generalized from certain living systems or constituent parts of them. He comes to the idea of an objective, 'natural,' creator-independent what-it-is-for for all individual living substances and possibly also for non-living ones. This is an idea hard to even grasp, much less submit to the tribunals of evidence. A lawn mower, sure; a kidney, acceptably so. In that former case, as we have said, its telos derives from those of its intelligent creators; in the latter, as we shall enlarge upon, the telos may be reducible to mechanical and non-teleological features of the world. However, to ask of a tulip, a tree, a lion, a human being, What is it for? What is it there to do (or be)? may well seem puzzling at best.

Aristotle, however, can give the idea greater motivation and point. Living objects can be in a thriving and flourishing condition. A plant can droop with its leaf tips brown or it can be strong, erect, with leaves fully green. Similarly animals are in a condition of health, thriving and flourishing, or otherwise. This suggests to Aristotle that an animal's telos might be held to be a matter of being the way the animal or plant is and perhaps doing the sorts of things the plant or animal does when it is thriving. Of course, it will be said, individuals, members of plant and animal species, differ in what they are like when they thrive. Well then, the Aristotelian response will be, take averages, generalities, characteristic states and patterns of a flourishing thing. However even this will vary with the sort of environment the organism is in; moreover, living things begin, develop, then age, wither, and die: shall we say the telos of an old decaying organism is to return to its more vigorous yesterdays? The Aristotelian response will be: we talk of normal and natural environments. The telos will be a function of those; artificially varied environments will be irrelevant to characteristic and normal conditions, within which there will be characteristic patterns of health, species by species. As for the growth and decay cycle: the organism's telos will be to enact precisely that, to have or have had a natural, thriving life that is characteristic of that species.

How far is this train of thought worth pursuing, and what will be its metaphysical significance? If the concepts of the normal and the natural are meant purely descriptively, it is difficult to believe that much of substance will survive counterfactual reflection. If the normal and natural are simply what happens most of the time it will be plain enough that circumstances which are now neither normal nor natural could easily become so. If nature for an organism is the condition in which that organism is in the highest state of health and vigour, for a maximum of its faculties and constituent systems, then the 'natural' condition for any organism could, in principle, be achieved by conscious manipulation by intelligent beings, using artificial means and inducements. There is no doubt a common-sense concept of the natural that would exclude the latter: it is supposed to be operative in determining whether an Olympic games victor has won fairly. It is difficult to believe, Aristotle and common sense notwithstanding, that there is a clear objective notion here. Is it natural to wear clothes, for men to shave, for people to perform non-procreative sexual acts? It is difficult to believe that there can be intelligent and plausible negative answers to these questions and virtually impossible to believe that there could be negative answers with metaphysical import. This is then a night in which all cats are black. Whatever is is natural, and if the normal is non-normative – i.e., isn't a matter of what ought to be the case – then being normal lacks metaphysical import because it can vary without variance in the internal states and properties (essential or otherwise) of substances. Objects do not have telea.

This does not of course have any direct bearing on the complex of problems in the philosophy of science, and for metaphysics, having to do with teleology: can all teleological and functional description and explanation be replaced with non-teleological and non-functional description and explanation? Or are there irreducibly teleological or functional facts of the world (apart from facts of conscious beings having purposes)?

It would seem that it almost defines a naturalist view of the world to hold that there are not, i.e., to hold that all purposiveness is the purposiveness of conscious beings, and that all appearance of end or function can be reduced to a reality of causal relationships. The divide between teleological and anti-teleological conceptions of the world runs very deep, and appears explicitly early in the history of philosophy, with Heraclitus, Anaxagoras, and the atomists appearing as anti-teleologists. The philosophy of Aristotle complicates the issue somewhat. As in so much he means to strike the middle ground and find a compromise between antithetical schools and positions. His idea of a natural telos, inherent in substances without need or benefit of exterior designers, may have been intended as a central instance of such a compromise. We have judged it unsuccessful. If the argument is sound and we continue to operate with naturalism as our working methodological assumption, the result is that we side with the anti-teleological perspective of Anaxagoras and Democritus. There will be no decisive knock-down argument that this is the correct way. Instead we adopt a position that seeks reductions of apparent ends or functions in science piecemeal.

It seems clear that – Aristotelian universal teleologism rejected – purpose is limited to living (or nonliving but conscious) beings or systems and their artefacts. The general position I advocate would accept purposiveness as literally accurate for conscious beings or systems, and dependently accurate for their artefacts: that is, applicable to those artefacts by virtue of conscious aims or purposes the creators of the artefacts had, and be eliminated in favour of causal relations, including possibly causal relations peculiar to living systems, in the cases of living but non-conscious beings or systems.

The last of these categories is one that involves special subtleties. Most promising is the idea that a biological system or subsystem has a purpose that is linked to roles this system plays in the survival or successful functioning of individuals or species of the system. It seems wrong to tie this idea conceptually to anything as specific as natural selection or any other mechanism of biological theory. However, the idea that the purpose of a bodily organ or an organic process is a matter of something without which the objects or systems with the organ or process would not function successfully or even survive seems right. The trick is to express the idea noncircularly. It is also necessary to contend with the possible claim that there could be a component in a system whose biological purpose is inimical to the system's success: a mechanism ensuring the individual's death, for example, or the species' extinction. It seems reasonable to reject the latter and argue that biological telea must be at least locally benign with items that promote thriving success or survival at least in the relatively immediate spatio-temporal environment in which the object or system operates. An alternative idea, which I will not take up in what follows, would be to take biological purposes to be essentially homeostatic, that is, to view them as causal mechanisms that tend to keep the biological system operating as it has generally.

There are also logical or categoreal complexities in the picture of purpose which we should favour. Individual purposes are specific and particular. My purpose may be to go to a restaurant to have curry because I hunger for one and want it now. The purposes that organs and organic processes have are not comparably individual. We differentiate event/state tokens and types. We need something more generic than the second of these: state/event/process kinds, of which state/event/process types will be relatively particularized instances. I assume such kinds are formally characterizable, although there is clearly a great deal of technical work involved in justifying this assumption.

Proceeding a little more formally, let us take E, E', ... to range over events, states, or processes, whether of token, type, or kind. Then we might offer the following proposed analysis of purpose: E is a purpose of E' if and only if (1) E' is a state of consciousness of some individual x, consisting of x wanting to bring it about that E occur, or (2) E is a state in an artefact y that a conscious individual x has created, and x intends that y should perform E' with a view to bringing it about that E, or (3) E' typically causes it to be the case that E occurs, and E and E' are states of living individuals, and without instances of E' those individuals would not sustain their species identity in the environments they currently occupy and in which they successfully function. If the foregoing works, then the purpose of something could be captured by utilizing Russell's theory of descriptions.[1]

This may be a reasonable place to make some additional informal remarks about reduction. Like takeovers of corporations in the economic sphere, reduction may take two forms, which we may think of as friendly and benign or hostile and malign. Benign reduction explains the reduced entity or trait as a special case of a larger category of thing with which it proposes an integration that will preserve salient features imputed to the reduced entity or trait before the reduction was proposed. You'll still have X's, and they'll still be F, even though we will now understand them better by seeing that they are also G's. With malign reduction the entity or trait is unmasked, so to speak. It had been viewed at special or immune with a character unlike anything else, and it is now seen that its special character is not only not special but in some sense fraudulent. Extreme malignity will of course produce elimination, not reduction at all. Maybe you do still have X's, but they are now seen not to be F or F-ishness not really as formerly understood. It appears clear that some central and important concepts, entities, and traits, are benignly reducible to others; and some are malignly reducible; with it being critical to recognize and signal which cases are which. Minds (the mental) are (is) benignly reducible to brains: the electro-chemical, central, neural system of the body. Freedom is benignly reducible to particular sorts of causality. It is possible, on the other hand, that acting in ethical rationality is malignly reducible to something else – so Hobbesians and other sorts of naturalists appear to argue. The reduction of natural telos to causal relations that tend to favour effective survival is, I would suggest, more malign than it is benign, for it revises how we look at the world in wholly naturalist directions.

II

The largest teleological question will, formally, be settled by the methodological resolve of seeking reductive elimination of purpose in nature piecemeal or wholesale. But the big question deserves to be addressed for its own sake, partly because it is one of the questions most often asked of philosophy by non-philosophers and most often evaded, by the professional philosophical practitioner. This is the second, grand and interesting question signalled at the beginning of the inquiry. Does the world, life, human life, or my life have a purpose, end, or meaning – and if so, what is it?

One of the most difficult things about this question is deciding just what it is. Or whether there may not be more than one question – perhaps quite different in kind – concealed in its formulation. Possibly a purpose or end that the universe might be held to have might be significantly different from a purpose or meaning that life might carry, and both different in turn from a meaning or purpose that I might come to believe my own life had. I will assume for now a single query for this topic but raise again whether its several cases may have their own features. Conceived as one question it is certainly not pellucid just exactly what it is that it asks. This is indeed the means or route by which academic philosophers typically dismiss and avoid this question. If the question is incoherent, ambiguous, or trivially answerable in the negative they can hardly be faulted for failing to satisfy this variety of inquiry.

Yet there is or can be something honest and searching in this question. It is evasion to trivialize and patronize this inquiry. It deserves sympathetic focus until a univocal question emerges from that process; whether or not, once rendered so, the question will have an answer.

I don't know how far I will be able to get with the attempt to formulate with some precision what may most plausibly be meant by the question, What is the purpose of (the world, life, my life)? still less what may be hoped for as a possible answer. However, some considerations do seem to emerge from reflection on this matter.

First, contrary to natural things to suppose and what certainly analytic philosophers would commonly suppose, the large teleological question is not, at least primarily, an ethical question. It may have ethical implications or dimensions, formal or informal, but many concerns quite obviously not ethical have ethical implications or dimensions. If one could know what the purpose of the world was, that would not, without providing additional normative principles, tell someone what they ought to do or what the good is. That something was the purpose of the world but not something we or someone should seek to reify or continue, might seem odd; but it's not impossible. Indeed if there is a normative component in matters of high purpose it could be isolated from other normative or ethical matters and one could be completely agnostic or sceptical about the latter.

Ethics is conceived along various categoreal lines by different philosophers. According to one point of view axiology or the theory of value is a part of ethics. According to another, things are the other way around and ethics is a part of axiology. While cosmic purpose may not seem directly connected to what I should do, it may be more plausible to link it to the study of intrinsic value. Perhaps the identification of something as the end or purpose of life or of the world attributes maximal intrinsic value to it. Intrinsic value or worth may be seen in turn as the same thing as, or very closely linked to, what is good in itself or the good.

I do not wish to make firm judgments in this conceptual territory. There are reasons, albeit not compelling ones, for both subsuming axiology in ethics and differentiating them. While it appears correct that whatever is good in itself is of intrinsic value, the converse is not so obvious. Moreover not quite self-evident is whether judging that something was the purpose, meaning, or end of the world (life or my life) should be held to imply that it had intrinsic value or worth.

Ethical normativity aside, high purpose queries seem to be the expression of a search for explanation or intelligibility of some kind. If one could know what the purpose of life is, something would have been rendered intelligible and not just tautologically. Moreover, high purpose queries are questions of comprehensive intelligibility. This above all makes them metaphysical in character. If someone could know what the purpose of the world is, something with systemic or systematic bearing on all of the parts of the world would be known too; and knowledge of the purpose of life, or of my life, would also – it seems clear – be fundamental and explicative knowledge of life and myself in relation to the whole of reality.

Of course all sorts of sceptical – or honestly inquisitive – queries suggest themselves. Why just one purpose? Why not a multiplicity? Might something have been the purpose of life once but no longer be? Could something be the purpose of the world or life but we are simply unable to discover it? Or able to guess that it might be but quite unable to know it? This is a quest easy to deride, dismiss, or be doubtful about. Yet earnest inquirers continue to search for something they hope this question or others like it to formulate.

Aristotle and his conception of a telos may be relevant to this matter. Aristotle meant telea to have a place within a naturalist understanding of the world; whereas the purpose of the world or life would not be that at all. It seems impossible in principle to be a specialist of detail – to have a Ph.D., for example, or a research grant – in the meaning of life. Yet the idea is that someone could get things wrong and think something was the purpose of the world but it wasn't, something else was. The purpose of the world should be something like an Aristotelian telos.

Should we perhaps see our question as more properly three or more questions? Might substance be given to the idea that a purpose for the universe could be one thing, a purpose for life another, and a purpose for my life still a third? Life is in any case indeterminate in this context, comprehending human life and all living things, and if we raised deep questions for both we would have perhaps a fourth teleological query.

Many thinkers, from extraordinarily different theoretical perspectives – Catholic, neo-Marxist, Schopenhauerian,[2] ecological, etc. – have seen a value and a conceptual centrality in life as such that others do not share or even understand. I confess that I am closer to the second constituency than to the first. I have argued, as many philosophers do, that there can be nonliving conscious beings, and consciousness, or, more widely, sentience, will seem more fundamental in significance to the second persuasion than will a cluster of DNA molecules. Some thinkers perhaps mean sentience when they speak of life or an inclusive disjunction of sentience and life.

The special case of myself and my life (that is, of course, for everyone, themselves and their life) poses its own teleological puzzles. A prominent philosophical constituency of recent years has made use of the literary notion of a narrative. Imbued with this conception, they have thought that an individual human life has meaning to the extent that it has a certain narrative structure with the 'closure' of what may have been critically wounding experiences or challenges at basic life-transitions, and an overall completion that resembles a satisfying work of fiction. Here too I find myself on the other side of the matter. I resist the idea that my life should aspire to pleasing literary structural features or that it has less value or meaning if it does not. The meaning of my life does not need to be a good tale or narrative. Of course this response may miss what the more thoughtful advocates of the idea of narrative have in mind.

I have no satisfying answers to the doubts that these queries and reflections raise. Yet I persist in the conviction that there is something significant in the fundamental teleological desire and something rational in the possibility of its resolution.

What are the possibilities for the purpose of the world/life/my life? What have some thought might be what it is all about? To do your duty, as Kantians, morally, in the widest sense suggest? Courage? This is the pre-Christian Norse idea, interestingly conceived conjointly with the conviction of approaching and final chaos, the moral equivalent of the heat death of the universe. Love? Some versions of Christianity, and the 1960s Woodstock ideal, advocate this. Knowledge? Many philosophers and scientists would affirm its claims as the telos. Endlessly expansive free rational consciousness, reflecting on reality and itself in relation to reality as Hegel speculated? An experience of ineffable union with the whole of reality as mysticism advocates?

I am willing to disclose my own leanings. If I could succeed in motivating, taking seriously, and having some confidence that I understood what this enterprise is – and I am honestly unsure whether I can, though I remain hopeful of its possibilities – I find myself drawn to some version of a Hegelian answer to these teleological questions for all three (world, life, my life). If anything, it is Absolute Knowledge itself which is Hegel's way of characterizing the idea of free rational consciousness, continuing toward knowledge and understanding, including ever-deeper self-understanding. However, I am of a philosophical temperament and I know that others, as fully citizens of the world as I, are not and with that I leave this serious and mystifying theme.

Chapter Thirteen

Persons, Personal Identity, and Metaphysical Luck

I

In this chapter I want to come to some conclusions about persons – ourselves and beings like us, if there are any that are in this respect like us. A good deal has already been said, in earlier chapters, about persons; and some views argued for in discussing essence and substance will now be set out more fully and defended. Let us, initially at least, begin afresh and bring the earlier discussion and results into the investigation as it proceeds.

The term 'person' has a number of uses or applications, both philosophical and extra-philosophical. I should say explicitly right at the beginning that I use the term to signify the being we refer to when we use the word 'I.' 'Persons,' in this sense, are, in effect, the plural of 'I.'[1] Other concepts of persons that may have a role in theories of various sorts – legal, juridical, moral, etc. – that do not coincide with the idea that a person is an 'I' (whether or not at a particular time and in particular circumstances, capable of conceiving of or referring to itself as an 'I') will not be what the present chapter is about.

A person is a substance that is conscious or has experiences. Persons are also characterized as selves. They are typically regarded as beings that are, at least at some stages of their existence, capable of deliberate action. Every reader of this book is a person as is its author. We are all human beings. So at least some human beings are persons.

It seems to me that many philosophers have over-mystified persons, and what it is to be one, from both ends of the philosophical spectrum. That is, many idealist, dualist, and hermeneutical and phenomenological philosophers have had mistaken and unjustifiably elevated notions of persons as inappropriately simple entities or as things that are not part of the natural world; and often allegedly tough-minded empiricist and materialist philosophers have had a similar conception usually as prelude to trying to make trouble for the idea. As I see it, person is a peculiar kind of classification we give to cases, all of which in our actual experience are cases of living terrestrial organisms but by virtue of which we pick out something we take to be distinctive of those and other possible beings that would not in fact need to be terrestrial or even, perhaps, living. *Person* does not identify a species or set of species; in that respect it resembles *quadruped* or, better, *multiped* which can apply to both giraffes and caterpillars. Something is a person by virtue of certain kinds of processes or states occurring in the thing or typically occurring in things of that sort. These processes do not imply genetic affinity, though of course there may be such an affinity. Being a person is conceived as a very central trait of the things to which it applies. Some hold it to be essential to those things, in the strongest metaphysical sense. Whether that is correct or not I shall side-step for now.

I want to emphasize what so many philosophers neglect: the species-like character and the naturalism of being a person. Persons can have sublime thoughts. They can also be photographed and hit by cars. A great many persons, at least in many modern societies, have birth certificates, which make it possible to infer how long the person has existed, at any rate what the duration of the person's existence is since their birth. I take it, moreover, that something is a human person if and only if it is a human being; and that this pattern holds for every natural species with members that are characteristically persons. Thus for every such species *F*, something will be an *F* person if and only if it is an *F*. The biconditional here may only be a material one but it does express something true.

The upshot of this will be, part of it at least, that the concept of a person should be expected to pose some of the conceptual and possible cases challenges that species natural kind concepts do, and should not be assumed to pose any other challenges than those concepts do; not unless special additional argument is given. Maybe *person* is an underdetermined concept: that is, one for the application of which there are sufficient but not necessary conditions. If so, and if currently prevailing views on species terms are correct, it will resemble *horse* and *frog* in that respect, neither of which seem any the worse for that, as correctly and literally applying to items of reality.

Further, there are complex and daunting challenges in trying to come to conclusions about personal identity, the problem of what it is for a person existing at one time to be numerically the same as a person existing at another time. Yet so there are for other cases of identity over time for kinds of things, e.g., human beings. Indeed, if some common-sense views are correct, the problem of personal identity is just about the same problem as the problem of human identity. Not quite, since some persons, it seems, are not or would not be human beings. However, for human persons, if you knew that human being x at time $t1$, was numerically identical to human being y at the time $t2$, and why (or that they were not and why not), you would know ipso facto the same things about human persons and conversely. Possibly as Derek Parfit and others argue, there are imaginable cases where no empirical or observational information could tell us that this case was or was not identical with an earlier person. The same thing is true of human beings. It will also I believe be found to be true of animals that aren't persons. Bizarre science fictional cases can readily be devised where we will hesitate and be unsure whether to affirm or withhold identity (over time) between one earthworm, moth, or spider, and another.

II

I want as much as possible to avoid merely semantic issues. Once we have targeted a set of individual substances which we take clearly to be persons – whatever else may be true of them – it is more important that we come to conclusions about basic and enduring features of those substances (and others like them), than that we reach consensus about what should be put in a philosophical dictionary for the term *person*. Is it analytic that, if something is a person then it is conscious and has experiences? I would say certainly not. However, Locke and some philosophers since have supposed otherwise.

I shall take it that most, possibly all, human beings are persons for all of the time that they are living. This will leave open whether a five-week-old fetus is a person; just as it is open whether a five-week-old fetus is a human being. I stipulate then – and invite the reader's concurrence that this is at least a plausible stipulation – that

$\forall x \, \forall t$ (if x is a human being at t, then x is a person at t).

Less clear is whether we ought to deny personhood to all other terrestrial creatures than humans. Are chimpanzees persons? Gibbons? Dolphins? Dogs? Amoebas certainly are not persons, I would say. Earthworms also are not. Where are the lines of demarcation to be drawn however?

Some want to limit persons to the class of things that are rational or potentially rational while others confine it to those that are conscious (or potentially so); and still others to those that act or are capable of action or that are capable of morality.

One of the curious, and striking things about the investigation of persons is that there is for the most part clarity and agreement about the facts of animal psychology that one would assume are relevant to deciding whether this or that living organism is a person. We may not know well what it would feel like to experience the world as other animals such as bats do, but we know that some non-human animals do experience the world, we know something of the sensory systems of most or all animals, and enough of their nervous systems to identify what, or who, experiences or can experience some degree of pain. Of course this information, like all empirical information, is imperfect and incomplete. On the whole animal psychology, particularly animal physiological psychology, is tolerably well-explored territory, with generally agreed results. This applies as well to that particularly controversial corner of that territory, the matter of the states that are (at least) on the way to becoming experiencing states of creatures that are (at least) on the way to becoming human beings, i.e., human persons, namely, zygotes and fetuses. We have largely pre-empted any need to decide whether or at what stage fetuses are persons, by identifying human persons with human beings. This of course to some degree simply passes the buck, i.e., the query of moral moment will then become, at what stage has something become a human being? In any case both classes of phenomena – human fetuses and 'higher' nonhuman animals (and the shading continuum from them to 'lower' nonhuman animals) – readily suggest reflections that will lead to philosophical conclusions. Virtually all relevant empirical facts are in, and they do not determine for us the precise boundaries of personhood. There is nothing particularly more to find out. So, we ought to infer, the concept of person is not defined for all possible, or even all actual cases, of its potential application. Whether, as Putnam has argued, this is true of natural species terms, it seems definitely to be the case that *person* is underdetermined. There are occasions wholly sufficient for the term's application, and likewise for its non-application; but there are also occasions where there is nothing in the 'logic' of the term that can ensure application or non-application. Dogs, dolphins, and chimpanzees seem to me such cases. If they seem to you certainly to be persons then continue down the mammal hierarchy and you will soon find cases that are indeterminate with respect to personhood. If you think dogs, dolphins, and chimpanzees are obviously not persons, then consider the extinct hominids, which are not ancestors to humans and significantly less advanced cerebrally than humans, though more advanced cerebrally than any living anthropoid ape. Would they be persons? What would or could decide the matter? *Person* is in this respect like being bald. Like the latter, there will be degrees of applicability, a continuum of overlapping states exhibiting traits that in increasing and decreasing degree would justify the term's assignment to the entity manifesting those states.

Baldness, though, would not appear to matter much metaphysically. In spite of the views of some philosophers who would advocate consigning personhood to the level of appearances that do not significantly resemble deeper underlying realities, most people, including most metaphysicians, hold views that would imply that personhood does matter metaphysically. Being me, being the self that I am, or (to take the indexical-free case) being a person is no merely superficial datum in the world for the things it applies to. It reveals a deep fact of the world that is at least fairly literally captured and expressed in the vocabulary of personhood, consciousness, and experiences.

Only a particular variety of physicalism, and physicalist methodology, would exclude that vocabulary from metaphysical, empirical, and scientific perspicuity. I shall assume that the concepts of personhood, consciousness, and experience (and cognates) only require a certain degree of defence or credentials-deployment. They do need some (in principle, every concept does); but I shall assume that their adequacy as potential descriptors of the world need not be conceived as tied to adequacy conditions for well-behaved postulates in contemporary physical theory.

III

There is however a deeper metaphysical problem. Granting that *person* and its companion concepts are potentially plausible candidates for accurate characterization of the real, how can it be that they are both metaphysically 'ultimate,' and underdetermined?

An adequate and sufficient answer to this query is I think the same as can and should be made for natural kind terms like *dog*, *horse*, and *tree*, all of which also appear both underdetermined yet accurate for parts of reality. It is not we, with either our language or our concepts, which determine anything but very small parts of the world. Neither our words nor our ideas make the world as it is; and our words and concepts may only be able to have apprehended, systematized, and internalized parts of what is objectively and determinately in the nature of things. This will not imply that some of our words and concepts may not, so far as they go, capture features of the world. And in the special case of *person*, we have good reason (and no incorrigibilist or foundationalist position need be embraced in affirming this) to think we are in a strong evidentiary position to suppose we have achieved such objective success. It may only be partial. That is, we may only have succeeded in grasping part of what being a person is. However, there seems little reason to doubt that we are indeed on to something.

Let me go on to remark parenthetically on some less central kinds of cases of persons or alleged persons. Although, for legal, ideological, or other purposes certain corporate entities – like business corporations, associations, clubs, societies, even the state – are or may be treated as having some of the important characteristics of persons, or as though they were persons, I shall take this as fiction (whether useful or not), or hyperbole. Similarly, nonliteral persons are the Rousseauian general will,[2] or the group identity that is said to obtain within tribal communities, families, or between or among lovers, friends, or with the mergers of selves held to occur when individuals are regarded as brainwashed or of subverted identity. I should say, in the last group of cases, that I do not mean to rule out a priori what may be real instances of pathology that may complicate or even sabotage locally, if I may put it like that, what a person may be. Indeed, as you will see in what ensues, my conception of persons will be open to such complications. I am assuming the viability of a plausible distinction between the literal and the nonliteral, and between standard or normal kinds of case and radically nonstandard ones; and in those terms there are cases we recognize without great difficulty to be literal and standard instances of persons, and contrasting ones that we see as not literally persons (even if treated for some purposes as though they were persons) or not persons of any standard sort.

Harder to comment on are notions from theology, Christian and non-Christian, of persons as possible components or aspects of a single importantly unitary being. The Christian doctrine of the trinity that affirms the reality of 'God in three persons,' is, for me, deeply opaque; similarly although possibly a little more comprehensible, notions of multiple aspects or manifestations of Hindu gods, and gods of other religious systems, pose a challenge. Notions of transformation (including very rapid transformation), or of presenting appearances (even simultaneous diverse appearances) to an experiencing other or group of others, where the appearances are appearances of a single underlying being – which may fit Hindu and other cases – seem imaginative options we can grasp. However the Christian God is evidently not supposed merely to be experiencable as Father or alternatively as Son, or to transform himself successively from one to the other, but somehow to be both persons. As I say, I cannot figure this one out but I have my doubts whether anyone else can either. In any event I want to put consideration of divine persons aside, at least where notions of them are not assimilable to those we have of the kinds of persons we take ourselves to be.

IV

Not dismissible or of minor significance for the metaphysics of persons, however, are theories of persons or selves as logical constructions, or as 'bundles' of experiences. This idea was introduced into philosophy by Collins, then, more famously, by Hume, who looked within for a self and failed to find one, discovering, instead, only states of experience. He concluded from the experiment that, strictly speaking, selves are fictions; that there are no such things as the stable continuing persons of common and of usual philosophical belief. Rather, Hume affirmed, a self or person, in a non-strict sense, may be held to be an aggregation of causally and spatio-temporally related experiences. Hume's twentieth-century empiricist successors enlarged upon this idea with the notion of a self as a   so-called logical construction out of sets of experiences to which that self is reducible.

As is well-known, Kant, in the *Critique of Pure Reason*, sought to prove that Hume was wrong about the reducibility of persons. The issue continues to be one that divides, and even defines modern empiricists and rationalists. It is, dialectically, if not strictly logically linked to another fundamental fissure between the same parties, also focused on persons: viz., the question of whether or not Descartes was on to something with the *cogito ergo sum* argument of the second *Meditation*.

Whether bundle theories of persons are defensible, or the Kantian argument for the transcendental unity of apperception is sound, are important issues but ones I shall mostly skirt here. I try to deal with Hume and Kant on persons essentially by seeking to go between them: I agree with Hume that we don't need to posit persons, but add that there are many sorts of things we don't need to posit or about which scepticism may be raised that there is nonetheless perfectly adequate reason to suppose real; and I agree with Kant that it is difficult to make sense of ongoing experience, experience understood as enduring and changing over time, except with reference to the idea of a subject whose experience it is, and yet I think that there could be an experience machine that did aggregate representational and affective states sequentially – so it is at least legitimate to ask whether we might not turn out to be instances of such machines.

However, I think Hume and Kant may be navigated between by again pointing out the species-like quality of personhood. One's animality and hominidity are just as phenomenologically elusive as one's selfhood. And yet there seems altogether adequate reason to believe that there are animals and humans. Animal specieshood seems to cut to some degree against both Hume and Kant. At any rate the deeper metaphysical issue seems to be whether there is good and sufficient reason to believe that there are what Bruce Aune and other philosophers call continuants. A continuant 'is a thing that persists through at least some interval of time and that is capable of undergoing change while remaining the same *thing* as before.'[3] In this context I shall simply assume that there are continuants. That assumption made, it seems plausible to acknowledge that among continuants may be reckoned animals, human beings, and persons.

V

I turn now to consideration of a part of the much-discussed problem of personal identity. In what follows, only a little of what I say will not be found elsewhere in this huge literature. Among recent philosophers whose work provides examples to illustrate the themes explored here are David Wiggins, Bernard Williams, Robert Nozick, Thomas Nagel, Derek Parfit, and Bruce Aune. Of the many dramatic imaginary cases these philosophers, and others, discuss, I give attention only to a particular variety, which I will develop in what may be distinctive ways.

Think back over your life to as far as your memories extend. Try to recall two or three particularly vivid occasions of three or more years ago. Focus on yourself, what it is to be you, your progressive, continuing identity as you; savour the ongoing, cumulatively enlarging saga of the set of experiences you have had over the passing years, and the being that has had those experiences. Now suppose – contrary doubtless to what will have been the facts – that two years ago you were awakened one night to find yourself having fallen with a thud onto the floor on the right side of your bed. Let us suppose as well that your bed is not firmly against a wall, so that there are clear open spaces on both sides of your bed. Let us suppose too that on the night in which this particular event occurred you were sole occupant of your room. Having fallen in this most undignified way onto the floor, let us suppose you get up, muttering a succession of expletives, and return to bed, to sleep and the continuing succession of experiences, the continuing life-story that you have had from that extremely minor episode of two years ago right up to the present moment.

Pursuing these imaginative forays further, turn from yourself and your experiences to a very different part of nature, the case of the humble unicellular organism, the amoeba. As you doubtless are aware, amoebas have something happen to them that is standardly called fission – not to be confused with the process that leads to atomic explosions. An amoeba exists for a while, and then it splits, into two new amoebas. At least, that seems to be a reasonably accurate way to describe what occurs. For one period of time there is one amoeba – we could call a particular such amoeba a – and at a time somewhat later there are amoebas, call them b and c, both of which have developed out of a. There has been no interruption in continuous, reasonably well-understood law-like processes, that have produced these two amoebas, b and *c*, from *a*. They are both made of the same organic matter as *a*, as well. Yet, of course, they cannot both be *a*, since neither is the same – i.e., numerically the same – as the other. Since they occupy different spaces, and one might perish while the other continued, etc., $b \neq c$. So at least one of them is diverse from *a*. And since either *b* isn't *a*, or *c* isn't *a* ('or' here is of course inclusive), the reasonable thing to conclude is that neither *b* nor *c* is *a*. It would be quite arbitrary to favour a candidacy of *b*'s identity with *a* over *c*'s, since both are in the same kind of position relative to *a*, and relative to identity with *a*. The right sort of thing to affirm, most students of identity over time will conclude, is that we should not understand the fission phenomenon for amoebas as involving a continuing numerical identity of an original amoeba through the course of one or more successive cases of fission; rather, we should say that, strictly speaking, by the time fission has been completed, at least, and there are two fully separate successor amoebas *b* and *c*, *a* no longer exists. Some time in the course of the fission process two new individuals have come into being. *B* and *c* have only started to exist then; they are new to the universe. This sounds, of course, a little odd. We want to, and can, supply context: although strictly speaking *b* and *c* are new individuals, diverse from anything else there has ever been, their presence in the world is to be explained by reference to their growth or development from *a*.

Now let us return to you. More specifically, and possibly more accurately, let us return to the episode imagined to have occurred two years ago: that thumping fall out of bed. Let us now enlarge the story, in science fictional ways. Let us imagine that human beings can resemble amoebas and undergo fission. Let us imagine that a human being can split, divide into two genetic replicas of the original, or at least earlier, human. Obviously the mechanics of human fission would be imaginatively, and scientifically, challenging. Aune, briefly discussing human fission, imagines a radiation process but without details. Something far more complicated even than cloning – the creation of a replica human from genetic material of a donor human – would be involved. Still, it is difficult to believe that the possible mechanics for adult human fission would be more than imaginatively and empirically challenging – that they would be metaphysically impossible, for example.

Parfit[4] explores at length a kind of fission case in which each of the two halves of the brain of one of a set of identical triplets – and whose body has otherwise been destroyed – is successfully hooked up as the brain for the bodies of the other two triplets – both of whose brains have been destroyed. His query is then: are the two resulting persons identical to any of the original triplets? This really is not fission in the full amoeba manner, since the radical surgery involved complicates the relevant continuities. It is certainly in the vicinity of the idea. David Wiggins and Bernard Williams also discuss variants of this idea.

Subject to an untold story as to how the mechanics of fission might go – and acknowledging that such a possible story would need to be able to be told, with details – let us grant ourselves, what surely is the case, that human beings could undergo fission. And now, let us suppose, when that thump and fall from bed occurred two years ago, what was happening was a case of fission, and when one human being – I said above, perhaps incautiously, that it was you – fell to the floor on the right side of the bed, another genetically 'identical' human being fell to the floor on the left side. Then – to seek to make the story fit what has been the experienced past and present as much as possible – let us suppose that passing extra-terrestrials, seeking a splendid human specimen for their intergalactic zoo back home, and happening to look in on the scene, noticed the human being on the floor on the left side of the bed, quickly grabbed him or her, and returned to their space ship with him/her in a trice, and before the human on the right side of that bed could have become aware of sentient company in the room. Maybe we should suppose too that you always sleep completely without clothing, so that both the fission and the seizure can have occurred without risk of complicating evidence being left behind. The left-side human – your genetic twin – has resided, let us further suppose, in that remote zoo ever since, his/her hosts having now abandoned any plans to return ever to earth.

Now if something along the lines imagined had actually taken place, it seems to me we ought to come to conclusions parallel to those reached about amoebas. If two years ago something like this had happened to a human person, then that human person did not survive the completion of the fission process. There will have been such and such a human, up until then, and then that person will have stopped existing and two new human persons will have come into the world – fully adult ones, never having been children. It will not affect this result that there is spatio-temporal continuity – as there is in the story – from the human that went to bed that night to the human that fell out of bed on the right side, and the human that woke up in the morning. Neither spatio-temporal continuity, nor even spatio-temporal continuity with the same (continuously changing, of course, as it always is) matter, will make a difference, since that genetic double, languishing in that intergalactically remote zoo, is also spatio-temporally and materially continuous, with the human that retired to bed. The same is true for the successor amoebas of an earlier amoeba following fission. That is what makes it a case of fission. This is the feature that defines fission metaphysically.

Nor does it affect the situation that there is continuity of consciousness and memory for the human that wakes up in that bedroom the next morning, back to the human that went to bed the previous night. If, as I am arguing, the human of the following day – call her Helen – is numerically distinct from the human of the day before – call her Ellen – then certain claims regarding memory and consciousness must be revised. It will not be true that Helen will remember having finishing reading a certain book three days before since Helen did not exist three days before. It was Ellen that read it, and Helen has an apparent memory – not an actual or veridical memory – of having read that book. However, she is correct to believe that a person continuous-in-consciousness with herself did that reading; and in general there will be revised phrasings or versions of all Helen's claims or beliefs about her past that will be in the same boat, epistemically and evidentially speaking, as if that fall out of bed had not occurred. Fission imposes, or would impose if it occurred, a duty of systematically careful description or re-description, sometimes to a point of technical and pedantic precision, to enable the things that happen to people to be talked about accurately.

Still such description or re-description being possible, you may say, would it matter very much if fission happened to someone? Even if I did not literally go to school in such and such a place, have so and so as parents and siblings, etc., a person at an earlier stage of 'development into' me, as we might put it, did. In a sense, at least, things that happened to Ellen are things that happened also to Helen; just as things that happened to amoeba *a* are, at least in a sense, things that happened to amoeba *b*. Maybe so but the fact remains that Helen is not Ellen, just as neither amoebas *b* and *c* are amoeba *a*. And it could make a considerable difference, as a little imaginative reflection should make clear. The genetic double need not conveniently disappear. It could stay around, and indeed enter into conflict with the genetic other. There could be legal disputes about which, if either, really owns that Ferrari, or is married to Robert, or owes those thousands to the bank; disputes that might be horrendously complicated, indeed impossible, to solve. Moreover, fission might be multiple. There might be more than two successors to the original person. There might be 3, 19, 804, over a billion of them.

The fact is, I think, we are all lucky that such things, fission, in any form, have not happened to us. That they have not is indeed a necessary condition of each of our personal identities over time. As a matter of fact, from moment to moment, throughout our lives, we only manage to continue to be ourselves by virtue of such luck. There will be, for each of us, possible worlds beyond number in which it does not. And this will be a central illustration of what I mean by metaphysical luck and why this idea is important.

Some will know a famous essay of Thomas Nagel's called 'Moral Luck.'[5]

Its theme is that things can happen that have moral significance that depend on completely fortuitous and morally insignificant circumstances; and that this is puzzling, indeed problematic, for thinking about morality. Metaphysical luck echoes Nagel's notion in similarly locating something puzzling or problematic for a central concept, from possible circumstances that should not have been able to make a difference for it. My continuation as myself is, we suppose, a firmly anchored datum of the world, and something that we see as in principle independent of what might happen externally to me. A sloughed-off person, that happens to be a genetic replica of what I take to be me, ought to count as something happening externally to me. If I manage to keep on being made of the right stuff, and have an ongoing and uninterrupted continuity of time and place and overlapping experience – continuous as subject – that should manage to be all it takes to be and continue as me. Yet, it seems, this is not so. Things that could happen involving other substances could dislodge the fact of my being, yet without changing the natural and law-like progression of things on the ground, as it were; the onward march of nature and of a subject's experiences.

VI

If I may slip briefly into the patois of semi-formal discourse, the idea of metaphysical luck may be given a certain precision. As we did in chapter 6, let us distinguish a thing's intrinsic from its non-intrinsic properties, by identifying an intrinsic property of something at a time t as one whose possession does not semantically imply that anything other than x exists, or that anything at all exists before or after t. (Roughly and briefly, 'p semantically implies q' iff 'if p then q' is analytically true, or the semantical content of q is contained in the semantical content of p.) We can then identify something's intrinsic property set at t as the set of all of the intrinsic properties x has at t. Let us call such a set F.

Then, where F is an intrinsic property set characterizing an object x at a time t, and x is in spatial region r at t, then that x exists at t is a matter of metaphysical luck iff there is a possible world w containing an object y existing at t, and y is not in r at t, and that y is in w at t entails that x is not in w at t.

Thus, metaphysical luck is a matter of something's being able to be 'dislodged into non-being,' necessarily precluded from existence, by the possible presence in the world of something else, with only such intrinsic properties as the extraneous being may have, in some other region than where the original something is.

I submit that the fact of metaphysical luck belongs in the odd but true category. I think its oddity is self-evident. Why should what may be true internally to something else, somewhere else, affect the being of something? Yet it is true, indeed true for every spatio-temporal particular, for any one of them can presumably do, at least in principle (i.e., in some possible world), what amoebas do. Thus, it will be true for each spatio-temporal particular that there is a world where that particular existed at times before our given designated time of focus t, and where, also before t, the particular 'split,' hence, at t that particular cannot exist – because some other competitor particular exists that branched off from it at an earlier stage.

Moreover, I submit that it is untrue that the existence of everything is in this way frail or tenuous. Stuffs or elements, for example – hydrogen, styrofoam, blood, etc. – is ontologically robust. Only particulars are subject to metaphysical luck it seems.

VII

Things are, I think, still more complicated and tenuous than indicated so far. In spite of what I have argued so far, mere fission, as such, might not, after all, terminate the existence of the substance, or object, that split up. Suppose that it was characteristic of a species – maybe even of humans – that it exhibited the or a fission pattern. Suppose also that such fission always – even almost always – resulted in the death of one of the genetic successor-partners very quickly after it occurred, whereas the other genetic successor-partner carried on normally. Suppose such a pattern was fairly regular – once every two years, for example, and the short-lived partner typically died within hours of the occurrence of the fission. Would not we then say that the continuing genetic successor-partner actually was numerically identical to the predecessor individual? Some might say we would not know what to say in the event of such bizarre things as we are imagining. Others might say that, from a metaphysical point of view, it is not what we would say that is important but what would actually be the case. I submit that, if there were these regularly occurring cases of short-lived, spinoff, fission-individuals for a species we would think that single, self-same individual members of the species continued in existence over a span encompassing the fission pattern. We might think that the substance's existence was in some sense in abeyance while the partner was there but once the partner had died we would not hesitate. It would be Fred remembering what it was like back in the old days and what he had done then, even though a fission episode or two had happened in the meantime.

There will, to be sure, be some surprising consequences of taking the view that I advocate here. Some will think them counter-intuitive. For example we might imagine the situation, brief though it might be, during which there are two genetic replicas of a person who had divided, and one of them saying to himself (or to others), with reference to the person who has divided, 'Gee, I wonder if it is me who is he.' That is, all current information might be available, and known to everyone on the scene, including the replicas, but until the death of one of the replicas it would not be known which one was the original all along. That someone is now the same as someone would turn out to be determined by (not just established by evidence that would not become available until) later events. There would be no reason to regard this as implying backwards causation. It cannot be caused to be the case that Cicero = Tully. Nonetheless, this may seem to some quite intolerable. It does not however appear to meet with formal difficulties (at least, not unless formal constraints on identity over time are devised, and imposed, that will ensure it). And the alternative intimated above, according to which we would regard the existence of the original person as in abeyance, or interrupted (compare the case of a disassembled watch, or car, that is later re-assembled), until the death of one of the doubles, seems still less plausible. On this latter construal, an identifying census of the persons in the world, or in the relevant part of it – an identifying census is one which indicates both how many people there are, and who they are – during the period when the doubles existed, and then another after one had died, would presumably need to affirm that a new person had come to existence in the second period, even though that new one was the same as one from the first. This seems intolerable. Whether or not metaphysical fusion is possible – two individuals becoming one through the reverse of fission – this would not be the situation envisaged. Rather we would have to think of an individual becoming the same as an individual that had not existed before. Just before then, it would seem, that individual both would and would not exist. So, I take it, we really need the first alternative, even with its somewhat odd results.

There would be oddities if we refused to allow that even the briefest fission episode could preserve the identity of the person that divided. That is, holding that fission always necessarily terminates the existence of the individual that divides carries costs. Suppose a 67-year-old human discovered that years before, as an 11-year-old, he had inadvertently walked through a radiation field that induced a fission phenomenon the following night. Unknown to him at the time, a genetic replica issued from his bed in the manner sketched in my original story, but the replica had died fourteen seconds after separation from the double, and the corpse consumed in a fire which happened (due to completely unrelated causes) to have broken out in the family house that evening, the double being rescued unharmed. Only, again quite independently, very sensitive recording and filming machinery had been on in the relevant room and graphically recorded the whole thing, the lost tape now being found, and correctly interpreted. If these things happened, should we believe that this allegedly 67-year-old person is in fact 56, and had never been an infant, or third-grade pupil, and began to exist only when the isolated fission incident had concluded? This would seem implausible and unattractive. Rather, we would rightly believe, I think, that a 67-year-old had had a fission episode occur when he was 11.

Now, if this is what would be right in this relatively clear case, what about the many muddier cases we can readily think of? Suppose the partner lives for many months or a few years? Suppose which successor will live and which will die is signalled by some characteristic trait – left-handedness or a slight cough – that the one typically has and the other lacks. What about a situation where the one that would normally live is accidentally killed while the partner is still alive, and the latter is kept alive and carries on? Would this near-miraculously preserved partner be the original creature? We might well say so but it must seem at least somewhat doubtful that we would be right.

The inference to draw from this is that personal identity – i.e., the conditions under which we should assign or withhold it – is underdetermined, just as the concept of being a person is. Concurrent with drawing that inference we should remind ourselves again that this is true of animal concepts, and animal identity over time. Yes indeed, things could happen such that we would not know what to say or that there would not be anything determinately the case with respect to concepts that had otherwise behaved perfectly satisfactorily. We are lucky such things have not happened. The world continues determinately, contingently, in its kinds, and with its stock of continuing substances, in the absence of such possibilities.

In affirming these views – indeed, in claiming that there is such a thing as metaphysical luck – I must disagree with a foundational position that Bernard Williams advocated for anything being able to be an adequate or successful criterion of personal identity. Williams held that any such criterion must satisfy two requirements. Parfit, discussing Williams, puts them like this: (1) 'Whether a future person will be me must depend only on the *intrinsic* features of the relation between us. It cannot depend on what happens to *other* people'; (2) 'Since personal identity has great significance, whether identity holds cannot depend on a trivial fact.'[6]

I think that the normative concepts – significance and triviality – that appear in the second requirement cannot be assumed to have obvious or metaphysically perspicuous meaning. What is significant or trivial for one set of minds, or occasion, may not be for another. However, the point about metaphysical luck is certainly that it is by virtue of the non-occurrence of phenomena – fission for a human being – the odds against the occurrence of which are astronomical, that we manage to preserve personal identity. A possibility as remote as this I would certainly be prepared to regard as trivial. Of course, if such an event as a human fission actually occurred, it would be anything but trivial. In that sense, I think, as does Parfit, that requirement 2 is false. And since I think that the non-survival, beyond a very short period of time, of a genetic double existing as a result of fission, would permit the continued existence (possibly the renewed existence) of a person, I think that requirement 1 is false as well.

And yet the fact of metaphysical luck, of our metaphysical luck, that certain things that could have happened but did not, does not diminish the reality of our personal identity over time, or the reality and significance of being a person. That a substance exists at all is fortuitous and contingent. For most things the merest breath of difference in the course of nature in the vicinity prior to the creation of the thing would have prevented its existence and typically would have destroyed it soon after its creation. However these counterfactual facts – if they are counterfactual, and the object has managed to come to existence, and continued in it, without (among other hazards) dividing – would not diminish the fact of the object's existence, and its properties, including the properties of being a person and being an adult person, and of having been a blue-eyed child, if those are properties that the object has.

VIII

To sum up: my purposes are essentially twofold. One is to bring attention to the fact of metaphysical luck itself for its own sake. Some things manage to be what they are, continue as they have been, have any history at all, as a function of happening to be in the right world. Conversely there are worlds where all of what happens to them (i.e., in the actual world) does happen, and in some manner 'out of' them but does not happen to them. The second general point is that the concept of an individual particular, a specific concrete substance, even when it is you or me, is more fragile metaphysically than much philosophy has supposed. Fission gives us reason to believe that individual substances – even when they are subjects, centres of consciousness – are not at the deepest level of metaphysical perspicuity. It certainly does not prove that there are no substances; and for my part I would want to resist strongly any argument that would imply that I do not exist. Some philosophers – Hume, Russell, some logical empiricists certain eliminative materialists – have viewed with equanimity the ontological elimination of persons or enduring particulars. I would like to affirm the reality both of persons and other enduring particulars.

However, fission and its implications do at least budge the ontological scales away from particulars. Possibly that may budge the scales towards the deeper, or more primary reality of elements, stuffs out of which things of the world are made, those things themselves having a somewhat perspective-relative being. Metaphysics would return then, in a sense, to Ionian cosmology.

IX

I conclude this chapter with some remarks on difficulties or complexities, raised for persons and personal identity by Derek Parfit. His discussion is rich in a range of examples, which I will not consider here. I take it that he successfully shows that things could happen to a person such that it would be problematic that the person had survived and still existed. As remarked earlier I think the same could be shown for giraffes and frogs. In none of these cases is there reason to believe that persons, giraffes, and frogs do not exist, or that they are not metaphysically significant kinds of things. That something could have become bemired in a fog which would have deprived it of its individuality or made it arbitrary and requiring a community of observers' decisions that it was or was not still there, will not have impact on the clarity of its continuity in the sunlight, if it had the metaphysical luck to do that.

I note further that issues of reduction and identity, that Parfit and others discuss, do not seem to have the pellucid clarity his account suggests. Identity seems most straightforward as a relation between individuals, or between sets: entities taken by one, in both cases. The assertion that an individual is identical to an aggregate is, I think, problematic. Parfit wants to defend the idea that a (human) person is identical to a (human) brain and body. This is supposed to be a reductionist thesis. There are aggregates or objects that are mereological sums of other objects. For example, a man's (or woman's) suit is the mereological aggregate of a jacket and a pair of trousers. A human person would seem not to be an entity of comparable type. Though our personhood, our being a substance that has experiences and is a self, is conveyed by our brains, it seems conceivable that these functions be transmitted, in gradual stages, to another bodily organ (perhaps an organ that became naturally or artificially developed for this role). The ancient philosophers debated whether the brain or the heart was where the soul was located (the Epicureans, for example, opting for the latter). As indicated it seems conceivable that what our brains do get gradually transferred elsewhere in the body. Whether persons could exist and be wholly nonphysical I defer to a later chapter.

Parfit claims that we have central beliefs about persons that are mistaken. Central beliefs could be of two kinds: conceptual beliefs, that is, beliefs about what the concept of a person includes; and contingent or empirical but very basic beliefs about persons. In the first of these cases it could be that we include in our concept of a person features that nothing in the world has. It could be that our concept is confused, incoherent, or contradictory on the other hand. Parfit does not apparently suppose the latter is the case. That neither of the other alternatives actually holds seems shown by the ready intelligibility of the plethora of imaginable cases that he, Williams, Aune, and others present. Person is underdetermined, as is personal identity itself. However, it seems doubtful that the 'logic' of the term, or deep and general beliefs of the community of cognizers that employ the term, had implied otherwise.

Chapter Fourteen

Mind

I

Of all categories of the real, the mental has undoubtedly received the most philosophical attention. This is doubtless due in the first instance to the fact that philosophers are human beings, with particularly cerebral leanings and orientations, and what has characteristically seemed most distinctive and impressive about ourselves (particularly when the selves are philosophical ones) is that we are thinking things, in Descartes's celebrated phrase. As in other spheres, human egoism has a lot to do with what inquiry chooses to focus upon.

However, there is clearly more to it. The mental is difficult and complicated, and has proved remarkably resistant to repeated attempts to come to summary theoretical judgment.

The foundational questions for the investigation of the mental may be stated as: what is it to be a thinking thing? and what is it to think? Moreover, how do both, being a thinking thing, and thinking, connect with other parts of the world?

The general investigation of mind is so multi-faceted that no attempt will be made here to exhaust even the contours of the topic. Moreover, partly for manageability of the inquiry and partly because they do seem evident to me, I will make assumptions that some philosophers would challenge. First, I assume without argument that there are thinking beings and mental states or events – thinkers and thinkings. (I will try not to assume anything in particular about what either is or involves.) This all by itself will put the themes and methodology of this chapter out of serious contention for some philosophical readers. Nonetheless, I shall assume (with most philosophers and non-philosophers) that there are thinkers and thinkings; or at least the latter (I shall pause, at least, to consider whether we ought to believe that there are thinkers). The mental is not merely appearance but reality. Second, I assume, contrary to Descartes, that there are non-human as well as human thinkers and thinkings: i.e., at least some other animals besides ourselves think. Third, I assume that the correct account of thinking is broadly naturalist. By this I do not mean that it is necessarily physicalist but that it is not merely consistent with but actively to be sought within the broad framework of a unitary system of natural processes and objects that science tries to explore. This is vague of course. Nonetheless I assume that the idea has intuitive resonance and that it is correct. I note, however, that the naturalist assumption does not, as I understand it, carry with it any assumption that the tools and resources for, much less the outline of the correct theory of, the mental are on the current conceptual agenda of 'hard' science.

Two features of mental states and events have seemed to some philosophers to make accommodation of the mental to even a broad naturalism problematic: the fine-grained character of mental states – e.g., the fact that someone's consciousness of a red Macintosh apple is, or can be, a different state from that person's consciousness of a red Spartan apple – and the representational character of mental states, their being of things (objects, states, or anything else; real or unreal), often called their intentionality. These features seem obviously related though they are logically quite distinct. Before giving paramount attention to thinking, let us say more about thinkers.

II

The most deeply metaphysical query we face here is whether thinking does require a thinker: not an enduring thinker but any thinker at all. We have ascribed to Hume the first articulation of the idea that there can be states or processes without objects – particulars – to which they are happening or which are performing or carrying out those states or processes.[1] Weather phenomena seemed to be candidates for such states or processes. When it snows or rains, it does not seem that we need an 'it' that is doing these things. Snowing or raining occurs (at place p and time t) but there is no snower or rainer.

Could there be thinking without a thinker? As intimated, Hume seems to have thought, rather obliquely, if he did, of this idea with reference to Descartes's cogito argument. For if there could be thinking without a thinker, while there might be confidence, even incorrigible certainty, that thinking was occurring, even in the face of a Cartesian evil demon, there could be no comparable confidence that it was I, or anyone, or anything, that did it. In the twentieth century Russell and Ayer took up this Humean idea, challenging both the Cartesian epistemic program and the common-sense views of persons as substances.

We need to confront the ontological issue that Hume-Russell-Ayer pose. However, this issue is not, at its deepest level, whether substances (persons, etc.) endure or continue but whether the logical structure of ψ-ing (where $\ulcorner\psi\urcorner$ is meant to apply to mental states or events) necessarily requires a logical subject. Does $\ulcorner\psi$-ing is occurring at p and $t\urcorner$ entail $\ulcorner(\exists x)(x$ is ψ-ing at p and $t)\urcorner$ – even if x exists only so long as the ψ-ing occurs (or even more briefly, if a single mental state could be conceived to include a series of logical-subjects)?

This question should perhaps be viewed in conjunction with the similar questions asked of the obtaining or exemplifying of a state or property at a momentary time. There would seem to be neither greater nor lesser reason to view $\ulcorner\psi$-ing is occurring at p and $t\urcorner$ as possible without a thing that ψs than to view $\ulcorner$redness obtains at p and $t\urcorner$ as possible without a thing that is red. If this is correct then the question of whether there need to be substances that think submerges in the wider metaphysical question of whether ontology can do entirely without particulars, even in the minimal sense of logical subjects. There have been philosophers who supposed that particulars are eliminable or non-basic: for whom a minimal, and Occamistically satisfactory, inventory of the real confines the categories of things to properties (and relations) exemplified or co-exemplified at places and times. Having earlier considered this project I shall say no more about it here. It does appear to point to nothing distinctive of thought and what it applies to: i.e., for this topic we take it that where thought obtains, there are things that are thinking.

Similarly, the question whether, even supposing that thought must always have a thinker, the $\ulcorner x\urcorner$ that thinks need be, or ought to be, conceived as more than a momentarily existing thing (persons to be regarded as logical fictions, or aggregative entities comprised of sets of such momentarily existing logical subjects), can be seen to be just a special case of the question whether continuing individual substances of any sort should be regarded as real or ontologically fundamental. There would seem to be nothing special about thinkers, in this regard, that would not apply equally to telephone poles, tigers, and planets. The concept of a continuant – an entity that exists through successive times, and capable of change as those times pass by – would seem no more and no less problematic for thinkers than for other particulars. So subject to the proviso of the general metaphysical acceptibility of continuants (and of some of them being particulars or substances), there are ongoing or continuing thinking beings.

III

However, there still remain serious metaphysical queries about the identities and natures of thinkers. Among candidates defended for thinkers have been persons, human beings, and other animals, human, and other animal (living) bodies, brains, and entities called minds.

Some of these seem satisfactorily assessable. Human beings, other animals, and brains, do unproblematically exist (if any macro-particular continuants do). Moreover, human beings and some other animals, we may boldly affirm, think. They, at least, are thinkers although something remains problematic about them. As for brains: their candidacy as things that think would appear to be like the candidacy of eyes as things that see. That is to say, we appear to have in both cases a derivative case of the applicability of a property to something: eyes see in virtue of, or derivatively from, the seeing that the human beings and animals they are the eyes of do, and brains think in virtue of, or derivatively from, the thinking that the human beings and animals they are the brains of do. There appears to be this difference between the cases: it is at least metaphysically possible that a brain exist, and think (or have thought take place in causal conjunction with it), with no other bodily parts continuing in existence;[2] whereas no one would likely be interested in arguing that eyes could see if no other bodily parts, once connected to those eyes, continued in existence. Even if the brain is 'the organ of thought,' as the eyes are 'the organ of sight,' this is not a 'just as' case: precisely because the brain is needed for sight as well as for thought, but, evidently, no other organ or bodily part than the brain is required for thinking to occur.

Still, a satisfactory way of putting the fact that a brain, without other bodily parts, might exist and have thought take place in causal conjunction with it, is that a human being, or other animal, might consist of just a brain. That is, all other bodily parts of an animal than its brain might be removed, and, provided the animal was still living, and still thinking, that animal may be said to have continued to be. The upshot of this is that it is acceptable to affirm that brains think, but this should be viewed as less than fully metaphysically perspicuous. Brains think, but it is because they are the brains of animals that think, that they do.

Would it be accurate to affirm that a thinking brain, in the cases where there is no other bodily part, is identical to the thinking animal? Here we come to the problematic matter signalled above. It seems correct, but puzzling, to deny the identity of animals, including human beings and animal bodies. Some philosophers have thought about this matter only in relation to human beings, and human bodies, but it seems as true of other animals, and their bodies: there is good metaphysical reason to deny their identity. This is not because life is essential to one but not the other: there is in fact no good reason to view life as essential to either, as I argued earlier. The best reason to believe that animals are not animal bodies is modal. An animal could have most or all of its matter altered – the chemical elements composing it reordered or wholly replaced – and the animal still exist. However this is untrue of an animal body. Drastically revise its chemistry, and the animal body ceases to be. Utilizing Aristotelian metaphysical vocabulary: bodies are matter, and animals are formed matter that can consist of matter of altogether different kind, or possibly no matter at all. A given animal can survive replacement of all its material components with components formed from different stuffs than previously. The replacements might need to be gradual, and piecemeal, over time; at any rate, if they, respectively, are, Alfred the alligator, as readily as Arnold the Australian, can continue to be even if now made of silicon, copper wiring, and plastic. It seems doubtful the same should be said of what were once their bodies. Of course this argument is held to beg the question. If Arnold was his body, then the one survives whatever transformations the other does. But this seems in the last analysis unconvincing. Arnold's body is that particular stuff there or that suitably arranged aggregate of stuffs: it is what one views in the funeral parlour after Arnold has died, and that might, at some time when Arnold no longer is, be in an advanced state of decomposition.

Even if this argument is persuasive, it is also puzzling. What kind of a world is it where we, animated beings, go around Doppelganger-like, paired with companions that we are so co-mingled with that we are, in a sense, one with them? If we really are stuck with such a view, it will, as Kripke saw, constitute a kind of resuscitation and vindication of much of Descartes's view of persons and bodies.[3]

I do not want to pause in this context to pursue this theme further, except to affirm again that its complexities attach not just to 'minds,' persons, or indeed to human beings but to every animal with (apparently) any degree of consciousness or mentality. We are prepared, in this context, to live with there being animals (humans among them), and quite reasonably so. And this can be our anchor, and fortress, whatever harrying counterfactual forces this datum must contend with.

Its being so smooths the pathway, I think, for persons. We argued earlier that 'person' is a non-biological descriptor for beings of a vaguely boundaried level of consciousness: a term for things that can have experiences, and can understand, whatever their domiciles, natural affinities, or other traits be. It will be, as was argued earlier, no more problematic to affirm the reality of persons than of human beings and chimpanzees. Indeed every human being is, we affirmed, a person. So persons too are thinkers.

IV

I take it that it is just a prejudice, and one with nothing to recommend it, that only living things could be thinkers. It seems quite obvious, when reflected upon, that things of varying chemistry could – in the metaphysical sense, at least, of 'could' (and probably in the empirical or causal one too) – think. Among the chemical variations must, there seems no reason to doubt, be ones not coinciding with living protoplasm, or DNA molecules.[4] Moreover, the occurrences in a natural system that produce thinking beings must be capable of wide variation too; certainly including deliberate manufacture by beings already endowed with thought (whether those beings were gods, or humans, or something else). The problem of artificial intelligence is, in other words, a quite uninteresting topic for metaphysics; though of course a hugely interesting one for technology (not to mention science fiction), and a somewhat interesting one – the jury is still out on this one (it has come in and gone back out several times in recent years) – for theoretical attempts to understand human thinking.

We must finally speak of 'minds.' The term *mind* has wide generic usage now as a collective for anything mental, anything involving thinking. While for a time it was extensively eschewed as a dangerously misleading term for something we were supposed to possess (or possibly, be), it is now again commonly used in that old way; with the difference now that hardly anyone understands it as a term of precision. It has now a more functional than ontic sense. Minds, now, are whatever it is that thinks, or that is centrally involved in thinking, the term being deliberately, and attractively neutral and non-disclosing about what such things might or must be.

Of course it was not so formerly. Once a mind was supposed to be either a person (a person 'qua thinking thing,' we might say), or a substance constituent of a human (or other conscious) being not identical with the latter, and regarded as immaterial, or an organ (or a sort of organ), used by a person to think – the organ of thought – and also, usually, regarded as immaterial. It should be quite clear, although the texts in the history of talk of minds are to a surprising degree unclear, that these three are distinct and non-equivalent ideas. The first is quite innocuous, and in this sense there are certainly minds, and they think. The third is fairly straightforward also. We can, and should, say that in the current state of evidence there is every reason to identify minds with brains. If it is insisted that minds must be immaterial, it can be affirmed with confidence that minds do not exist; and even dualists – both substance and property (or state/process) dualists – can, and should, take this position. The brain is the only organ of thought.

The middle variety of mind is less straightforward. First of all, it is not altogether clear what is intended in this theory. For it is supposed to deny the identity of a (human) mind and a human being. Rather, the mind, in this sense, is supposed to be a constituent of a human being. So, it would seem, minds, in this sense, are not persons, since some persons are identical to human beings, and all human beings are identical to persons.[5] So neither you nor I literally are minds. Instead we are supposed to have or be (partly) comprised of minds. However these minds are not mere organs, not even extraordinary and immaterial organs. These minds are individual substances which, together with bodies, are supposed to make up human, and possibly some other, persons. Of course organs as such would seem to be plausible candidates as individual substances. They can exist independently of other particulars; and they are particulars. However, an organ, as such, would seem insufficient to constitute one of the two logical halves of a person or human animal. Just as there are theories, sciences, and therapies, concerned with the body, there are theories, sciences, and therapies allegedly concerned with the mind. The latter are not merely, if at all, confined to a better understanding or treatment of brains.

It seems to me that our thinking about minds, in this sense, has gradually, and subtly, become de-substantialized and de-literalized, over the course of the past century or so. This has happened before naturalistic ontology came to any firm sense of what the theoretical alternatives might be, to be considered, rejected, or embraced. There were partial, or developed theories of persons, thinking animals, and thought-organs but not of the minds of classical psychophysical substance dualism. This is odd, since the latter has been around since Pythagoras in philosophy. Under probing, Pythagorean and Cartesian views of minds seem to collapse them into persons (and occasionally into thought-organs), with a conviction of the inessentiality of corporeality to the latter particulars: a conviction that we have by no means argued or declared to be false. A different kind of probe produced behaviourism, by way of rejection of immaterial substance minds that are proper parts of human (or other) persons. However, there is a curious insubstantiality about there ever having been much of a theory that was there to reject or transcend.

At any rate, we can happily and plausibly reject, transcend, or ignore such minds as these. They do not exist or they are just persons, rather misleadingly described, or they represent a *façon de parler*, a way of collectivizing and personifying the dimension of us that experiences or thinks.

V

I proceed to thinking, the state, processes, and events that make thinking beings deserve that label. Although we have assumed that there are thinkings, this by no means identifies what they are. Views have differed so considerably that we must proceed carefully, with judicious attention to their range and variation.

A first position to assess is the view that thinking exists only in an attenuated, non-literal, or logical fictional sort of way: perhaps as some kinds of minds do. Indeed, put too forcefully, or literally, this position will contravene the assumption we said we were making, viz., that there are thinkings. But the advocates of the position intended here have hardly ever put their view as baldly as that. This position is behaviourism, in either of its two chief varieties, empirical or ontological behaviourism, and logical behaviourism. Actually we might do well to identify a wider genus of view, not given a name in the literature, of which both varieties of behaviourism are just one instance. This is the negative position that whatever thinkings are, they are not states, processes, or episodes in a literal way comparable to physical states, processes, or episodes; that thinkings have a different 'logic,' and are only misunderstood and distorted if construed literally as happenings, occurrences or states in a manner resembling what obtains for the physical.[6]

I will consider a modified form of this view in a moment. In full, unqualified, and universally quantified form, it seems false. The proof of this is that individual thinkings – individual cases of mental states or events – are as precisely locatable in time as physical events, and enter into causal relations as fully as physical events. 'I will always remember the moment when I realized that Beatrice could not have been present when Randolph telephoned. The evidence had been before me in its complexity for days, and only and precisely, at 4:15 p.m. (I remember the clock chiming) on January 4th, it all came together and I knew that Beatrice was then in a taxi on her way to Randolph's house ...' could well represent, accurately, a sequence of reflection some detective or lawyer could experience in autobiographical reconstruction of a celebrated case. It might continue: 'I immediately telephoned my assistant Watkins to let her know ...' A mental episode or event, S realizing that Beatrice was not there when Randolph telephoned, takes place in a very brief temporal interval, at a set of microseconds converging on 4:15 p.m., January 4th; hardly discernible in these features of its 'logic,' from the boiling of a pot of water that might have occurred in a neighbouring room at the same time. Further, S's realization has a direct causal consequence: it, together with relevant additional beliefs (some of them doubtless constituting knowledge), desires, and abilities (with stable background factors) causing movements on a telephone to occur.

Some mental phenomena are, then, events or occurrences. Their being actions may give them distinctive properties that non-actions do not share; arguably some of those properties may almost constitute a difference in kind between actions and other events. At least some mental events, actions, are events, take place at times, and intersect causally with the non-mental world. Let me remark in passing that I do not mean by this to seek to settle, casually and in passing, what has often been thought a major problem of philosophy, indeed by some dubbed the mind-body problem as such: viz., whether mental and (non-mental) physical states or events can and do interact causally. In fact, I take this allegedly major problem to be a non-issue. Of course the mental and the physical interact causally. One can hardly have been awake during an adult span of years and not had empirically overwhelming evidence of this. Indeed, I take it that the fact of interaction is a contingent, and empirical datum, that any theory of the mental that has hope of adequacy must accommodate. The point made here is rather a claim as to modest progress with the logic of the mental; namely, that at least some mental phenomena have similar structure, in extensional logical space – i.e., ignoring intentionality – to physical phenomena.

I take it that this result will go some distance in helping refute behaviourism, as a global thesis about mental phenomena, as well. Behaviourism, we have said, takes two fundamental forms. Empirical or ontological behaviourism holds that mental states and events are identical to aggregates of actual or possible behaviourial states and events (which are themselves to be understood in terms of physical motions of animal bodies or bodily parts, together, possibly, with other physio-chemical states and events in those bodies or parts). Logical behaviourism is the thesis that all statements about mental events and states are synonymous with, or at least strictly equivalent to, statements about behaviour (in the sense indicated).

If at least some mental events are temporally and causally parallel to non-mental physical events, including some of relatively simple structural type, it should seem implausible to believe that they, at least, would have, contingently or necessarily, the considerable structural complexity that any behaviourial aggregate that would even seem to offer prospect of invariable correspondence with mental events, would have to have.

Behaviourism is in any case wholly implausible. No actual behaviourist analysis of a mental state or event has ever been offered in the literature, which has not turned out – usually rather easily – to be subject to counterexample. I do not propose to explore this; global behaviourism, in any form, is no longer seriously held by any philosopher of mind.

VI

What has not been refuted, or perhaps adequately discussed, are positions, some behaviourist, some not, that are less than global, and that see wide difference of type among mental phenomena. Some philosophers think there are important distinctions to make between mental states and mental events, or between occurrent and dispositional mental states.

Mental events, including mental acts, have seemed the most securely anchored of mental phenomena, and the most like their non-mental physical counterparts. This seems true whether or not the mental event is one of 'propositional attitude,' i.e., is adequately characterized by means of a psychological verbal expression followed by a 'that' (or cognate) clause. If S is realizing, at p and t, that q is the case, this is as securely dateable and as straightforwardly able to be in causal relation with other events or states, as $S's$ suddenly having an anxiety attack, or thinking of a favourite food. Activity and passivity also seem irrelevant to the security of occurrent mental events: $S's$ adding two three-digit numbers in his or her head, or being terror-struck by a disagreeable sight, seem equally capable of perspicuous well-behaved respectability.

It is not my purpose here – and it would be folly if it were – to attempt even the outline of a full theory or typology of mental states and phenomena. That endeavour remains an extraordinarily sketchy and incomplete enterprise, even after so much labour and ingenuity expended on it. That there is a secure class of mental states is, I think, real progress. Beyond noting that fact I will indicate what some of the problematic cases are, why they are so, and in some cases what might be plausible views on them.

VII

A first category of challenging mental states (and events) consists of those that seem as appropriately conceived as bodily states (and events) as they are mental: namely, sensings and perceivings. In this group I do not mean to include what in one vocabulary are called *appearings to perceive*. Appearings to perceive are sensory or perceptual states – or isolable components of them – that do not as such imply anything as to the nature or reality of the objects or causes of those states. If someone sees a red apple, that implies that there is a red apple there to be seen. If they appear to see a red apple – or in so far as they appeared to see a red apple (possibly as a constituent or isolable past of some experience they are having) – that will not imply that there is a red apple there to be seen, or an apple, or anything else. Appearings to perceive are maximally neutral perceptual or sensory states, in respect of the aetiology or objective correlates of those states. They – or at least a proper subset of them – are what Hume (usually) called impressions. Hume is not always clear that impressions are states or events and not supposed objects of those states or events. Also, while seeming to see something red would appear to qualify as a Humean impression, it is not so evident that seeming to see a second-hand VCR, would.

Impressions, and other appearings to sense or perceive, are plausibly taken to be logically isolable constituents of actual sensings and perceivings. Both categories of state (or event) are somewhat problematic from an ontological perspective. It may be doubted whether the former ever genuinely occur 'neat,' unalloyed, in the real world, and if that is the case whether there actually are, at any rate in an ontologically perspicuous sense, things such as these. The latter seem genuine but of dubious pure mental status. *Seeing* is (for example) among other things your eyes doing something, and highly complex events in your nervous system, quite apart from interpretive operations in your brain, taking place. Sensing, it seems, is not obviously more a case of mind than of matter (whether or not materialism is true); at any rate it is not a pure act of mind.

Non-occurrent mental states and events seem satisfactorily mental, but less obviously real. If I am not now thinking, consciously or unconsciously, about Paris or France, it may still be said of me, truly, now, that I know that Paris is in France. Does this involve – anyway, is there – a mental state going on in some way in me, consisting of my knowing (or believing) that Paris is in France? A merely counterfactual conditional analysis of my so-called dispositional state seems unsatisfactory. It is doubtless true that were I asked about Paris and France and I had no reason, or inclination, not to be truthful, I would affirm my view that Paris is in France. Yet this, even if true, does not address the conviction of something going on 'in the mind,' involving Paris and France (or ideas of them) prior to the activation of the 'disposition' (or dispositional knowledge). No account of what this might be seems altogether plausible. The problem is essentially that of giving an empirically satisfactory account of memory (rather than a wider theory of the sort of property of which solubility in water is the standardly used example). It may be that information theory, and cognitive science broadly, should reasonably be expected to offer the brightest prospect of resolution of this problem. However they do not seem yet to have done so.

VIII

That thinking involves, sometimes at least, reference as well as representation does not seem to me as philosophically significant as very many contemporary philosophers think that it is (among them Putnam and Burge). There can be no serious doubt that we do really refer; that is, some of the things we think, and say, do reach right out to the world. Certainly there could be no adequate account of language, meaning, and thinking, that did not encompass that fact. However solipsistically isolated thinkers and language-users are possible metaphysically. The world could have come into being fifteen minutes ago, with apparent evidence of greater age; as Russell supposed.[7] We know that it did not, and that there are other thinkers (and language-users), and that some of our words really refer to, and name, objects we have direct contact with. Yet we do not know this infallibly or incorrigibly. There are worlds with persons in them who would think such things, and think they knew such things, and be wrong. So the fact that we (and our words, and thoughts) refer cannot be all that important metaphysically. It is not an anchored datum to which any satisfactory account of the world and our place in it simply must accommodate itself. Maybe we think we refer but do not really ever.

We do however certainly represent. The intentional character of thought is central and challenging. Possibly a wholly reductive account of representation, that will explain it and subsume it within the wider physical categories of representation typified by barometers, and non-artefactual indicators of physical states of the world, will succeed. None seems to have yet, and the possibility of the representation of non-existent things typical of thought (and its extensions, like art), may make the prospects seem unpromising, for this is not misrepresentation, or anything obvious that natural monitoring or calibrating systems exhibit, but the great ingenuity that has been expended in this direction may yet bear fruit.

Whether representational or intentional states are reducible to a wider class of states exhibited by non-mental entities, the question of the strictly physical character of mental states and events has had great attention. A series of prevailing or nearly prevailing positions since the 1950s has reached at least a temporary hiatus in the literature of the subject in philosophy of mind. Briefly a now classical reductive psycho-physical identity theory which identified every mental state/event (type and token) with some brain process or complex of them found the field contested by eliminative materialism, which advocated jettisoning thoughts as mere, and soon to be superseded, folk psychology. Materialist thesis and antithesis then found synthesis (for few were prepared to reject thought) in functionalist materialism according to which thinkings are 'higher-order' 'functional' states of certain physical systems or substances, linked in systemic causal (and logical) nexus, those functional states exemplified in human (and other animal) organisms in certain of their brain states. However functionalism too has been found wanting. The requisite systematicity seems unnecessary for thinkings. Moreover functionalist materialism appears to lose direct linkage with the world and fail to capture consciousness: a system of states could exhibit the relevant functionality but not be intuitively mental.

Do we return then to dualism? Few naturalist philosophers would find this a palatable dialectical outcome. Its least unpalatable form, for many, is the surprisingly long-lived position called epiphenomenalism. Epiphenomenalism is a theory – there are others in other areas of philosophy, which share this feature – which seems quite implausible to a majority of philosophers but which does not go away, because a small coterie of thinkers – who always manage to have intellectual heirs – find it deeply persuasive and cling tenaciously to what they see as its special merits. Epiphenomenalism is strictly and formally a dualist theory: it holds that no mental state is a physical one; they are sui generis and real. In spirit and motivation epiphenomenalism is deeply naturalist, and nearest cousin to materialism, for it holds that mental states and events have a reality similar to shadows or echoes. All are 'mere' epiphenomena. An ongoing purely physical world-system is self-contained, and wholly sufficient to produce all world states at micro- or macro-levels. Epiphenomenalism in metaphysics is similar to historical materialism in social philosophy. For both the mental is real, and non-physical, but largely or wholly ineffacious causally. If the mental has causal results, it does so only unnecessarily, alongside physically determining causes. All cases of mental causation are cases of causal overdetermination in which the other determining causes are non-mental.

The uncomfortable reality, for both epiphenomenalism and historical materialism, is that genuinely mental and ideational phenomena have causal effect, with no obvious accompanying physical determinant. Of course both positions can be made unfalsifiable, but if they are not – if they are defended as empirical, or contingent – the evidence seems definitely to be contrary. Cleopatra's nose – shorthand for key Roman beliefs about Cleopatra's nose – really did change the course of history, in directions there is no plausible reason for assigning an independent non-mental co-determining cause. Nonetheless, epiphenomenalism endures, and will doubtless continue to do so.

I am myself drawn to the idea of a favourable re-consideration of classical identity theory, with some modifications. Some of the first advocates of the identity theory were more modest than their successors were soon to be: they limited the candidates for identity with brain processes to some mental states, chiefly sensings, including sensings of pain. The original idea seems to have been programmatic and piecemeal. If a case for identifying certain reasonably simple sensory, or para-sensory, states with brain states proved successful, one might go on to consider other classes of mental cases with respect to a tentative hypothesis of mental-brain identities.

Among the objections to the full psycho-physical identity theory that resulted was the implausibility of supposing that the fine-grained structure, and the discriminability, of intentional mental states, especially those of 'propositional attitude,' would be matched with or mirrored by brain processes. If George thinks (at time t) about a heavy leather-covered eighteenth-century book then he is thinking (then) also about a leather-covered eighteenth-century book. These are evidently distinct mental events, even if the one is performed while doing the other.[8] Is it credible that there are distinct, in principle empirically isolable brain processes to be candidates for identity with these mental events? Similarly, if he believes that Hesperus is a very bright planet while believing that it is a bright heavenly body, can we plausibly expect a textbook of brain physiology, in however remote and sophisticated a future, to identify the part(s) of the brain – or processes occurring there – that are these different states?

The firmest anchor for identity theory is with relatively 'coarse-grained' or gross mental states. This was the central intuition of the first formulators of the original version of the theory. There is no reason not to extend the foundational sensory range of cases envisaged to 'coarse-grained' propositional and ideational ones. For example, if S believes that the fruit in front of him is an apple, then S believes something. The latter, at least, if not the former, ought in principle to turn out to be an identifiable brain process. It seems reasonable to expect that all major psychic modes should be distinct brain processes. Perhaps believing something pleasing might also; feeling betrayed by someone one had trusted; enjoying tranquil music; and very many more increasingly 'calibrated' states. How far the fine-grained specification of states may continue to permit identification with actual discrete brain activity cannot be said in advance of the relevant neurophysiology. We might take prospects to licence a very modest revived identity theory, that would hold that:

For every mental state or event M, there is a mental state or event M', such that M occurring at a time t causally or logically implies M' occurring at t, and there is a brain state or event, or aggregate of them, B, such that B occurs at t and $B = M'$.

It is clear how modest a claim this is but it should also be evident that, if it is true, the mental will be tied to the physical in a stronger sense than any classical version of dualism, or for that matter behaviourism, could concede. Possibly stronger theses than this will be formulable and defensible.

However, two dimensions of what we have learned about the mental in the attempt to understand the plausibility of its alternative mappings onto the physical must be registered. First, no matter how far the road from our modest identity principle may run, there will be many fine-grained mental states which will defy identification with a brain state. Second, referential mental states (and possibly others) seem identifiable as states that essentially involve objects and systems external to the subject of the mental state; and this must mean that these states cannot be purely states of those subjects or of their brains or bodies. If noticing Roger, for example, essentially involves Roger, then noticing Roger cannot be purely a brain state, even if the part of noticing Roger that is purely in or connected to a person that does this might be purely a brain state.

One way or another we have to accept that there are mental states that are not functional states of persons, brains, or bodies, and that – even if wholly physically conditioned, as epiphenomenalism holds – are not purely physical states of those persons, brains, or bodies. We have distinguished two kinds of such mental states: referential mental states and mental states of some unspecified but complex degree of fine-grained content. In the case of the first something external to the mind is involved, as well as something in or of the mind; these states are essentially relational states. It may be defensible that the part or element of referential states that is purely in or of the mind is a brain state (or set of them). In the case of mental states of rich (i.e., extremely fine-grained) content, we argued that identity with a unique brain state is most likely an unavailable option. If this is so, and if we want nonetheless to hold that such states are real – and it seems that we should – we will find ourselves with a partial, or qualified, version of psycho-physical dualism. It is, to be sure, a somewhat pale and truncated variety of dualism, but it is dualism nonetheless.

IX

Two last comments on this. One is that, quite independent of the ontological ditches we fall into, or want to defend, and independent of a general naturalistic physicalism, that holds that in some sense we are physical beings located in a physical world – which I take to be indisputable – then waiting for sophisticated and plausible completed cognitive science looks like waiting for socialist world revolution or the second coming of Christ. Let it be said quite explicitly: there is no prospect on the table that a state like remembering the halcyon days of youth, and people one knew who looked and acted like characters in a Renaissance tableau vivant – and a thousand like states that one can find named on the pages of a thousand novels – will undergo interesting theoretical reduction in anyone's cognitive theory. The result, I think, is that philosophers should allow themselves to rejoin those who articulate, and think about, nuanced subtleties of the mind. Whether ontological dualists or not, it is wholly appropriate to regain, and reclaim, what can be called methodological dualism.

The second comment is to remind the reader of one of the major themes of this book, viz., that existence is an unjustifiably inflated concept. That something exists does not imply that it is at some determinate place, or indeed at any place at all. Even ideal total science may be best conceived as limited to existents that are at determinate places (even if in many cases it will be undetermined that they are at those places). In any case, if there are non-physical mental states – more precisely, if (ontological) dualism, in an etiolated version, is true – it is not clear that this need be any threat to naturalism or the unity of science.

X

A recent reformulation of an old notion has been held to have decisive bearing on fundamental mind-body issues, perhaps (some claim) providing the possibility of settling the fundamental mind-body issue, viz., whether a human person is an altogether physical entity.[9] The recent formulation is of the concept of a so-called zombie, understood as something observationally indistinguishable from a human being but lacking consciousness and failing to have experiences. Like so many philosophical conceptions, a version of this notion appeared among the ancient Greeks. In one of the accounts of the Trojan War story, Paris runs off with a standardly human Helen, but the gods replace her with a phantom Helen (made of cloud), whisking the real Helen off to Egypt, where she is kept safely until her husband Menelaos can find her after Troy has been besieged and sacked.[10] In the meantime, for a considerable span of years (Homer says twenty)[11] Paris lives with the phantom Helen, and his fellow Trojans also interact with this being on a regular basis as a genuine flesh-and-blood human being. The gods have not induced systematic hallucinations in the Trojans so that they merely think they perceive a real Helen. Nor is the phantom Helen a spirit disguised as a human being; rather, the creature is a physical entity the gods have fashioned with such skill that it mimes a human being, undetected by the people among whom it is placed. After the fall of

Troy, when Menelaos regains the real Helen in Egypt, the phantom Helen disappears, evaporating into the air.

The mythographers do not make this absolutely clear but the phantom Helen does not have feelings, sensations, or episodes of consciousness of any sort: she only seems to. Let us suppose that this is definitely the idea. The Trojans do not perform DNA, serological, or radiological analyses or tests on phantom Helen. We of course could do such things. It is instructive to ask whether, even if we might discover from such analyses and tests that the phantom Helen was not a human being – the gods had not troubled (even if they could have) to ensure that our science, just that Trojan science, would not have detected that phantom Helen was not a human person – it is at least metaphysically possible for phantom Helen really not to be conscious and have experiences, even though she appears for so long to the Trojans to do so. This seems an instructive question because it asks whether we can have phenomenological guarantees from human being-indicating behavioural interactions that we are dealing with a conscious experiencing human being.

Obviously behaviourist views will be implicated in this query. For a behaviourist it is evidently unintelligible that something like our supposed phantom Helen not be a conscious, thinking, feeling person. We have, I think, abundant reason to believe that behaviourism is false. At the centre of the case against it is the self-validating fact of the interior experience of consciousness that each physiologically normal adult human being knows. Still, it might be argued, even if not by a behaviourist, that such experience is distinct from but necessarily accompanies relevant behaviour. The phantom Helen case, as we construe it, is a putative counterexample to this latter claim.

Could the gods intend, and succeed in the intention, that phantom Helen should be an unthinking physical object that appears to be a living thinking human being – seeming to utter meaningful sentences, perform actions, respond to others, and otherwise and generally appear to be intelligent? Could the gods pull this off?

There is, I think, good reason to believe that they could. Various sorts and kinds of imaginative science-fiction scenarios could be devised to show this. In the end they amount to the following: we can imaginatively project ourselves into the body of another, and imagine doing so drawing a (psychological) blank. We do actually imaginatively perform such projections, into the bodies of others whom we take to be very much like ourselves, or very well known to us, and into the bodies of others who seem more remote or different from ourselves. We imagine what it would be like to be in that person's shoes (as we say), with their feelings, memories, values, physical traits. There may be more challenges in such imaginings than we think of – more challenges for the subject, person S imagining himself or herself in the skin of person S'; or more challenges for a philosopher, claiming the general idea feasible. Yet something along these lines is feasible, and all we need for present purposes is something along these lines. We can imagine stepping into the other's shoes, and it turning out to be as we have imagined it or quite surprising, alien, different. We can also imagine stepping into some other's shoes in this way and it being a complete and total blank. Nothing is felt, sensed, or experienced. Yet we can also imagine that concurrent with what might be an extended blank period third parties observe the other into whose shoes we have stepped exhibit behaviour taken by those third parties to be animate, purposive, human. We imagine something from the inside, and something from the outside: the latter the behaviour of an apparently normal awake and conscious active human being; the former a complete absence of anything. Were something like the situation described actually to happen to someone for an interval, we might imagine that interval as flanked by two others, each of several hours' duration, the whole three-part sequence involving standard active behaviour, including verbal behaviour, observed (perhaps filmed) by several others, but only the first and third interval, being felt and remembered by the 'subject' as something that happened and had been experienced.

Of course the subject could have been conscious during the middle interval, and had memory of this experience effaced. But to insist that this must have occurred is dogmatic apriorism. Possibly the subject was not conscious, but nonetheless exhibited seemingly conscious behaviour.

I take it that this result is correct. A phantom Helen in the strong metaphysical manner intended is possible. There are worlds with such beings. There are possible worlds, that is to say, with zombies.

What seems not to follow from this modal fact is anything that compromises the full physicality of actual human beings in the actual world.

The most plausible view about mental states is, I believe, the following. Some features of mental states will be true for wide varieties of kinds of things that may exhibit those states as their subjects (some indeed doubtless holding for all actual subjects of mental states; some perhaps holding for all possible cases); and some features of mental states will be true distinctively for particular kinds of subjects: for example, for particular living species, like human beings. Moreover, some mental states are complex states that involve objects or states outside the subject of the mental state – for example, seeing the pool of water on the floor. All such states will however include component substates which are also mental and do not involve objects or states outside the subject of the mental state. And some mental states do not at all involve 'referentiality' beyond their subject – for example, feeling elated. The pure mental states are the ones that are, in this sense, internal. A general theory of mental states may otherwise not have much further content, or may be elusive. We may nonetheless make progress with theorizing about human mental states. Of these there may be a case for viewing some of these as epiphenomenal, that is, nonphysical causally inefficacious states of the subject. And there is certainly a case, in my view a compelling case, for viewing others (and possibly all of them) as (identical with) brain states or aggregations of brain states. I would advocate not mere token identity but type-identity in these cases. Holding that human mental states are (identical with) human brain states does not preclude those same mental states, in other life-forms, nor nonliving machines of suitable complexity and configuration, nor indeed in noncorporeal entities (if they are metaphysically possible), from having a different biochemistry or no chemistry at all. Floating, being within the boundaries of New York City, and being discussed in an encyclopedia, do not require much that is interesting and common in the chemistry of their subjects; nor need thinking.

I think further that the human internal mental states that are physical – unless some are epiphenomenal this is all of them – are likely essentially physical: physical in every possible world those states are in (and conversely those same individual states will be essentially mental). This will leave open possibilities – possible worlds – in which their human subjects have (internal) mental states that are qualitatively identical to such states in respect of all of their mental properties, but which are nonphysical; and still other mental states, in those worlds, which are physical, and others again, not qualitatively identical to any mental state in the actual world, which are nonphysical. Some such worlds as these will have zombies in them, as will some worlds with human beings in them all of whose mental states (in the internal sense indicated) will be physical.

A theory of the nature of mental states needs to specify whether it means to be of actual mental states or, in addition, possible ones; and whether of all cases of subjects or merely human ones. There are no zombies, even if there could be some. And, so I will argue, there are no afterlives for once-living human beings, even if there could be such states of being. A purely materialist (or that weaker, paler cousin, an epiphenomenalist) theory of human mental states is caused no insuperable difficulties by modal options for humans, or human-like, things; or by altogether nonhuman thinkers, actual or possible. Such a theory is almost certainly true, although, as we may go on to note, there have been serious philosophical doubters, who have had reservations about the possibility of systematic general knowledge about mind at all.

XI

A number of positions on the mental have been what may be called inscrutabilist. That is, they have held that the mental is in one degree or other opaque,
in principle opaque, to the possibility of our having systematic and comprehensive knowledge of it. Three variants of this idea may briefly be noted.
Kant, of course, held that reality is inscrutable root and branch: we cannot, the
critical philosophy asserts, have any knowledge at all of things in themselves.
That said, Kant went on (in the *Critique of Practical Reason*, and similar
works) to demarcate and explore a whole territory, the territory of free rational
agency, which at least may be, Kant holds, noumenal (i.e., reality, not merely
concerned with appearance). Certainly, for Kant, the domain of free rational
agency cannot be subsumed in natural science, or understood as part of our
empirical knowledge of the world. The territory of free rational agency is
moreover not to be confused with the object domain of empirical psychology
– which is a legitimate and constituent part of science, aiming, like all science
does, to produce exceptionless deterministic laws. Further, for Kant, the
bounds of the scientific enterprise are limitless: the whole experienceable
world is subject to causality, and the rest of the mind's categories and forms.
The full picture has seemed to many commentators inconsistent. Either total
science is a possible project, whose successful realization would come to
deterministic laws for all of experienced reality, including the mental; or it is
not, and some part of the encountered world resists the embrace of causality.
More concretely, either our actions issue from deliberation and free choice –
in which case they will not for Kant (and many other philosophers) be fully
pre-determined, or they are fully pre-determined, and rational deliberation and
its outcome are illusions, epiphenomenal at best. To be succinct: how can my
act (or my conscious state) be at the same time noumenally free and phenome-
nally unfree?

Donald Davidson's much-discussed anomalous monism[12] is an interesting
attempt to represent and defend what may have been the point Kant endeav-
oured to articulate.[13] For Davidson our mental states are brain states, but there
is no systematic general fit between these brain states, and such general laws
as may apply to them by virtue of being brain states, and the character they
have as psychological states. There are no psychological or psycho-physical
laws of nature. And, like Kant, Davidson understands the psychological (in
this primary sense) as involving an entire web or network of concepts and
principles that have to do with deliberation, rational choice, consciousness,
and intentional action. There may be a significant conceptual geography for
this territory but it is not to be confused with the kind of result the natural sci-

ences aspire to. Yet, at the same time – and thus Davidson's resolution of apparent Kantian inconsistency – the individual identifiable items of our mental lives are actually in fact physical states, parts of the comprehensive physical world that all things are part of.

Still a third inscrutabilist view is a position Chomsky briefly formulates in one context.[14] It may be, Chomsky suggests, that we humans simply do not have the cerebral equipment to come to truly theoretical scientific understanding of the sphere of consciousness. It may be that mathematics, and mathematical physics (with similar subordinate theories they engender), are the only really successful contentful bodies of theoretical knowledge we are capable of; and our attempts at systematic psychology – systematic knowledge of consciousness, and agency – are, in the large scheme of things, feeble and futile gropings, childlike in character, and will never be more than that.

None of these positions affirms or implies a view stemming from Aristotle which still has its advocates, according to which objective parts of the world, including parts involving states of consciousness and free rational agency, are inherently without determining causes. For the Aristotelian position, there is nothing particularly inscrutable about the mental. On the contrary, we know as much as there is to know in this sphere, at least in general outline. The inscrutabilist views do not imply that the Aristotelian view is wrong. They are neutral about it formally, but they do, all three of them considered above, embrace scientific modernism, the position that there are no genuine competitors to broad naturalist (i.e., Galilean and post-Galilean) natural science for understanding and explaining the experienced world (the position, as we might put it, that science is untrumpable) in a general way – a position which the followers of Aristotle contest. For the inscrutabilists discussed, wherever the conceptual content which covers consciousness and agency is to be placed, it is neither as a rival nor an allied companion of natural science, contrary to the Aristotelian stance.

I will not undertake to assess the plausibility of the inscrutabilist views, beyond saying that I believe they are premature, and that goals of a total science that would include the domain of consciousness and free agency within its comprehensive naturalist (and non-eliminativist) embrace are by no means known to be misguided. As I have indicated in earlier chapters, I think variants of several Kantian positions – and I believe this also of these ones – are quite serious and important. I believe that they are mistaken but I would not claim to know that they are.

Chapter Fifteen

God

I now consider the first of Kant's three central metaphysical topics – God. There are things that it is appropriate, and important, to note before turning to the substance of the topic, that are different in kind from preliminaries to other metaphysical themes. As on most if not all subjects they explore, philosophers differ considerably with respect to whether there is a God. What is distinctive in this case is that for many philosophers there is not a serious topic posed by the question. I think it is important to be very candid about this. It is not simply that a great many philosophers are atheists. Many among them have in fact the view that the existence of God is on a par, with respect to its serious content and probability, with the existence of a tooth fairy. I do not of course mean to say that philosophers with such a view are correct. I mean that it is important to pierce what may be a veil of silence, occasioned by elemental courtesy for views with which one disagrees. Many will tacitly feel that it is rude to say that some belief dear to someone is completely infantile, not something an adult person ought to entertain even for a moment. Yet many philosophers have, I think, precisely this view about God. Others have a somewhat less rude view. Russell, for example, said that he thought the existence of the Judaeo-Christian God no more probable than that of the pagan gods Zeus, Aphrodite, or Thor. H.L. Mencken, in similar vein, insists that we recognize how very many gods humans have believed in, and how readily all are dismissed, forgotten, and viewed as below the salt of credible attention, except for one's own.[1]

At the same time – and this is, I think, quite as arresting a fact as the one just noted – a considerable number of philosophers, including some of the most intelligent, well-educated, and philosophically sophisticated members of the profession, are theists. As in the general population, so among philosophers, belief in God simply does not go away. The demise of theism in an educated scientifically informed society has been predicted by successive waves of thinkers, of otherwise differing views, since the eighteenth century. These predictions seem to be as far from fulfilment today as they were 250 years ago. A sizeable constituency of philosophers continue to be among the believers, year after year. There can only be the expectation that this fact of demographics of philosophers will continue into a foreseeable future.[2] Not only that: any philosopher who is honest will acknowledge that he or she knows philosophers that he/she respects who are convinced theists (just as a comparably honest philosopher will acknowledge respect for at least some philosophers of their acquaintance for whom God and the tooth fairy are on an evidentiary par).

There is a kind of cognitive dissonance in confronting this contrasting pair of facts, which I will not try to resolve. I want to proceed to examine 'the metaphysics of God' in an open, analytical way, exploring the nature, or possible nature, of God as well as his existence. That mode may seem breezy, or insouciant, a response that will be reinforced when the reader duly arrives at my perhaps predictable verdict on this metaphysical topic. Let me say only, in concluding these prefatory comments, that I share Hume's view that the singularity of the universe makes it quite difficult to conceive what may have been involved in its coming into existence – if it came into existence – or its eternal existence, if that is the case; and why it is here, now. Of course there are many possible hypotheses for what was or is involved, and a great many involve gods, just as a great many do not, as Hume also pointed out. As I argued in Chapter 5, there is a mystery of the world – why it exists – which seems to be unanswerable. Some of the grounds for the spiritual impulse in people, among them intelligent and sophisticated philosophers, do not seem plausibly reduced to their psychological needs. Of course, neither of these vague facts will yield either genuine theism or its rationality.

Proceeding in an organized structured way, there will be, as with other ontic quarries, three matters on which to focus. With respect to any category of a putative entity, we ought to ask: (1) what would such a thing be if there were one? (2) is a thing like that possible? (3) is a thing like that actual?

Metaphysically speaking, God is quite interesting if understood in specific kinds of ways. So understanding it, or 'him,' – I will conform to the (arguably sexist) convention of using the masculine pronoun for reference to the deity – has been intertwined with some of the subtlest, most conceptually fine-grained and imaginative philosophy that the western tradition has produced, over the course of the eleventh to the eighteenth centuries especially. Indeed, if God does not exist, then (to paraphrase Voltaire (1694–1778)), it would be necessary to invent him, for thought experiments and conceptual models, and puzzles, of different kinds. He is useful and fun. These are of course intellectualist kinds of reflections on the deity. The God of the philosophers has seldom been the God of people at large. They do not seem to be incompatible but much that philosophers have had to say for or against their God seems to have little to do with the God of other believers (or non-believers).

A few parenthetical remarks in the history of ideas may not be inappropriate. The Christian religion has been, it is reasonable to claim, the most metaphysical of all religions. Just why this has been so is unclear but the fact is striking: since the eleventh century Christian thinkers in western Europe were allowed, indeed encouraged to think closely and analytically about matters that others of the world's religious traditions insisted be left fearful and mysterious. The Western inheritance from Greece and Rome doubtless had much to do with this. The result, as the work of Anselm (1033–1109), Abelard (1079–1142), Aquinas (1225–74), and dozens of later thinkers shows, was analytic philosophical work of the first order, focused on the nature of God.

It seems to me inappropriate to take the abstract reflections of many dozens of priest-philosophers at Western European universities to be authoritative for the conception of God. The God of whom Kant and the priest-philosophers speak is the Judaeo-Christian-Islamic God, the God of the Believers. This being may or may not, if existent, be literally perfect, all-powerful, or all-knowing; and it is doubtful whether necessary existence in the technical sense or senses (existence in all possible worlds or existence such that literal self-contradiction is involved in denying that existence) is any part of the concept of this being.

The God of the believers, it seems, is to be conceived fundamentally with reference to power and personhood. It is doubtful whether the ordinary believer's concept of God includes the notions of omnipotence, omniscience, or total goodness. It appears that ordinary believers sometimes wonder whether God is fair about something, or whether he can be aware of something – usually, something bad – that has happened, or whether he really has the power to bring about some desired change. Ordinary geometers do not wonder whether triangles have three sides. Whether or not literally all-powerful, this being is supposed to have power sufficient to create, guide, and maintain the entire (physical) universe, including both macro-power, over the whole thing, and at least some degree of micro-power, permitting monitoring and interventions at the small-scale level of the activities of individual substances. This does not imply that such interventions would occur, just that they could. This being is also supposed to be a kind of person, with states of knowledge (both knowledge that and know-how), memory, and some degree of emotion (love) and morality (a sense of goodness, and of justice, notably) or states that resemble such states.

Things get abstrusely metaphysical when the idea of there being no limit at all to the power or perfection of God is pursued. This pursuit is joined here only in so far as doing so seems metaphysically interesting or problematic. What appears chiefly to be so is the idea of omnipotence as such. Is it logically possible that there be a being that was able to do everything that it is logically possible to do?

The question requires being able to identify action types. This is a huge and difficult topic which can only be partly explored here. I suggest that an action (type) is to be identified by reference to a possible agent's intentions. Such identification would be circular if claimed to afford an analysis, definition, or explication, of an action type. But that is not what is intended. Rather action (type) x is identical with action (type) y iff an agent's intending to do x is identical with that agent's intending to do y.

An action is something someone can mean to do. There are of course unintended actions and (apparently) unintentional ones. Yet it would not seem that there could be an action that someone could not intend to perform. This seems to apply even to reflex or immediate actions.

Actions are events. Like all events they are concrete. They occur in time. Something an agent does might be a case simultaneously of tying a left shoe and an action of an eleven-year-old. Being an eleven-year-old tying a left shoe: is this an action type? It is, of course, true of some particulars at some times and places, and of others false. Intuitively the act's performance by an eleven-year-old does not seem to be part of the act. The tying of the shoe is; however, a state or condition of the agent that the agent cannot intend or will is not part of it. How about being the first person to climb Mt. Everest? This does seem to designate an action: an action performed in fact by Hillary in 1953. This precludes it ever being performed again by anyone.

Since Hillary did that, and Hillary is not all-powerful, will that prove that no being is omnipotent? Does the existence of Hillary disprove the existence of God? If Hillary is the first person to climb Mt. Everest no one else can be, ever, then there is something that God, were he real, cannot do: viz., be the first person to climb Mt. Everest?

No, one reasonably responds: that will not disprove the possibility of omnipotence. There is a possible world, we may say, in which someone else than Hillary first climbs Everest: in many such worlds it is God (assuming he exists in any world).

On the other hand it seems wrong to insist simply on identifying an action with its 'internal constituents' – the sequence and structure of movements and subordinate events it contained, independent of any of their relations with other actions or agents. One of the things Hillary did was climb Everest first.

So, to turn now to alleged problems for divine omnipotence, it appears to be wrong to say that, e.g., making an object too heavy for the agent to lift must be the same as making an object of weight w (for some weight w).[3] If a being really could not make something that would be too heavy for it to lift, there would seem to be something it could not do. We can make things too heavy for us to lift, so if there were a being that could not do that, then there would be something we can do that that being could not. Hence that being at least would not be omnipotent.

Old challenges to divine omnipotence chiefly have been variants on the problem of God and the stone (could God make a stone too heavy for him to lift?): could God sin? know doubt? know what strawberry ice cream tastes like? be surprised? commit suicide?

Mediaeval, Renaissance, and Enlightenment responses to such queries were uniformly ones insisting that God could not do any of these things, yet that this did not impair his omnipotence. Basically the line taken was that God was essentially perfect, and it would be unreasonable to regard abilities to act as lessened or limited by incompatibilities with the agent's essence.

In fact these philosophers were revising omnipotence, although they were seldom straightforward about it. Omnipotence as ability to do anything at all, even logically impossible acts, seemed clearly inappropriate. A being with omnipotence in this sense would have to be able, for example, to cause it to be the case that it had never existed and did not now exist. Save for a very few thinkers, this notion of omnipotence was overwhelmingly rejected. Omnipotence should mean being able to do anything at all that is a thing that can or could be performed, i.e., by someone.

The philosophically interesting thing about a trait such as this is whether anything at all could have this trait; not whether a particular being invested with a special dignity and role within a cultural context (or series of contexts) in which he is accorded reality and worshipped, could have it. The term God presumably is a term for an office or role, like king or mayor; it is not a proper name, and only comes to resemble one under monotheistic assumptions being taken for granted. At the same time it is a term for an office or role that differs importantly from other such terms. God does not require, semantically, that there be a world over which he is god. There are worlds in which there is a God but no other substance nor any physical state, if there are worlds with a God at all.

There would not in fact seem to be any grave difficulty along the lines of God and the stone. Someone can have a power that is left always unexercised. Some of the powers we never exercise we fail to exercise for the very good reason that it would be deeply against our best interests to do so. I have the ability to mutilate myself but I would not, so far as I can tell, exercise this ability. I would not want to do so. I would have no reason to and finally I would be a fool to do so. And some abilities are such that if someone exercises them, they won't thereafter have that ability that they did formerly. Thus, I have the ability to commit suicide but if I exercise it, I will not have the ability to commit suicide any longer, nor will I have the ability to butter toast (or to exercise any other of my abilities) any longer. Yet this does not show that I do not now have the ability to commit suicide.

If a being were all-powerful, the fact, if it were a fact, that if it created something such that, once that thing were created, it could not lift it would show that, at least from then on the being was no longer all-powerful. But it would not show that that being was not formerly all-powerful. Possibly making such an object would require, for such a being, activity directed to itself more than to the world exterior to it; a sort of self-diminishing. Making oneself weaker while making something would be one way of ensuring for the right object (and subject, and process of self-diminishing), that the creator would not be able to lift the object later.

Mutatis mutandis an all-powerful being could doubt, commit suicide, be surprised, etc. It might have to do some other things first, in order to be able to do these things.[4] If it did these things, it would presumably no longer be omnipotent. How about be surprised while remaining unchanged with respect to internal states? That is something, we may say, we can do. How about our candidate for omnipotence? That is where our earlier remarks about the eleven-year-old tying his or her shoes come into operation. That one has or has not changed internally does not seem accurately included in a conception of a possible action, of what it is that an agent does, means to do, or might do.

I do not want to suggest that ingenuity might not produce a case of a possible action – an action that someone or other really could do (in some possible world exercises the ability to do) – that would demonstrate literal omnipotence to be logically impossible. For example, setting in motion a chain of events that will result in being weaker without doing or having done anything to oneself would seem trickier for omnipotence; and many other perplexing cases seem conceivable. Conjoint actions seem definitely legitimate action candidates: chewing gum while walking, for example.

My purpose here is to probe the modalities of divinity. The primary aim is to see how flexible these modalities are, how little is actually demonstrable from the root conception of a divine nature. Omnipotence, for example, does not imply omniscience. An all-powerful being would have to be able to know everything (or perhaps: everything knowable – everything that anyone could know); but not to have chosen to exercise that ability. Nor indeed need perfection (if that trait could be given precision) imply omniscience, though I would think it should require omnipotence. Maybe a perfect and all-powerful being might have reason to draw a veil over some of what it could know should it wish to.

Some conclusions then: a literally all-powerful being probably is logically impossible but there seems no difficulty with the idea of a being with powers only a shade short of omnipotence, and morally speaking no less impressive. Put differently, if literal omnipotence is logically impossible then logically possible power that is maximal – no additional power could be added to it without logical impossibility resulting (there might well be a large variety of cases of possible maximal power) – is going to be as good as and as much as any theist (other than one of Anselmian mind set) could or would desire. Just as being able to do anything quite readily gives way, on more sophisticated reflection, to being able to do anything logically possible, so the latter, if contradictory, appropriately gives way to having a logically consistent set of powers so great that any addition to them would imply inconsistency.

In fact, as indicated above, most Christians, at least, have preferred that their God not even be able to err, sin, know indecision or surprise, etc. They have wanted his perfection to be essential to him. It is hard to see why this should be regarded as theologically, metaphysically, or morally desirable. However, if wanted, this notion too seems to permit the possibility of a being with quite staggering abilities and powers. At least it would if it truly were possible. It does not always seem to be appreciated that metaphysical modality is not something always available for legislative or stipulative purposes. Someone who says, suppose it were logically impossible for humans to be left-handed, does not suppose something that could be. Similarly, someone who says, suppose there were a person that was morally good in every world it existed in (or had amazing powers in every such world), seems to be supposing something that could not be. Traits of character, and power, seem simply inevitably to be characteristics that will be had varyingly in some of the indefinitely many possible worlds an individual with such traits will be found in. This appears to be a central part of what is wrong with the ontological argument. A person – any person, however extraordinary – is not a thing that could not not exist. Given that it is a person one is thinking of, one will be thinking of a thing that has, necessarily, contingent existence.[5] Similarly one will be thinking of a thing that could – in some worlds does – fail to be morally good or powerful.

God, then, if real, is contingently as his supporters can and should want him to be. And that seems to be perfectly all right. There is a viable and substantive concept formulable – likely more than one – for a being that could fit what non-Anselmian sorts of theistic believers have had in mind. Moreover, it seems that little is lost if such a being were only contingently as he is held to be.

One may reasonably query other divine traits than any we have yet discussed. How about omnipresence? God is supposed to be in some manner simultaneously everywhere. And how about immateriality? The former seems no problem metaphysically: it seems easy to conceive an aggregate sum of all perspectives – the view from everywhere, in total sum – with an extraordinary mind able to coordinate and integrate the whole set. Immateriality, for a person or mind, we deal with in Chapter 17.

Other themes and queries with respect to God than the familiar and exhaustively discussed ones may also have metaphysical interest, and deserve remark if only to illustrate the continued fecundity of the idea of God. One is the idea of what we might call a 'naturalist' God. The standard theological conception is of a God who does no work, in a physicist's sense. His knowledge, and the exercise of his power, are instantaneous. They involve neither mechanics nor dynamics. There are not ways by which his will is implemented. His power is total, and literally irresistible. That a proposition is true is enough to guarantee that God knows it, without attention needing to be paid to how he might do so (indeed, where there is no such how; he is conceived as not doing anything to bring it about that he knows the proposition).

It is interesting to think of a God who actualizes the world through an instrumentality, the translation of whose will involves a method, even if instrumentality and method are suitably divine, involving infinite power, for example. A God for whom there are mechanics, and dynamics. A God who works, in short (and not simply one who acts). Such a God, if there were one, would have a place in total physics. He would have an explanatory role in an adequate understanding of the nature of things. He would be restored, indeed, to an older place in natural theology, and folk philosophy, that he has had where hyper-rationalist over-clever over-pious philosophizing has not obtruded.

Further to this conception would be the possibility that there might be truths that God could not know, because they were inherently unknowable. These might include some cases of free choices. They might also include cases of subatomic physical states, where there is no sense in which the exact features of an outcome (if there are exact features) have issued from its predecessor, and no way by which precisely it has been produced; and perhaps also no precise or determinate way that the state was during the interval that produced that outcome. If the idea was that even God must have some means by which he can do whatever it is that he does, and knows whatever it is that he knows – where the means need not be one consonant with any known, or indeed (for us) intelligible natural principles, but nonetheless an inherently coherent means – there would seem then to ensue a world only mostly constrained by God's volitions and only mostly constrained to have the contents of its states known by him. In fact a plausible version of omniscience could still be retained in such a 'naturalized theology': just as the inability to do what is logically impossible is no limitation, so too the inability to know what is inherently unknowable is none. In some cases of such unknowability, there will in fact be nothing to know; in others, an unknowability because there is no determinative relation between a prior state of a system and a genuinely quantum random subsequent state. The overall resulting theological conception might in fact be argued to be consistent with orthodox Judaeo-Christian conceptions.

An independent line of theistic reflection may also be of interest to pursue. The specially Lutheran Christian conception (with roots in Stoicism and original Biblical Christian thought as well as in Luther (1483–1546)), most fully formulated in Kant, is the idea of a moral republic of free rational beings, subjects of consciousness and conscience, created not because God, the prince of this republic, was lonely or desirous of adoration, but because it was intrinsically valuable or good that such a community exist. Its goodness or value in this deeply Kantian understanding is the goodness of autonomous rational subjects, with inherent dignity and the potential for self-directing inwardness. A community of such beings, even if only able to be brought into existence by something like divine agency, has its greatest value in the fact of the resulting individual minds, in their individuality and in their mutual communion. Such mutual communion, even when with the prince of this community, may be held to be of the highest value where that prince has eschewed options of playing tricks – e.g., making miraculous interventions (even to help out a deserving mind in distress). Indeed he once having opted for a natural world with tenuousness and indeterminacies that he has willed, partly out of respect for his fellow citizens of the republic of minds, shall be the setting for this republic, it may seem persuasive that his own role would be compromised were he to contravene or reverse that natural world.

If there is a plausibly coherent divine nature formulable, and the nature so set out is possible, and even if there are notions of a possible God that have depth, moral and existential substance, we still must confront the direct and unevadable question: is God in fact actual?

The answer, I think, is, No. There is not the slightest serious good evidence for such an individual as the Judaeo-Christian-Islamic God. None of the historic or traditional 'proofs' has any genuine force, as students in introductory philosophy classes discover, and show, year after year.[6] To be sure, new arguments, sometimes quite complex, are developed from time to time by philosophers, and they will receive a brief round of consideration in the literature. But none appears to make any serious or longterm impression. 'Sire, I have no need of that hypothesis,' Laplace said to Napoleon when the latter asked where God was in his scientific system. The theistic scholium to Newton's *Principia*[7] notwithstanding, science has had no need or explanatory role for God in its hypotheses at any time since the seventeenth-century scientific revolution.[8] To be sure the fortuitousness of habitat for living systems on earth and some of the features of economy and apparently improbable conjunction in fundamental natural law, seemed naggingly still to speak for large-scale teleology in the world even to the anti-theistic Hume, who was an intellectually honest as well as a highly original thinker.[9] Darwin's discovery of natural selection put, if not the final nail, a significant fistful of further nails in the coffin of final causes – that is, of plausible evidence of final causes – in the world. It should seem odd, in fact, that if there were such a being as God, he would not have made his reality somewhat clear over the years. Moreover, if arguments from the problem of evil do not decisively refute the theistic hypothesis, they surely confer an extremely low probability on it.

Not only that, we can explain with some plausibility why people have so widely wanted to believe (as they still widely continue to believe) that there is a God, even in the more or less total absence of serious evidence. Anthropomorphic projection, fear of personal extinction and the hope that another person with enough power and concern for oneself might prevent it, and a desire that there be a father for the world as there was a father in one's childhood, to afford security, regulation, and love, together perhaps with an inherent psychological conservatism, a desire to preserve and maintain old ways (including old beliefs) that have been held widely and long, all seem sufficient to explain why so many have believed, in the face of non-evidence, and contrary evidence.

The foregoing affirmed, it seems to me that while the existence of God is improbable and implausible, it is not impossible. Like Leibniz, and Hume, I think that the atheist argument from the problem of evil is not a sound refutation even of standard or orthodox theism. An extraordinarily powerful and extremely morally impressive God could have reasons for allowing even gratuitous cruelties and other evils in a world he had created. That there exist free choices in the created world is not an adequate or sufficient reason. Many possible worlds with free will are clearly much morally superior, over all, to the actual world. One such reason is implied in the naturalizing Kantian theistic position sketched above. Inevitably 'prince' of the universe – creator, wildly disproportionately most excellent of its beings – a God might through 'moral republicanism' decline to be the universe's king, and bind himself to consequences of that abdication in a naturalistic developing of the world through its own causal logic.

Leibniz had a distinct ground for rejecting the argument from the problem of evil. He held that the universe contains – must contain – such an amplitude of being, so many systems, subsystems, and supersystems of actuality, that what we may know as the worst evils of the world may be held to be in fact among its worst evils anywhere, only allowed into total creation by the imperative the deity acts from to actualize as much as can be compossibly actualized, save only moral cesspools so extreme that not even the earth displays them. Interestingly, this is a version of 'many worlds' hypotheses entertained or advocated by a number of contemporary cosmologists.

It seems to me in fact not only possible (if improbable) that standard theism be true but possible – if still less probable – that some reasonably orthodox version of one of the major religions be true, among them Christianity. It is an interesting exercise for the philosophical imagination, with dimensions of philosophical history (Hegelian-style) as well as of moral, cosmological, and metaphysical theory, to try to work out, with details, a world-story that is both Christian and capable of fitting what we seriously know to be the empirical facts of the world.

Although the probability of some version of standard theism seems to be low, and particular world religions' versions of it still lower, that of many or most alternative theisms seems to me substantially lower still. The Russellian position that Olympian deities are at least as probable is unpersuasive. Those spirits have no assignable reasons for being hidden, for example, whereas the standard God has at least some. Moreover, the standard God, if actual, would provide a certain kind of explanation for the world, and would give it meaning, including, perhaps, axiological meaning. There seems no good reason to believe that the world needs that meaning or explanation. And I have argued that the existence of a God would not solve the riddle of existence, only relocate the place where the riddle is to be posed. So, I think, these are not good arguments or reasons for believing in God. Yet if – against the odds – it turns out that there is a God, this would not be without parallel. Sometimes an improbable hypothesis is nonetheless correct.

Chapter Sixteen

Freedom and Determinism

I

The term *libertarianism* has two primary meanings in philosophy. In political philosophy, libertarianism (a view associated with Locke, and with people like Ayn Rand (1905–82) and Robert Nozick in this century) is the theory that there ought to be only minimal states, whose functions would be limited to protecting property rights (conceiving one's life and body, as Locke does, as part of one's property). In the philosophy of mind and action, libertarianism is the view that human persons perform actions that are both free and undetermined.

The latter terminological usage seems unfortunate since it leaves without a name the view that human persons perform actions that are free (whether or not those actions are also determined). A few philosophers simply appropriate libertarianism for the latter idea. However, this seems to lead to some confusion, and as indicated, libertarianism as the conjunction of freedom and indeterminism for actions is already centrally and firmly in place.

We clearly need a term for this fundamental notion that virtually everyone takes to be grounded in everyday experience, that we can and do perform free actions, which issue from us, that are within our power to do or not do as we may choose or prefer, actions that we do for reasons (more or less) consciously and deliberately. Some use the ungainly term free will-ism for this theory. I prefer to use a slightly more euphonious term. I will call the theory that we sometimes act freely *libertism*.

Incompatibilism is the thesis that determinism and libertism are logically incompatible. Or (a way of expressing the view that will imply but not be implied by the latter), it is the view that if determinism were true, it would follow from that fact alone that libertism was false; and that if libertism were true, it would follow from that fact alone that determinism was false. Obviously, then, we need to proceed to indicate what is meant by determinism, and to say more than already said, about libertism.

It is to be remarked right away that some people, including both philosophers and non-philosophers, have meant by these two theories something such that it would indeed follow immediately, and in fact trivially, that the one was inconsistent with the other. Some people have said that they understand the idea that we act freely as implying, if true, that some events occur without any cause or explanation whatever: that this was part of the meaning of 'free will' or 'free act' for them. Similarly some have meant by determinism a theory which, by definition, would include the idea that there are no free choices, no capacities for a person doing otherwise than as they do. Clearly notions such as these two theories would establish the truth of incompatibilism very quickly, and, as I have said, trivially.

I think however that neither of these concepts or definitions of determinism and free acts or free will is in fact what most people who have thought about either have in mind. First, people have usually meant by determinism something that does not explicitly say anything about free action or free will or for that matter anything about human beings or rational agents of any kind. Determinism is a thesis about the structure of the universe (or some isolated part of it), and the world could have been a deterministic one whether there were any human beings, or thinking beings of any kind, in it. Determinism involves the idea of a natural law, or law of nature. For now it is sufficient to note that the kind of natural law relevant for determinism is an exceptionless general law, a principle or general truth asserting that whenever an instance of one set of circumstances obtains, then a certain event, state, or process occurs. This provides a necessary condition of being a deterministic natural law. Enlarging conditions until there is reached a set of conditions which will be jointly sufficient for being a deterministic natural law is more complicated, and remains still in some respects controversial.

There are probably more theses than one that can be erected on the base identified so far, and which might all with some plausibility be called determinism. Certainly many contemporary philosophers would assert that there are more determinisms than one, some regarded as stronger than others. I want to talk about the strongest possible determinism: so long as it is not a theory that says explicitly that every single event in the universe, considered all by itself and without reference to any other event or any general law, is something that occurs necessarily. In fact the latter is a view that no one, I think, would want to make part of their definition of determinism. Some think it would follow from a good definition of determinism, but that is a different matter.

I want to consider and, for the sake of argument, accept the idea that laws of nature of the kind I have been referring to – deterministic laws – include a type of necessity. It will not, and cannot, involve what is usually called logical necessity. One of the most important contributions that empiricist philosophy has made to the philosophy of science is the idea that natural laws are not (and fundamentally are not like) truths of logic: that the discovery and confirmation of a natural law requires observation and experience, and could not be reached a priori. This contribution is associated especially with Hume. Hume, and the empiricist tradition in the philosophy of science that stems from him, hold that it is a complete mistake to regard natural laws as including necessity of any sort; or at least that there is no warrant in experience for believing that they do. The entire logical empiricist tradition in twentieth-century philosophy of science held that the necessity commonly supposed to be involved in what science teaches us about the world – the 'must' of 'a piece of copper must expand if heated' or 'heavy objects must go more slowly than the speed of light' – is simply something that is superimposed on what science actually teaches us. According to this view, what science teaches us is what does occur; in fact – at least in the cases of deterministic events and processes – what always does occur, in every case without exception; but never what must occur. The latter is something we read into nature or what science tells us about nature. When we do so we exceed our evidence and perhaps become illogical. According to some logical empiricists, and Hume himself, we are being anthropomorphic, and transferring ideas we have of coercive social laws and human institutions to nature. Or we are, equally unjustifiably, transferring ideas of logical or mathematical necessity to nature. Of course scientists themselves talk this way when they are talking loosely but never when they are actually engaged in science.

This Humean-logical empiricist view may or may not be true. Its critics include philosophers who have attempted to develop, sometimes in highly complex and formal ways, notions of a natural necessity that would go with being a law of nature but would not be anthropomorphic or anthropocentric. With this line of thought, we could say that deterministic natural law does not merely say that whenever an instance of a set of circumstances of a certain kind obtains, then a certain event (state, process) occurs, but that whenever the circumstances obtain, then the event necessarily occurs. Let us assume that this line of thought is sound or, at least, let us incorporate this idea into what we mean by determinism and assert that by deterministic laws we shall mean necessary, exceptionless general principles (or facts).

Let us also move directly to the idea of a deterministic system. A deterministic system will be a system all the elements in which are events, states, or processes that are instances of deterministic laws as we now understand the latter, reminding ourselves that we have still provided only an incomplete account of the conditions involved in a deterministic law. Let us continue to what may be called, for good historical reasons, a Laplacean system.[1] A Laplacean system will be a deterministic one in which, from the set of all the deterministic laws of the system, together with a complete assertion of the state of all the individuals in the system at a given time, all states of all individuals in the system at any time, may be logically deduced. There are more or less technical difficulties that are involved with this idea of a complete state description – the term is Carnap's – that a Laplacean system includes. We want a complete state description, in the sense relevant here, to contain no references to any other times than the time to which the description is supposed to apply, for example. This is I think an intuitive idea. We have the notion of the way the system is at a specified time – the state it is in then, without reference to any other states or times – and this is what is most centrally meant by a complete state description.

Determinism then is the thesis that the actual universe is a Laplacean system. I remind you that this is meant to be a strong version of determinism, the strongest possible non-trivial version, I would say. Some would hold that any developed version of determinism would lead to or imply Laplacean determinism. I do not know if this is true, though I suspect that it is; or at least that the further assumptions necessary to reach Laplacean determinism from weaker forms would be wholly uncontroversial. This may be over-sanguine. Bertrand Russell argued[2] that relativity theory renders incoherent or meaningless the concept of a complete state of the universe at a time, since the latter requires an absolute, non-relative notion of simultaneity, something relativity theory precludes. More than the present concern requires that Russell is wrong about this. If determinism is true, then every event, state, and process in the universe, including every human action, is an instance of a necessary exceptionless general law or a set of such laws; and such that the occurrence of that event, state, process, or action could have been predicted or retrodicted from any earlier or later (respectively) state of the universe – so long as everything in the earlier or later state is included – together with a complete set of the laws of nature. In more vivid and immediate terms for ourselves, it means that, if determinism is true, then every action that every human being ever performs could, in principle, have been predicted with 100 per cent accuracy 20 million years ago; and that each action is a case of natural law, such that, given the law and the conditions antecedent to the action, the action necessarily occurs.

Now we know, or apparently know, that determinism is in fact false. This is one of the most important and exciting results of twentieth-century physical theory. There is evidently good reason to believe that there are events whose occurrence is genuinely random and in principle unpredictable. These events have no causes at all. Modern physical theory is indeterministic since determinism is false.

However, it is only gradually in the course of that century that this has come to be seen. There is some evidence, I believe, that many social scientists still do not know, or perhaps they have heard but do not believe, that the universe is partly undetermined, and that the most that could in principle be attained for many varieties of phenomena that science investigates is probabilistic natural law. In any case there is no firm evidence as yet that any distinctively human phenomena are indeterminate, so perhaps diehard deterministic social scientists are merely being parochial. Maybe all distinctively human behaviour is subject to deterministic law; hence, even if determinism is false for the whole world, it may be true for specific subsystems of the universe, including those relevant for social science (or particular parts of social science).

Further, determinism was believed to be true or at least was a guiding general presupposition of inquiry, in the natural sciences at least, from Galileo in the early 1600s, into the early 1900s: the three hundred years during which the disciplines we know, and the general framework of assumptions and procedures that have shaped and guided intellectual inquiry, were formed. We are the heirs of a civilization in which scientific investigation was the search for deterministic laws and in which, in the natural sciences at least, there was and continues to be a remarkable degree of success in this search.

II

The conception and conviction that science implies determinism leads to the case of human behaviour, especially what we take in everyday life to be deliberate, chosen, free human actions. What about them?

Libertism is the theory that human beings sometimes act freely, i.e., that they perform actions which they choose to perform and which are such that they – the human agents performing the actions – could have done otherwise. It is I think misleading and unnecessary to make any special reference to a so-called free will in explaining libertism. We may or may not have a will and it may or may not be free. What we are really concerned about is ourselves, other human beings, and our actions and choices. We think and act. We perform a certain action on a particular occasion and we suppose that we could have behaved differently; that it was up to us, within our power, to have done something other than what we did. Could we ever have acted differently? Libertism is the view that sometimes, at least, we can.

As I have indicated, some philosophers have actually defined a free act as one that is, among other things, uncaused or undetermined. Such definitions seem unwarranted, if they reflect what we commonly believe about ourselves, our actions, and freedom. By this I do not mean to imply that ordinary notions imply that free actions are caused or determined; rather that they are silent or agnostic about the matter, explicitly. Let us stress that the freedom we are concerned with here is not a philosopher's technical concept. Its root is in everyday lived experience. It is the feature of our actions whereby, as we suppose – and whatever the right analysis of this turns out to be – our actions are up to us, within our power, issue from our choices, are done for reasons we have and are such that we could have done something else. None of that means that our actions, while free, are thereby uncaused or undetermined. If the latter really obtains, then it remains to be shown. It cannot be assumed or subsumed as part of the concept of a free act.

Let me note parenthetically that libertism (and libertarianism) as such says nothing about morality. Many people interested in human freedom in the sense meant here are primarily interested in ethical issues. It will evidently be the case that if human beings are ever morally responsible for their actions, then libertism must be true. However, the converse does not hold: it does not follow from the assumption that people are free, i.e., sometimes act freely, that there is moral responsibility, or that anyone has the property of being good or bad. If libertism is true, it provides no evidence whatsoever for the objectivity of ethics or the truth of any view about morality.

III

Returning to our central theme, it is I think a fact that most people, philosophers and non-philosophers, who have thought about determinism and libertism have supposed that the truth of the former would preclude the truth of the latter. They have not, as I have shown, thought that this was true by definition of the constituent terms but as a consequence of those definitions together with uncontroversial principles. I shall try to show that this widespread belief is untrue. I shall also try to explain how this erroneous belief has become so widespread.

Before that however I want to set out some speculative hypotheses about the history and development of social science over the course of the 300 years of Galilean-Newtonian supremacy in the natural sciences. My hypothesis is that the belief in incompatibilism – the belief that human action is (sometimes) free only if determinism is false – led to two fundamentally distinct and incompatible outcomes. One group felt that the case for determinism and the achievements of deterministic natural science were too impressive to be credibly denied and that it must therefore be supposed that human behaviour is as fully determined as the behaviour of a mollusc or a chunk of iron; and hence that the belief in free action is an illusion. In this group, some were scientifically disposed and some were not. For the latter there was already available predestinarian religious theories – Calvinism, for example – to fill in a worldview that could cheer or terrify, according to the temperament of the individual. For those scientifically disposed this internalized incompatibilism led to the ideal and the pursuit of naturalistic social science. This took many forms most strikingly in nineteenth-century sociology and psychology. I take Marx (1818–83) and Freud (1856–1939), respectively, to be particularly clear instances of this pattern.

In saying so, however, this should be accompanied by the observation that determinism as such is not a materialist or physicalist theory, in the metaphysical sense. Metaphysical materialism holds that every existing individual, state, event, and process – in sum, the whole of the real – is physical or material in nature. It is usually contrasted with metaphysical idealism, which holds that everything real is mental in nature; and with metaphysical dualism, which holds that reality divides into two fundamentally and irreducibly distinct classes of phenomena, things (including objects, events, etc.) which are physical in nature, and those which are mental, together possibly with some compound phenomena which have elements of both – these elements remaining unconquerably distinct. Someone could be an idealist and a determinist, and someone could be a dualist and a determinist. As it happens, idealists and dualists have typically been anti-determinists, and materialism and determinism have tended to go hand in hand, but this is an accident. Marx and Freud prove this as well as illustrating my historical case, since both were determinists and professed to be anti-libertists. Each offered what they claimed were frameworks for and much of the content of the sciences of man. Both also claimed to be materialists, but the claim in both cases does not survive scrutiny. Marx's materialism is not metaphysical materialism but the supremacy of the material over the mental in the causal order. In fact his contrast is not between the material and the mental in the metaphysical sense, but between the concrete and practical, and what is concerned with human well-being and advantage (all of which will include some mental phenomena), on the one hand, and the abstract, the spiritual and the ideational, on the other. In any case Marx regards both as real; it is just, for him, that whatever occurs is determined by the material (in his sense). As for Freud, though he professed that his theories would eventually give way to biological theories, he made absolutely no contributions to this development. His theories remain entirely dualist methodologically, and provide a rich and interesting illustration of how a dualist, determinist, anti-libertist theory of human behaviour can work.

In general the phenomenon I describe may seem familiar and persuasive. Naturalistic social science has taken other forms as well; it is, usually in methodologically unstated or understated, form the general framework for the prevailing schools and movements in academic psychology in the twentieth century. Approaches tend now to be heuristic and there is little commitment generally to trying to prove anti-libertism. Part of the moral of these remarks will be that naturalistic social science is the right model within which to operate, but that, since incompatibilism is false and determinism so very general a theory (as well as being false) that it offers no research directives whatsoever, there has been a good deal of misplaced dichotomizing in the social sciences.

However, that looks ahead. It is the second contingent of pre-twentieth-century incompatibilism I am interested in now. These people, unwilling to surrender human liberty, took a different path. It is the theorists among them I really focus on, those wanting to understand the world and have an integrated picture of it. These people formed, and in the nineteenth century more fully developed, the idea of two distinct spheres of inquiry: the realm of nature, which is subject to determinism and is mechanistic, and the realm of freedom, which is indeterminist. The earliest thinker to really assert this view is Descartes. I shall call the general position I have in mind cognitive dualism. It opposes itself very naturally to what is standardly called the Unity of Science view in the philosophy of science. Descartes was unusual among cognitive dualists in actually being more interested in the material and natural half of the duality than in the mental. At least his systematic theoretical work was in the direction of contributions to natural philosophy. Most cognitive dualists have been far more interested in the realm of freedom than nature. At any rate, this bifurcation, in full flower, saw – and still sees, for this is a continuing legacy in the contemporary world of philosophy and social science – the two realms as involving not only distinct subject matter but distinct methodologies, and even a distinct logic. The *Naturwissenschaften*, or sciences of nature, are deterministic and involve the subsumption of particular cases to be explained or predicted under exceptionless general law; and the *Geisteswissenschaften*, or sciences of spirit (or mind), are indeterminist and involve the faculty of intuitive understanding. Both are sciences, both legitimate, rational, and wholly sui generis, unique and irreducible, each to the other. Since Dilthey (1833–1911), the nineteenth-century historicist who drew this contrast in the way I have indicated, cognitive dualists have tended to see cognitive monists (the unity of science people), especially when they are social scientists or philosophers of science, as enemies wrongly treading on what is not their terrain.

Prominent twentieth-century schools of cognitive dualism are hermeneutics and phenomenological psychology.

If I am right about incompatibilism – that is, right in believing that incompatibilism was the primary historical reason for the rise of cognitive dualism and its manifestation in *Geisteswissenschaftliche* schools of social science, and right in believing that incompatibilism is false – then this polarity in the history of nineteenth- and twentieth-century philosophy and social science was misconceived and ought to be dissolved or at least redirected. Let me turn now to the purely philosophical issue of whether incompatibilism is false.

If determinism is false, one may feel, why bother? The answer, as already indicated, is that though universal determinism is untrue, comprehensive subsystems are deterministic and all those involving human action may be among them. Further, the question of the conceptual relations between determinism and libertism has intrinsic interest and, I shall try to show, much to teach us.

IV

Let us begin with this question as many feel inclined to do: if determinism is what I have said it is, then is it not obvious that no one could act differently than they do? However, it is not in fact obvious. The burden of proof lies at the door of the incompatibilist to make his or her case because determinism as such is so very general a thesis. As we said, it does not mention people, their abilities, or actions in the explication of the idea.

If incompatibilism is true, then a sound argument ought to be constructible from premises asserting determinism and the relevant laws of nature to the conclusion that no one can do other than they do. Strictly speaking, to the conclusion that if there are persons performing specified actions, then those persons cannot do other than they do. It is unlikely prima facie that such an argument can be constructed and this is the first part of the proof that incompatibilism is false. That this is unlikely can be seen by noting again just what determinism does and does not assert. As we have characterized it, determinism asserts that every event is explainable (and predictable) as an instance of necessary laws of nature, that is, of assertions (or facts – there are grounds for regarding laws as both) of the form, ⌜necessarily, if instances of $C_1, C_2 ... C_n$ occur then an instance of E obtains⌝ – where the C's are relevant prior conditions, and E is the event in which we are interested. The laws that we are allowing to be necessary in some manner – a manner appropriate for natural laws – but this alone will not of course establish the necessity either of the C's or of E.

David Hume was one of the first clear compatibilists[3] and the very first to

say that the apparent problem of liberty and necessity and their alleged conflict is a pseudo-problem: specifically that the apparent problem stems from a
semantic confusion. This is the sort of claim that in the two centuries following Hume has become stock-in-trade in philosophical polemics and is deserv-
edly, at least in the general case, viewed with suspicion. It seems to me
however that this is indeed a good part of how people come to be incompatibilists, and that Hume was perfectly correct.

The core set of ideas that incompatibilism and its opposite number involve
are the ideas of modality: i.e., those of necessity, possibility, and contingency.
There is good reason to believe that in English and related languages there is a
great measure of imprecision in the manipulation of modal concepts. There is
a remarkable richness of alternatives in the family of modal expressions –
'necessarily,' 'must,' 'has to,' 'has got to' all express one of the key ideas;
'might,' 'may,' 'can,' 'possibly' and others express another of them – and yet
this lexical variety fails to disclose the fact that there seem to be radically dissimilar kinds of necessity and possibility. There are other counter-productive
features of typical modal discourse. Consider this argument (call it A):

(1) If Jones is a bachelor, then, necessarily, Jones is unmarried.
(2) Jones is a bachelor.
∴ (3) Necessarily, Jones is unmarried.

Let us suppose that the second premise is in fact true, and that the individual
referred to as Jones is a bachelor. The first premise is also true. At least, taken
as it seems most natural, it says something that appears true. The conclusion
however is false. It, does not affirm (merely) that Jones is unmarried. It affirms
that it is a necessary truth that Jones is unmarried, that this is something which
could not be false. However, it is easy to suppose (3) to be false. It is easy to
suppose that Jones gets married.

Yet, rather oddly, the argument may have looked at first as obviously valid,
a simple instance of the classic valid inference pattern called *modus ponens*,
viz.,

if *p* then *q*
p
∴ *q*

What has happened? Are we saying then that *modus ponens* is not always
valid? No. What has happened is this: the reasoning involved in *A* is fallacious. The fallacy involved is sometimes called Sleigh's fallacy, after a philos-

opher who does not commit it frequently but rather who often points it out.[4] Premise (1), in *A*, is actually equivalent to

(1)′ Necessarily, if Jones is a bachelor, then Jones is unmarried.

Thus the necessity asserted in (1) is supposed to be something which attaches to the link between Jones' being a bachelor and his being unmarried, not something which will attach to his being unmarried, if it should happen that Jones is a bachelor. That is, the more syntactically revealing equivalent of (1) is (1)′, and not

(1)″ If Jones is a bachelor, then: it is something that is necessarily true that Jones is unmarried.

The resources of modal logic bring this out more sharply. A standard symbol for necessity in modal logic is a square or a box. The general form of argument *A* then is (*B*)

(i) $\square$ (if *p* then *q*)
(ii) *p*
∴ (iii) $\square$ *q*

This is the argument form that is invalid and fallacious. Simply because it is a necessary truth, something that absolutely has to be, that if *p* is true than *q* is true, and also because it happens to be true that *p*, it will not follow that *q* is, all by itself, something that is necessarily true, something that has to be. The valid argument form will be (*C*)

(i) if *p* then $\square$ *q*
(ii) *p*
∴ (iii) $\square$ *q*

This one is valid. The only thing is that there is typically no reason to believe that instances of its first premise are true. Certainly, there will not be if *p* stood for 'Jones is a bachelor' and *q* for 'Jones is unmarried.' Another way to say all this is to say that from the absolute, iron necessity of it having to be that if Jones is a bachelor then Jones is unmarried, together with Jones really being a bachelor, it will follow – will really, necessarily follow – that Jones is unmarried. However, it will not follow that Jones is necessarily unmarried. That is, argument form *D*

(i) $\square$ (if p then q)

(ii) p

$\therefore$ (iii) q

is a valid pattern of reasoning.

How will all of this prove or help prove the falsehood of incompatibilism? The necessity of our examples is evidently what is called logical or conceptual necessity, not the natural necessity we are interested in. Nonetheless the patterns discussed are paralleled exactly in assertions of determinism and the conclusions drawn from them. Let us use the symbol $\boxed{C}$ to express natural or causal necessity: the impossibility of something not occurring in the natural sense. Then we can express deterministic laws as having the form

$\boxed{C}$ (if an instance of C_1, C_2, ... , C_n occurs, then an instance of E obtains)

and the appropriate statement of relevant prior conditions, the sort of thing we have in mind as comprising (jointly) the cause of cases of E occurring, as follows:

An instance of C_1, C_2, ... C_n has occurred/will occur.

And the corresponding conclusion will be:

An instance of E obtains.

That is to say, from the necessity of all the laws of nature, and the assertion that every event is explainable as an instance of such laws, and the assertion that the appropriate causal conditions have obtained, it will follow, definitely and unerringly, that the event we are interested in – that is, for our concerns, some human action – does occur. It will not follow – and more, we will have been given no reason whatsoever to believe that the event – the action – had to occur.

V

Some complicated arguments for incompatibilism have appeared in recent years, developed chiefly by Peter Van Inwagen, intended to show that determinism implies features of the past that preclude freedom. I will turn to these arguments subsequently. Apart from them, it is reasonable to claim I think that only by committing Sleigh's fallacy can a case for incompatibilism be mounted. Only in this way can one be mounted that will not simply assert, without argument, that if an action follows from conditions such that given the conditions, the action necessarily occurs, that then the action was something the person performing it could not have avoided doing.

The compatibilist claims that resolving the free will-determinism issue, even just understanding it, requires a degree of semantic sensitivity finer-grained that people normally bring to the philosophical topics they consider, specifically a finely honed modal awareness. Compatibilism, as argued here, leads to the conclusion that we have no alternatives given the conditions in which we act, we cannot do other than as we do given the antecedent background, and results similarly expressible. This may appear serious and heavy. Incompatibilism requires though the conclusion that we cannot do other than we do and this the compatibilist denies. Thus he or she says that from instances of the schema

(i) S cannot do otherwise than perform action A given relevant antecedent
    conditions $C_1, \ldots , C_n$

it does not follow, nor is there afforded any reason to believe

(ii) S cannot do otherwise than perform action A

Nor will (ii) follow form (i) together with the conjoint statement of all the laws of nature and the assertion that $C_1, C_2, \ldots , C_n$ have obtained.

Moreover the compatibilist insists (i) is misconceived if taken to limit agent $S's$ powers of action. For what does an assertion of type ⌜unavoidably true given C⌝ mean? It means, the compatibilist says, ⌜it is unavoidably true, and beyond the power of an agent to alter, that if C, then p⌝. That *given*, in short, makes all the difference in the world.

At the risk of overkill, let me restate the matter still more fully. Consider the following set of patterns of argument. In this set we have alternative possibilities for the first premise, which may or may not be equivalent to each other.

I. C causally necessitated S ϕ-ing

    or

    S couldn't avoid ϕ-ing, given C

    or

    S necessarily ϕ-ed, given C

or

If C occurred, then, necessarily, S φ-ed.

II. C occurred

∴ III. S had to φ or couldn't avoid φ-ing or necessarily φ-ed.

About this pattern of argument, in any of its forms, one asks the question: Is it valid? Incompatibilists – except for Peter van Inwagen and Storrs McCall (for different reasons in each case), and those like-minded – answer Yes. And in so answering, they betray their confusion, since the correct answer is the compatibilist answer, No: i.e., this pattern of reasoning is invalid. The conclusion does not follow from the premises, and supposing that it does, commits a form of Sleigh's fallacy (p, if p then, necessarily, q, ∴ necessarily q). Virtually all incompatibilists, in the history of the issue – so I contend and would be prepared to document – have committed this fallacy, and are only incompatibilists because they do so. Van Inwagen has quite different arguments against compatibilism and might well accept the invalidity of this pattern of reasoning. McCall offers a different perspective According to him the argument is neither valid nor invalid, but defective or ill-formed since the conclusion is so. According to McCall 'S had to φ/could not avoid φ-ing/necessarily φ-ed' is always elliptical for 'S had to φ/could not avoid φ-ing/necessarily φ-ed, given some set of circumstances C'.[5] This view seems implausible; we certainly seem able to understand 'necessarily φ-ing' without reference to attending circumstance.

VI

Peter van Inwagen's 1975 paper, 'The Incompatibility of Free Will and Determinism,'[6] and several subsequent publications have generated a·new sub-literature on the subject. Van Inwagen's new defence of incompatibilism has the virtue of clarity and technical proficiency. He at least does not commit Sleigh's fallacy and defends himself with vigour and ingenuity against compatibilists who have thought his views easily refuted.

Nonetheless, it is difficult to believe that van Inwagen makes good his claims of refuting compatibilism. By his own account the elaborate argument he produces is a rendering of the idea that since we cannot causally affect either the past or the laws of nature, and since determinism implies that every act issues causally from past states of the world (plus the laws of nature), hence, eventually in the chain of causal linkage, from states of the world prior to the agent's birth, since the agent can do nothing to affect or prevent those states, he or she can do nothing to prevent or affect the putatively free present act. Van Inwagent calls this the Consequence Argument.

It seems clearly to be a bad argument. It rests on the unstated assumption that states transmit their properties to their effects. Thus: the state-of-the-world-prior-to-my-birth P had the property of being unable to be affected or modified by me. My (allegedly free) act A issues directly, deterministically, from P (doubtless through a very large number of intermediary states). Therefore A has the property of being unable to be affected or modified by me. However this assumption is certainly false. P will have many properties – e.g. occurring (or obtaining) in the fourteenth century (for some cases of P) – which A will not have. States transmit some of their properties to their causal successors. They definitely do not transmit all of them. Van Inwagen offers no adequate reason for believing either that agents' powers of modifying (some part of) the world or, the complementary case, being beyond the power of agents to affect, are among the first rather than the second group of cases. He does argue, as other incompatibilists have, that if determinism were true, we would have to have the power to alter the past. Since we don't, it can't be true. However (as Gilbert Ryle argued usefully long ago in *Dilemmas*)[7] in one sense our freedom has to involve a sort of 'power to alter the past,' independently of determinism. Thus, if it is up to me whether to buy a plane ticket to Tangier, and I do, then in a sense it will have been up to me whether it will have been the case a million years ago that I would buy that ticket. However, there is no reason to regard this as implying backwards causation. I do not cause something to have been the case (or not) long ago by my acts. As for 'temporally pure' states in the past, states that involve no reference to earlier or later events, van Inwagen again gives no non-question-begging reason to think that they would need properties (like modifiability by an agent living and acting now) that their remote causal descendants have.

VII

The case against incompatibilism can be augmented. As I have said, determinism as such is an exceedingly general thesis about the structure of the universe. As such it says nothing about the kind of laws of nature there are. It will be – as we have seen already in the cases of Marx and Freud – perfectly possible that there turn out to be psychological or sociological laws of nature, some or all of which might be irreducible to laws of any other kind, e.g., to laws of physics, biochemistry, or evolutionary biology. There may even be laws of freedom – that is, laws which express under what circumstances someone will freely choose to perform certain actions and invariably succeed in exercising this choice. Nothing about determinism as such rules this out. If freedom, in the libertist sense, is an ability or capacity that at least some human beings have, possibly some other animals occasionally have, but that definitely other animals do not have, and no un-thinking non-living physical objects ever have, then, it seems plausible to suppose, possibly, like other abilities and capacities it is something that develops in species of animals that achieve a sufficiently sophisticated degree of complexity, and functions of the right sort, in their cerebral cortex. Some have proposed thinking of freedom as an emergent property. Possibly there are laws of the emergence of this very capacity: the capacity to act freely, to act in such a way that you choose, act for reasons, and can act otherwise than as you do. These would presumably be laws of evolutionary biology.

What might such laws be like? What might a law of freedom look like? Let me attempt to provide the skeletal framework of an answer at least to the second of these questions. A law of freedom, at least in very general form, might say something like:

© (if a human being is alert, awake, in a choice situation where his or her alternatives are A, B, and C, and he or she strongly prefers A to either B or C, dislikes both B and C, has no reason not to choose A, and knows this, believes he or she will be benefited by choosing A, but disadvantaged by choosing B or C, and is correct in both beliefs, and is such that nothing in his or her vicinity will impede his or her obtaining A if he or she were to choose it, and has the ability freely to choose any of A, B, or C, then the human being will choose and obtain A).

Now: complex as the C's – the prior relevant circumstances – are in this case, it is still possible that with sufficient ingenuity someone might find a counterexample to the proposed form of a law of freedom. If they did, one may simply take whatever general feature the counterexample involved and add the absence of that feature to the antecedent of the conditional. Ad hoc? Not at all. This is an example of how the enterprise of seeking to replace a merely statistical or probabilistic law of nature with a genuinely deductive or deterministic law in any area of scientific investigation, typically goes. We would aim to arrive at all those conditions which are invariably there whenever a person successfully acts upon a choice for reasons – the paradigmatic context of free action.

The advance predictability of an action is clearly no bar to its being free. We sometimes know what choice situations other people, or ourselves, will be in on future occasions; and we sometimes know, in advance, what the people in question will do. Because of knowledge of their character and values but also because of knowledge of the choice situations. There are situations where someone would, as we say, be a fool not to choose a certain option that will be available to them and where we know that the person is not a fool. We cannot of course make predictions that will have anything approaching 100 per cent accuracy. However, this is because we cannot know all relevant factors. We cannot know for example whether the earth will be struck by a comet or the agent suffer a fatal heart attack before the choice situation occurs. But the idealized predictor of the Laplacean model suffers no such limitations. He or she knows all the laws of nature and all the circumstances obtaining, throughout the universe, at some given point in time. His or her predications will be 100 per cent certain. Yet they will predict unerringly what will occur – not what must happen.

There remain many dimensions to my theme I have not addressed. I have not said enough, for example, about the nature of the ability that I have argued constitutes freedom. Is it like the ability to run, for example, or the ability to memorize poetry? And how similar or dissimilar? What is the proof that the agent can do other than he or she does? This question does seem answerable. The proof – all the proof that there could be of such a matter and it is a sufficient proof – is that in relevantly similar circumstances the agent does do otherwise, or can be conceived as doing so. This too deserves more extended discussion. There will be nothing about determinism that will prevent such discussion and analysis from proceeding.

VIII

I go on to elaborate upon freedom and address the views of another recent contributor to the compatibilism/incompatibilism issue, Daniel Dennett. Consideration of his views will be seen I think not materially to alter the views already defended. But we may have an enlarged picture of what our freedom is, and its extent.

In his book *Elbow Room*,[8] subtitled 'The Varieties of Free Will Worth Wanting,' Daniel Dennett, without using this term, revives a compatibilist position weaker than the one I have been defending called 'soft determinism.' The latter holds that we do not have the ability or power to act otherwise than we do but that that is all right since we nonetheless act (sometimes) for reasons, and not subject to external constraint or irrational internal constraint, and this is enough to justify our being characterized as free. Soft determinism contrasts with the compatibilism defended here, which holds that we do, in typical free cases, have the ability to act otherwise than we do, and that there is nothing about determinism which would preclude this.

Libertism as I have explained (I will not say defined) it, involves centrally the idea that if you were free you must have the ability, power, or capacity to do something other than anything you can correctly be said to have done freely. Indeed, the most useful or effective way of explaining (and perhaps even defining) what freedom is seems to be as a very general ability, capacity, or power, which beings of a certain degree of complexity and a certain range of mental functioning can have. Some beings have the ability to run a three-minute mile. Some can walk and chew gum at the same time. Better cases possibly are located with abilities that go by species. Some beings have the capacity to swim while others do not. Some can add three digit numbers in their heads. Some have an ability to fall in love with others of their species. None of these abilities need of course be exercised in the cases of particular members of the species. Other abilities – like the ability to walk or use language – will in the general, non-handicapped case, always be exercised.

In this mode of thinking, free will or freedom is a very generic ability, which, we suppose, the typical human possesses. This leaves open the question whether this ability might come in degrees, and whether some might lack it entirely. Perhaps freedom can and should be viewed as an emergent property, developed in the course of our species' evolution. An ability is an ability to do something. This ability will be, it would seem, the ability to perform actions that have been thought about and intended that would be, if done, performed for reasons that the human performing them had, and, that the human could have refrained from doing. The latter is of course what is primarily at issue here. Is it important, necessary, desirable, or plausible to identify as a constituent in the frame of abilities that we have in mind as freedom a power to do otherwise or differently?

Dennett, in *Elbow Room*, argues that there is no convincing reason to think that free will – at least (in his phrase) a free will worth wanting – should be conceived as including such an ability as this. He argues that the usual 'could' of the 'could have done otherwise' standardly ascribed to agents, is usually epistemic or ought to be so construed. That is, according to Dennett, when we say that someone could have acted differently than they did we really mean to say, or ought to mean, that it is consistent with our evidence or the agent's evidence, that they have done otherwise. For all we know, or could have predicted in advance, they would have done otherwise. One of the many salutary features of Dennett's book is its eloquent depiction of how remote from reality the old conception of a Laplacean predictor is. Nature is far more complicated than classical deterministic models ever allowed for; quite apart from the genuine indeterminacies and randomness we apparently now know to be present in the universe. There is no practical possibility of predicting even very restricted portions of the universe's coming history, not even with anything foreseeable as a knowledge gain. So if we say that someone in an anticipated choice situation could do *a*, or refrain from doing so, we are confessing honest ignorance. We just do not know how nature will force the agent to act.

It seems to me that Dennett's intuitions are off in the case of the ability to do otherwise. He may be right that we have no such ability – it is to that that I wish to turn in a moment – but the case he makes in Chapter 6 ('Could Have Done Otherwise') of his book, that is to say, the intuitive perspective that is urged there, seems to me unsound. Dennett argues that in central, paradigmatic cases of freedom, cases we all acknowledge to be such, there is plainly and avowedly no ability to do otherwise. One of his cases is Martin Luther's declaration 'Here I stand. I can do no other.' I will not take the time to argue this here but Luther's 'can' seems to me very definitely a deontic 'can.' He means that his conscience, his duty as he sees it, requires that he not do otherwise; not that he might not be able to get himself to do otherwise, were he (as no doubt, as a fallible and sin-disposed human, he could) to prefer to fail to do what conscience says he should. Dennett also discusses and endorses Frankfurt's cases of overdetermined actions, where the agent (though he does not know it) could be forced to do what he freely intends and wants to do, were he to have a change of heart.[9] These seem to me to be (*pace* both Frankfurt and Dennett) cases where the agent really could have done otherwise (if there are any such cases), even though were the agent to seek to exercise this ability, doing so would trigger or set in motion a chain of events (in Frankfurt's examples the chain is very short, and operates very quickly; but these facts are irrelevant to the logic of the case) that would result in the loss of that ability. But that this consequence would ensue from attempting to exercise the agent's ability in a particular way will not show that in the microsecond prior to undertaking action the agent does not have the abilities both to act and refrain. Dennett's remaining cases are of situations where the agent really could not do otherwise (or so it appears); but where, according to me, it is correspondingly doubtful that the agent is free. These are cases where education, upbringing, and possibly inherent predispositions of character have led to an individual who, in a certain situation, could not bring themselves to do other than they do. However these are cases where we can, and on reflection will, doubt that the agent really is at liberty. This may be posed in the following manner: one may argue (as I have argued) that it is precisely, and only, in life's trivial and mundane contexts of choice that freedom obtains: whether to go round a telephone pole in one's path by the right or the left, which of three dessert options one will prefer in a restaurant, whether to wear this sweater or that one, to go to this film or that one – these are the most intuitively anchored cases of freedom, the ones where we would be most surprised were we to be shown (somehow) that we were not free in these cases. Yet the great existential questions: whether to commit suicide or not; whether to continue a course of study leading to renumerative employment (having completed five years of that study), or to abandon it all in favour of a life of beachcombing in Pago-Pago; whether to suddenly throw the contents of the punch-bowl at the person to whom one is amiably talking at a party, or to just carry on the discussion – about such matters as these, one may reasonably doubt whether whatever is opted for is something with respect to which one was free. Some people, it would seem, are not capable of suicide. They feel too content in the world, too much at home, like themselves too deeply, or perhaps are too squeamish, or imbibed the injunctions of educators too thoroughly, for this to be a genuine possibility for them. They are condemned to seek to live. And so it is with others of the major social and personal questions. Perhaps we really are not free with respect to all sorts of these; though we are free, really free, with respect to many less grand and character-expressing matters.

I prefer then to confine my attention to the trivial and commonplace cases, like the four itemized above. These seem to me the real paradigms of freedom, together perhaps with others where there will more obviously be reasons for acting that the agent is aware of, like walking to the corner store for a loaf of bread, when one wants to make oneself a sandwich and there is no bread at home. In these kinds of cases, can the agent do otherwise than he or she does? Is it crucial to his/her freedom that he be able to?

What is the argument (endorsed, by the way, by Dennett) that the agent cannot do otherwise? It is this: a highly plausible way to conceive of the human agent is as a naturally evolved structure or system of beliefs, goals (or intentions), and attempted actions. (All three of these are intended in the act/state/process sense(s) of these terms, not the product or object senses.) These three major subsystems seem logically independent of each other (although certainly a number of philosophers would not agree with this). That is to say, it is logically possible that there is a centre of consciousness with beliefs but no desires and that is wholly inert. It seems equally possible that there is a blindly striving being, a mere *conatus*, without a belief or identified goal. Perhaps having goals or intentions implies having some beliefs but they need not be beliefs rationally germane to the satisfaction of those intentions. At any rate the agents we discover ourselves to be have all three: beliefs, intentions, and physically expressible impulses to states that will fulfil those intentions. Moreover this system is in us highly rational or reality-oriented. Our beliefs tend to be true and practically relevant to the realization of our goals, which in turn tend to be (with, of course, many exceptions) on the whole feasible for realization in the environments we occupy and with the physical equipment we possess or can marshal.

All of the preceding is intended to be understood in a manner wholly compatible with a physicalism of either reductive, eliminative, or functionalist variety. Possibly there are more adequate theoretical models for characterizing what have here been characterized along belief-intention lines. That will be as the future of neuroscience reveals. We may turn out to be as appropriately conceivable as (of course idiosyncratic) computing machines as Dennett and other cognitive science advocates hold; or it may turn out that we really operate radically differently, as others maintain.

At any rate at the middle level of intelligent reasonably sharp analysis that this is intended to be couched in, we are belief-intention-action systems that are as-though-designed or as-though-programmed.[10] Nature or natural selection, given some very specific starting material, and some very specific environmental circumstances has fashioned us, over a long period of time, in a manner analogous to the workings of human cyberneticists over very short periods of time. It may be recalled that the opening chapter of *The Origin of Species* explains how Darwin arrived at the idea of natural selection through the example and model of agriculturalists' controlled breeding programs, with both plants and animals. It is then as though we had been programmed or designed to deal with our habitat in highly specific ways, though they are also highly flexible and wholly focused on species success. In very compressed form, the general structure of the program we have been encoded with is something like this: (1) if in situation S, in which goal or intention G is the primary member of the then active goal set (i.e., G is the thing then most sought), and in which action A is believed to be the most preferred means to the realization of G, and A is an acceptable course to take, seek to implement A; (2) if in situation S', in which no member of the then active goal set is discerned as primary, seek a reason or consideration for determining one to be, then act as in (1); (3) if in situation S'', in which there is a preferred goal but uncertainty as to its realization, seek information as to this, then act as in (1); and so on. This is a very schematic program and no doubt only one of the general structures of our encoding. However, something like this may be conceived as how we are programmed with respect to belief-intention-action contexts in which we have some possibility of acting for reasons, and choosing – i.e., some possibility of acting freely.

The case against an ability to behave otherwise than we do may now emerge. It basically involves saying that where we know what we want, know the means to get it, find the means acceptable, are able to perform the means, are in no conflict, do not change our minds or lose our attention and grasp of belief state and context of projected action, we have no ability to do other than seek to implement our primary goal. We have not been programmed for alternatives to the highest acceptable goal with acceptable means within our power. We could have been (contrary to the views of those who think it is a matter of logic or conceptual necessity, that highest goal, etc., issues in seeking to implement that goal). But we have not been. We do not know anything else but to go for it, in contemporary jargon, where our situation is read, by us, as permitting us (in all ways of concern for or to us) to do as we most want to do or most have as an aim or goal.

Now, if this is correct – and it seems to be (although many details in this very schematic picture are missing, and providing them might, really might, change the picture we have reached) – then, it is to be noted, our inability to do otherwise than we do, in the sense indicated, is not a function or consequence of determinism as such. The logical content of the compatibilist thesis remains wholly unimpaired. Moreover, we could describe a sort of agent that would be at least somewhat like ourselves, and that would have been programmed to sometimes do other than it wanted to do, maybe even programmed always to have a reason for so acting, when it did. (Such an agent would I think be clearly different from the agents we are.) But as we are, when we act – freely, as we want to say – , when we are in a situation where all the cards are up, and the situation one of ideal choice, we just do not have an ability to say no to pursuing the course of rational intention. (And possibly we would be in an important sense irrational if we did have such an ability.)

Now all of the foregoing has been put very loosely, schematically, and incompletely. I think however it is something like the argument Dennett accepts and gives implicitly in *Elbow Room*, which I think is sound.

What seems to me to be the case is this: if we had a complete description of the entire physical and psychological state of an agent for a time interval of a period of time (varying from action to action) up to a microsecond before the actual taking of action by the agent (i.e., right up to an instant before the point of no return, where action has been launched), then, if we are dealing with a situation in which no physical indeterminism occurs, there will in fact be a deterministic general law asserting that anyone in the condition the agent is in will do what the agent is about to do. Moreover – though this is not implied by the latter – the agent will at that final moment, the instant before leaping, have no ability or power to do otherwise than what he is about to do. Yet he will, in the typical case, be free with respect to what he is about to do.

Further there will be a sense in which the agent could have done otherwise, even at the crucial instant. We are concerned here with how we conceive agents and their circumstances, and the fact is that not only do we lack the fine-grained and complex information that would comprise the immediate situation for an agent prior to acting; but much of this information would be irrelevant to what we would be assessing and describing. We mean to characterize agents, their beliefs and desires, and the actions they issue in, only at a macro level, a level of broad, gross, or approximate detail of state. For purposes of assigning or withholding agency, responsibility, freedom, and a capacity for doing otherwise, we neither want nor need the full story that is there, and in whose terms there really will be no such capacity to do otherwise.

Being able to act differently must be a matter of some subtlety. In determining whether someone can do otherwise than they are going to do, it is necessary to ask: when? when can the agent act otherwise? There will be a point, evidently, prior to which the agent could still do otherwise (according to the free will view of common sense and which there seems no good reason to dispute), and after which he or she cannot. In many standard cases, it would appear that point is at the instant or a fraction of a second prior to the event, when the action is about to be launched. It seems right that there will be a point of no return, when the die is cast, and an alternative course is no longer within the agent's power – perhaps no more than a millisecond before the action is happening but nonetheless, before it is under way. And affirming this fairly evident fact will not compromise the agent's having a power of reversing course at times prior to that critical point; hence, a fortiori, it will not compromise the general possession of free will.

Another subtlety with being able to do otherwise remains to be elaborated. It seems clear that one will have this ability where a single simple action is involved. Someone eats an apple, and they could have done otherwise, we suppose rightly. They could have refrained and eaten something else or nothing at all. Could they have done otherwise than eat the apple having really wanted the apple? Presumably we can refrain from doing things we want to do. This is what self-restraint and will-power are all about. How about this: could someone refrain from – do something other than – eat an apple having wanted to do that more than any other available alternative, including the alternative of exercising self-control?

Sometimes the idea that advocates of free will have is that, when someone is free, all the background and causal factors leading up to a certain point – perhaps just prior to that point of no return – could occur and the agent, in one scenario carry out action A – one of his or her alternatives – and in another scenario not do so, do something other than A, or nothing at all. However, this conception does not usually give explicit details as to what all the background and causal factors includes. Perhaps it is unnecessary. They did say *all*, didn't they? It would of course be wrong and unfair to take the all to include future-indicating factors: e.g., that the agent will do A (if in fact this is the case). The idea has to be that all the factors up to that critical point that occur in the situation inherently, without reference to other situations, should have been able to occur and again in one possible scenario the agent does *A*, and in another refrains from doing so, in both cases as the exercise of free will or free choice.

If all factors are meant – otherwise one is not talking about the same situation occurring – it would seem that we cannot limit those factors to such matters as where various molecules were located, and what the electro-chemical situation was, or the physiological one. If the two scenarios to be compared are to be the same, the agent has to be in all respects in the same state, as well as the background circumstances; including then all the same psychological states, with the same beliefs and desires. This will be a matter independent of what theory we prefer as to the explanation of human actions. We might prefer one theory or another, or not know how it is that people manage to do things that they do or why. However, if we have this idea of exactly this situation up to that critical point obtaining, and then he/she does *A*, or does not, then everything in the situation has to be relevant and available, and the same.

One may say that we have to allow one difference at least, in the scenarios, for in the one *A* is done, and in the other non-*A*, and since we want to think of both as free acts, we need to regard what is done, in each case, as chosen. So in one scenario the agent chooses to do *A*; but in the other, obviously, s/he doesn't. So the scenarios, up to that critical point, cannot be identical.

Here we come to a dilemma. On the one hand we may think that no one does, or perhaps can, just choose. We choose for reasons, or at least by virtue of considerations that we allow to weigh with us. If there isn't anything at all that we adduce in resolving to do something we will do, we could not do anything. So many suppose. If that is correct, then it will be harder, not impossible but certainly harder, to describe, with the details, that exact same scenario which forks into two alternatives, as time marches forward and the agent chooses to act, and then acts. For the agent either had such and such a reason or he/she didn't, and that will modify the background situation. And if that reason was there it had such and such weight for the agent or it didn't. Some situations involve changes of mind. Is the situation one where a change of mind occurs? Whichever it is, a common, detailed, past situation will need to be identified and it will need to include facts about the agent's beliefs, desires, values specific to the particular occasion, and perhaps general values. Such a detailed past situation will need to be describable whether the past stops at the point of the agent's choosing, or at the point where the reasons that will make the difference have appeared (or have failed to) or at the point where those reasons have a certain weight and priority (or not). On this fork of the dilemma, it looks like we may have a difficult time in such identification; at least without going well back before the agent chooses. If this is the picture, it is problematic whether there can be that common course of history for our agent, up to that branching scenario, because there will start to be differences – differences which will make a difference – well before (maybe minutes or hours before) the choice begins.

On the other hand some hold that on certain occasions, we just choose; and indeed, that our freedom must include the possibility of such occasions. Sometimes, according to this constituency, we act with no particular reason. There are bald, or bare, acts of willing and choosing. A situation presents itself, we do come to that fork in our path, and we go for this or that alternative as we will. Now even if it is true that there are such acts and choices as these, it clearly cannot be and is not the case that they are the only cases where we act and choose freely. Lots of cases where we act in a certain way because we wanted to, and where we had particular reasons, are perfectly good and clear cases of free acts, and cases where we can do otherwise. There isn't anything problematic with freely doing something you wanted to do for excellent reasons.

Perhaps there are, in addition, cases of choosing for no reason. Someone extends a fistful of cards with their backs (all of them the same) facing you. 'Pick a card, any card,' they say. And you do. You choose card 15 and could have picked another or declined to play. You acted and chose freely. Yet why did you pick card 15? No reason. You resolved to pick one of the cards and there it was: you happened to pick that one.

So we say. And indeed you may have had no reason or no particular reason, to pick the one you did. However, this is not the same as, nor is it a good reason for holding that there was no reason that you picked the card you did, i.e., that it was a genuinely random act, or something without cause. Something is involved in choosing it – perhaps something that makes you shun the extreme ends of a sample (so you would pick a card somewhere in the middle), and other factors of the angle you were at relative to the card, the musculature it required to reach it, the light that illuminated it in such a way that made it stand out for you, and perhaps a variety of other comparable factors of circumstance that were cumulatively the cause of your action.

If we stop the receding, revising journey backwards into the background at the point just prior to choosing, and allow all the factors to be the same, we have to be prepared to say: someone could want to do A more than any alternative known to him or her, in fact not like any of the other alternatives, be able, physically and psychologically, to do A, not wish, on this occasion, to exercise self-restraint or to demonstrate self-denial (or, particularly, to offer a proof of free will by doing something undesired), believe, correctly, that A is morally desirable as well as desired by the agent, be a person, in general, of character and integrity, not, on this occasion, change his or her mind, not be masochistic or self-destructive or self-frustrating, believe, correctly, that none of the alternatives to A would have consequences that the agent would desire more than A and its consequences, believe that there is no good reason, from duty or desire, or anything else, to do anything other than A, and yet, with all that, choose non-A. Could there be a human being who had the ability to do all of that? I think not. I think that no one would be capable of doing this complex act. This would be a matter of our specifically human nature. It would not, contrary to what some have held, be logically self-contradictory for someone to act as described. If someone did, we would be mystified, but logic would remain intact. I hold that, in fact, no human being is capable of getting themselves to do, or to try to do, the complex act described. And yet, I think there remains no doubt whatever that an agent, qua agent, even in the complex situation described, could have acted otherwise than A.

One of the morals of these reflections is that just as we said that when confronted with the idea of an agent's ability to do otherwise we should think to ask: when is it that the agent has that ability? We should also ask: ability to do other than what? For someone could have the ability to do other than B and have the ability to do other than B while p and q, but not have the ability to do other than B while p and q and r and s. That someone can act differently than A implies that in relevantly similar possible circumstances they do other than A; not that in the exact same circumstances, in a possible scenario they do; and where relevant similarity has got to include some possible changes in agent's preferences.

We learn as well that it is wrong to suppose that it is only our choices that determine what we will do. That is to say, we make our choices for reasons, either reasons that we have had, or 'reasons' that are in causal operation in the circumstances in which we act. An act of choice, all by itself, cannot be causally efficacious for a human being. We are not the sort of creatures for which they could be.

We learn also, I think, that being able to act otherwise is being able to do other than the act we performed, where the act we performed is the one we conceived ourselves to perform, meant to perform. If so and so meant to walk, and walked, at time t, then to say that this agent could have done otherwise than they did at t is to say that they could have done other than walk at t. If, rather, the agent meant to walk while chewing gum at t, and did that, what they could have done other than do at t, was walk while chewing gum.

The claim that they can, could, or will be able to act otherwise does not extend, without examination or qualification, to any and every true description of what they were doing at the time at which they acted. It may not extend to descriptions that the agent would not recognize as capturing what they were doing, and it will not extend, I think it has been shown, to instances of the description form ⌜φ-ing, while C⌝, where C includes everything true of the agent and the agent's circumstances up to the microsecond before the actual choice took place.

IX

An objection to my argument comes to mind. In the circumstances we will be envisaging, it will be said, performing action A (at t) is identical to performing A (at t) while C – where C is all causally relevant factors antecedent to A. That is, even if doing A is a different action type from doing A while C, in fact that chunk of space-time, in the world, consisting of agent s doing A at t is the very same event as s doing A at t while C. If so, they cannot of course differ in their properties. So if the one has the property of being unable to be done otherwise by s – as, we have argued, s doing A at t while C, has – then so will – must – the other. In that event s will be unable to do other than A, contrary to what we have claimed.

This objection, however, is spurious. It rests on a more general fact than it discloses, viz., that something's being the case is materially equivalent or factually (contingently) identical to its being the case and P, where P is any true proposition including therefore true propositions that characterize the complete state of the universe at times in the remote past. However, that someone can modify an event's occurrence does not imply that they can modify a state of the universe prior to their birth. An equivocation or ambiguity is involved in the objection's claim (an equivocation of scope). *Doing A while C* is not identical to *doing A* while C. The former has the property of being unable to be done otherwise by s (the performer of A); and while the latter does also, its italicized constituent does not have this property.

How can we capture or express a macro-level capacity for acting differently? This will not, and is not intended to, correspond to ordinary or common sense intuition, but perhaps the following will do. Let us utilize again the conjunction of Dennett's design-stance and his intentional stance that were employed above. I shall use a technical term *design** to stand for what natural selection has produced for the belief-intention-action structures of agents of our kind. I shall also speak of situations foreseen* in the design* of some machine or some agent to identify prospective or anticipated possible choice and action contexts that natural selection and experience have encoded in the design* of a machine or agent of our type. Further, I shall talk of situations being relevantly similar to each other. Situation S is relevantly similar to situation S' for agent a iff some object that a would be aware of in S is replaced by an object of the same kind that a would also be aware of in S' (but otherwise S and S' are identical), or a's gross emotional state (happy, unhappy, anxious, etc.) is very similar in S and S', as are a's gross cognitive, valuational, and physical states (but otherwise S and S' are identical). Then: if a is in situation S, and a performs action x at t in S, then a can do other than perform x at t iff a is an agent, with beliefs, goals, and the ability to act, and a is so designed* that there are situations foreseen* in a's design*' that are relevantly similar to S and in them a does x and there are situations foreseen* in a's design* that are relevantly similar to S and in them a fails to do x.

That is, we can act otherwise if and only if we are programmed to anticipate similar contexts, in which – provided that different objects are located in those contexts or our cognitive, affective, valuational, or physical states differ but only slightly – we will (so we are programmed) sometimes do one thing and sometimes another thing. Those anticipated different contexts may of course never arise. But we are programmed for a great variety of situations which we will in fact never encounter.

This proposal may seem trivial. Isn't it saying that we can act otherwise if we are so set up that sometimes we do one thing, and sometimes, in similar circumstances, do another – or would do so if the situation arose? However, what one wants to know is how, in some detail, beliefs and intentions may vary, and still permit our acting differently. The long and the short of the answer to this is that the proposal is not trivial and will permit a plausible and non-epistemic sense in which we are able to do otherwise, but that there is a great deal more work to be done in setting out the details.

X

I shall conclude this chapter by setting out and distinguishing eight positions on free will and determinism that involve subtleties, some of which have been addressed here but which a thorough examination of the topic would need to explore further and come to certain conclusions about. The reader is urged to reflect on which seems to him or her most accurately to fit the real facts of our condition.

Positions on free will and determinism.

1. Whether or not our universe is a deterministic system, the concept of free will is incoherent and unintelligible.
2. Compatibilism: free will and determinism can both obtain and (we have every reason to suppose) actually do.

3. Strong compatibilism: free will implies determinism, i.e., that some act or state is free implies that it was pre-determined, and there are free acts.
4. Incompatibilism: free will implies the falsehood of determinism, and contrariwise.
5. Free will is formally compatible with determinism, but in fact we are never free.
6. Free will is formally compatible with determinism, but in fact we are free only in trivial mundane acts of everyday life.
7. Free will is formally compatible with determinism, but in fact we are free only sometimes, in contemplative or cognitive states. (This position might be called Spinozist compatibilism.)
8. Free will is generally incompatible with determinism, but the latter is not strictly universally true; some contemplative or cognitive states are epiphenomena, and they are free.

Chapter Seventeen

Immortality

As I have indicated at the beginning of this book, my aim has been to investigate and reach at least tentative conclusions about each of the fundamental topics of metaphysics identified by Kant in the historical rationalist tradition. For him what the inquirer qua metaphysician would like to know about most, if he could – Kant of course thinks that he cannot – are God, freedom, and immortality. We will consider the last of these here. What, if anything, can we reasonably suppose with respect to whether human persons, or any persons, are or can be immortal?

First of all we may affirm, modestly and negatively (and in accord with Kant), that we do not in fact know that we, human persons, are immortal, nor that any persons, if there are any persons besides ourselves, are immortal either. In fact, this puts the matter so modestly as to seem almost coy. Many philosophers now, and in the past, would assert emphatically that there is no plausible evidence whatsoever that human existence extends beyond the existence of human bodies. Some philosophers in fact – this view seems first to appear explicitly only in the twentieth century[1] – take the position that there could not be a continued existence of an individual human person beyond the term of existence of that individual human person's body or of a body that is a successor substance to that human person's body; where the modality – the 'could' – is intended to be a metaphysical, or logical, or 'in principle' one. Such philosophers as these regard immortality as a non-question.

I shall presently consider this latter position. Let us first note some fairly obvious matters. Human bodies are in fact of only finite duration. It is hard to see why it would be metaphysically impossible that there be a human body that continued indefinitely to exist. It would seem to be naturally impossible that this occur. That is, there are no possible worlds in which all and only the actual laws of nature hold which contain bodies which in this, actual, possible world would be correctly identified as human bodies, where any of those bodies exists for all times. However, with different laws of nature it is hard to see why an actual human body, animated by (and perhaps identical with) an actual human being, might not exist at all times.[2]

At any rate such possibilities are clearly not the issue in this topic. This was not what Kant supposed humans generically yearn to know of, but cannot.

More on target metaphysically would be the question whether an individual human person might continue to exist indefinitely through successive alterations, which never involve an interruption in spatio-temporal continuity, of what had been originally (whether or not it always continued to be) that human person's human body. Here we would start to find divided opinions, with intelligent positions on either side. Some think it essential to human persons that they be alive, and there would be conceivable alterations to human persons' material composition that would produce a moving, acting, and apparently thinking being that was not biologically living. Such philosophers might suppose that immortality might be possible if life were never lost. Others see life as non-essential to human persons. For some it is not so much life that is essential to human personal identity as it is the continued possession of a numerically self-same brain (whether or not that brain came to be, or could come to be, primarily or wholly composed of non-living tissue).

This cluster of issues too I shall postpone. We need first to point out that, though Kant (and others) see the metaphysical issue as immortality, it is more fundamentally the issue whether the identity of a human person can extend beyond the existence of that person's body, whether or not the extension is literally unending. The metaphysical topic is really survival of bodily extinction, however long the survival. It is the question whether there could be a time when I exist, even though my body no longer exists.

As I have indicated, there is one position on this matter which reaches an affirmative answer: it holds that I could exist, and in some possible worlds do exist, where and when my body did not, because enough transformations of my (current) body were made, including alterations of the material substance of my brain, which eventuated in a material body for me that is not numerically identical to the material body I had originally but where I continue to exist because I am the person whose body that later body is, and have (perhaps) memories and a consciousness that extends back into the past to states of memory and consciousness of the earlier person. Now this seems to me an exciting and interesting metaphysical theme, and I will want to defend the affirmative answer just sketched. I think I could survive a brain transplant where I received a resulting brain made of quite different, and nonliving, chemical elements than my current brain possesses. I certainly do not think it is obvious that this view is correct, and a very formidable position on the essences of human beings (indeed, of every material thing) stands on the opposing side of the issue. I shall try to show that this opposing position is mistaken.

However, it must be said that even if the view I, and others, defend on this topic of (human) personal identity and essence is correct, it still does not arrive at Kant's topic: what he would like to know but thinks no one can.

The survival issue that Kant is interested in is whether a human person could continue to exist where no material body, spatio-temporally continuous with a body the person had, is in existence. It is commonly supposed that this would be a purely disembodied personal existence (i.e., existence as a person): existence as a thinking or conscious being with no anchorage to any material state of the world. I am not sure, however, that this needs to be supposed for Kant's query. First, it might be held that someone, even if totally disembodied (assuming, of course, that that was metaphysically possible), would always – must always, perhaps – be at some region of space, from which a (temporally) backwards trajectory would reach regions of space the individual occupied when living. If this were the case, a disembodied person would always be at some location and hence, at least in that sense or degree, material; somewhat, for instance, as sound waves are material. Some cultures' beliefs conceive survival of death along such lines. Second, it is difficult to see why the advocate of the spiritualist view that we are trying to identify and evaluate cannot suppose or be agnostic regarding the possible existence of a materiality quite different from familiar ones; and the possibility of a thinking substance that would be disembodied in the sense of no longer having material-stuff composition but would always have some exotic variety of materiality. One of the chief arguments against the spiritualist survivalist view, if I can call it that, is that it is difficult to conceive of what the mechanics of survival might be like. This seems to be a serious problem for spiritual survivalism. At any rate it does seem unreasonable to saddle the spiritual survivalist with having to suppose that the mechanics he or she needs involve utter immateriality. She or he wants to suppose it is possible that there is a condition or state of my existence, and thinking, feeling, and remembering that is profoundly different from anything that currently obtains materially for me. Who knows, and why need the spiritualist know, whether there might not be a sort of ethereal body that involves a cascading echo of my current materiality, which a God or the natural order of things might need to avail himself or itself of to have me continue? The Christian hope, and some Christian theology, can accommodate a survival that would be, in principle, materially traceable, and possessing what true (ideal) physics would recognize as material states.

Now is any such survival possible, thinkable, coherent? Does it occur in any possible worlds? What is key to a reasonable view on this matter is what we make, metaphysically, of states of consciousness or states of experience. If they do exist in the world, and their being states of consciousness or experience really characterizes them intrinsically – which is compatible with their turning out to be brain states or functional states of certain material bodies – then it would seem that spiritual survivalism, as a metaphysical possibility, is defensible. If an actual state in the world is (such a thing as) what it is (feels like) to remember someone (for a human being), what it is (feels like) to feel love, sorrow, pleasure in solving an algebra problem, etc., and they at least closely resemble what they seem to be, then there will be facts of consciousness, at the metaphysically most perspicuous level of reflection on the world. This does not require a dualist or irreducibly mentalist view of such facts. In our world, such facts might all be material states of an already known type. So at least I wish to argue, i.e., dualism is not a priori true, and probably is contingently false.

If there are fundamental facts, of type *S experiencing X*, or even *experiencing X* taking place, we appear to have licensed or be stuck (or blessed) with, subjective facts that involve something's feeling or seeming so for a subject. Just as there are non-existent 'intentional objects,' as we argued, there might also be non-existent 'intentional subjects,' and the views and arguments set out here are intended always to be compatible with that possibility. Experiences seem generically to need to be of something structurally, even if, in some cases, there is no such thing as that being; and they seem to need to be of, by, or for someone, and we ought to remain open to at least the possibility that there is no such thing as that someone in some cases. If there are fundamentally subjective facts – facts like my feeling exultant at *t* and *p* or wondering whether 973 is prime – where the 'how it feels for the subject' is accorded ontic and epistemic legitimacy, then, it would seem, we can construct possible scenarios where it looks like there is consciousness without (at least familiar) physicality. Take the following example (most such examples seem inevitably to be somewhat gruesome). Suppose you are kidnapped by medically skilled criminals who, to convince your family of their fell intent, sever one of your ears and send it to them. Suppose too that these kidnappers made use of amputation techniques that involved no pain for you, then or later. They have discovered an anaesthetic that permanently dulls or destroys nerve endings in the vicinity of the excision but leaves normal consciousness unaffected, and they give you this anaesthetic. Suppose your relatives remain unmoved by the sight of your ear, and are still unwilling to hand over large sums for you. So the kidnappers up the ante. This time they amputate your left arm. This too fails to produce results. (We must suppose your relatives not to be exceptionally fond of you.) Your remaining three limbs follow in due course, and now, though your family is at last prepared to act, the family fortune is wiped out in a market crash and the money doesn't exist to send the criminals. In disgust the latter decide to give you a particularly heavy dose of the anaesthetic, and put what remains of you in their furnace. (They don't mind killing you, but they hate the idea that you might suffer.) Now our hypothesis has been that, though you know the anguish of your situation – captivity with desperadoes, fear of mutilation and death, actually witnessing your own dismemberment – you have not been in the slightest physical pain. You have been conscious and thinking of various things – what you'll do to Uncle Fred if you ever get out alive, for example, how you'll be able to compete in the Olympics without your legs, etc. – and have experienced clinically normal mental states. Imagine now that you find yourself thinking (no doubt in a state of some agitation): My goodness, they're coming to get me, they're picking me up, leading me to the furnace, I'll surely be dead presently, and so on. It appears quite easy to continue the story of what we are imagining with two divergent perspectives: how it all looks and seems for you, and how it looks and seems for the kidnappers (and anyone else who might be present). For the latter, we suppose that they witness a limbless human being being thrown into a furnace and quickly consumed by the flames, leaving a residue of ash, which they then scatter. For the former – it is you, remember – it seems easy to imagine consciousness continuing. You no longer hear, see, or otherwise sense features of the environment you had been perceiving. Maybe you have new sensory states or sensory-miming states (like those in dreams); or maybe you have new varieties of consciousness, hitherto unknown to you; or maybe it is as if you are now in a sensory deprivation situation and your consciousness must chiefly consist in what you can manage to remember, imagine, or conceive.

The point is that you can imagine this happening to you. You can imagine remaining conscious, continuing to have experiences, even if realizing – maybe even having witnessed – the destruction of your body including your brain. Perhaps there was a mirror opposite the furnace door, and you see what is being done to you up to the destruction of your eyes and brain, then switch to a dream-like apparent perception of what happens to what remains of your body after that. You wouldn't, doubtless, understand what was happening, but that, of course, isn't the point. If there are 'subject facts,' some of which we are acquainted with as subjects ourselves, then there can be an overlapping sequence of subject facts – its being and feeling thus and so for me – that accompany the coming into non-existence of any even approximately familiar physical system that can be regarded as having constituted the 'housing' for the occurrence of such facts. At any rate, we can imagine such things happening to ourselves. We have just done it.

Still, it might be granted that there are perspectival or subjective facts (facts of the 'what it's like to be/feel F' type) but insisted that they supervene upon facts of brain chemistry and should be viewed as identical to them or as their causal products. This might be held to be not merely contingently so, but part of what they are essentially or necessarily.

That perspectival facts are not essentially body-bound (this seems a reasonable term for the relevant property) seems proved by our thought experiment. The rationale is as follows: the proof (all the proof that there can be) that something x is not essentially F is there being consistently and coherently described, imagined, or conceived, x's lacking F. We described, imagined, and conceived subjective facts that existed without being body-bound. So at least one such fact is not essentially body-bound. If one isn't, there is a presumptive case that none is. So subjective facts as a class are not essentially body-bound. So the relation between subjective facts and facts of brain physiology is at most causal or physical necessity. However, that is in turn to say again that, since causal necessities hold in at most some possible worlds, there is a metaphysical possibility of disembodied personal survival of death.

Thoughtful philosophers will remind us that matters of essence are matters *de re*, matters in things and not merely in how we think about or classify things. There are essential properties which things have that may come as a surprise to many philosophers. Kripke and Putnam's properties of material composition – claims that, for example, a table wholly made of wood is essentially made of wood – come to mind here. Even if, as argued in the earlier chapter on essence, Kripke and Putnam are mistaken about the essentiality of such properties to their bearers, the insight is surely correct, viz., that the strong (metaphysical) necessities are by no means necessarily going to be found to correspond to what may be merely cultural, linguistic, psychological convictions, or intuitions but should be hard, world-grounded facts of things that couldn't be otherwise. Perhaps we should hesitate before accepting the 'kidnapping' argument as conclusive. I take that argument incontestably to have a certain force, even a prima facie presumption in its favour. Perhaps matters of essence, even for subjective or perspectival facts, aren't to be taken to be conclusively decided by a subject's phenomenological convictions.

Eschewing conclusiveness, and in suitably tentative or presumptive mode, I have argued for the metaphysical possibility and the coherence of personal continuity, survival and continuation as a person and moreover the same person that one was, beyond the extinction or destruction of the whole of one's physical body (and without the acquisition of a successor body). That continuity involved, as it was conceived and imagined in the possible-case scenario that generated it, uninterrupted experience, with uninterrupted memory of having been the subject of that experience as well as previous experiences in the background of those occurring in the vicinity of becoming disembodied. Critics and objectors want to know soon what replies there may be to the difficult, but apparently possible, complicating options. They must indeed have their reply, but I wish first to underscore that part of the point of the way the story was set up was to make things as easy as they could be. In someone else's story there might be rival claimants to being the disembodied survivor of a formerly disembodied self; but in mine there is only one such claimant, and he or she does not become amnesiac or suffer a lapse in the continuity of consciousness and memory, indeed of consciousness and memory of the self-same self as a person formerly alive and embodied and apprehended under a name and personality which have continued. If the scenario had happened to you, you would be feeling it as something that had happened to you and you would not have paused, slept, rested, or turned off the ongoing flow of the occurrent experience-sequence since the catastrophic demise of your body. The point is to win acknowledgment at least this far. The point is to have described a coherent possible state of affairs which would be sufficient for disembodied survival of death. At least presumptively, this has, I think, been done.

Immortality is, of course, something else again. I actually argue elsewhere that literal immortality, even in embodied form, is a conceptually problematic idea.[3] Disembodied immortality will clearly be a still more challenged notion. But here I shall not explore the metaphysical possibility of literally unending existence for a person as the same individual that person was. Our endorsement even of a brief disembodied survival of death was tentative, and it is time to return to the actual world and our prospects at and beyond our deaths.

Are we, in fact, as in the dark on what our actual prognoses are as Kant supposes? Kant holds that we have no possibility of coming to any conclusion on the basis of argument or evidence about immortality. Surely the answer to this is clear. Kant and many human individuals' fond hopes notwithstanding, it is extremely persuasive to believe that this is an empirical question on which there is abundant, if negative, empirical evidence. There is not the slightest serious reason in the world to believe that any person we know of continues in consciousness beyond the death or destruction of their bodies. We could so continue but the evidence is that we don't.

In fact the best empirical case against spiritual survival was given long ago by the ancient Epicureans. It is set out effectively in Lucretius's *On the Nature of the Universe*. Lucretius observes that we find that our mental states correlate significantly with our bodily states. When we are infants we have feeble minds and bodies. Both are new and undeveloped. The normal human life's path then presents a profile that shows, characteristically, vigour and activity, bodily and mental, coinciding through the course of youth and adult maturity. There are of course variations, but they do not favor spiritualism: everything we know about the mind shows that it constitutes a system that is decidedly relative to body-chemistry. In old age, finally, both mental and bodily systems undergo decline and diminution. All of this speaks, as Lucretius argues, for a mind system that dissolves when life does.

Notes

Preface

1 Wilfrid Sellars, 'Philosophy and the Scientific Image of Man,' in Sellars, *Science, Perception and Reality*, 32.
2 See Horwich, *Truth*, ch. 2.

1: What Is Metaphysics?

1 Bradley, *Appearance and Reality*, x.
2 Jean-Paul Sartre (1905–80), a leading existentialist thinker, held that human beings are radically free – unable to avoid or escape the ongoing condition of free choice in matters large and small. The attempt to evade our freedom is for Sartre one of the varieties or instances of personal or existential *inauthenticity* (a pervasive condition of self-deception). Benjamin Lee Whorf (1897–1941) was an American linguist who developed what is called the Whorf (sometimes the Sapir-Whorf) hypothesis, which holds that structures in particular human languages shape our conceptions of reality, indeed, largely or significantly imprison members of very diverse cultural-linguistic communities within the ontological frameworks these structures supply.
3 Cf. Wilfrid Sellars' characterization of what he calls 'the philosophical quest': 'The aim of philosophy, abstractly formulated, is to understand how things in the broadest possible sense of the term hang together in the broadest possible sense of the term. Under "things in the broadest possible sense" I include such radically different items as not only "cabbages and kings", but numbers and duties, possibilities and finger snaps, aesthetic experience and death. To achieve success in philosophy would be, to use a contemporary turn of phrase, to "know one's way around" with respect to all these things' ('Philosophy and the Scientific Image of Man,' in Sellars, *Science, Perception and Reality*, 1). Philosophy, in Sellars' sense, is at least

somewhat wider and not quite as clearly focused ontologically, as metaphysics in the sense meant above. On the other hand, it is very much the intent of the conception of metaphysics pursued in the present volume that the full range of items Sellars lists be included within its reach.

4 Science, I would say, is both a process (or activity, or praxis), and a product of that process. As product, science may be said to be *systematic public knowledge*. Natural science is systematic public knowledge of nature – the observable and physical world (even if some of *that* knowledge will posit unobservable entities). Biological science is systematic public knowledge of living objects and systems. Social science is systematic public knowledge of human behaviour, apart from human behaviour studied by biological science. Mathematical science is systematic public knowledge of quantifiable structures. This list is not meant to be exhaustive; and it will be obvious that many of its key terms invite clarification, expansion, and commentary – perhaps especially the notion of *public knowledge*. Since the seventeenth century, 'natural science' is often abbreviated to 'science,' in a kind of synecdoche. I will often conform to this usage.

Although the foregoing characterization of science may be said to be broadly *realist*, it does not imply realism in specific detail or application; it is compatible with it, for example, to deny (or be agnostic about) the reality of unobservable theoretical entities in particular scientific theories, insisting only that whatever the science's pronouncements involving such putative entities they aim to constitute (public) *knowledge*. Similarly, although this characterization might be held to impute to science the goal of *truth*, this is not to make commitment to what the correct theory of truth is.

Turning to the other aspect of science: as process, or praxis, science is the organized endeavor of trying to achieve or produce science in the product sense.

5 On the conception of metaphysics advocated here, cf. Alfred Tarski, 'The Semantic Conception of Truth and the Foundations of Semantics' (originally published in *Philosophy and Phenomenological Research*, vol. 4, 1944; reprinted in H. Feigl and W. Sellars, eds., *Readings in Philosophical Analysis* (New York: Appleton-Century-Crofts, 1949) – the page citation is to this reprint – and frequently elsewhere): 'For some people metaphysics is a general theory of objects (ontology) – a discipline which is to be developed in a purely empirical way, and which differs from other empirical sciences only by its generality. I do not know whether such a discipline actually exists (some cynics claim that it is customary in philosophy to baptize unborn children); but I think that in any case metaphysics in this conception is not objectionable to anybody, and has hardly any connections with semantics' (72). I do not of course share Tarski's uncertainty whether metaphysics in this sense has historically been practised or pursued. As noted above, I think Aristotle, and a large number of successors, up to the present, have been metaphysicians in the

sense intended. As I make clear, metaphysics in my sense is not *purely* empirical; like mathematical science some of its projects are abstract, conceptual, or a prioristic ones; and it has a concern with the *modal* that would be seen as rare, and perhaps extravagant, in the special sciences. I would also not quite share the identification of metaphysics with ontology, the relations between the two being more like genus to species in my view. Nonetheless, Tarski's characterization is certainly in the vicinity of what is intended in these pages. Also in the vicinity are some remarks of Russell's: 'I believe the only difference between science and philosophy is, that science is what you more or less know and philosophy is what you do not know. Philosophy is that part of science which at present people choose to have opinions about, but which they have no knowledge about. Therefore every advance in knowledge robs philosophy of some problems which formerly it had' ('The Philosophy of Logical Atomism' (1918), in Russell, *Logic and Knowledge*, 281). These remarks appear in the final section – 'Excursus into Metaphysics: What There Is' – of the logical atomism lectures.

6　Spinoza's primary metaphysical work, which sets out his view of the universe along the model of Euclid's *Elements*, with definitions, axioms, and what are intended to be mathematically rigorous proofs of propositions and theorems.

7　Thales held that all things consist of water. Only some things of course *appear* to be, or present themselves as, water; and some things that appear to be water really are water.

2: Metaphysics and Its Critics

1　*A Treatise of Human Nature*, 113f.

2　Idealism – at least as usually understood (there are important distinct deviant versions) – is the metaphysical thesis that everything real is a thinking substance, or mind, or a mental existent (a mental state or process, or a subjective image) dependent on a mind. Probably the most famous of all idealists is Berkeley (1685–1753).

3　*The Autobiography of Bertrand Russell*, vol. 3, 130 (Letter to A.J. Ayer (1910–89). Russell must be understood to intend an implicit *ceteris paribus* clause in the alleged entailment. For I might, e.g., have looked at a bunch of blue objects, then put on blue spectacles, etc.

4　See Devitt, *Realism and Truth*, 347 and passim.

5　The early pragmatists, including Peirce (1839–1914) and Dewey (1859–1952), shared the wide later nineteenth-century acceptance of a broad or basic Kantianism. Kant's claims as to the inscrutability of the world beyond our apprehensions of it were taken as permanent philosophical results, and what was at issue was what else, philosophically, there was to say, pragmatism making novel contributions with respect to a praxis component in theory. Current pragmatists are not as unblinkingly Kantian; but there can be no doubt of their anti-metaphysics. Rorty is an especially clear case, since his writings are rife with claims about the 'things-in-themselves' enterprise and its follies. One passage may suffice to give the flavour of the pragmatist anti-metaphysical stance, in Rorty's rendering of it: 'philosophers like me ... have learned (from Nietzsche and James, among others) to be suspicious of the appearance-reality distinction. We think that there are many ways to talk about what is going on, and that none of them gets closer to the way things are in themselves than any other. We have no idea what "in itself" is supposed to mean in the phrase "reality as it is in itself." So we suggest that the appearance-reality distinction be dropped in favor of a distinction between less useful and more useful ways of talking' (Rorty, *Truth and Progress*, 1).

6 Verificationism is the position (or family of positions) which holds that a declarative sentence only has meaning where there are public means for verifying or falsifying it.

7 Putnam's work, over the course of a long and productive career, may be viewed – at least from a metaphysical point of view – as dividing into four broad periods. In the earliest, Putnam is an outstanding creative contributor to naturalist analytic philosophy, and to a range of metaphysical realist enterprises. The middle period (the 1970s, approximately) is transitional, with Putnam critical of much of his own and others' earlier work. It is in the third period (whose avatar Devitt names, provocatively, 'the renegade Putnam') – dating from his 1981 book *Realism, Truth and History* – that the neo-Kantian philosophy Putnam calls 'internal realism' develops. This is the position referred to in the present context. Putnam's fourth and most recent position – natural realism – is set out in his 1994 'Dewey Lectures.' Although he continues there to affirm opposition to metaphysical realism and the project of theoretical metaphysics, it is difficult not to view this opposition as equivocal or merely nominal. Putnam characterizes his own philosophical odyssey, in this work, as a voyage from realism back again to realism, and he makes clear and unequivocal, that he thinks some stances, including some of his own, have insufficiently included the world and its operations independent of will or thought on our part, in constituting the nature of things. This anti-idealism is notably *not* coupled with a Kantian inscrutabilism – that is, with any affirmation that reality is beyond the possibility of our gleaning. To the contrary, Putnam speaks for common-sense knowledge of the world. Even if there remains an insistence that natural (or common-sense) realism is not a theory, and that it is just what (according to Putnam) Wittgenstein had been telling us all along, one wants to say: welcome back, Professor Putnam. It is good to have you back on side.

8 *The Earlier Letters of John Stuart Mill 1812–1848* (vol. 12 of *The Collected Works of John Stuart Mill*), ed. F.E. Mineka (Toronto: University of Toronto Press, 1963), 48. (Letter to Gustave d'Eichthal)

9 The advocates of linguistic contextualism have been legion. Particularly extreme versions of this idea have been commonplace outside academic philosophy most notably among practitioners of several varieties of literary study often grouped under the collective label of critical theory, above all the post-structuralist movement. Derrida's famous line, 'there is nothing outside the text' (*Of Grammatology,* 157f.), while apparently intended as hyperbole (and to have also other purposes), is an extension of linguistic contextualism to an enframement of thought and being within a particular form of the linguistic. Within analytic philosophy some positions especially identified with the Wittgensteinian and so-called ordinary language schools have been expressions of linguistic contextualist convictions.

10 Cf. Putnam's even stronger formulation of this idea: '*thinking* is not something only one person *could* do.' (H. Putnam, 'The Dewey Lectures 1994,' 492; first emphasis in original; second is mine.) Putnam is explaining and endorsing Wittgenstein.

11 Referential semantics is, briefly, the theory that many linguistic expressions are only successfully and meaningfully in place in language where those expressions directly refer to items of the world. The germ and the original formulation of the idea is due to Russell, in whose version of it the referential role was limited to (genuine) proper names and demonstrative pronouns.

12 Inscrutabilism may be defined as the position that a world independently of the mental exists (one might add: and is known to exist), and in some way or to some degree corresponds to our apprehensions of reality, but we are entirely unable to determine how it does so, or what its actual character is, this inability being something no future development of science or technology will lead to our overcoming. Cf. what Devitt calls 'weak, or fig-leaf realism' (Devitt, *Realism and Truth,* 17).

13 In a number of recent publications or interviews, Rorty's chief 'argument' against metaphysics appears to be that the subject is boring, and that it is immature to be interested in it. See, for example, an interview with Rorty in *The Philosophers' Magazine,* no. 8 (Autumn 1999), 40.

14 These remarks may seem cryptic as well as polemical. For an extended discussion of some of the issues posed – whether, and to what degree, various contemporary philosophers, particularly those aligning themselves with pragmatism, are antimetaphysicians, how literally, or otherwise, to take their stated views, and what those views' implications are – the reader is referred to Devitt's *Realism and Truth,* especially chapters 11, 12, and 13, and the Afterword.

15 Kant, *Critique of Pure Reason,* 29. (It may be noted that this passage is from the Preface to the second – 1787 – edition of the *Critique.* The spirit of the view expressed is less evident in the first edition.)

16 Putnam is, to be sure, an exception. In the most recent stage of his thinking he has, evidently, embraced a Kierkegaardian version of Judaism, with, presumably, com-

mitments to the existence of God. See Giovanna Borradori, *The American Philoso-pher*, 64–9.

3: Metaphysical Systems

1 In the case of Judaism these historical claims require qualification. Only some strands of Judaism may be regarded as Pythagorean (in the sense intended), and it is arguable whether they include earlier Old Testament theological stances.
2 This is the year of the Edict of Milan, from which the established position of Chris-tianity in the Roman Empire is conventionally dated.
3 Sallust, *The Jugurthine War*, 35f.
4 Complex issues of scholarship are involved in attributions of explicit and fully lit-eral immaterialism to souls and numbers as Pythagoras and his school conceived them. The relevant ancient texts are fragmentary and obscure, and it cannot be cer-tain that Pythagoras may not have believed that souls and numbers are both in some manner material. What is clear is that Plato thought souls and numbers – and other abstract things – wholly non-bodily, and that he developed these views from Pythagorean bases. It is altogether certain that both Pythagoras and Plato believed in the 'transmigration' of immortal souls.
5 Dante, *Inferno*, 4.136.
6 Ironically, while Democritus is found among those in the first circle of hell, Dante places 'Epicurus with all his followers, who make the soul die with the body,' in the much lower and darker sixth circle (*Inferno*. 10.14f.). Doubtless we shouldn't infer from this that Dante supposes that God prefers determinists to indeterminists. Less frivolously, we may see here a reflection of the fact that the austere philosophy of Democritus has never had the sort of influence – pernicious influence, of course, for a Christian – that the humanist, even populist, naturalism of Epicureanism has had.
7 I do not mean by this to imply that sizeable numbers of Catholics have cons-ciously formulated Aristotelian metaphysical views; rather, that the theology they formally (if in very many cases only ritually) assent to has Aristotelian meta-physical content and commitments, at least some of which most Catholics become aware.
8 Another interpretive option would be to take the Stoics to have anticipated not Meinong, but his interesting contemporary Vaihinger (1852–1933), who advo-cated the idea that many, indeed most, of the postulates of most theories are strictly speaking fictional, but nonetheless useful. His philosophy, the philosophy of *as if*, proposes that we utilize these fictions for our purposes of theory, though never losing sight of their strictly or literally fictional character. Aligning the Stoics more with Vaihinger than with Meinong would have the merit of keeping

their views, in logic and elsewhere, more 'classical' and realist; but we really do not have enough textual evidence to decide issues of such subtlety.

9 An attempt to provide an analysis of Cartesian essence is the central topic of my doctoral dissertation (University of Pittsburgh, 1972).

10 Solipsism is usually understood as the theory that only the self – i.e., in my case, only *my* self – is real, together perhaps with mental states of the self whose contents do not imply the reality of any other object or substance. The theory is revised here to the view that some set of states none of whose contents imply the reality of any object or substance is alone real, together possibly with the reality of at most one self.

11 Foundationalism is the thesis that knowledge has certain and secure foundations. Typically these foundations are held to be immediate deliverances of consciousness, in sensation – e.g., that someone seems to see something red on a particular occasion. Incorrigibilism is the view that these or other states, or the beliefs they yield, are self-certifying, unable to be erroneous. Foundationalism sees all knowledge as deriving from these allegedly secure foundations.

4: Categories and First Principles

1 Whitehead, *Process and Reality.*

2 Sommers' work in category theory appears in many publications. Among them may be cited Sommers, *The Logic of Natural Language.*

3 Devitt and Sterelny, *Language and Reality*, 3.

4 The word *thing* is sometimes used as a synonym for *entity*, and sometimes only for particular sorts of entities, usually what we will call individuals or else the category of particulars. Moreover, in English, 'thing' is often contrasted in a mutually exclusive sense with 'person' (in compounds usually appearing as 'one' – 'everyone,' 'someone,' etc.). In this book 'thing' and 'entity' will be used interchangeably.

5 For some there are problematic cases (or putative cases) – e.g., points in space, and supposed 'concrete universals' – that are (according to some views) abstract and (according to others) nonabstract. Some empiricist philosophers have I think believed that perceptible qualities are concrete and particular properties, directly experienced by the senses, where other philosophers will insist that it is objects that are directly perceived, and their so-called perceptible qualities are really abstract universals, no less abstract and universal than typical mathematical properties of numbers are. Some of these complexities are discussed, briefly, below. I want in this context only to affirm that some putative entities seem clearly and intuitively to be abstract, among them examples of the kinds listed.

6 This version of empiricism will be entirely compatible with metaphysical realism. Other, more positivist species of empiricism, will not.

7 See Quine, 'Two Dogmas of Empiricism.'

8 It should be remarked that some philosophers do not share the intuition or the view that actual geometrical objects like the points of space are abstract entities. They are imperceptible, wholly without physical or mental properties; they are also causally inefficacious – entirely without causes or effects. These seem impressive grounds for assigning them abstract status. On the other hand they are particular which some see as sufficient for being concrete.

9 Lewis, *On the Plurality of Worlds*, 81–6.

10 The vocabulary with which properties and their applications are characterized is variable and complex. Thus, some conceive an instance as a variety, and would prefer to say that the instances of redness are properties like being crimson and being scarlet. These matters appear to be merely terminological. The usage in the present context is to take the instances of a property to be the members of the set which comprises the extension of predicates which express the property. Those items, we say, instantiate the property. Still another view is that instances of properties are so-called tropes or 'concrete universals': for example, a particular redness which only one of the instances (in my sense) of redness can have. As I indicate below, I share the view that this conception is of doubtful coherence and unnecessary even if able to be rendered intelligible.

11 This will be to claim that the existence of relations with instances or exemplars will imply the existence of sets, indeed, of ordered sets. Nothing further will follow as to the character of a set theory that may or should be built upon or house the relevant sets.

12 Some prefer to take the view that there are – indeed, can be – no contradictory properties. This seems implausible (though, of course, making the right terminological arrangements can secure this result if desired strongly enough). The core intuitive idea of a property, as I see it, is the idea of something which can be true or false of something. Since being a round square is definitely false of every geometric figure, and indeed of everything else, it can be false of something, and hence can be true or false of something, and hence is a property.

13 Where the idea of the ordering is taken seriously – i.e., where entities have been typed, such that universals (also, possibly, such things as propositions) cannot be taken as values of the individual variables.

14 This will be provisional because of metaphysical theories that affirm the reality of ultimate simples – objective sensory qualia, for example – out of which ordinary physical objects are alleged to be constructions.

15 According to the view developed by Frege and Russell, and widely accepted since, the natural numbers are not particulars but sets. If numbers are analyzable as sets, then of course they won't fall under this category; in any case they might be thought to be things with instances, in which event they would (if not sets) fall under (6).

16 A haecceitous property is one involving a proper name concept, the name being used not mentioned in a predicate expressing the property. An expression is mentioned if something is said about it as an expression; otherwise it is used. Accordingly, examples of haecceitous properties are: being Aristotle, being taller than Fred, not being as wise as Martha. Haecceitous propositions are to be understood analogously.

17 Some historical considerations may be useful to insert here, at least in a footnote. Russell, guided chiefly by ontological economy (but also by that 'robust sense of reality' which seems to motivate most philosophers to jettison abstracta wherever they think they can), proposed taking the objects of psychological states of 'propositional attitude' (like knowing or believing that something is the case), when they correspond to reality, to be facts, not true propositions, as earlier more classically Platonistic analyses had held. This has also the advantage of hooking such states more directly to the world, and the objects and properties those states are about. It has the disadvantage of making it difficult to say what the objects are when the belief is false, or the state's object otherwise fails to correspond to reality. For Russell it was altogether clear that facts were concrete entities – as concrete as events, states, or processes. Some more recent philosophers have wanted to proceed in a 'reverse-Russell' direction, and to construe facts as true propositions.

18 We won't define a substance as contingent, since some have wanted to argue that God, for example, is a necessary substance. It does remain the conviction probably of the majority of philosophers (a conviction I myself share) that it is necessarily true that no substance is necessary.

19 Further discussion of this principle (which I call 'causalism'), and of the idea of basic, fundamental, or primary being will be found in the next chapter.

20 Let it be noted as well that some of the kinds enumerated will pose a challenge for the attempt at a categoreal theory that the present chapter has undertaken.

21 Among the many philosophers who do from time to time write in scare-quoted mode may be mentioned Ryle, Wittgenstein, Putnam, Rorty, and Dennett.

22 Wittgenstein, *Tractatus Logico-Philosophicus*; but I quote, above, from the earlier English translation of 1922, which, like the King James version of the Bible, is often apter, if less literalistically accurate, than its successors.

23 Gilbert Ryle (1900–76) coined this term. The 'Fido'-Fido fallacy is supposing or inferring that because 'Fido' is a name of a dog Fido (any other proper name/ object-named-by-the-proper-name pair would do just as well), any other meaningful or successfully functional expression must be a proper name of an object of some kind. In fact it is doubtful whether anyone has ever inferred that because some expression properly named something, it followed that every expression properly named. Presumably Ryle meant the term 'fallacy' here more loosely, comprehensively, or elliptically to signify either such a fallacy (were anyone to commit

it) or what he supposed was the error of thinking that every meaningful or successfully functioning expression is a proper name or a kind of proper name. The latter view, whether or not an error, was certainly held by some philosophers, most famously (at least in modern times) by Frege.

5: Existence

1 The question seems first to have been formulated explicitly, at least in this way, by Leibniz.

2 Among those who have viewed the problem or question, in this way, is Heidegger (1889–1976). It is posed, and confronted, among other places in his work, in *An Introduction to Metaphysics*, ch. 1. Although he complicates the question in ways that lead to a somewhat different answer to the question than the one that will be defended here, Heidegger both accords the question deep seriousness and affirms (as will the discussion below) the conviction of its ultimate unanswerability.

3 Others prefer requiring that, to be a property, a candidate case must be able both to have and to lack instances. It will fall out automatically on such a view as this, it will be clear, that there can be no properties that nothing lacks – hence that existence is not a property, since everything has it. One can of course choose to understand 'property' in this way. It will have the consequence that there are neither contradictory nor universal properties (whereas in my usage there will be innumerable properties of both types). But we will still need, and be able to find some way to avail ourselves of, some conception, and accompanying term, for what it will be that properties (in this sense) and contradictory or otherwise strictly impossible affirmables, together with universal affirmables, have in common. We could just call them, presumably, affirmables. And then one will say that I am using the term 'property' for 'affirmable.' Any way the pie is sliced, it will turn out – I argue – that an affirmation of existence is a saying something (with content) of whatever it is said of.

4 For a valuable historical discussion of the question, providing also a thematically structured account of its possible answers, including the one he himself favours, see Rescher, *The Riddle of Existence*.

5 So to claim is to align oneself with the explicitly formulated positions of Russell and Quine – the latter, in a famous essay, decrying 'those philosophers who have united in ruining the good old word "exist"' ('On What There Is,' in Quine, *From a Logical Point of View*, 3).

6 Not that some revisions to classical logic don't seem highly plausible. It is hard to believe that universal instantiation is a valid inference pattern, for example. There is a good case also to be made against disjunctive addition.

7 Causalism is called, by some writers, the Eleatic Principle – after a passage in one

of Plato's dialogues (the *Sophist*) in which the Eleatic stranger (one of the dialogue's characters) takes causal power to be the signifier of being. This usage evidently stems from David Armstrong's *Universals and Scientific Realism* (Cambridge: Cambridge University Press, 1978), vol. 2, p. 45f. Armstrong has been a leading causalist.

8 'An Argument for the Identity Theory,' in Lewis, *Philosophical Papers*, vol. 1, p. 100; my emphasis.

9 Ellis, *Truth and Objectivity*.

10 Field, *Realism, Mathematics and Modality*. In Field's case a modified causalism is defended, according to which something is real if and only if it either has causal efficacy or is spatio-temporally located. The extra-causalism defended in the present chapter will oppose both of the latter disjuncts.

11 Minneapolis: University of Minnesota Press, 1985.

12 Spatiotemporalism appears in an explicit early formulation in Samuel Alexander's *Space, Time, and Deity* (The Gifford Lectures at Glasgow, 1916–18), vol. 1, ch. 2: ('Being is the occupation of space-time which also excludes other occupancy of space-time.'), 195; ('Since existence is occupancy of a space-time in exclusion of other occupancy, and since such occupation is always temporal, existence must not be limited to present existence but includes past and future.'), 200; and passim.

13 R. Sylvan, 'Existence II: Existence and Non-Existence,' in Burkhardt and Smith, eds., *Handbook of Metaphysics and Ontology*, vol. 1, p. 263.

14 Originally expressed (in something like this form) in Quine, 'On What There Is,' 21–38 (and widely reprinted thereafter).

15 Dennett, *Consciousness Explained*, 460.

16 The earliest, clearest, and certainly most famous philosopher to multiply senses of being – and beyond, as I argue, necessity – is Aristotle (in *Metaphysics* Gamma).

17 Moore argues, in *Principia Ethica*, ch. 1, that a property (Moore's example is the property of being good) is indefinable if a putative analysis or definition, which should, by rights, have produced a tautology, nonetheless invites or leaves open, the question whether it really does apply to or define what it purports to.

18 For a fuller enumeration than I have provided, and a useful (and, I believe, successful) independent case against causalism, see Mark Colyvan, 'Can the Eleatic Principle Be Justified?'

19 'Empiricism, Semantics, and Ontology.'

6: Essence and Possible Worlds

1 This historical claim is interestingly and impressively supported in Knuuttila, *Modalities in Medieval Philosophy*.

2   It is discussed, and attacked, in an interesting, if highly polemical paper, by James F. Ross called 'The Crash of Modal Metaphysics.'

3   In several significant papers on tense and modal logic.

4   As signaled, *being able* ... is meant in a (strongly) modal sense; not as signifying so-called natural or physical possibility.

5   A logically proper name – the term and concept is Russell's – is a proper name without a sense or intension whose entire semantical role is to denote something actually existing. The intended idea is that such a name is a purely referring expression which will be without any semantical role – hence, strictly, meaningless – unless it successfully refers or denotes.

6   The possibility of logically proper naming all individuals is assumed. Not all entities are individuals. Sets are not individuals, for example. If sets as well as individuals were regarded as logically properly nameable, the theory sketched here would risk paradox, as it is evidently formally provable that there cannot be a set with all the sets in it. Just what the identity conditions for individuals are, and whether a hierarchical typing of entities (possibly including orders of individuals) would be feasible and necessary, are technical issues not explored here. I assume that they are soluble but appreciate that the difficulties are complex. The metaphysical conviction that sets (and possibly other kinds of entities) are in some sense supervenient upon discriminable countable nameable individuals seems sound, however involved the difficulties of justifying it may be.

7   Chisholm, 'Possibility without Haecceity.'

8   A more detailed and formally precise account of the kinds of worlds discussed here would proceed as follows:

We specify four kinds of 'worlds' – comprehensive compossible modal properties.

For our metalanguage, we require a naming of all individuals in the actual universe, $a_1, a_2, a_3, ...$

We also require a set of propositional variable letters, $ncp_1, ncp_2, ncp_3, ... ,$ ranging over non-contingently existing propositions.

And a set of propositional variable letters relativized to individuals that may be named in contingently existing propositions they range over: $\{cp_1, cp_2, ... cp_n\}/$ $\{ ... a_i, a_j, ... \}$ designates a set of contingently existing propositions and individuals such that no other individuals are named in any member of the set.

Then we specify property schema *PS*:

(PS) being able to (1) contain $\{a_k, a_1, ... \}$

(2) contain only the individuals identified in (1)

(3) be such that each member of $\{ncp_1, ncp_2, ... \}$ or its negation is true, the entire set being compossible.

(4) be such that where $\{cp_r, cp_{r+1}, ... \} / \{a_k, a_1, ... \}$, each

member of $\{cp_r, cp_{r+1}, \dots\}$ / $\{a_k, a_1, \dots\}$ or its negation is true, the union of the entire set with the set of propositions in (3) being compossible.

Any property that is an instance of (*PS*): (1), (2), (3), (4) is a 'possible world.'

Any property that is an instance of (*PS*): (1), (3), (4) but not (2), is an 'incomplete world.'

Any property that is an instance of (*PS*): (3), but not (1), (2), or (4) is a 'Ramsey world' [this notion will be explained and motivated more informally below].

Where $\{a_t, a_u, \dots\}$ are all individuals not in (1), a 'possible world' becomes a 'possible-world-from-without' when there is conjoined to the relevant instance of (*PS*) the relevant instance of

being able to   (5) lack $\{a_t, a_u, \dots\}$

(6) be such that where $\{cp_q, cp_{q+1}, \dots\}$ / $\{a_t, a_u, \dots\}$ is the set of contingently existing propositions save those – if any – containing constants naming individuals not in the set $\{a_t, a_u, \dots\}$, each member of $\{cp_q, cp_{q+1}, \dots\}$ / $\{a_t, a_u, \dots\}$ or its negation is true, the union of the entire set with the sets of propositions in (3) and (4) being compossible.

Where $\{a_v, a_w, \dots\}$ is a set of individuals not in (1), an 'incomplete world' becomes an 'incomplete-world-from-without' when there is conjoined to the relevant instance of (PS): (1), (3), (4) the relevant instance of

being able to   (7) lack $\{a_v, a_w, \dots\}$

(8) be such that where $\{cp_s, cp_{s+1}, \dots\}$ / $\{a_v, a_w, \dots\}$ is a set of contingently existing propositions save those, if any, containing constants naming individuals not in the set $\{a_v, a_w, \dots\}$, each member of $\{cp_s, cp_{s+1}, \dots\}$ / $\{a_v, a_w, \dots\}$ or its negation is true, the union of the entire set with the sets of propositions in (3) and (4) being compossible.

9 Graeme Forbes, *The Metaphysics of Modality*, 75.

10 Set out initially in Lewis, *Counterfactuals*, 84–91, and frequently subsequently, most fully, in *On the Plurality of Worlds*.

11 Plantinga, *The Nature of Necessity*, 44–5.

12 Humberstone, 'From Worlds to Possibilities,' 313–39.

13 This is the idea which Chisholm characterizes, and likewise opposes, of 'a realm of *possibilia* falling between being and nonbeing' ('Possibility without Haecceity,' 157).

14 Adams, 'Actualism and Thisness,' 7.

15 Plantinga, 'De Essentia'; Plantinga, 'On Existentialism,' 1–20.

16 See Prior, *Objects of Thought*; Bull, 'An Axiomatization of Prior's Modal Calculus Q,' 211–14; Loptson, 'Logic and Contingent Existence,' 171–85; Loptson,

'Q, Entailment, and the Parry Property,' 305–17; Loptson, 'Prior, Plantinga, Haecceity, and the Possible,' 419–35. It is a three-valued logic, the basic semantical
principle of which is that a compound sentence with a component with the third
(indeterminate) truth value takes that third value but that otherwise everything
behaves classically.

17 '$\Diamond\alpha$' symbolizes 'α is possibly true (*de dicto*),' and '$\Box\alpha$' symbolizes 'α is
necessarily true (*de dicto*).' The standard interdefinability principle then holds
that a proposition is possibly true if and only if it is not necessarily true that it
is false.

18 The founder of modern modal logic, C.I. Lewis (1883–1964), developed five basic
modal systems – called S1, S2, S3, S4, S5 – each included in its successor with the
successor adding a 'stronger' thesis or principle unprovable in the predecessors.
The 'characteristic' S4 principle is $\ulcorner\Box\,\alpha \to \Box\Box\,\alpha\urcorner$ – if α is necessarily true, then
it had to be so (it is necessarily true that it is necessarily true) – and the 'character-
istic' S5 principle is $\ulcorner\Diamond\,\alpha \to \Box\,\Diamond\,\alpha\urcorner$ – all the possibilities are necessarily possible. Since Lewis's foundational work it has been realized that there are many other
distinctive and philosophically as well as formally interesting modal systems than
just his five.

19 For those unfamiliar with the relevant logical vocabulary: an atomic sentence is one
ascribing a property to an individual or affirming a relation among individuals (like
'Aristotle is a philosopher' or 'Heather is sister of Emma'). An existential generalization of a sentence is a sentence that replaces one or more proper names it contains with an individual variable, and prefixes an existential or particular quantifier
expression to the result. Thus, if 'Ann is wise' is an atomic sentence, then 'Something is such that it is wise' (or just 'Something is wise') will be an existential generalization of it.

20 See Kripke, *Naming and Necessity*, 15, 42, 76.

21 Set out most fully in *Naming and Necessity* (1980).

22 I will note that the 'logic' intended here and in the discussion that follows is the
logic of Kripkean modal semantics: the logic of *de re* possibility, i.e., of possible
worlds.

23 See Adams, 'Primitive Thisness and Primitive Identity.'

24 On the Putnam-Kripke view evidently, we could imagine two distinct branches of
the proto-English-speaking community, both of which encountered cats for the first
time at about the same time but completely independently of each other, and both
of which, through sheer coincidence, happened to dub or baptise the creatures
encountered 'cats,' and continued (let us suppose) successfully to employ their language for some while without hook up or interaction with the other group: the term
'cat' would have only homonymous relationship between the two communities,
even though both were in the course of developing English, both were referring to

cats by means of the term, and both would eventually reunite. Synonymy of terms, for the Putnam-Kripke view, requires a shared usage history.

25 This does not of course mean or imply wholly different laws of nature than ours. Many might be exactly the same.

26 Shared by Chisholm. See Chisholm, *On Metaphysics,* 109f.

7: Substance

1 Anaximander (d. ca. 547 B.C.), second of the Ionian cosmological philosophers, believed that everything in the world was comprised of a single stuff, which did not correspond to any familiar element of the experienced world but was rather what he called 'ton apeiron,' or 'the boundless.'

2 The term 'neutral monism' was coined by William James, though it seems reasonable to apply it to Anaximander's and perhaps to some other theories in the history of philosophy before James's notion of a single stuff or element of the world, of which mental and material things are variant formations or cases. Russell was also for a time drawn to neutral monism.

3 Jeff Pelletier is perhaps the philosopher who, of those who have worked closely on mass terms and mass entities, most emphatically takes this view. See (principally) Pelletier, 'Editorial Introduction,' 'Non-Singular Reference: Some Preliminaries,' and 'Sharvy on Mass Predication,' in Pelletier, *Mass Terms*; Pelletier and Schubert, 'Mass Expressions'; and Pelletier, 'Mass Terms,' 495–9. Pelletier devises and makes effective deployment of the imaginative construct of a 'Universal Grinder,' which can produce a stuff from the referents of any count noun, and argues as well, plausibly, that for any mass term a conventionalized count noun can be engendered. Yet, the ingenuity notwithstanding, it will not follow, nor will these premises even suggest, that there are no such things as gold or alligators, or, more broadly, that (at least some) mass entities are not deeply different kinds of things from (at least some) countable particulars.

4 Quine puts the point with splendid succinctness: 'Even the tightest object, short of an elementary particle, has a scattered substructure when the physical facts are in.' (*Word and Object*, 98)

5 Some particulars, e.g., atoms, may not be directly perceptible. Some will argue that sensory qualities are cases of properties that are directly perceptible. Unless we believe in so-called tropes, the latter view seems wrong, and indeed, confused. Instances of particulars having sensory qualities may be directly perceived but not the qualities themselves.

6 The only comparable terms seem to be the terms for musical notes, like $C^{\#}$. Thanks to Robert Muehlmann for reminding me of this apparently singular companion case.

7 Quine, *Word and Object*, 91.

8 See Roeper, 'Semantics for Mass Terms with Quantifiers,' 251–65; Lønning, 'Mass Terms and Quantification,' 1–52; Needham, 'Stuff,' 270–90.

9 One example of such limitations is the inability of any of these logics to give formal expression to cases of terms with both count and mass noun use. E.g., 'Every cake is made of cake, but not everything made of cake is a cake' should have a structural rendering in an adequate logic of mass terms, i.e., one that utilizes the commonality of the two uses of 'cake.'

10 Paul Needham, 'Stuff.'

11 'Concrete mass nouns should basically be taken as denoting properties of individuals.' '*Abstract* mass nouns (correctly delimited ...) would be treated in exactly the same way as concrete mass nouns.' ('The Proper Treatment of Mass Terms in English,' 173, 177.)

8: Universals

1 Georg Cantor (1845–1918) was the primary creator of modern set theory, the foundational theory for mathematics. Cantor proved that no matter what size a given set is, there must be a distinct set with more members. So if there were a set with everything in it, there would have to be another larger set – contradicting the assumption that the first set contained everything.

2 See his interesting 1919 essay 'On Propositions: What They Are and How They Mean.'

3 Affirmed in Devitt and Sterelny, *Language and Reality*, 3 and passim. (They actually say 'boots' rather than 'britches.')

4 Putnam introduced this argument in 'Brains in a Vat' in *Reason, Truth and History*. Putnam argues that we could not be (lifelong) mere brains in a vat, hooked up to systematic illusion-producing machinery, because 'brain' and 'vat' are (something like) logically proper names, only available where they have had successful reference; which will mean not only not available for individuals in fanciful stories but also for philosophical theorists attempting to describe genuine possibilities.

5 The particular meanings of particular expressions contained in a sentence can of course show that the sentence is, for example, logically self-contradictory, but that is a different point.

6 Strictly, the appropriate participial nominalization requires, grammatically, the subject in possessive form – 'Socrates's being wise' (rather than 'Socrates being wise'), etc. If less grammatically apposite, the rendering without possessive appears more metaphysically perspicuous, lacking the possessive formation's (Aristotelian) tilt to individual substance ontology.

9: Space

1 Displacement 'identity' occurs where there seemed (or had been supposed, in some
theory) to be items of a certain kind but strictly, or literally, there are no such
things; where, in fact, the items mistakenly or inaccurately referred to by the term
for the fictional item are actually items of a distinct kind. The standard formula for
a displacement 'identity' (quotation marks are used because it is not a genuine
identity) is: (for relevant F and G) so-called 'Fs' are really Gs. Eliminative materialists, for example, hold that so-called 'mental states' are really brain states. That
is, for them, mental states are displacement 'identical' with brain states.

2 The historian and philosopher of science Thomas S. Kuhn (1922–96) achieved
fame and considerable influence on the strength of his 1962 book, *The Structure of
Scientific Revolutions.* Kuhn argued that the history of science should discourage
belief in a cumulative and increasingly accurate total body of scientific results.
Rather, Kuhn holds, science goes through successive stages of theory, none of them
significantly closer to a supposed objective truth than the others, and which replace
each other through conceptual 'revolutions,' that are not prompted fundamentally
by new evidence. Kuhn has many critics as well as supporters. See Weinberg, 'The
Revolution That Didn't Happen,' 48–52.

3 Georg Riemann (1826–66) developed the non-Euclidean geometry that figures in
Einstein's theory of general relativity. Non-Euclidean geometry defines itself by
denying the so-called parallels postulate – for any straight line, and point not on
that line, there is exactly one line going through the point that is parallel to the
first line. In Riemannian geometry there are no lines parallel to the original line.
There are many popular accounts that explain how this will work. One that may
be recommended is Carnap's *An Introduction to the Philosophy of Science,*
ch. 14.

4 Abbott, *Flatland: A Romance of Many Dimensions.*

5 Strawson, in *Individuals,* 54–80, explores the idea of a subject whose experience is
purely auditory, and explicitly conceives this as probing the possibility of a No-
Space world. Strawson's project, in what he calls 'descriptive metaphysics,' is
explicitly Kantian. He only studies fundamental contours of our 'conceptual
scheme,' without the consequences pursued (or for a good Kantian able to be pursued) for how things may be other than for-us. Nonetheless, it is striking that
Strawson too comes, if tentatively, to the conclusion that the notion of a thinking
being in an aspatial world is coherent.

10: Time

1 'What, then, is time? I know well enough what it is, provided that nobody asks me;

but if I am asked what it is and try to explain, I am baffled' (Saint Augustine, *Confessions*, 264).

2 Bergson supposed both that time is real and that its nature and reality depend on consciousness.

3 Tense or temporal logic was developed chiefly by A.N. Prior, with many roots and partial anticipations among ancient, medieval, and nineteenth-century philosophers. In the work of Prior, Rescher, Urquhart, and others a range of rich formal models of alternative temporal structures is developed.

4 It will not do simply to hold that the laws of physics, plus the hypothesis of backwards time travel, rule out such a world as logically impossible. The coherence of backwards time travel is part of what is under consideration. If there is a possible world in which human being A confronts human being *B* with a loaded revolver, then there must be a possible world (some possible world or other) in which *A* successfully shoots *B*, and *B* is killed and does not revive, no matter who *A* and *B* are. If *A* does or does not succeed in killing *B*, there are necessarily features of local mechanics involved in success or non-success, and some world or other will exhibit all variations of these mechanics. Only if one imputed a magical power of the laws of logic to bend bullets could one suppose otherwise.

5 M.C. Escher (1898–1972) was an artist whose best-known and most frequently reproduced work shows impossible or illusionary architectural and other structures.

6 I argue against this standard interpretation in 'Was Leibniz an Idealist?'

7 Newton-Smith, *The Structure of Time*.

8 In his science-fiction novel *Slaughterhouse-Five*, Kurt Vonnegut describes what purport to be recurrences of the same events, though whether these are supposed to be repetitions of event tokens, or occurrences of event tokens exactly similar to earlier ones (or even event tokens largely similar to earlier ones) is never made altogether clear.

9 Van Fraassen, *An Introduction to the Philosophy of Time and Space*, 61.

10 McTaggart, *The Nature of Existence*, 14.

11 This is the view of the future advocated and defended with similar arguments by C.D. Broad in *Scientific Thought*, 66f.

11: Causality

1 That facts enter into causal relationships may seem problematic, and I do not wish to commit the present account to the idea that they do. Assertions that appear to imply such relationships may all be analysable as or displaced by assertions about states, processes, or events. At any rate we do assert that facts have both causes and effects.

2 There is a certain naturalness about affirmations that objects are effects in some

contexts. Thus, old Christian catechisms included the query, Who made thee? (The answer of course, was supposed to be, God.) And some non-visual sensory assertions and questions – e.g., What caused that smell? Who produced that noise? – suggest something similar. In these cases, however, it seems particularly clear and obvious that the alleged object-effect is really an effect that is the existence of an object.

3 These two primary theories of subjunctive or counterfactual conditionals are set out in Lewis, *Counterfactuals*; and Stalnaker, *Inquiry*. Cf. Nortmann, 'Counterfactuals,' 189–93.

4 'Laws and Causal Relations.'

5 'On the Nature and the Observability of the Causal Relation.'

6 See Anscombe, 'Causality and Determination.'

7 Trimmer, *Response of Physical Systems*, 1–3.

8 Bunge, *Causality*, 46–8.

12: Purpose

1 The general view of teleology in biology outlined here is by no means original. It is in fact rather standard and now almost old-fashioned empiricist and naturalist fare, even if some details of the analysis proposed above may be distinctive. The general stance is set out admirably and more fully than is attempted above in Ernest Nagel's *The Structure of Science*, 401–28.

2 Schopenhauer (1788–1860) believed that the 'thing-in-itself' is a blind, striving, life-force, which he conceived as will.

13: Persons, Personal Identity, and Metaphysical Luck

1 The 'in effect' is critical. 'I' is an indexical term; 'person' is not. Properly the plural of 'I' is, of course, 'we'; and the singular of 'persons' is 'person.'

2 Rousseau (1712–78) had the idea of a society undertaking to act in its deliberations as though one person with a common or shared 'general will.'

3 Aune, *Metaphysics*, 78. Aune's emphasis.

4 Parfit, *Reasons and Persons*.

5 In fact priority for this idea belongs properly to Bernard Williams. Williams' original paper, 'Moral Luck,' appeared in the *Proceedings of the Aristotelian Society*, supplementary volume 1 (1976), 115–35, and Nagel's paper of the same name appeared in the same place as a reply to Williams. Nagel's paper is reprinted in his *Mortal Questions*; Williams' paper reappears in his *Moral Luck*.

6 Parfit, *Reasons and Persons*, 267. The citation is from Williams, *Problems of the Self*, 20.

14: Mind

1 The idea that there can be states without subjects of those states – and specifically mental states without subjects – appears explicitly in the remarks of Georg Christoph Lichtenberg (1742–99). Discussing the Cartesian *cogito*, Lichtenberg comments: 'It thinks, we really ought to say, just as we say, it thunders.' Cited in Ted Honderich, ed., *The Oxford Companion to Philosophy*. (Oxford: Oxford University Press, 1995), 487.

2 This is the central metaphysical thought experiment whose possibility is the theme of Putnam's 'brain in a vat' paper.

3 See Kripke, *Naming and Necessity*.

4 It should perhaps be noted that some use the term, *life*, loosely and non-biologically, such that anything that thinks would count ipso facto as living. Such usage seems unhelpful.

5 They could, I suppose, be non-human persons contained within the human person: truly (if not in the etymological sense) homunculi!

6 An interesting non-behaviourist thinker who takes a view of this kind is the psychiatrist Thomas Szasz. See his book *The Myth of Mental Illness*.

7 Bertrand Russell, *Human Knowledge*, 178.

8 It seems plausible to suppose that the identity of a conscious and deliberate mental event – a 'thinking about' will be a paradigm case – is determined by what were intended to be its contents. So, if George meant to be thinking about something that would be, inter alia, heavy, his thinking about something where he hasn't focused (one way or the other) on its being heavy, will be a distinct thinking about, even if the contents are otherwise identical. Still, when George thinks about the heavy book, he is also thinking about the book.

9 This is a central part of the anti-materialist argument of Chalmers, *The Conscious Mind*.

10 See Apollodorus, *Epitome* iii.5; Euripides, *Electra* 1280 and *Helen* 31ff. and passim. The story apparently originated with the sixth century B.C. poet, Stesichorus.

11 Homer, *Iliad*, xxiv.765.

12 See 'Mental Events,' in Davidson, *Essays on Actions and Events*.

13 I am unaware whether Davidson explicitly links anomalous monism and Kant. He does explicitly connect the theory, interestingly, with Spinozist metaphysics. In a 1999 conference paper, for which I was among the audience, Davidson made a passing reference to 'anomalous monism, which is what I call my version of Spinoza.' ('Past, Present, and Future of Action Theory,' University of Saskatchewan, 16 Oct. 1999.) Dissimilarities between anomalous and Spinozist monism seem, Davidson's words notwithstanding, evident.

14 Chomsky, *Language and Responsibility*, 64–9.

15: God

1 Mencken, 'Memorial Service,' in *Mencken Christomathy*.
2 Philosophers may or may not exhibit patterns comparable to natural scientists in these respects. Results of an interesting survey of American scientists' views on God are reported in *Scientific American* (Edward J. Larson and Larry Witham, 'Scientists and Religion in America,' *Scientific American* 281, no. 3 (Sept. 1999), 88–93). Larson and Witham asked significant numbers of natural scientists and mathematicians whether they believed in a (personal) God or an afterlife. This repeated an earlier similar survey done by a psychologist in 1914 and again in 1933. All surveys divided the pool of scientists into ordinary and 'elite' groups – Larson and Witham's elite being the 1,800 members of the National Academy of Sciences, all of whose members were polled. The responses show that about 40 per cent of the responding scientists believe in God, and the same number believe in an afterlife. Some 60 per cent therefore are nonbelievers. The figures are dramatically higher among the elite group. The survey showed that over 90 per cent of the top scientists and mathematicians are atheists (with biologists in this group at 95 per cent, and mathematicians, interestingly, at 83 per cent).
3 It is also wrong to say that making something too heavy for the agent to lift is the same as making something too heavy for the ϕ to lift – where 'the ϕ' is intended to abbreviate some description not synonymous with 'agent' (like 'omnipotent being'). There clearly are self-referring actions, that are essentially such ('doing something that will make me happy,' for example, can identify an intended class of possible actions even if, as it happens, I am constitutionally incapable of being happy).
4 Typically there are enabling actions that some agent may need to perform in order to carry out some action that we will say that agent can, now, do. An ability, to be exercised, requires opportunity. In some cases it is other actions that the agent can perform which will create that opportunity. The agent will have the ability in question, at least typically, even if the relevant opportunity has not been created.
5 A weaker claim than this but which will still secure the intended outcome, may seem to some preferable, viz., that the burden is on he or she who would regard the necessarily-existent person as a possible concept to show this. There can certainly be no prima facie presumption that this concept is possible.
6 The core conceptions of the traditional arguments seem to be three in number, viz., that the experienced universe needs an explanatory cause, that it is likewise with the universe's being sustained in being, and that features of the general structure (e.g., the natural laws) or the constituent systems (e.g., life, consciousness, environ-

mental adaptation, morality) strongly point to or require extraordinary purposive agency as their ground. The general drift of the dissenting response is to point to flaws in the logic of the arguments or a natural accountability for the data supposed in the arguments' premises; it is pointed out as well that the supposed ground, source, or cause of the allegedly surprising or explanation-requiring data would not need to bear much resemblance to the divine being.

7 See Newton, *Principia*, vol. 2, pp. 543–7.

8 For an interesting recent summary overview by a prominent contemporary physicist, see Weinberg, *Dreams of a Final Theory*, ch. 11, and 'A Designer Universe?'

9 See Hume, *Dialogues Concerning Natural Religion*, Part XII.

16: Freedom and Determinism

1 Named for the mathematician and astronomer Pierre Simon, Marquis de Laplace (1749–1827), who conceived the model described here in terms of an omniscient predictor.

2 Russell, *An Outline of Philosophy*, 114–19.

3 The term 'compatibilist' (originally spelled by them 'compatiblist'), for the philosophical position intended, seems to have been coined by Cornman and Lehrer in their *Philosophical Problems and Arguments*.

4 In the middle ages it was identified as the failure to differentiate between *necessitas consequentiae* (the necessity of the consequence) and *necessitas consequentis* (the necessity of the consequent). Leibniz, who was also a compatibilist, defends the position by reference to this distinction.

5 This view is set out, with reference to physical modality, in McCall, 'Time and the Physical Modalities,' 427f.

6 *Philosophical Studies*, 185–99.

7 Ryle, *Dilemmas*, ch. 2.

8 Dennett, *Elbow Room*.

9 Frankfurt, 'Alternate possibilities and moral responsibility.' See also the two successor essays in *The Importance of What We Care About*.

10 Credit for the central role of the 'as though,' or 'as if,' notion, which plays so large a part in Dennett's philosophical work (in the key concept of a 'stance') ought to be accorded Hans Vaihinger. See his *The Philosophy of As If*, passim. Dennett, we might say, is (in part) the Vaihinger of our time.

17: Immortality

1 Hobbes may have anticipated it, in the seventeenth century, with his emphatic claims that the concept of an immaterial or incorporeal substance is absurd, insig-

nificant, contradictory, inconsistent nonsense (all of these are terms he uses for the indicated conjunction). See Thomas Hobbes, *Leviathan*, 18, 22, 236.

2 It does bear reminding that, just as we (rightly) affirm that metaphysical possibilities and necessities are not automatically available for the asking ('let's just suppose we've got the concept of an extraordinary person such that it would be logically impossible that that person not exist'), comparable caution is necessary in respect of worlds where the actual laws of nature are revised. Maybe if we invite consideration of a world where copper doesn't expand when heated, we will have unwittingly unleashed consequences we didn't anticipate or want; for surely some laws of nature *are* tied to, and will have consequences for, others. That said, and the need for radar-like vigilance acknowledged, it appears, at least, that we can conceive of worlds whose natural laws are generally and mostly like those of the actual world, but in which there are, say, preservative substances (balms of an extraordinary sort) that can keep living animal bodies, human bodies among them, from decay, indefinitely.

3 Loptson, 'The Antinomy of Death.'

Works Cited

Abbott, Edwin A. *Flatland: A Romance of Many Dimensions*. New York: Barnes and Noble, 1963.

Adams, Robert Merrihew. 'Primitive Thisness and Primitive Identity.' *The Journal of Philosophy* 76, no. 1 (Jan. 1979).

– 'Actualism and Thisness.' *Synthèse* 49 (1981), 5–26.

Alexander, Samuel. *Space, Time, and Deity* (The Gifford Lectures at Glasgow, 1916–1918). London: Macmillan, 1920.

Anscombe, G.E.M. 'Causality and Determination.' In E. Sosa, ed., *Causation and Conditionals*. Oxford: Oxford University Press, 1975.

Aristotle. *The Complete Works of Aristotle*. 2 vols. Edited by J. Barnes. Princeton: Princeton University Press, 1984.

Aristotle. *Metaphysics*. H.G. Apostle, translator and commentator. Grinnell, Iowa: Peripatetic Press, 1979.

Armstrong, David. *Universals and Scientific Realism*. 2 vols. Cambridge: Cambridge University Press, 1978.

Augustine. *Confessions*. Trans. by R.S. Pine-Coffin. Harmondsworth: Penguin Books, 1961.

Aune, Bruce. *Metaphysics: The Elements*. Minneapolis: University of Minnesota Press, 1985.

Borradori, Giovanna. *The American Philosopher*. Chicago: University of Chicago Press, 1994.

Bradley, F.H. *Appearance and Reality*. Oxford: Oxford University Press, 1962 (first edition, 1893).

Broad, C.D. *Scientific Thought*. London: Routledge & Kegan Paul, 1923.

Bull, R.A. 'An Axiomatization of Prior's Modal Calculus Q.' *Notre Dame Journal of Formal Logic* 5 (1964), 211–14.

Bunge, Mario. *Causality*. Cambridge, Mass.: Harvard University Press, 1959.

Carnap, Rudolf. *An Introduction to the Philosophy of Science*. New York: Basic Books, 1966.

– *Meaning and Necessity*. Chicago: University of Chicago Press, 1956.

Chalmers, David J. *The Conscious Mind: In Search of a Fundamental Theory*. Oxford: Oxford University Press, 1996.

Chisholm, Roderick M. *On Metaphysics*. Minneapolis: University of Minnesota Press, 1989.

– 'Possibility without Haecceity.' In Peter A. French, Theodore E. Uehling, Jr., and Howard K. Wettstein, eds., *Midwest Studies in Philosophy*. Vol. 11. *Studies in Essentialism*, 157–63. Minneapolis: University of Minnesota Press, 1986.

Chomsky, Noam. *Language and Responsibility*. New York: Pantheon, 1977.

Colyvan, Mark. 'Can the Eleatic Principle Be Justified?' *Canadian Journal of Philosophy* 28, no. 3 (1998) 313–35.

Cornman, James W., and Keith Lehrer. *Philosophical Problems and Arguments*. First edition. New York: Macmillan, 1968.

Dante. *The Divine Comedy*. 6 vols. Trans, with commentary, by Charles S. Singleton. Princeton: Princeton University Press (Bollingen Series), 1970.

Davidson, Donald. *Essays on Actions and Events*. Oxford: Clarendon Press, 1980.

Dennett, Daniel C. *Consciousness Explained*. Boston: Little, Brown, 1991.

– *Elbow Room: The Varieties of Free Will Worth Wanting*. Cambridge, Mass.: MIT Press, 1984.

Derrida, Jacques. *Of Grammatology*. Baltimore: Johns Hopkins University Press, 1974.

Devitt, Michael. *Realism and Truth*. Second edition, with a new afterword. Princeton: Princeton University Press, 1997.

Devitt, Michael, and Kim Sterelny. *Language and Reality*. Cambridge, Mass.: MIT Press, 1987.

Ducasse, C.J. 'On the Nature and the Observability of the Causal Relation.' *Journal of Philosophy* 23 (1926); reprinted in E. Sosa, ed., *Causation and Conditionals*. Oxford: Oxford University Press, 1975.

Ellis, Brian. *Truth and Objectivity*. Oxford: Blackwell, 1990.

Field, Hartry. *Realism, Mathematics and Modality*. Oxford: Blackwell, 1989.

Forbes, Graeme. *The Metaphysics of Modality*. Oxford: Clarendon Press, 1985.

Fosl, Peter. Interview with Richard Rorty. *The Philosophers' Magazine* no. 8 (Autumn 1999), 40–2.

Frankfurt, Harry G. *The Importance of What We Care About*. Cambridge: Cambridge University Press, 1988.

Heidegger, Martin. *An Introduction to Metaphysics*. New Haven: Yale University Press, 1959.

Hobbes, Thomas. *Leviathan*. London: Everyman, 1994.

Honderich, Ted., ed. *The Oxford Companion to Philosophy.* Oxford: Oxford University Press, 1995.

Horwich, Paul. *Truth.* 2nd ed. Oxford: Oxford University Press, 1998.

Humberstone, L. 'From Worlds to Possibilities.' *The Journal of Philosophical Logic* 10 (1981): 313–39.

Hume, David. *Dialogues Concerning Natural Religion.* Norman Kemp Smith edition. Indianapolis: Bobbs-Merrill, 1947.

– *A Treatise of Human Nature.* Selby-Bigge and Nidditch edition. Oxford: Oxford University Press, 1978.

Kant, Immanuel. *Critique of Practical Reason.* Translated by L.W. Beck. Indianapolis: Bobbs-Merrill, 1956.

– *Critique of Pure Reason.* Kemp-Smith edition. London: Macmillan, 1933.

Knuuttila, Simo. *Modalities in Medieval Philosophy.* London: Routledge, 1993.

Kripke, Saul. *Naming and Necessity.* Cambridge, Mass.: Harvard University Press, 1980.

Kuhn, Thomas S. *The Structure of Scientific Revolutions.* Second edition, enlarged. Chicago: University of Chicago Press, 1970.

Lewis, David. *Counterfactuals.* Oxford: Blackwell, 1973; rev. ed., 1986.

– *On the Plurality of Worlds.* Oxford: Basil Blackwell, 1986.

– *Philosophical Papers.* Vol. 1. New York: Oxford University Press, 1983.

Lønning, Jan Tore. 'Mass Terms and Quantification.' *Linguistics and Philosophy* 10 (1987), 1–52.

Loptson, Peter. 'The Antinomy of Death.' In J. Malpas and R.C. Solomon, eds., *Death and Philosophy.* London: Routledge, 1999.

– 'Leibniz, Sufficient Reason, and Possible Worlds.' *Studia Leibnitiana* no. 2 (1985).

– 'Logic and Contingent Existence.' *History and Philosophy of Logic* 1 (1980), 171–85.

– 'Prior, Plantinga, Haecceity, and the Possible.' In B.J. Copeland, ed., *Logic and Reality,* 419–35. Oxford: Clarendon Press, 1996.

– 'Q, Entailment and the Parry Property.' *Logique et Analyse* 90–1 (1980), 305–17.

– 'Was Leibniz an Idealist?' *Philosophy* 74 (1999), 361–85.

Lucretius. *On the Nature of the Universe.* Trans. by R.E. Latham. Harmondsworth: Penguin, 1951.

McCall, Storrs. 'Time and the Physical Modalities.' *The Monist* 53, no. 3 (July 1969).

McTaggart, J.E. *The Nature of Existence.* 2 vols. Cambridge: Cambridge University Press, 1927.

Mencken, H.L. *Mencken Christomathy.* New York: Alfred Knopf, 1949.

Mill, John Stuart. *The Earlier Letters of John Stuart Mill, 1812–1848.* Edited by F.E. Mineka. Vol. 12. *The Collected Works of John Stuart Mill.* Toronto: University of Toronto Press, 1963.

Montague, Richard. 'The Proper Treatment of Mass Terms in English.' In Francis Jeffry Pelletier, ed., *Mass Terms: Some Philosophical Problems*. Dordrecht: Reidel, 1979.

Moore, G.E. *Principia Ethica*. Cambridge: Cambridge University Press, 1903.

Nagel, Ernest. *The Structure of Science*. Second ed. Indianapolis: Hackett, 1979.

Nagel, Thomas. *Mortal Questions*. Cambridge: Cambridge University Press, 1979.

Needham, Paul. 'Stuff.' *Australasian Journal of Philosophy* 71, no. 3 (Sept. 1993), 276–90.

Newton, Isaac. *Principia (Mathematical Principles)*. 2 vols. Berkeley: University of California Press, 1934.

Newton-Smith, W.H. *The Structure of Time*. London: Routledge & Kegan Paul, 1980.

Nortmann, Ulrich. 'Counterfactuals.' In H. Burkhardt and B. Smith, eds., *Handbook of Metaphysics and Ontology*, vol. 1, 189–93. Munich: Philosophia Verlag, 1991.

Parfit, Derek. *Reasons and Persons*. Oxford: Clarendon Press, 1984.

Pelletier, Francis Jeffry. 'Mass Terms.' In H. Burkhardt and B. Smith, eds., *Handbook of Metaphysics and Ontology*, vol. 4. Munich: Philosophia Verlag, 1991.

– ed. *Mass Terms: Some Philosophical Problems*. Dordrecht: Reidel, 1979.

Pelletier, Francis Jeffry, and Lenhart K. Schubert. 'Mass Expressions.' In D. Gabby and F. Guenthner, eds., *Handbook of Philosophical Logic*, vol. 4. Dordrecht: Reidel, 1989.

Plantinga, Alvin. 'De Essentia.' In E. Sosa, ed., *Essays on the Philosophy of Roderick M. Chisholm*. Amsterdam: Rodopi, 1979.

– 'On Existentialism.' *Philosophical Studies* 44 (1983), 1–20.

– *The Nature of Necessity*. Oxford: Oxford University Press, 1974.

Prior, A.N. *Objects of Thought*. Edited by P.T. Geach and A.J.P. Kenny. Oxford: Clarendon Press, 1971.

Putnam, Hilary. 'The Dewey Lectures 1994.' *The Journal of Philosophy* 91, no. (9 Sept. 1994), 445–517.

– *Reason, Truth and History*. Cambridge: Cambridge University Press, 1981.

Quine, W.V.O. 'On What There Is.' In *From a Logical Point of View*. Cambridge: Harvard University Press, 1961.

– 'Two Dogmas of Empiricism.' In *From a Logical Point of View*. Cambridge: Harvard University Press, 1961.

– *Word and Object*. Cambridge, Mass.: MIT Press, 1960.

Rescher, Nicholas. *The Riddle of Existence*. Lanham, MD: University Press of America, 1984.

Roeper, Peter. 'Semantics for Mass Terms with Quantifiers.' *Noûs* 17 (1983), 251–65.

Rorty, Richard. *Truth and Progress*. Cambridge: Cambridge University Press, 1998.

Ross, James F. 'The Crash of Modal Metaphysics.' *Review of Metaphysics* 43, no. 2 (Dec. 1989), 251–79.

Russell, Bertrand. *The Autobiography of Bertrand Russell*. 3 vols. London: Allen and Unwin, 1967–9.

– *Human Knowledge*. New York: Simon and Schuster, 1948.

– *Logic and Knowledge*. London: Allen and Unwin, 1956.

– *An Outline of Philosophy*. London: Allen and Unwin, 1927. Published in the U.S. as *Philosophy*. New York: W.W. Norton, 1927.

Ryle, Gilbert. *The Concept of Mind*. London: Hutchinson, 1949.

– *Dilemmas*. Cambridge: Cambridge University Press, 1954.

Sallust. *The Jugurthine War*. Translated by S.A. Handford. Harmondsworth: Penguin, 1963.

Schopenhauer, Arthur. *The World as Will and Representation*. 2 vols. Payne Translation. New York: Dover, 1966.

Sellars, Wilfrid. *Science, Perception and Reality*. London: Routledge & Kegan Paul, 1963.

Sommers, Fred. *The Logic of Natural Language*. Oxford: Clarendon Press, 1982.

Spinoza, Baruch. *The Ethics and Selected Letters*. Translated by Samuel Shirley; edited and introduced by Seymour Feldman. Indianapolis: Hackett Publishing Company, 1982.

Stalnaker, Robert. *Inquiry*. Cambridge, Mass.: MIT Press, 1984.

Strawson, P.F. *Individuals*. London: Methuen, 1959

Sylvan, Richard. 'Existence II: Existence and Non-Existence.' In H. Burkhardt and B. Smith, eds., *Handbook of Metaphysics and Ontology*. 2 vols. Munich: Philosophia Verlag, 1991.

Szasz, Thomas. *The Myth of Mental Illness*. New York: Harper and Row, 1961.

Tarski, Alfred. 'The Semantic Conception of Truth and the Foundations of Semantics.' In H. Feigl and W. Sellars, eds., *Readings in Philosophical Analysis*. New York: Appleton-Century-Crofts, 1949.

Tooley, Michael. 'Laws and Causal Relations.' In P.A. French, T.E. Uehling, Jr., and H.K. Wettstein, eds., *Midwest Studies in Philosophy*. Vol. 9. *Causation and Causal Theories*. Minneapolis: University of Minnesota Press, 1984.

Trimmer, John D. *Response of Physical Systems*. New York: 1950.

Vaihinger, Hans. *The Philosophy of 'As If'*. London: Routledge & Kegan Paul, 1924.

van Fraassen, Bas C. *An Introduction to the Philosophy of Time and Space*. New York: Random House, 1970.

van Inwagen, Peter. 'The Incompatibility of *Free Will* and Determinism.' *Philosophical Studies* 27 (1975); reprinted in Gary Watson, ed., *Free Will*. Oxford: Oxford University Press, 1982.

Vonnegut, Kurt. *Slaughterhouse-Five*. London: Cape, 1970.

Weinberg, Steven. 'A Designer Universe?' *New York Review of Books* 46, no. 16, 21 Oct. 1999.

– *Dreams of a Final Theory*, New York: Vintage Books, 1994.

– 'The Revolution That Didn't Happen.' *New York Review of Books* 45, no. 15, 8 Oct., 1998, 48–52.

Whitehead, Alfred North. *Process and Reality*. New York: Macmillan, 1929.

Whitehead, Alfred North, and Bertrand Russell. *Principia Mathematica*. 3 vols. Cambridge: Cambridge University Press, 1910.

Williams, Bernard. *Moral Luck*. Cambridge: Cambridge University Press, 1981.

– *Problems of the Self*. Cambridge: Cambridge University Press, 1973.

Wittgenstein, Ludwig. *Tractatus Logico-Philosophicus*. Translated by D.F. Pears and B.F. McGuinness; introduction by Bertrand Russell. London: Routledge & Kegan Paul, 1963.

Index